HAND BOOK
of Physics

Complete

NCERT in
One Liner Format

for NEET/ JEE/ CBSE
Class 11 & 12

Corporate Office

DISHA PUBLICATION
45, 2nd Floor, Maharishi Dayanand Marg,
Corner Market, Malviya Nagar, New Delhi - 110017
Tel : 49842349 / 49842350

Typeset by Disha DTP Team

Write to us at **feedback_disha@aiets.co.in**

Contents

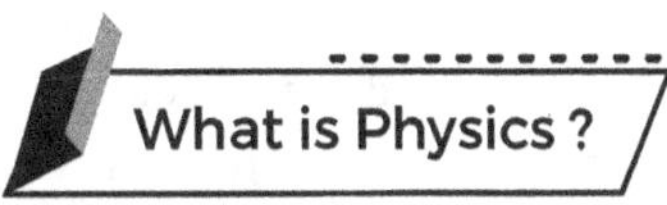

1   Physical World

- **Science** is a systematic attempt to understand natural phenomena. Science is exploring, experimenting and predicting from what we see around us.

- The **scientific method** involves several interconnected steps : Systematic observations, controlled experiments, qualitative and quantitative reasoning, mathematical modelling, prediction and verification or falsification of theories. Speculation and conjecture also have a place in science.

- **Physics** is a basic discipline in the category of **Natural Sciences,** which also includes other disciplines like Chemistry and Biology.

- In Physics, we attempt to explain diverse physical phenomena *in terms of a few concepts and laws.* The effort is to see the physical world as manifestation of some universal laws in different domains and conditions.

- There is two principal thrusts in physics **unification** and **reduction**.

- The attempts to unify fundamental forces of nature reflect this same quest for **unification**.

- A related effort is to derive the properties of a bigger, more complex, system from the properties and interactions of its constituent simpler parts. This approach is called **reductionism** and is at the heart of physics.

- Basically, there are two domains of interest : **macroscopic** and **microscopic.** The macroscopic domain includes phenomena at the laboratory, terrestrial and astronomical scales. The microscopic domain includes atomic, molecular and nuclear phenomena.

- **Classical Physics** deals mainly with macroscopic phenomena and includes subjects like **Mechanics, Electrodynamics, Optics** and **Thermodynamics.**

- Mechanics is concerned with the motion (or equilibrium) of particles, rigid bodies.

- Electrodynamics deals with electric and magnetic phenomena associated with charged and magnetic bodies.
- Optics deals with the phenomena involving light. The working of telescopes and microscopes, colours exhibited by thin films.
- Thermodynamics, is concerned with changes in internal energy, temperature, entropy, etc., of the system through external work and transfer of heat.
- The scope of physics is truly vast. At one end, physics deals with phenomena at the very small scale of length (10^{-14} m or even less) involving electrons, protons, etc.; at the other end, it deals with astronomical phenomena at the scale of galaxies or even Physics is the study of nature and natural phenomena.
- Physicists try to discover the rules that are operating in nature, on the basis of observations, experimentation and analysis. The entire universe whose extent is of the order of 10^{26} m. The two length scales differ by a factor of 10^{40} or even more. The range of time scales can be obtained by dividing the length scales by the speed of light : 10^{-22} s to 10^{18} s.
- The range of masses goes from, say, 10^{-30} kg (mass of an electron) to 10^{55} kg (mass of known observable universe).
- It was realised that for scientific progress, only qualitative thinking, though no doubt important, is not enough. Quantitative measurement is central to the growth of science, especially physics, because the laws of nature happen to be expressible in precise mathematical equations.
- The most important insight was that the basic laws of physics are universal — the same laws apply in widely different contexts. Lastly, the strategy of approximation turned out to be very successful.
- A good strategy is to focus first on the essential features, discover the basic principles and then introduce corrections to build a more refined theory of the phenomenon.

Physics, Technology and Society

- Physics deals with certain basic rules/laws governing the natural world.
- An important example of physics giving rise to technology is the **silicon chip** that triggered the computer revolution.
- A most significant area to which physics has and will contribute is the development of alternative energy resources.

Table: Some physicists from different countries of the world and their major contributions

Name	Major contribution/ discovery	Country of Origin
Archimedes	Principle of buoyancy; Principle of the lever	Greece
Galileo Galilei	Law of inertia	Italy
Christiaan Huygens	Wave theory of light	Holland
Isaac Newton	Universal law of gravitation; Laws of motion; Reflecting telescope	U.K.
Michael Faraday	Laws of electromagnetic induction	U.K.
James Clerk Maxwell	Electromagnetic theory; Light-an electromagnetic wave	U.K.
Heinrich Rudolf Hertz	Generation of electromagnetic waves	Germany
J.C. Bose	Ultra short radio waves	India
W.K. Roentgen	X-rays	Germany
J.J. Thomson	Electron	U.K.
Marie Sklodowska Curie	Discovery of radium and polonium; Studies on natural radioactivity	Poland
Albert Einstein	Explanation of photoelectric effect; Theory of relativity	Germany
Victor Francis Hess	Cosmic radiation Austria	Austria
R.A. Millikan	Measurement of electronic charge	U.S.A.
Ernest Rutherford	Nuclear model of atom	New Zealand
Niels Bohr	Quantum model of hydrogen atom	Denmark
C.V. Raman	Inelastic scattering of light by molecules	India
Louis Victor de Borglie	Wave nature of matter	France
M.N. Saha	Thermal ionisation	India
S.N. Bose	Quantum statistics	India

Wolfgang Pauli	Exclusion principle	Austria
Enrico Fermi	Controlled nuclear fission	Italy
Werner Heisenberg	Quantum mechanics; Uncertainty principle	Germany
Paul Dirac	Relativistic theory of electron; Quantum statistics	U.K.
Edwin Hubble	Expanding universe	U.S.A.
Ernest Orlando Lawrence	Cyclotron	U.S.A.
James Chadwick	Neutron	U.K.
Hideki Yukawa	Theory of nuclear forces	Japan
Homi Jehangir Bhabha	Cascade process of cosmic radiation	India
Lev Davidovich Landau	Theory of condensed matter; Liquid helium	Russia
S.Chandrasekhar	Chandrasekhar limit, structure and evolution of stars	India
John Bardeen	Transistors; Theory of super conductivity	U.S.A.
C.H. Townes	Maser; Laser	U.S.A.
Abdus Salam	Unification of weak and electromagnetic interactions	Pakistan

Fundamental Forces in Nature

- In the macroscopic world, besides the gravitational force, we encounter several kinds of forces: muscular force, contact forces between bodies, friction the forces exerted by compressed or elongated springs and taut strings and ropes (tension), the force of buoyancy and viscous force the force due to pressure of a fluid, the force due to surface tension of a liquid, and so on.
- In the microscopic domain again, we have electric and magnetic forces, nuclear forces involving protons and neutrons, interatomic and intermolecular forces, etc.
- There different forces arise from only a small number of fundamental forces in nature.

Table: Link between technology and physics

Technology	Scientific principle(s)
Steam engine	Laws of thermodynamics
Nuclear reactor	Controlled nuclear fission
Radio and Television	Generation, propagation and detection of electromagnetic waves
Computers	Digital logic
Lasers	Light amplification by stimulated emission of radiation
Production of ultra high magnetic fields	Superconductivity
Rocket propulsion	Newton's laws of motion
Electric generator	Faraday's laws of electromagnetic induction
Hydroelectric power	Conversion of gravitational potential energy into electrical energy
Aeroplane	Bernoulli's principle in fluid dynamics
Particle accelerators	Motion of charged particles in electromagnetic fields
Sonar	Reflection of ultrasonic waves
Optical fibres	Total internal reflection of light
Non-reflecting coatings	Thin film optical interference
Electron microscope	Wave nature of electrons
Photocell	Photoelectric effect
Fusion test reactor (Tokamak)	Magnetic confinement of plasma
Giant Metrewave Radio Telescope (GMRT)	Detection of cosmic radio waves
Bose-Einstein condensate	Trapping and cooling of atoms by laser beams and magnetic fields.

Gravitational Force

♦ The gravitational force is the force of mutual attraction between any two objects by virtue of their masses.

♦ It is a universal force. It plays a key role in the large-scale phenomena of the universe, such as formation and evolution of stars, galaxies and galactic clusters.

Electromagnetic Force

♦ Electromagnetic force is the force between charged particles.

♦ Like the gravitational force, electromagnetic force acts over large distances and does not need any intervening medium.

♦ It is enormously strong compared to gravity. The electric force between two protons, for example, is 10^{36} times the gravitational force between them, for any fixed distance.

♦ Since the electromagnetic force is so much stronger than the gravitational force, it dominates all phenomena at atomic and molecular scales.

♦ It underlies the macroscopic forces like 'tension', 'friction', 'normal force', 'spring force', etc.

♦ Gravity is always attractive, while electromagnetic force can be attractive or repulsive.

Strong Nuclear Force

♦ The strong nuclear force binds protons and neutrons in a nucleus. It is evident that without some attractive force, a nucleus will be unstable due to the electric repulsion between its protons. This attractive force cannot be gravitational since force of gravity is negligible compared to the electric force.

♦ The strong nuclear force is the strongest of all fundamental forces, about 100 times the electromagnetic force in strength.

♦ It is charge-independent and acts equally between a proton and a proton, a neutron and a neutron, and a proton and a neutron.

♦ Its range is, however, extremely small, of about nuclear dimensions (10^{-15}m). It is responsible for the stability of nuclei. The electron does not experience.

Weak Nuclear Force

♦ The weak nuclear force appears only in certain nuclear processes such as the β-decay of a nucleus. In β-decay, the nucleus emits an electron and an uncharged particle called neutrino.

♦ The weak nuclear force is not as weak as the gravitational force, but much weaker than the strong nuclear and electromagnetic forces.

♦ The range of weak nuclear force is exceedingly small, of the order of 10^{-16} m.

Table: Fundamental forces of nature

Name	Relative strength	Range	Operates among
Gravitational force	10^{-39}	Infinite	All objects in the universe
Weak nuclear force	10^{-13}	Very short, Sub-nuclear size $(\sim 10^{-16}\,\text{m})$	Some elementary particles, particularly electron and neutrino
Electromagnetic force	10^{-2}	Infinite	Charged particles
Strong nuclear force	1	Short, nuclear size $(\sim 10^{-15}\,\text{m})$	Nucleons, heavier elementary particles

Towards Unification of Forces

♦ Newton unified terrestrial and celestial domains under a common law of gravitation.

♦ Recent decades have seen much progress on this front. The electromagnetic and the weak nuclear force have now been unified and are seen as aspects of a single 'electro-weak' force. Attempts have been (and are being) made to unify the electro-weak and the strong force and even to unify the gravitational force with the rest of the fundamental forces. Many of these ideas are still speculative and inconclusive. Table summarises some of the milestones in the progress towards unification of forces in nature.

Table: Progress in unification of different forces/domains in nature

Name of the physicist	Year	Achievement in unification
Isaac Newton	1687	Unified celestial and terrestrial mechanics; showed that the same laws of motion and the law of gravitation apply to both the domains.
Hans Christian oersted	1820	Showed that electric and magnetic phenomena are
Michael Faraday	1830	inseparable aspects of a unified domain; electromagnetism.

James Clerk Maxwell	1873	Unified electricity, magnetism and optics; showed that light is an electromagnetic wave.
Sheldon Glashow, Abdus Salam, Steven Weinberg	1979	Showed that the 'weak' nuclear force and the electromagnetic force could be viewed as different aspects of a single electro-weak force.
Carlo Rubia, Simon Vander Meer	1984	Verified experimentally the predictions of the theory of electro-weak force.

Nature of Physical Laws

- Physicists explore the universe. Their investigations, based on scientific processes, range from particles that are smaller than atoms in size to stars that are very far away.
- In any physical phenomenon governed by different forces, several quantities may change with time. A remarkable fact is that some special physical quantities, however, remain constant in time. They are the conserved quantities of nature. Understanding these conservation principles is very important to describe the observed phenomena quantitatively.
- The concept of energy is central to physics. When all forms of energy e.g., heat, mechanical energy, electrical energy etc., are counted, it turns out that energy is conserved.
- The general law of conservation of energy is true for all forces and for any kind of transformation between different forms of energy.
- The law of conservation of energy is be valid across all domains of nature, from the microscopic to the macroscopic. It is applied in the analysis of atomic, nuclear and elementary particle processes.
- According to **Einstein's theory, mass m is equivalent to energy E given by the relation $E = mc^2$, where c is speed of light in vacuum.**
- Energy is a scalar quantity. But all conserved quantities are not necessarily scalars. The total linear momentum and the total angular momentum (both vectors) of an isolated system are also conserved quantities.
- Symmetries of space and time and other abstract symmetries play a central role in modern theories of fundamental forces in nature.

The International System of Units

- Measurement of any physical quantity involves comparison with a certain basic, arbitrarily chosen, internationally accepted reference standard called **unit**. The result of a measurement of a physical quantity is expressed by a number (or numerical measure) accompanied by a unit.
- The units for the fundamental or base quantities are called **fundamental** or **base units**.
- The units of all other physical quantities can be expressed as combinations of the base units. Such units obtained for the derived quantities are called **derived units**.
- A complete set of these units, both the base units and derived units, is known as the system of units.
- The base units for length, mass and time in the CGS, the FPS (or British) and the MKS system were as follows:
  - In CGS system they were centimetre, gram and second respectively.
  - In FPS system they were foot, pound and second respectively.
  - In MKS system they were metre, kilogram and second respectively.
  The system of units which is at present internationally accepted for measurement is International System of Units, abbreviated as SI.
- Because SI units used decimal system, conversions within the system are quite simple and convenient.
- In SI, there are seven base units as given in Table. Besides the seven base units, there are two more units that are defined for (a) plane angle $d\theta$ as the ratio of length of arc ds to the radius r and (b) solid angle $d\Omega$ as the ratio of the intercepted area dA of the spherical surface, described about the apex O as the centre, to the square of its radius r.

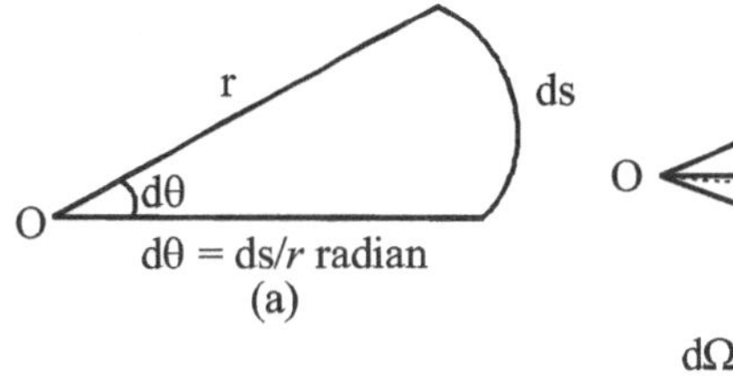

$d\theta = ds/r$ radian
(a)

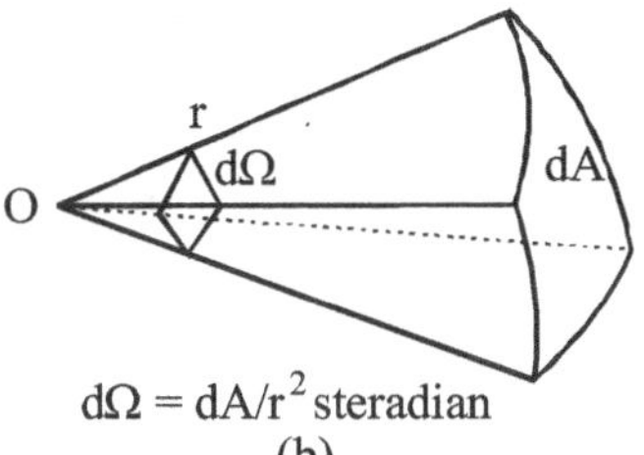

$d\Omega = dA/r^2$ steradian
(b)

Fig.: Description of (a) plane angle dθ and (b) solid angle dΩ.

Table: SI Base Quantities and Units

Base quantity	SI Units		
	Name	**Symbol**	**Definition**
Length	metre	m	The metre is the length of the path travelled by light in vacuum during a time interval of 1/299, 792, 458 of a second. (1983)
Mass	kilogram	kg	The kilogram is equal to the mass of the international prototype of the kilogram (a platinum-iridium alloy cylinder) kept at international Bureau of Weights and Measures, at Sevres, near Paris, France. (1889)
Time	second	s	The second is the duration of 9,192,631,770 periods of the radiation corresponding to the transition between the two hyperfine levels of the ground state of the cesium-133 atom. (1967)
Electric current	ampere	A	The ampere is that constant current which, if maintained in two straight parallel conductors of infinite length, of negligible circular cross-section, and placed 1 metre apart in vacuum, would produce between these conductors a force equal to 2×10^{-7} newton per metre of length. (1948)
Thermo-dynamic Temperature	kelvin	K	The kelvin, is the fraction 1/273.16 of the thermodynamic temperature of the triple point of water. (1967)

Amount of substance	mole	mol	The mole is the amount of substance of a system, which contains as many elementary entities as there are atoms in 0.012 kilogram of carbon-12. (1971)
Luminous intensity	candela	cd	The candela is the luminous intensity, in a given direction, of a source that emits monochromatic radiation of frequency 540×10^{12} hertz and that has a radiant intensity in that direction of 1/683 watt per steradian. (1979)

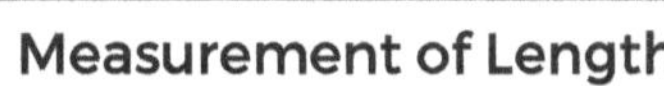

Measurement of Length

- To measure the distance D of a far away planet S by the **parallax method,** we observe it from two different positions (observatories) A and B on the Earth, separated by distance AB = b at the same time as shown in Fig. We measure the angle between the two directions along which the planet is viewed at these two points. The $\angle ASB$ in Fig. represented by symbol θ is called the **parallax angle** or **parallactic angle.**

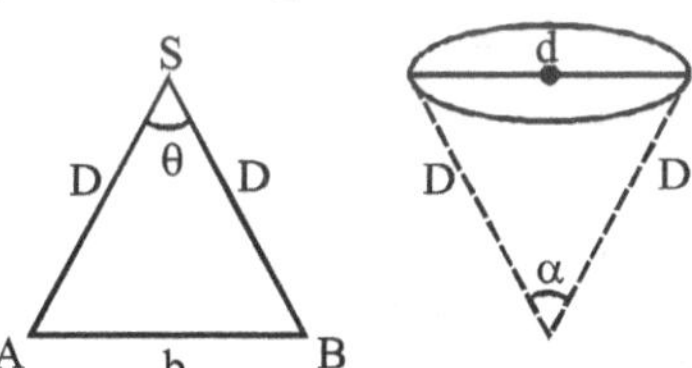

Fig.: Parallax method.

- As the planet is very far away, $\dfrac{b}{D} \ll 1$, and therefore, θ is very small. Then we approximately take AB as an arc of length b of a circle with centre at S and the distance D as the radius AS = BS so that AB = $b = D\theta$ where θ is in radians. $D = \dfrac{b}{\theta}$

- Having determined D, we can employ a similar method to determine the size or angular diameter of the planet. If d is the diameter of the planet and α the angular size of the planet (the angle subtended by d at the earth), we have
$\alpha = d/D$
α is the angle between the two directions when two diametrically opposite points of the planet are viewed through the telescope. Since D is known, the diameter d of the planet can be determined.

- **Estimation of very small distances: size of a molecule.**
- Dissolve 1 cm^3 of oleic acid in alcohol to make a solution of 20 cm^3. Then we take 1 cm^3 of this solution and dilute it to 20 cm^3, we put one drop of this solution in the water. The oleic acid drop spreads into a thin, circular film of molecular thickness on water surface. Then, we measure area A. Suppose we have dropped n drops in the water.
  Volume of n drops of solution $= nV$ cm^3
  Amount of oleic acid in this solution

$$= nV\left(\frac{1}{20 \times 20}\right) \text{cm}^3$$

- The thickness of the film $t = \dfrac{\text{Volume of the film}}{\text{Area of the film}}$

  or, $t = \dfrac{nV}{20 \times 20\text{A}}$ cm

- If we assume that the film has mono-molecular thickness, then this becomes the size or diameter of a molecule of oleic acid.

- Range of length
1 fermi	$= 1$ f $= 10^{-15}$ m
1 angstrom	$= 1$ Å $= 10^{-10}$ m
1 astronomical unit	$= 1$ AU (average distance of the Sun from the Earth)
	$= 1.496 \times 10^{11}$ m
1 light year	$= 1$ ly $= 9.46 \times 1015$ m (distance that light travels with velocity of 3×10^8 m s^{-1} in 1 year)
1 parsec	$= 3.08 \times 10^{16}$ m

Measurement of Mass

- While dealing with atoms and molecules, there is an important standard unit of mass, called the **unified atomic mass unit** (u), which has been established for expressing the mass of atoms as
  1 unified atomic mass unit $= 1$u

  $= (1/12)$ of the mass of an atom of carbon-12 isotope $\left(^{12}_{6}\text{C}\right)$ including the mass of electrons $= 1.66 \times 10^{-27}$ kg

Measurement of Time

- The **second** is taken as the time needed for 9,192,631,770 vibrations of the radiation corresponding to the transition between the two hyperfine levels of the ground state of cesium −133 atom.
- The cesium atomic clocks are very accurate. A cesium atomic clock is used at the National Physical Laboratory (NPL) New Delhi to maintain the Indian standard of time.

Accuracy, Precision of Instruments and Errors in Measurement

- The result of every measurement by any measuring instrument contains some uncertainty. This uncertainty is called **error**.
- The **accuracy of a measurement** is a measure of how close the measured value is to the true value of the quantity. **Precision** tells us to what resolution or limit the quantity is measured.
- Suppose the true value of a certain length is near 3.678 cm. In one experiment, using a measuring instrument of resolution 0.1 cm, the measured value is found to be 3.5 cm, while in another experiment using a measuring device of greater resolution, say 0.01 cm, the length is determined to be 3.38 cm. The first measurement has more accuracy (because it is closer to the true value) but less precision (its resolution is only 0.1 cm), while the second measurement is less accurate but more precise.

Systematic errors
- The **systematic errors** are those errors that tend to be in one direction, either positive or negative.
  - (a) **Instrumental errors**
  - (b) **Imperfection in experimental technique or procedure**
  - (c) **Personal errors**

Random errors
- The **random errors** are those errors, which occur irregularly and hence are random with respect to sign and size. These can arise due to unpredictable fluctuations in temperature, voltage supply, mechanical vibrations of experimental set-ups, etc.

Least count error
- The smallest value that can be measured by the measuring instrument is called its **least count**.
- The **least count error** is the error associated with the resolution of the instrument. For example, a vernier callipers has the least count as 0.01cm; a spherometer may have a least count of 0.001 cm.

Absolute Error, Relative Error and Percentage Error
- Suppose the values in several measurements are $a_1, a_2, a_3...., a_n$.

$$a_{mean} = (a_1 + a_2 + a_3 + ... + a_n)/n = \sum_{i=1}^{n} a_i / n$$

- **The magnitude of the difference between the individual measurement and the true value of the quantity is called the absolute error of the measurement (Δa).**
- Errors in the individual measurement values are

$\Delta a_1 = a_1 - a_{mean}$,
$\Delta a_2 = a_2 - a_{mean}$,
$\Delta a_n = a_n - a_{mean}$

The arithmetic mean of all the *absolute errors* is taken as the *final or mean absolute error* of the value of the physical quantity a.

$$\Delta a_{mean} = (|\Delta a_1| + |\Delta a_2| + |\Delta a_3| + ... + |\Delta a_n|)/n = \sum_{i=1}^{n} |\Delta a_i|/n$$

♦ If we do a single measurement, the value we get may be in the range $a_{mean} \pm \Delta a_{mean}$

$$a = a_{mean} \pm \Delta a_{mean}$$
$$a_{mean} - \Delta a_{mean} \leq a \leq a_{mean} + \Delta a_{mean}$$

♦ The **relative error** is the ratio of the mean absolute error Δa_{mean} to the mean value a_{mean} of the quantity measured.

Relative error $= \Delta a_{mean} / a_{mean}$

♦ When the relative error is expressed in per cent, it is called the **percentage error.**

Percentage error

$$\delta a = (\Delta a_{mean} / a_{mean}) \times 100\%$$

Combination of Errors

♦ **Error of a sum or a difference**

Suppose A and B have measured values $A \pm \Delta A$, $B \pm \Delta B$ respectively error ΔZ in the sum

$Z = A + B$.

$Z \pm \Delta Z = (A \pm \Delta A) + (B \pm \Delta B) = A + B \pm (\Delta A + \Delta B)$

The maximum possible error in Z

$\Delta Z = \Delta A + \Delta B$

For the difference $Z = A - B$, we have

$Z \pm \Delta Z = (A \pm \Delta A) - (B \pm \Delta B)$

$= (A - B) \pm \Delta A \pm \Delta B$

$\pm \Delta Z = \pm \Delta A \pm \Delta B$

The maximum value of the error ΔZ is again $\Delta A + \Delta B$.

When two quantities are added or subtracted, the absolute error in the final result is the sum of the absolute errors in the individual quantities.

♦ **Error of a product or a quotient**

$Z = AB$ measured values of A and B are $A \pm \Delta A$ and $B \pm \Delta B$.

$Z \pm \Delta Z = (A \pm \Delta A) (B \pm \Delta B)$

$= AB \pm B \Delta A \pm A \Delta B \pm \Delta A \Delta B$.

Dividing LHS by Z and RHS by AB

$1 \pm (\Delta Z/Z) = 1 \pm (\Delta A/A) \pm (\Delta B/B) \pm (\Delta A/A)(\Delta B/B)$.

$\Delta A \Delta B$ is very small, neglect product.

The maximum relative error

$\Delta Z/ Z = (\Delta A/A) + (\Delta B/B)$.

When two quantities are multiplied or divided, the relative error in the result is the sum of the relative errors in the multipliers.

♦ **Error in case of a measured quantity raised to a power**

$Z = A^2$,

$\Delta Z/Z = (\Delta A/A) + (\Delta A/A) = 2 (\Delta A/A)$.

In general, if $Z = A^p B^q / C^r$

$\Delta Z/Z = p (\Delta A/A) + q (\Delta B/B) + r (\Delta C/C)$.

Percentage error of Z

$= P (\% \text{ error in A}) + q (\% \text{ error in B}) + r(\% \text{ error in C})$

The relative error in a physical quantity raised to the power k is the k times the relative error in the individual quantity.

Significant Figures

- The reported result of measurement is a number that includes all digits in the number that are known reliably plus the first digit that is uncertain. The reliable digits plus the first uncertain digit are known as **significant digits** or **significant figures**.
- **A choice of change of different units does not change the number of significant digits or figures in a measurement.**
  - **All the non-zero digits are significant.**
  - **All the zeros between two non-zero digits are significant, no matter where the decimal point is, if at all.**
  - **If the number is less than 1, the zero(s) on the right of decimal point but to the left of the first non-zero digit are not significant.**
  - **The terminal or trailing zero(s) in a number without a decimal point are not significant.**
  - **The trailing zero(s) in a number with a decimal point are significant.**
- In scientific notation, every number is expressed as $a \times 10^b$, where a is a number between 1 and 10, and b is any positive or negative exponent (or power) of 10. Exponent (or power) b of 10 is called **order of magnitude**
$$4.700 \text{ m} = 4.700 \times 10^2 \text{ cm}$$
$$= 4.700 \times 10^3 \text{ mm} = 4.700 \times 10^{-3} \text{ km}$$
  The power of 10 is irrelevant to the determination of significant figures. All zeroes appearing in the base number in the scientific notation are significant. Each number in this case has *four* significant figures.
  - **For a number greater than 1, without decimal, the trailing zero(s) are not significant.**
  - **For a number with a decimal, the trailing zero(s) are significant.**

Rules for Arithmetic Operations with Significant Figures

- **In multiplication or division, the final result should retain as many significant figures as are there in the original number with the least significant figures.**
- Density should be reported to *three* significant figures.

$$\text{Density} = \frac{\text{Mass}}{\text{Volume}} = \frac{4.237 \text{ g}}{2.51 \text{ cm}^3} = 1.69 \text{ g cm}^{-3}$$

- **In addition or subtraction, the final result should retain as many decimal places as are there in the number with the least decimal places.**
- The sum of the numbers 436.32 g, 227.2 g and 0.301 g by mere arithmetic addition, is 663.821 g. But the least precise measurement (227.2 g) is correct to only one decimal place. The final result should, be rounded off to 663.8 g.
- Similarly, the difference in length can be expressed as:
$$0.307 \text{ m} - 0.304 \text{ m} = 0.003 \text{ m} = 3 \times 10^{-3} \text{ m}.$$

Rounding off the Uncertain Digits

- **Preceding digit is raised by 1 if the insignificant digit to be dropped is more than 5, and is left unchanged if the latter is less than 5.**
- **If the preceding digit is even, the insignificant digit is simply dropped and, if it is odd, the preceding digit is raised by 1.**

Dimensions of Physical Quantities

- **The dimensions of a physical quantity are the powers (or exponents) to which the base quantities are raised to represent that quantity.**
- Force = mass × acceleration

    = mass × (length)/(time)^2

    The dimensions of force are $[M]\ [L]/[T]^2 = [M\ L\ T^{-2}]$.

    The force has one dimension in mass, one dimension in length, and -2 dimensions in time.

Dimensional Formulae and Dimensional Equations

- The expression which shows how and which of the base quantities represent the dimensions of a physical quantity is called the *dimensional formula* of the given physical quantity. For example, the dimensional formula of the volume is $[M^\circ\ L^3\ T^\circ]$, that of speed or velocity is $[M^\circ\ L\ T^{-1}]$.
- An equation obtained by equating a physical quantity with its dimensional formula is called the **dimensional equation** of the physical quantity.
- For example, the dimensional equations of volume $[V]$, speed $[v]$, force $[F]$ and mass density $[\rho]$ may be expressed as

    $[V] = [M^0\ L^3\ T^0]$

    $[v] = [M^0\ L\ T^{-1}]$

    $[F] = [M\ L\ T^{-2}]$

    $[\rho] = [M\ L^{-3}\ T^0]$

Dimensional Analysis and its Applications

- Only those physical quantities can be added or subtracted which have the same dimensions.

Cheking the Dimensional Consistency of Equations

- The magnitudes of physical quantities may be added together or subtracted from one another only if they have the same dimensions. We can add or subtract similar physical quantities. Velocity cannot be added to force, or an electric current cannot be subtracted from the thermodynamic temperature. This simple principle called **the principle of homogeneity of dimensions** in an equation is extremely useful in checking the correctness of an equation. If the dimensions of all the terms are not same, the equation is wrong.

$$x = x_0 + v_0\, t + (1/2)\, at^2$$

- **Conversion of one system of unit into another**

    Let the numerical values are n_1 and n_2 of a given quantity Q in two unit systems and the units are –

$$u_1 = M_1^a L_1^b T_1^c \text{ and } u_2 = M_2^a L_2^b T_2^c$$

Therefore, by the principle, $nu = constant$

$$n_2 u_2 = n_1 u_1$$

$$n_2 [M_2^a L_2^b T_2^c] = n_1 [M_1^a L_1^b T_1^c]$$

$$\Rightarrow \quad n_2 = \frac{n_1 [M_1^a L_1^b T_1^c]}{[M_2^a L_2^b T_2^c]}$$

$$\Rightarrow \quad n_2 = \left[\frac{M_1}{M_2}\right]^a \left[\frac{L_1}{L_2}\right]^b \left[\frac{T_1}{T_2}\right]^c n_1$$

Deducing Relation among the Physical Quantities

♦ **To derive the formula by dimensional analysis method**

Let a physical quantity x depends on the another quantities P, Q and R. Then

$$x \propto (P)^a (Q)^b (R)^c$$

or, $x = k (P)^a (Q)^b (R)^c$ .....(1)

Now consider dimensional formula of each quantity in both sides.

$$M^x L^y T^z = [M^{x_1} L^{y_1} T^{z_1}]^a [M^{x_2} L^{y_2} T^{z_2}]^b [M^{x_3} L^{y_3} T^{z_3}]^c$$

$$\Rightarrow M^x L^y T^z = M^{ax_1} L^{ay_1} T^{az_1} M^{bx_2} L^{by_2} T^{bz_2} M^{cx_3} L^{cy_3} T^{cz_3}$$

$$\Rightarrow M^x L^y T^z = M^{ax_1+bx_2+cx_3} L^{ay_1+by_2+cy_3} T^{az_1+bz_2+cz_3}$$

Now comparing the powers of both sides –

$$ax_1 + bx_2 + cx_3 = x \qquad ....(2)$$
$$ay_1 + by_2 + cy_3 = y \qquad ....(3)$$
$$az_1 + bz_2 + cz_3 = z \qquad ....(4)$$

After solving equations (2), (3) and (4) value of a, b and c will be m, n and o may be find out

Now substitute the values of x, y and z in equation (1)

Then obtained formula will be

$$x = (P)^m (Q)^n (R)^o$$

♦ **Limitations of dimensional Analysis :**

(i) While deriving a formula the proportionality constant cannot be found.

(ii) The formula for a physical quantity depending on more than three other physical quantities cannot be derived. It can be checked only.

(iii) The equations of the type $v = u \pm at$ cannot be derived. They can be checked only.

(iv) The equations containing trigonometrical functions ($\sin \theta$, $\cos \theta$, etc), logarithmic functions ($\log x$, $\log x^3$, etc) and exponential functions (e^x, e^{x^2}, etc) cannot be derived. They can be checked only.

Past Years ONE-LINERS
NEET/JEE Main/Board

- Energy, $E = F.S$ and $G = Fr^2/M.m$
- For screw guage diameter reading $= MSR + (CSR \times LC)$
- $\text{L.C.} = \dfrac{\text{Pitch}}{\text{No. of division on circular scale}}$
- Subtraction result has least number of decimal places of components
- For $Z = a^x b^y, \dfrac{\Delta z}{z} = \dfrac{x\Delta a}{a} + \dfrac{y\Delta b}{b}$
- Dimension of a physical quantity can be expressed in terms of fundamental quantities dimension
- In the relation $[v_C] = [\eta^x \rho^y r^x]$, express the all quantities in fundamental quantity, then power in LHS = power in RHS
- Exponential $e^{-\frac{x^2}{\alpha KT}}$ is dimensionless
- For density, relative error is $\dfrac{\Delta d}{d} = \dfrac{\Delta m}{m} + \dfrac{3\Delta L}{L} \quad \because d = \dfrac{m}{v} = \dfrac{m}{L^3}$
- Diameter of ball $= MSR + CSR \times (LC) \pm$ Zero error
- Measured value = mean value $\pm$ LC
- Zero error in screw guage is negative if zero of main scale is not visible
- In relation $T = 2\pi\sqrt{\dfrac{l}{g}}$

$$\dfrac{\Delta g}{g} = \dfrac{\Delta l}{l} + \dfrac{2\Delta T}{T}$$

Tips/Tricks/Tecchniques ONE-LINERS
(Exam Sample)

- The dimensions of a physical quantity do not depend on the system of units. The units of force in S.I. unit is newton and dyne in C.G.S. unit but its dimensions $[MLT^{-2}]$.
- A physical quantity that does not have any unit must be dimensionless. *e.g.*, refractive index.
- The physical relation involving logarithm, exponential, trigonometric ratios, numerical factors etc. cannot be derived by the method of dimensional analysis.

- Physical relations involving (+) or (–) sign cannot be derived by dimensional analysis.
- If units or dimensions of two physical quantities are same, these need not represent the same physical characteristics like torque and work have the same units (joule) and dimensions $[ML^2T^{-2}]$ but their physical characteristics are different.
- The order of magnitude of a physical quantity is its value in suitable power of 10 nearest to the actual value of the quantity.
- Angle is a physical quantity, which though is a ratio of two similar physical quantities (angle = arc / radius) but still requires a unit (degree or radian) to specify it along with its numerical value.
- Measurement is accurate if the systematic error in its measurement is relatively very low and measurement precise if the random error is small.
- A measurement is most accurate if its observed value is very-very close to the true value.
- The absolute error in each measurement is equal to the least count of the measuring instrument.
- The unit and dimensions of the absolute error are same as that of quantity itself.
- Least Count (L.C.) = $\dfrac{1 \text{ part on main scale}}{\text{number of parts on vernier scale}}$
- Least count of vernier callipers = 1 MSD – 1 VSD
  MSD = Main Scale Division
  VSD = Vernier Scale Division
- Least count of screw guage

$$= \dfrac{\text{pitch}(p)}{\text{no. of parts on circular scale } (n)}$$

Diameter of a spherical body like a ball measuring by a screw-guage = MSR + CSR($\times$ L.C.)-zero error.

- Significant figures are the number of digits upto which we are sure about their accuracy.
- Errors are always additive in nature.

For example, if a physical quantity (A) is related to four observations a, b, c and d as $A = \dfrac{a^2 b^3}{c\sqrt{d}}$ then percentage error in A = 2(% error in a) + 3(% error in b) + (% error in c) + $\dfrac{1}{2}$(% error in d)

- Significant figures retained after mathematical operations (+, –, $\times$ and $\div$) should be equal to the minimum significant figures involved in the operation.
- In an expression, if a quantity appears with a power less than one, its error contribution in the final result is reduced.
- To obtain dimensions formula of a physical quantity, first define its relation with other quantities where dimensions in M, L and T are known.
- The form of expression for a given physical quantity can be obtained using principle of homogeneity if we know the factors upon which that physical quantity depends.

3 Motion in a Straight Line

Position, Path Length and Displacement

- Motion is change in position of an object with time.
- Motion of objects along a straight line, is known as **rectilinear motion.**
- In **kinematics** we study ways to describe motion without going into the causes of motion.

Position

- In order to specify position, we need to use a reference point and a set of axes.
- A rectangular coordinate system consisting of three mutually perpenducular axes, labelled X-, Y-, and Z- axes. The point of intersection of these three axes is called origin (O) reference point. The coordinates (x, y. z) of an object describe the position of the object. This coordinate system along with a clock constitutes a **frame of reference.**
- For describing motion in one dimension, we need only one axis. To describe motion in two/three dimensions, we need a set of two/three axes.
- To describe motion along a straight line, choose an axis, say X-axis, so that it coincides with the path of the object. We then measure the position of the object with reference to a chosen origin, say O, as shown in Fig. Positions to the right of O are taken as positive and to the left of O, as negative.

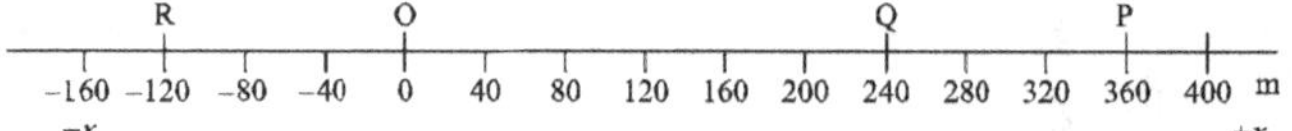

Fig.: x-axis, origin and positions of a car at different times.

- The position of point P and Q in Fig. are +360 m and +240 m. Similarly, the position of point R is –120 m.

Path Length

- Consider the motion of a car along the x-axis, the car was at $x = 0$ at $t = 0$.
- Consider two cases of motion. First the car moves from O to P. The distance moved by the car is OP = +360 m. This distance is called the path length.
- Second case, the car moves from O to P and then moves back from P to Q. Path length is OP + PQ = + 360 m + (+120 m) = + 480 m. Path length is a scalar quantity & equals to total length of path.

Displacement

- Displacement is the change in position. Let x_1 and x_2 be the positions of an object at time t_1 and t_2. Then its displacement, denoted by Δx is given by the difference between the final and initial positions :

$$\Delta x = x_2 - x_1$$

Delta (Δ) denote change in a quantity.

- Displacement of the car in moving from O to P is:
$$\Delta x = x_2 - x_1 = (+360 \text{ m}) - 0 \text{ m} = +360 \text{ m}$$

♦ The displacement of the car from P to Q is 240 m – 360 m = – 120 m. Negative sign indicates the direction of displacement.

♦ The magnitude of displacement may or may not be equal to the path length traversed by an object. Consider the motion of the car from O to P and back to Q. In this case, the path length = (+360 m) + (+120 m) = + 480 m. The displacement = (+240 m) – (0 m) = + 240 m.

♦ The magnitude of the displacement for a course of motion may be zero but the corresponding path length is not zero. If the car starts from O, goes to P and then returns to O, the displacement is zero. However, the path length of this journey is OP + PO = 360 m + 360 m = 720 m.

♦ A car is standing still at x = 40 m. The position-time graph for this car is a straight line parallel to the time axis.

♦ If an object moving along the straight line covers equal distances in equal intervals of time, it is said to be in **uniform motion.**

Average Velocity and Average Speed

♦ How fast is the position changing with time and in what direction? To describe this, define the quantity average velocity. **Average velocity** is defined as the change in position or displacement (Δx) divided by the time intervals (Δt), in which the displacement occurs:

$$v = \frac{x_2 - x_1}{t_2 - t_1} = \frac{\Delta x}{\Delta t}$$

where x_2 and x_1 are the positions of the object at time t_2 and t_1, respectively. Like displacement, average velocity is also a vector quantity. The x-t graphs for an object, moving with positive velocity, moving with negative velocity (Fig.) and at rest.

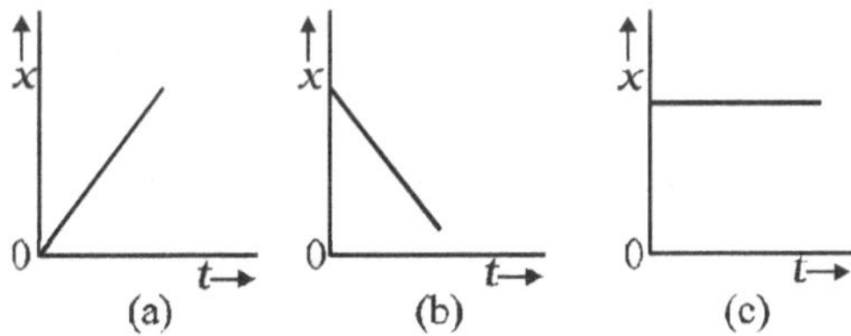

♦ Average speed is defined as the total path length travelled divided by the total time.

$$Average\ speed = \frac{Total\ path\ length}{Total\ time\ interval}$$

♦ If the motion of an object is along a straight line and in the **same direction**, the magnitude of displacement is equal to the total path length. The magnitude of average velocity is equal to the average speed. This is not always the case, speed is, in general, greater than the magnitude of the velocity.
Speed ≥ |velocity|

Instantaneous Velocity and Speed

Instantaneous Velocity

♦ The velocity at an instant is defined as the limit of the average velocity as the time interval Δt becomes infinitesimally small.

$$v = \lim_{\Delta t \to 0} \frac{\Delta x}{\Delta t} = \frac{dx}{dt}$$

♦ Slope of tangent on position time graph gives velocity at that instant $\dfrac{dx}{dt} = \tan\phi$

♦ For uniform motion, velocity is the same as the average velocity at all instants.

♦ Instantaneous speed or simply speed is the magnitude of velocity. For example, a velocity of $+\,24.0$ m s^{-1} and a velocity of -24.0 m s^{-1} — both have speed of 24.0 m s^{-1}.

♦ Instantaneous speed at an instant is equal to the magnitude of the instantaneous velocity at that point.

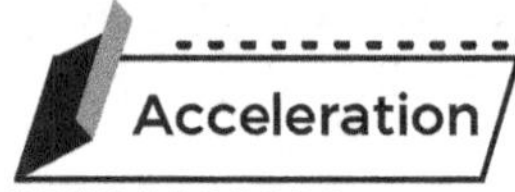

Acceleration

♦ The **average acceleration** $\bar{a}$ over a time interval is defined as the change of velocity divided by the time interval :

$$\bar{a} = \frac{v_2 - v_1}{t_2 - t_1} = \frac{\Delta v}{\Delta t}$$

♦ **Instantaneous acceleration** is defined as $a = \lim_{\Delta t \to 0} \dfrac{\Delta v}{\Delta t} = \dfrac{dv}{dt}.$

♦ The acceleration at an instant is the slope of the tangent to the v–t curve at that instant.

♦ Velocity is a quantity having both magnitude and direction, a change in velocity may involve change in either or both of these factors. Acceleration, therefore, may result from a change in speed (magnitude), a change in direction or changes in both.

♦ Position-time graphs for motion with positive, negative and zero acceleration are shown in Figs. (a), (b) and (c), respectively.

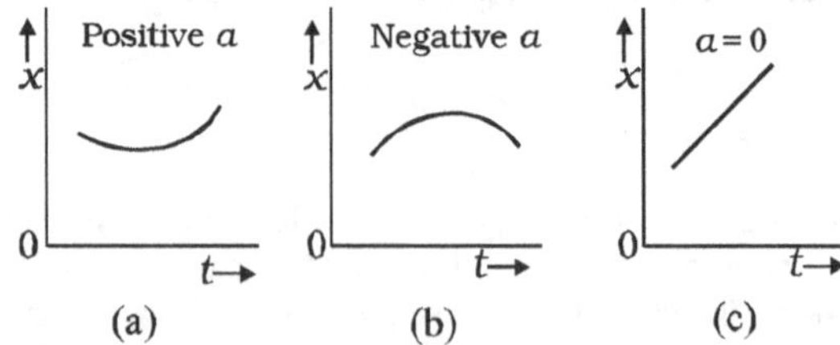

♦ The area under the curve represents the displacement over a given time interval.

Kinematic Equations for Uniformly Accelerated Motion

♦ For uniformly accelerated motion, we can derive some simple equations that relate displacement (x), time taken (t), initial velocity (v_0), final velocity (v) and acceleration (a).

(i) $v = v_0 + at$ (ii) $x = v_0 t + \dfrac{1}{2} at^2$ (iii) $v^2 = v_0^2 + 2ax$ (iv) $x_{nth} = V_0 + \dfrac{a}{2}(2n-1)$

Relative Velocity

♦ Consider two objects A and B moving uniformly with velocities v_A and v_B in one dimension, along x-axis. If $x_A(0)$ and $x_B(0)$ are positions of objects A and B, respectively at time $t = 0$, their positions $x_A(t)$ and $x_B(t)$ at time t are given by:

$$x_A(t) = x_A(0) + v_A t \; ; \; x_B(t) = x_B(0) + v_B t$$

♦ The displacement from object A to object B is given by

$$x_{BA}(t) = x_B(t) - X_A(t) = [x_B(0) - x_A(0)] + (v_B - v_A)t$$

Equation tells us that as seen from object A, object B has a velocity $v_B - v_A$:

♦ Velocity of object B relative to object A is; $v_{BA} = v_B - v_A$

Similarly, velocity of object A relative to object B is:

$$v_{AB} = v_A - v_B$$

Past Years ONE-LINERS
NEET/JEE Main/Board

♦ Distance travelled in n^{th} second, $S_n = u + \dfrac{a}{2}(2n-1)$.

♦ 3rd equation of motion $v^2 = u^2 + 2as$

♦ Angle swimmer makes with perpendicular to river flow to reach across river is

$$\sin\theta = \dfrac{\text{Velocity of river}}{V_{man}\,\text{w.r.t. river}}$$

♦ Total displacement (Δx) = $\Delta x_1 + \Delta x_2 + \Delta x_3$

♦ Velocity of man on a moving escalator = $V_m + V_{es}$

♦ Displacement = $\int V dt$

♦ Acceleration, $a = V\dfrac{dv}{dx}$

♦ Acceleration at any point is given by slope of tangent to velocity-time graph.

♦ To cross river straight $V_s \sin\theta = V_r$

♦ Tangent to distance time graph given idea of speed at that point.

♦ For a body thrown upward $v = u - gt$

♦   Motion under gravity displacement $\Delta x = ut - \dfrac{1}{2}gt^2$

Tips/Tricks/Tecchniques ONE-LINERS
(Exam Sample)

♦   An object is said to be point object if its mass is very small as compared to its velocity.

♦   The angle between acceleration and velocity is either 0° or 180° in one dimensional motion and it does not change with time.

♦   The speed of the particle increases when the angle between $\vec{a}$ and $\vec{v}$ lies between 0° and 90°.

♦   The speed of the particle decreases, when the angle between $\vec{a}$ and $\vec{v}$ lies between +90° and 180°.

♦   The speed of the particle remains constant when the angle between $\vec{a}$ and $\vec{v}$ is equal to 90°.

♦   The ratio of distance and displacement is equal or greater than 1.

♦   Displacement of a particle gives no information regarding the nature of the path followed by the particle.

♦   Average speed of a body is equal or greater than the magnitude of the average velocity of the body.

♦   The average speed of a body is equal to its instantaneous speed if the body moves with a constant speed.

♦   If a particle travels with speed v_1 for first half time of its total motion and with speed v_2 for next half time then $v_{av} = \dfrac{v_1 + v_2}{2}$.

♦   When a particle covers first half of a distance with speed v_1 and another half with speed v_2 then $v_{av} = \dfrac{2v_1 v_2}{v_1 + v_2}$.

♦   When a particle covers first one-third distance with speed v_1, next one third with speed v_2 and last one third with speed v_3, then $v_{av} = \dfrac{3v_1 v_2 v_3}{v_1 v_2 + v_2 v_3 + v_3 v_1}$

♦   If displacement time graph of two particles moving with velocities v_1 and v_2 are straight line with slopes θ_1 and θ_2 then $\dfrac{v_1}{v_2} = \dfrac{\tan\theta_1}{\tan\theta_2}$.

♦   Area enclosed by $v - t$ graph = displacement of the particle.

♦   Slope of velocity-time graph = acceleration.

♦   If a particle travels for a time t_1 with acceleration a_1 and for time t_2 with acceleration a_2 then average acceleration is $a_{av} = \dfrac{a_1 t_1 + a_2 t_2}{t_1 + t_2}$

♦   If a body is starting from rest and is moving with uniform acceleration then distance travelled by the body in t second is proportional to t^2 ($i.e., s \propto t^2$). For example : the ratio of distance covered in 1 sec, 2 sec and 3 sec is $1^2 : 2^2 : 3^2$ or $1 : 4 : 9$.

4. Motion in a Plane

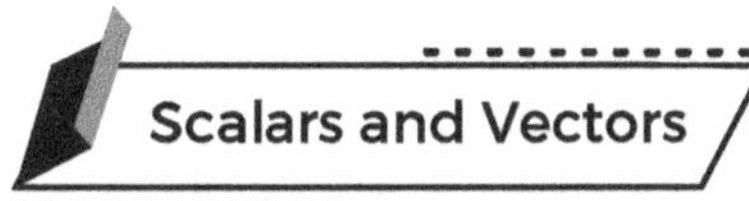

- In order to describe motion of an object in two dimensions (a plane) or three dimensions (space), we need to use vectors.
- We can classify quantities as scalars or vectors. Basically, the difference is that a direction is associated with a vector but not with a scalar.
- A **scalar** quantity is a quantity with magnitude only. It is specified completely by a single number, along with the proper unit. Examples are : the distance between two points, mass of an object, the temperature of a body and the time at which a certain event happened.
- The rules for combining scalars are the rules of ordinary algebra. Scalars can be added, subtracted, multiplied and divided just as the ordinary numbers.
- A **vector** quantity is a quantity that has both a magnitude and a direction and obeys the triangle law of addition or equivalently the parallelogram law of addition.
- A vector is specified by giving its magnitude by a number and its direction. Some physical quantities that are represented by vectors are displacement, velocity, acceleration and force.
- A vector is represented by an arrow placed over a letter, say $\vec{v}$. Vector is also represented by bold face.
- The magnitude of a vector is often called its absolute value, indicated by $|v| = v$.

Position and Displacement Vectors

- **Displacement vector** is the straight line joining the initial and final positions and does not depend on the actual path undertaken by the object between the two positions.

  In fig. (a) OP and OP' are **position vectors** and PP' is the **displacement vector**.
- The magnitude of displacement is either less or equal to the path length of an object between two points.

  | Displacement | $\leq$ Path length or distance

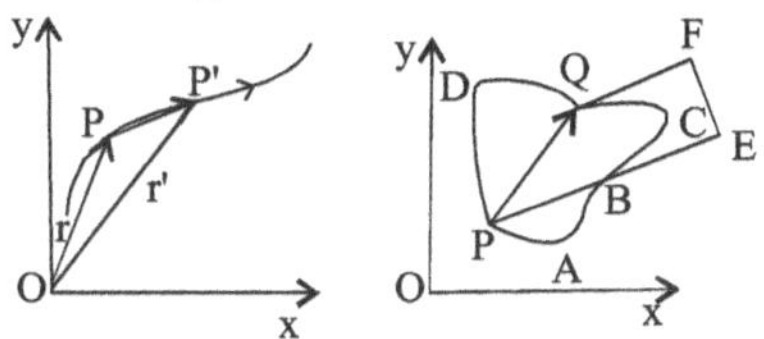

Fig.: (a) Position and displacement vectors. (b) Displacement vector PQ.

Equality of Vectors

♦ Two vectors A and B are said to be equal if, and only if, they have the same magnitude and the same direction.

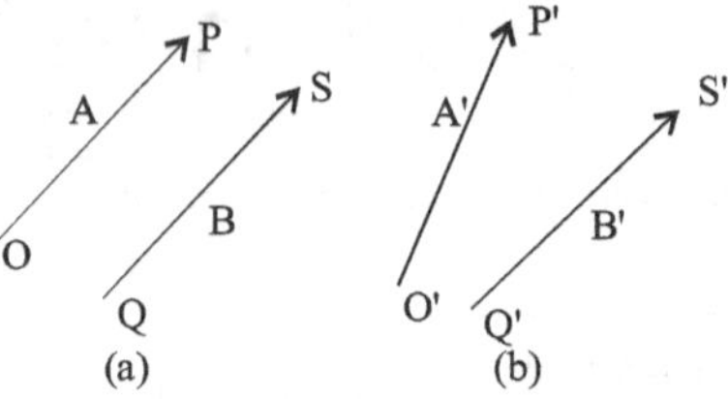

Fig.: (a) Two equal vectors **A** and **B**. (b) Two vectors **A'** and **B'** are unequal though they are of the same length.

Multiplication of Vectors by Real Numbers

♦ Multiplying a vector A with a positive number λ gives a vector whose magnitude is changed by the factor λ but the direction is the same as that of A :
$$|\lambda\mathbf{A}| = \lambda\,|\mathbf{A}|\ \text{if}\ \lambda > 0.$$

♦ Multiplying a vector **A** by a negative number-λ gives another vector whose direction is opposite to the direction of **A** and whose magnitude is λ times $|\mathbf{A}|$.

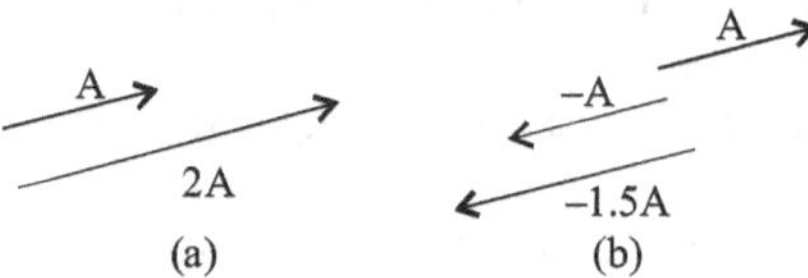

Fig.: (a) Vector **A** and the resultant vector after multiplying **A** by a positive number 2. (b) Vector A and resultant vectors after multiplying it by a negative number -1 and -1.5.

Addition and Subtraction of Vectors-Graphical Method

♦ Vectors are arranged head to tail, this graphical method is called the head-to-tail method.

♦ The two vectors and their resultant form three sides of a triangle, so this method is also known as triangle method of vector addition.

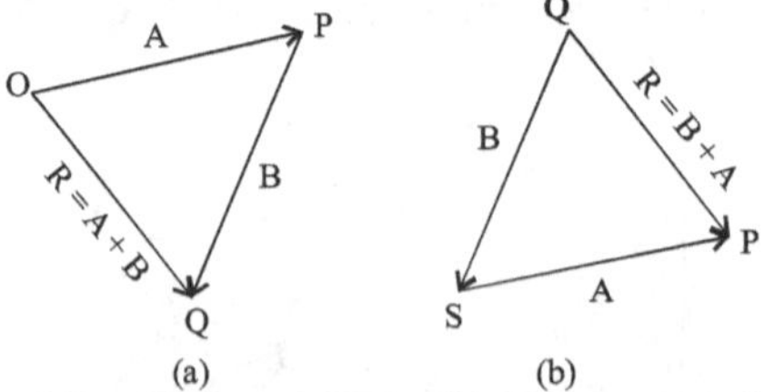

Fig.: (a) Vectors **A** and **B** added graphically. (b) Vectors **B** and **A** added graphically.

♦ **Subtraction of vectors** can be defined in terms of addition of vectors. We define the difference of two vectors **A** and **B** as the sum of two vectors **A** and $-\mathbf{B}$:

$$\mathbf{A} - \mathbf{B} = \mathbf{A} + (-\mathbf{B})$$

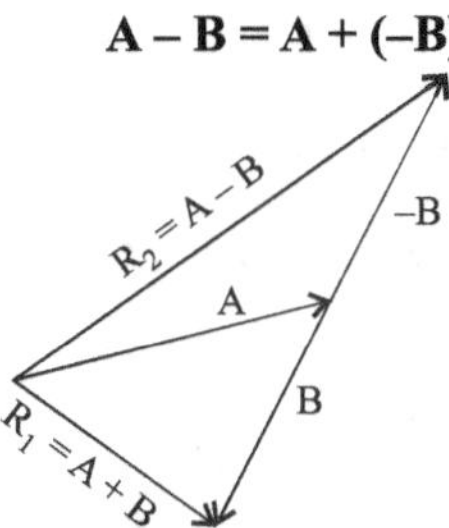

Fig.: (c) Subtracting vector B from vector A, the result is R_2. For comparison, addition of vector A and B, i.e. R_1 is also shown

♦ If we find the resultant of **B + A,** the same vector **R** is obtained. Thus, vector addition is **commutative:**
$$\mathbf{A} + \mathbf{B} = \mathbf{B} + \mathbf{A}$$

♦ The addition of vectors also obeys the **associative law**
$$(\mathbf{A} + \mathbf{B}) + \mathbf{C} = \mathbf{A} + (\mathbf{B} + \mathbf{C})$$

♦ If the magnitudes of the two vectors are the same, but the directions are opposite, the resultant vector has zero magnitude and is represented by **0** called a null vector or a zero vector :
$$\mathbf{A} - \mathbf{A} = \mathbf{0} \quad |\mathbf{0}| = 0$$

♦ Since the magnitude of a null vector is zero, its direction cannot be specified.

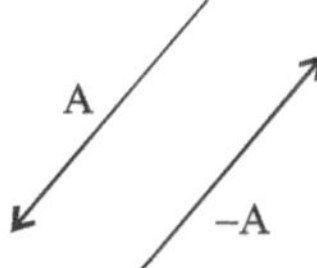

Fig.: Two vectors A and − A is shown.

♦ The null vector also results when we multiply a vector **A** by the number zero. The main properties of **0** are :
$$\mathbf{A} + \mathbf{0} = \mathbf{A}; \quad \lambda\, \mathbf{0} = \mathbf{0}; \quad 0\, \mathbf{A} = \mathbf{0}$$

♦ We can also use the **parallelogram method** to find the sum of two vectors.

Resolution of Vectors

♦ Let **a** and **b** be any two non-zero vectors in a plane with different directions and let A be another vector in the same plane. **A** can be expressed as a sum of two vectors — one obtained by multiplying a by a real number and the other obtained by multiplying b by another real number.
$$\mathbf{A} = \lambda\, \mathbf{a} + \mu\, \mathbf{b}$$

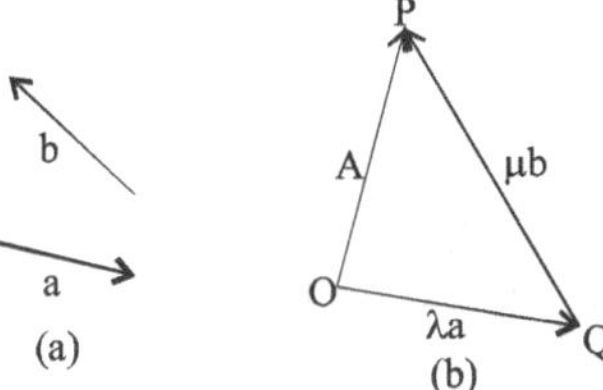

Fig.: (a) Two non-colinear vectors **a** and **b**.
(b) Resolving a vector **A** in terms of vectors **a** and **b**.

- One can resolve a given vector into two component vectors along a set of two vectors.
- A **unit vector** is a vector of unit magnitude and points in a particular direction. It has no dimension and unit.
- It is used to specify a direction only. Unit vectors along the x-, y- and z-axes of a rectangular coordinate system are denoted by $\hat{i}, \hat{j}$ and $\hat{k}$ respectively. Since these are unit vectors, we have

$$|\hat{i}|=|\hat{j}|=|\hat{k}|=1$$

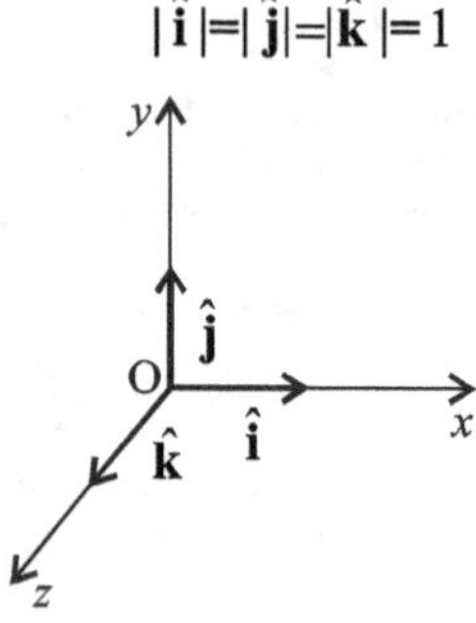

Fig.: Unit vectors $\hat{i}, \hat{j}$ and $\hat{k}$ lie along the x-,y- and z-axis

- If we multiply a unit vector, say $\hat{n}$ by a scalar, the result is a vector $\lambda = \lambda\hat{n}$. In general, a vector can be written as $A = |A|\hat{n}$

  where $\hat{n}$ is a unit vector along **A**.
- A component of a vector can be positive, negative or zero depending on the value of θ.

Vector Addition – Analytical Method

- If two vectors **A** and **B** in x-y plane with components A_x, A_y and B_x, B_y:

$$A = A_x\hat{i} + A_y\hat{j};$$

$$B = B_x\hat{i} + B_y\hat{j}$$

Let **R** be their sum. We have

$$R = A + B = (A_x\hat{i} + A_y\hat{j}) + (B_x\hat{i} + B_y\hat{j})$$

$$\Rightarrow R = (A_x + B_x)\hat{i} + (A_y + B_y)\hat{j}$$

$$\Rightarrow R = (A_x + B_x)\hat{i} + (A_y + B_y)\hat{j}$$

Since $R = R_x\hat{i} + R_y\hat{j}$

$$\therefore R_x = A_x + B_x, \; R_y = A_y + B_y$$

Parallelogram Law of Vector Addition

- Let **OP** and **OQ** represent the two vectors **A** and **B** making an angle θ. Then, using the parallelogram method of vector addition, **OS** represents the resultant vector **R** :

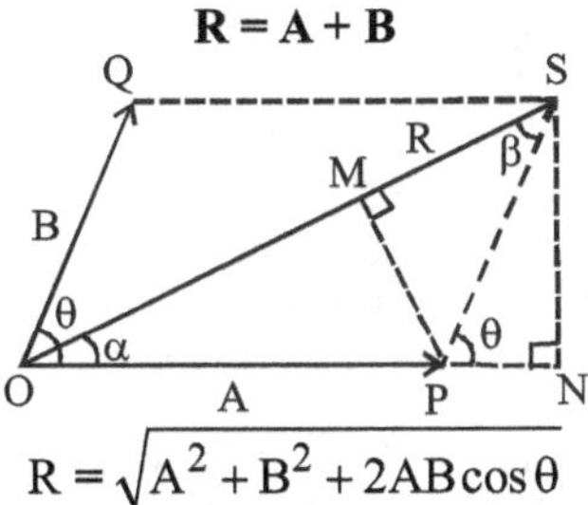

$$R = \sqrt{A^2 + B^2 + 2AB\cos\theta}$$

The above equation is known as **law of cosines** and $\dfrac{R}{\sin\theta} = \dfrac{A}{\sin\beta} = \dfrac{B}{\sin\alpha}$ is **law of sines**.

Motion in a Plane

Position Vector and Displacement

♦ The position vector r of a particle P located in a plane with reference to the origin of an x-y reference frame is given by $\mathbf{r} = x\,\hat{\mathbf{i}} + y\,\hat{\mathbf{j}}$

where x and y are components of **r** along x, and y axes or simply they are the coordinates of the object.

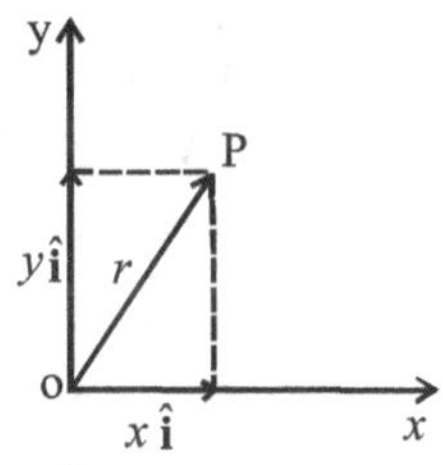

Fig.: Position vector r

Velocity

♦ **The average velocity** $(\overline{\mathbf{V}})$ of an object is the ratio of the displacement and the corresponding time interval :

$$\overline{\mathbf{v}} = \frac{\Delta\mathbf{r}}{\Delta t} = \frac{\Delta x\,\hat{\mathbf{i}} + \Delta y\,\hat{\mathbf{j}}}{\Delta t} = \hat{\mathbf{i}}\frac{\Delta x}{\Delta t} + \hat{\mathbf{j}}\frac{\Delta y}{\Delta t}$$

Or, $\overline{\mathbf{v}} = \overline{v}_x\hat{\mathbf{i}} + \overline{v}_x\hat{\mathbf{j}}$

♦ **The velocity (instantaneous velocity)** is given by the limiting value of the average velocity as the time interval approaches zero :

$$\mathbf{v} = \lim_{\Delta t \to 0}\frac{\Delta\mathbf{r}}{\Delta t} = \frac{d\mathbf{r}}{dt}$$

♦ **The direction of velocity at any point on the path of an object is tangential to the path at that point and is in the direction of motion.**

♦ We can express **V** in a component form:

$$\mathbf{v} = \frac{d\mathbf{r}}{dt} = \lim_{\Delta t \to 0}\left(\frac{\Delta x}{\Delta t}\hat{\mathbf{i}} + \frac{\Delta y}{\Delta t}\hat{\mathbf{j}}\right) = \hat{\mathbf{i}}\lim_{\Delta t \to 0}\frac{\Delta x}{\Delta t} + \hat{\mathbf{j}}\lim_{\Delta t \to 0}\frac{\Delta y}{\Delta t}$$

Or, $\mathbf{v} = \hat{\mathbf{i}}\dfrac{dx}{dt} + \hat{\mathbf{j}}\dfrac{dy}{dt} = v_x\hat{\mathbf{i}} + v_y\hat{\mathbf{j}}.$

where $v_x = \dfrac{dx}{dt}, v_y = \dfrac{dy}{dt}$

The magnitude of velocity, $v = \sqrt{v_x^2 + v_y^2}$

Direction of $\vec{v}$, $\tan\theta = \dfrac{v_y}{v_x} \Rightarrow \theta = \tan^{-1}\left(\dfrac{v_y}{v_x}\right)$

Acceleration

♦ **The average acceleration a** of an object for a time interval Δt moving in x-y plane is the change in velocity divided by the time interval :

$$\overline{a} = \frac{\Delta v}{\Delta t} = \frac{\Delta\left(v_x\hat{i} + v_y\hat{i}\right)}{\Delta t} = \frac{\Delta v_x}{\Delta t}\hat{i} + \frac{\Delta v_y}{\Delta t}\hat{j}$$

Or, $\overline{a} = a_x\hat{i} + a_y\hat{j}$

♦ The **acceleration** (instantaneous acceleration) is the limiting value of the average acceleration as the time interval approaches zero :

$$a = \lim_{\Delta t \to 0} \frac{\Delta v}{\Delta t}$$

Since $\Delta v = \Delta v_x\hat{i} + \Delta v_x\hat{j}$ we have

$$a = \hat{i} \lim_{\Delta t \to 0} \frac{\Delta v_x}{\Delta t} + \hat{j} \lim_{\Delta t \to 0} \frac{\Delta v_y}{\Delta t}$$

Or, $a = a_x\hat{i} + a_y\hat{j}$

♦ **In one dimension, the velocity and the acceleration of an object are always along the same straight line (either in the same direction or in the opposite direction). However, for motion in two or three dimensions, velocity and acceleration vectors may have any angle between 0° and 180° between them.**

Motion in a Plane with Constant Acceleration

♦ If an object is moving in *x-y* plane and its acceleration **a** is constant. Let the velocity of the object be V_0 at time $t = 0$ and V at time t then.

$$a = \frac{V - V_0}{t - 0} = \frac{V - V_0}{t} \Rightarrow V = V_0 + at$$

In terms of components:

$v_x = v_{ox} + a_x t$
$v_y = v_{ox} + a_y t$

$$x = x_o + v_{ox}t + \frac{1}{2}a_x t^2$$

$$y = y_o + v_{oy}t + \frac{1}{2}a_y t^2$$

♦ Motion in a plane (two-dimensions) can be treated as two separate simultaneous one-dimensional motions with constant acceleration along two perpendicular directions.

Relative Velocity in Two Dimensions

♦   Two objects A and B are moving with velocities $\mathbf{v_A}$ and $\mathbf{v_B}$ (each with respect to some common frame of reference, say ground.). Then, velocity of object A **relative to that of B is:** $\mathbf{v_{AB}} = \mathbf{v_A} - \mathbf{v_B}$
and similarly, the velocity of object B relative to that of A is : $\mathbf{v_{BA}} = \mathbf{v_B} - \mathbf{v_A}$
Therefore, $\mathbf{v_{AB}} = -\mathbf{v_{BA}}$
and, $|\mathbf{v_{AB}}| = |\mathbf{v_{BA}}|$

Projectile Motion

♦   An object that is in flight after being thrown or projected is called a **projectile**.
♦   The motion of a projectile is the result of two separate, simultaneously occurring components of motions. One component is along a horizontal direction without any acceleration and the other along the vertical direction with constant acceleration due to the force of gravity.
♦   The projectile is launched with velocity $\mathbf{v_0}$ that makes an angle θ_0 with the x-axis. After the object has been projected, the acceleration acting on it is that due to gravity which is directed vertically downward:

$\mathbf{a} = -g\hat{\mathbf{j}}$

$a_x = 0, \ a_g = -g$

The components of initial velocity $\mathbf{v_0}$ are :

$v_{ax} = v_0 \cos\theta_0$
$v_{ox} = v_0 \sin\theta_0$

The components of velocity at time t can be obtained

$v_x = v_{ox} = v_0 \cos\theta_0$
$v_y = v_0 \sin\theta_0 - gt$

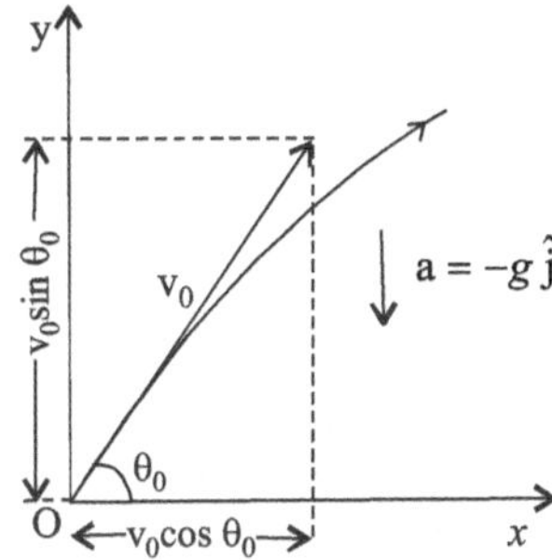

Fig.: Motion of an object projected with velocity $\mathbf{v_0}$ at angle θ_0.

♦   At the point of maximum height of the projectile, $v_y = 0$

$$\therefore \theta = \tan^{-1}\frac{v_y}{v_x} = 0$$

Time of maximum height

- Let time to reach at highest point be denoted by t_m. Since at this point, $v_y = 0$,

  $v_y = v_0 \sin \theta_0 - g t_m = 0$ or, $t_v = v_0 \sin \theta_0/g$

- The total time T_f during which the projectile is in flight can be obtained by putting $y = 0$

$$0 = v_0 \sin \theta T_f - \frac{1}{2} g T_f^2 \Rightarrow T_f = 2(v_0 \sin \theta_0)/g$$

T_f is known as the time of flight of the projectile. We note that $T_f = 2\, t_m$,

Maximum Height of a Projectile

- The maximum height h_m reached by the projectile can be calculated by substituting $t = t_m$

$$y = v_0 \sin \theta T_m - \frac{1}{2} g t_m^2$$

$$\text{or } y = h_m = (v_0 \sin \theta_0)\left(\frac{v_0 \sin \theta_0}{g}\right) - \frac{g}{2}\left(\frac{v_0 \sin \theta_0}{g}\right)^2$$

$$\text{or, } h_m = \frac{(v_0 \sin \theta_0)^2}{2g}$$

Horizontal Range of a Projectile

- The horizontal distance travelled by a projectile from its initial position ($x = y = 0$) to the position where it passes $y = 0$ during its fall is called the **horizontal range, R**. It is the distance travelled during the time of flight T_f.

  $R = (v_0 \cos \theta_0)\,(T_f)$

  $= (v_0 \cos \theta_0)\,(2 v_0 \sin \theta_0)/g$

$$\text{or, } R = \frac{v_0^2 \sin 2\theta_0}{g}$$

- R is maximum when $\sin 2\theta_0$ is maximum, i.e., when $\theta_0 = 45°$. The maximum horizontal range is, therefore,

$$R_m = \frac{v_0^2}{g}$$

Uniform Circular Motion

- When an object follows a circular path at a constant speed, the motion of the object is called **uniform circular motion.**
- An object is moving with uniform speed v in a circle of radius R as shown. Since the velocity of the object is changing continuously in direction, the object undergoes acceleration.
- Therefore, the **centripetal acceleration** a_c is:

$$a_c = \left(\frac{v}{R}\right) v = v^2/R$$

- The acceleration of an object moving with speed v in a circle of radius R has a magnitude v^2/R and is always directed towards the centre. This is why this acceleration is called centripetal acceleration.

- We define the angular speed ω (Greek letter omega) as the time rate of change of angular displacement :
$$\omega = \frac{\Delta\theta}{\Delta t}$$

- **Relation between linear velocity and angular velocity is**
$v = R\omega$

- Centripetal acceleration a_c in terms of angular speed:
$$a_c = \frac{v^2}{R} = \frac{\omega^2 R^2}{R} = \omega^2 R \; ; \; a_c = \omega^2 R$$

- The time taken by an object to make one revolution is known as its time period T and the number of revolution made in one second is called its **frequency v** **(=1/T).**

- Distance moved by the object in one time period is $s = 2\pi R$. Therefore, $v = 2\pi R/T = 2\pi Rv$

  In terms of frequency v, we have
  $\omega = 2\omega v$; $v = 2\omega Rv$; $a_c = 4\omega^2\, v^2 R$

Past Years ONE-LINERS NEET/JEE Main/Board

- In two dimensional motion, magnitude of velocity, $V = \sqrt{V_x^2 + V_y^2}$

- Maximum height in projectile motion, $H = \dfrac{u^2 \sin^2\theta}{2g}$

- When object shot from inclined plane kept at $\theta°$ and velocity say u, then distance travel $x_1 = \dfrac{u^2}{2g\sin\theta°}$

- Cross product of two vector $\vec{a}$ and $\vec{b}$
$$\vec{a}\times\vec{b} = (a_x\hat{i}+ a_y\hat{j}+a_z\hat{k})\times(b_x\hat{i}+b_y\hat{j}+b_z\hat{k})$$
$$= (a_y b_z - a_z b_y)\hat{i}-(a_x b_z - a_z b_x)\hat{j}+(a_x b_y - a_y b_x)\hat{k}$$

- Velocity along x direction $v_x = \dfrac{dx}{dt}$, velocity along y direction, $v_y = \dfrac{dy}{dt}$

  Acceleration along x direction, $a_x = \dfrac{dv_x}{dt}$, acceleration along y direction, $a_y = \dfrac{dv_y}{dt}$

  $\vec{a} = a_x\hat{i}+a_y\hat{j}$

- Resultant of vector $\vec{A}$ and $\vec{B}$, $R = |\vec{A}+\vec{B}| = \sqrt{|\vec{A}|^2 + |\vec{B}|^2 + 2\vec{A}\vec{B}\cos\theta}$

♦ $\vec{r} \cdot \vec{v} = 0$ hence $\vec{r} \perp \vec{v}$ and $\vec{a}$ is directed towards the origin.

♦ Shortest distance $= \dfrac{d}{v \cos \theta}$

♦ In circular motion, acceleration vector is along $-\vec{R}$ and its magnitude $= \dfrac{V^2}{R}$ Velocity of particle, $V = \omega R$

♦ For two vectors $\vec{A}$ and $\vec{B}$ to be orthogonal, $\vec{A} \cdot \vec{B} = 0$

♦ Range $R = \dfrac{u^2 \sin 2\theta}{g}$, height in projectile motion, $H = \dfrac{u^2 \sin^2 \theta}{2g}$

♦ $V_x = \dfrac{dx}{dt}, V_y = \dfrac{dy}{dt}, V = \sqrt{V_x^2 + V_y^2}$

♦ $t_{minimum} = \dfrac{\left| (\vec{r}_{BA}) \cdot (\vec{v}_{BA}) \right|}{\left| (\vec{v}_{BA}) \right|^2}$

Tips/Tricks/Tecchniques ONE-LINERS
(Exam Sample)

♦ In a plane, a vector can have only two rectangular components and only three rectangular components are possible in space.

♦ Vectors can be added and subtracted geometrically.

♦ We cannot divide vectors as directions cannot be divided.

♦ Unit vector of given vector acts in the direction of vector.

♦ Minimum number of collinear vectors of equal magnitude whose resultant can be zero is two.

♦ Minimum number of coplaner vectors of unequal magnitude whose resultant can be zero is three.

♦ Tensors are those physical quantities which have different values in different directions. For example : Moment of inertia.

♦ For three vectors $\vec{A}$, $\vec{B}$ and $\vec{C}$ if $\vec{A} + \vec{B} = \vec{C}$ and $\vec{A} + \vec{B} + \vec{C} = \vec{0}$, then $\vec{A}$, $\vec{B}$ and $\vec{C}$ lie in one plane.

♦ If the vectors $\vec{A}$ and $\vec{B}$ are such that $\vec{A} \times \vec{B} = \vec{C}$, then $\vec{C}$ is perpendicular to $\vec{A}$ as well as $\vec{B}$.

♦ If two vectors $\vec{A}$ and $\vec{B}$ are such that $|\vec{A} \times \vec{B}| = |\vec{A} - \vec{B}|$, then angle between $\vec{A}$ and $\vec{B}$ is 90°

♦ If $\vec{A} + \vec{B} = \vec{C}$ and $A^2 + B^2 = C^2$, then the angle between $\vec{A}$ and $\vec{B}$ is 90°.

♦ The projectile follows parabolic path.

♦ In projectile motion, momentum is never zero throughout the motion.

♦ At highest point of the projectile path, acceleration due to gravity acting vertically downward makes an angle of 90° with the horizontal component of the velocity of the projectile.

♦ Time of flight and maximum height of projectile motion depend on the vertical component of the velocity of projection.

♦ When a particle moves along the circular path with constant speed, its linear velocity and linear momentum changes at every point of motion but its angular speed and kinetic energy remains constant.

♦ If an object moves in a circular path with constant angular velocity, the object will possess only centripetal acceleration.

♦ If an object moves in a circular path with increasing angular velocity, the object will possess both centripetal and transverse acceleration.

♦ Uniform circular motion is a case of uniformly accelerated motion.

♦ For a given vector $\vec{A}$, $\vec{A} \times \vec{A} = \vec{0}$ and $\vec{A} - \vec{A} = \vec{0}$ but $\vec{A} \times \vec{A} \neq \vec{A} - \vec{A}$ because $\vec{A} \times \vec{A} \perp \vec{A}$ and $\vec{A} - \vec{A}$ is collinear with $\vec{A}$

♦ Projection of a vector $\vec{A}$ in the direction of vector $\vec{B}$ is given by $= \dfrac{\vec{A}.\vec{B}}{|\vec{B}|}$

♦ If two vectors $\vec{A}$ and $\vec{B}$ makes an angle of 45° with each other, then $\vec{A}.\vec{B} = |\vec{A} \times \vec{B}|$

♦ The horizontal range of projectile is maximum when $\theta = 45°$

$$R_{max} = \dfrac{u^2}{g}$$

♦ For maximum range of projectile, the height attained by the projectile is :

$$H = \dfrac{u^2}{4g} = \dfrac{R_{max}}{4}$$

♦ For maximum range of the projectile, the time of flight is: $T = 2t = \dfrac{\sqrt{2}u}{g}$

♦ The maximum height attained by a projectile is given by $H_{max} = \dfrac{u^2}{2g}$

It is twice of height attained, when the range is maximum.

♦ If velocity of projection is made n times, the maximum height attained and the range become n^2 times and the time of flight becomes n times the initial value.

♦ A projectile is projected with a velocity u at an angle of α with the horizontal direction up the inclined plane. If β be the angle of inclination of plane, then

Time of flight, $T = \dfrac{2u\sin(\alpha - \beta)}{g\cos\beta}$, Range, $R = \dfrac{u^2}{g(1 + \sin\beta)}$

Range of projectile along the inclined plane

$$R = \dfrac{2u^2 \sin(\alpha - \beta).\cos\alpha}{g\cos^2\beta}$$

5 — Laws of Motion

Aristotle's Fallacy

- A force is required to put a stationary body in motion or stop a moving body, and some external agency is needed to provide this force.
- The external agency may or may not be in contact with the body.
- Aristotle (384 B.C– 322 B.C.), held the view that if a body is moving, something external is required to keep it moving.
- Aristotelian law of motion may be phrased as: An external force is required to keep a body in motion.
- In fact, force is necessary in practice to counter the opposing force of friction.
- The opposing forces such as friction (solids) and viscous forces (for fluids) are always present in the natural world. This explains why forces by external agencies are necessary to overcome the frictional forces to keep bodies in uniform motion. Here Aristotle went wrong.

The Law of Inertia

- Galileo concluded that an object moving on a frictionless horizontal plane must neither have acceleration nor retardation, i.e. it should move with constant velocity.
- The state of rest and the state of uniform linear motion (motion with constant velocity) are equivalent. In both cases, there is no net force acting on the body.
- Inertia means **resistance to change**. If the net external force on the body is zero, a body at rest continues to remain at rest and a body in motion continues to move with a uniform velocity. This property of the body is called inertia.

Newton's First Law of Motion

Law of inertia

- Every body continues to be in its state of rest or of uniform motion in a straight line unless compelled by some external force to act otherwise.
- If the net external force on a body is zero, its acceleration is zero. Acceleration can be non zero only if there is a net external force on the body.

Newton's Second Law of Motion

♦ The second law of motion refers to the general situation when there is a net external force acting on the body.

♦ It relates the net external force to the acceleration of the body.

Momentum

♦ Momentum of a body is defined to be the product of its mass m and velocity **v**, and is denoted by **p**:

p $= m$**v**

Momentum is clearly a vector quantity.

♦ The greater the rate of change of momentum, the greater is the force not only depends on the change in momentum but also on how fast the change is brought about.

♦ Force is necessary for changing the direction of momentum, even if its magnitude is constant. We can feel this while rotating a stone in a horizontal circle with uniform speed by means of a string.

Newton's Second Law of Motion

♦ The rate of change of momentum of a body is directly proportional to the applied force and takes place in the direction in which the force acts.

♦ If under the action of a force **F** for time interval Δt, the velocity of a body of mass m changes from **v** to **v** $+ \Delta$**v** i.e. its initial momentum **p** $= m$**v** changes by Δ**p** $= m\Delta$**v**. According to the Second Law,

$$\mathbf{F} \propto \frac{\Delta \mathbf{p}}{\Delta t} \quad \text{or} \quad \mathbf{F} = k\frac{\Delta \mathbf{p}}{\Delta t}$$

where k is a constant of proportionality.

For a body of fixed mass m,

$$\frac{d\mathbf{p}}{dt} = \frac{d}{dt}(m\mathbf{v}) = m\frac{d\mathbf{v}}{dt} m\,\mathbf{a}$$

i.e the Second Law can also be written as

$$\mathbf{F} = k\,m\,\mathbf{a}$$

which shows that force is proportional to the product of mass m and acceleration **a**.

For simplicity, we choose $k = 1$. The second law then is

$$\mathbf{F} = \frac{d\mathbf{p}}{dt} = m\,\mathbf{a}$$

♦ In SI unit force is one that causes an acceleration of 1 m s^{-2} to a mass of 1 kg. This unit is known as newton
$1 \text{ N} = 1 \text{ kg m s}^{-2}$.

- If a force is not parallel to the velocity of the body, but makes some angle with it, it changes only the component of velocity along the direction of force. The component of velocity normal to the force remains unchanged.
- The second law of motion is applicable to a single point particle.

Impulse

- The product of force and time, which is the change in momentum of the body remains a measurable quantity. This product is called impulse:
  Impulse = Force × time duration
  = Change in momentum
- A large force acting for a short time to produce a finite change in momentum is called an *impulsive force*.

Newton's Third Law of Motion

- According to Newtonian mechanics, force never occurs singly in nature. Force is the mutual interaction between two bodies. Forces always occur in pairs.
- The mutual forces between two bodies are always equal and opposite.

Newton's Third Law

- **To every action, there is always an equal and opposite reaction.**
- There is no cause effect relation implied in the third law. The force on A by B and the force on B by A act at the same instant.
- Action and reaction forces act on different bodies, not on the same body. Consider a pair of bodies A and B. According to the third law,

$$\mathbf{F}_{AB} = -\mathbf{F}_{BA}$$

(force on A by B) = – (force on B by A)

Conservation of Momentum

The **total momentum of an isolated system of interacting particles is conserved.**

- Two bodies A and B, with initial momenta P_A and P_B collide, get apart, with final momenta $\mathbf{p}'_A$ and $\mathbf{p}'_B$ respectively.

$$\mathbf{p}'_A + \mathbf{p}'_B = \mathbf{p}_A + \mathbf{p}_B$$

This is true whether the collision is elastic or inelastic.

- In elastic collisions, there is a second condition that the total initial kinetic energy of the system equals the total final kinetic energy.

Equilibrium of a Particle

- Equilibrium of a particle in mechanics refers to the situation when the net external force on the particle is zero.
- If two forces $\mathbf{F}_1$ and $\mathbf{F}_2$, act on a particle, equilibrium requires

$$\mathbf{F}_1 = -\mathbf{F}_2$$

- Equilibrium under three concurrent forces F_1, F_2 and F_3 requires that the vector sum of the three forces is zero.

$$F_1 + F_2 + F_3 = 0 \qquad \text{...(i)}$$

Common Forces in Mechanics

- A contact force on an object arises due to contact with some other object: solid or fluid. When bodies are in contact (e.g. a book resting on a table, a system of rigid bodies connected by rods, hinges and other types of supports), there are mutual contact forces (for each pair of bodies) satisfying the third law.
- The component of contact force normal to the surfaces in contact is called normal reaction.
- The component parallel to the surfaces in contact is called friction. The viscous force, air resistance, etc are also examples of contact forces.
- For an inextensible string, the force constant is very high. The restoring force in a string is called tension.
- Spring force $F = -kx$ where x is the displacement and k is the force constant.
- It is customary to use a constant tension T throughout the string. This assumption is true for a string of negligible mass.
- At the microscopic level, all bodies are made of charged constituents (nuclei and electrons) and the various contact forces arising due to elasticity of bodies molecular collisions and impacts, etc.

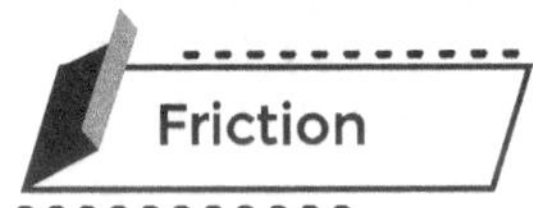

Friction

- **Static friction** does not exist by itself. When there is no applied force, there is no static friction.
- It comes into play the moment there is an applied force. As the applied force F increases, f_s also increases, remaining equal and opposite to the applied force (up to a certain limit), keeping the body at rest. Hence, it is called static friction.
- **Static friction opposes impending motion**. The term impending motion means motion that would take place (but does not actually take place) under the applied force. if friction were absent.

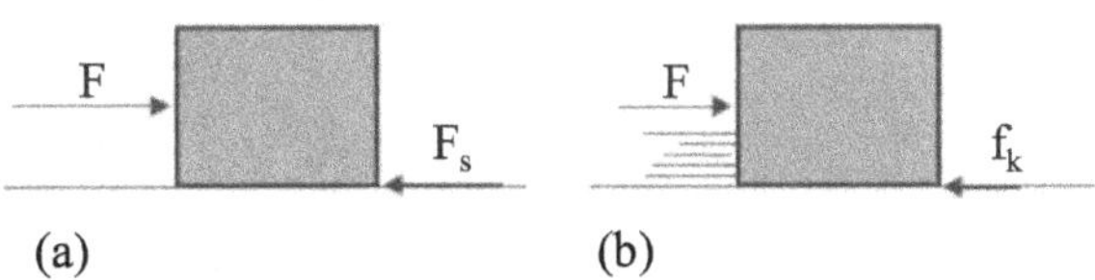

(a)   (b)

- Limiting value of static friction $(f_s)_{\max}$ is independent of the area of contact and varies with the normal force(N) approximately as :

$$(f_s)_{\max} = \mu_s N$$

where μ_s is a constant of proportionality depending only on the nature of the surfaces in contact.

♦ The law of static friction may thus be written as

$$f_s \le \mu_s N$$

♦ Frictional force that opposes relative motion between surfaces in contact is called **kinetic** or **sliding friction** and is denoted by $\mathbf{f_k}$.

♦ Kinetic friction, like static friction, is found to be independent of the area of contact. Further, it is nearly independent of the velocity. It satisfies a law similar to that for static friction:

$$\mathbf{f_k} = \mu_k \mathbf{N}$$

where μ_k the coefficient of kinetic friction, depends only on the surfaces in contact.

♦ μ_k is less than μ_s. When relative motion has begun, the acceleration of the body according to the second law is $(F - f_k)/m$.

♦ For a body moving with constant velocity, $F = f_k$. If the applied force on the body is removed, its acceleration is $-f_k/m$ and it eventually comes to a stop.

♦ Friction, by definition, is the component of the contact force parallel to the surfaces in contact, which opposes impending or actual relative motion between the two surfaces.

♦ Static friction provides the same acceleration to the box as that of the train, keeping it stationary relative to the train.

Rolling friction

♦ A body like a ring or a sphere rolling without slipping over a horizontal plane will suffer no friction, in principle. At every instant, there is just one point of contact between the body and the plane and this point has no motion relative to the plane. In this ideal situation, kinetic or static friction is zero and the body should continue to roll with constant velocity.

♦ For the same weight, rolling friction is much smaller than static or sliding friction. This is the reason why discovery of the wheel has been a major milestone in human history.

♦ During rolling, the surfaces in contact get momentarily deformed a little, and this results in a finite area (not a point) of the body being in contact with the surface. The net effect is that the component of the contact force parallel to the surface opposes motion.

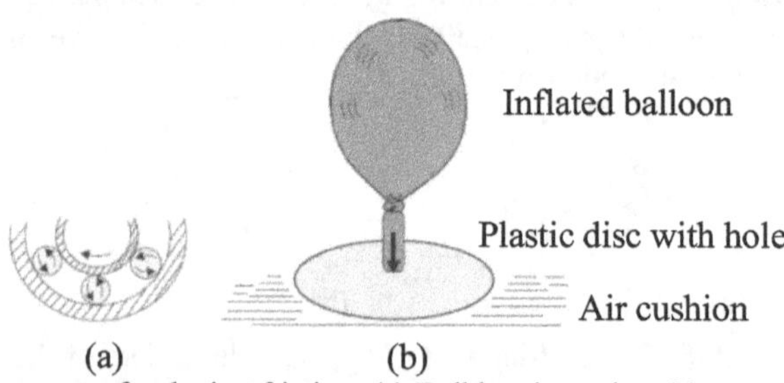

Fig.: Some ways of reducing friction. (a) Ball bearings placed between moving parts of a machine. (b) Compressed cushion of air between surfaces in relative motion.

- $M_S > M_K > M_R$
- In many situations, like in a machine with different moving parts, friction does have a negative role. It opposes relative motion and thereby dissipates power in the form of heat, etc.

Methods of Reducing Friction

- Lubricants are a way of reducing kinetic friction in a machine.
- Another way is to use ball bearings between two moving parts of a machine. Since the rolling friction between ball bearings and the surfaces in contact is very small, power dissipation is reduced.
- A thin cushion of air maintained between solid surfaces in relative motion is another effective way of reducing friction.
- Similarly, static friction is important in daily life. We are able to walk because of friction.
- It is impossible for a car to move on a very slippery road. On an ordinary road, the friction between the tyres and the road provides the necessary external force to accelerate the car.

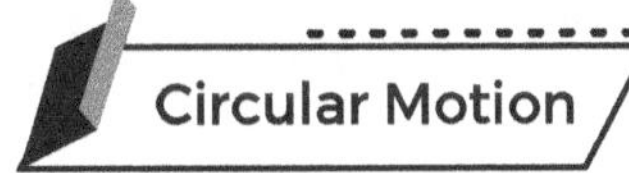

Circular Motion

- Acceleration of a body moving in a circle of radius R with uniform speed v is v^2/R directed towards the centre. According to the second law, the force f_c providing this acceleration is :

$$f_c = \frac{mv^2}{R}$$

where m is the mass of the body.
- This force directed forwards the centre is called the centripetal force.

Motion of a car on a level road

- Three forces act on the car
  - (i) The weight of the car,
  - (ii) Normal reaction, N
  - (iii) Frictional force, f

As there is no acceleration in the vertical direction

$N - mg = 0; N = mg$

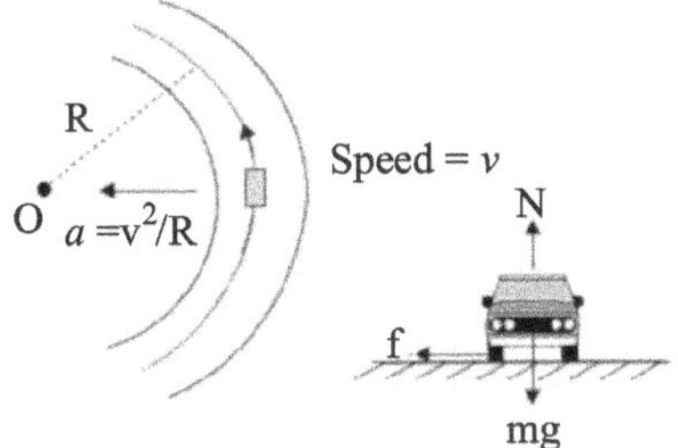

Fig.: Circular motion of a car on a level road

- The centripetal force required for circular motion is along the surface of the road, and is provided by the component of the contact force between road and the car tyres along the surface.
- It is the static friction that provides the centripetal acceleration. Static friction opposes the impending motion of the car moving away from the circle.

$$f \le \mu_s N = \frac{mv^2}{R}$$

$$v^2 \le \frac{\mu_s RN}{m} = \mu_s Rg \qquad\qquad [\because N = mg]$$

- For a given value of μ_s and R, there is a maximum speed of circular motion of the car possible, namely

$$v_{max} = \sqrt{\mu_s Rg}$$

Motion of a car on a banked road

- There is no acceleration along the vertical direction, the net force along this direction must be zero. Hence,

$$N \cos\theta = mg + f \sin\theta \qquad\qquad ...(i)$$

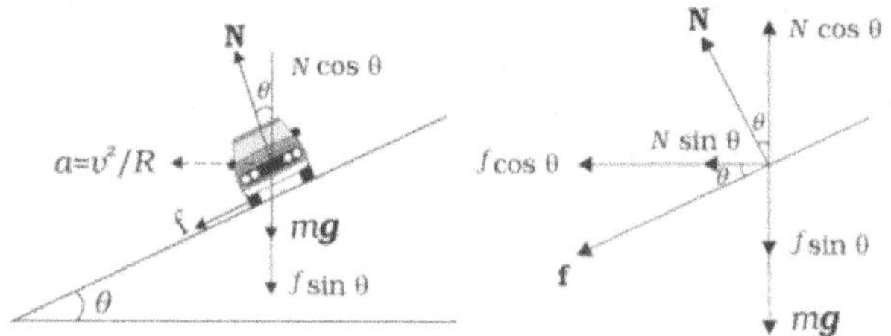

Fig.: Circular motion of a car on a banked road

The centripetal force is provided by the horizontal components of N and f.

$$N \sin\theta + f \cos\theta = \frac{mv^2}{R} \qquad\qquad ...(ii)$$

But $f \le \mu_s N$

Thus to obtain v_{max} we put

$f = \mu_s N.$

Then equation (i) and (ii) become

$N \cos\theta = mg + \mu_s N \sin\theta$

$N \sin\theta + \mu_s N \cos\theta = mv^2/R$

Solving equations, we obtain

$$N = \frac{mg}{\cos\theta - \mu_s \sin\theta}$$

Substituting value of N we get

$$\frac{mg(\sin\theta + \mu_s\cos\theta)}{\cos\theta - \mu_s\sin\theta} = \frac{mv_{max}^2}{R} \quad \text{or} \; V_{max} = \left(Rg\frac{\mu_s + \tan\theta}{1 - \mu_s\tan\theta} \right)^{\frac{1}{2}}$$

♦ The maximum possible speed of a car on a banked road is greater than that on a flat road.

For $\mu_s = 0$

$v_0 = (Rg\tan\theta)^{\frac{1}{2}}$

♦ At this speed, frictional force is not needed at all to provide the necessary centripetal force. Also, for $V < V_0$ frictional force will be up the slope and that a car can be parked only if $\tan\theta \le \mu_s$.

Solving Problems in Mechanics

♦ A typical problem in mechanics usually does not merely involve a single body under the action of given forces. More often, we will need to consider an assembly of different bodies exerting forces on each other. Besides, each body in the assembly experiences the force of gravity.

♦ We can choose any part of the assembly and apply the laws of motion to that part provided we include all forces on the chosen part due to the remaining parts of the assembly.

♦ The practice of drawing **free-body diagrams** is of great help in solving problems in mechanics. It allows you to clearly define your system and consider all forces on the system due to objects that are not part of the system itself.

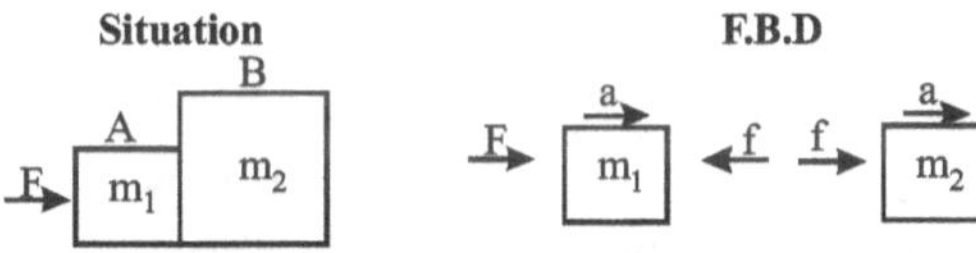

Past Years ONE-LINERS
NEET/JEE Main/Board

♦ Impulse = Change in linear momentum

♦ Acceleration of the system, $a = \dfrac{(m_1 - m_2)g}{(m_1 + m_2)}$ where $m_1 > m_2$

♦ Tension in vertical circle motion, $T = mg + \dfrac{mv^2}{r}$

♦ The velocity is maximum at lowest point so tension is maximum at the lowest position of mass, so the chance of breaking is maximum.

♦ Static friction, $f = \mu_s N \Rightarrow \mu_s = \dfrac{f}{N}$

♦ Acceleration on smooth inclined plane, $a = g\tan\theta$

♦ Net force on particle in uniform circular motion is centripetal force $\left(\dfrac{mv^2}{l}\right)$ which is provided by tension T.

♦ Maximum safe velocity on a curved road, $V_{max} = \sqrt{Rg\left[\dfrac{\mu_s + \tan\theta}{1 - \mu_s \tan\theta}\right]}$

♦ To complete the loop a body must enter a vertical loop of radius R with the minimum velocity $v = \sqrt{5gR}$.

♦ Coefficient of static friction, $\mu_s = \tan\theta$
Acceleration on rough inclined plane, $a = g\sin\theta - \mu_k(g)\cos\theta$

♦ Acceleration of system $a = \dfrac{F_{net}}{M_{total}}$

♦ Tension in the string, $T = \dfrac{m_1 m_2 g\,(1 + \mu_k)\,g}{m_1 + m_2}$

♦ The block will not fall from the wall if $f = mg$

♦ Angle of repose $= \tan\theta = \dfrac{dy}{dx}$

Tips/Tricks/Tecchniques ONE-LINERS
(Exam Sample)

♦ Inertia of a body is proportional to mass of the body.
♦ A body is in equilibrium, when sum of all the force acting on it is zero.
♦ A single isolated force cannot exist. Force always exists in pair.
♦ Newton's laws can be applied only in inertial frame of reference. In non inertial frame, pseudo force exists.
♦ The number of normal force acting on a body depends on the number of points of contact.
♦ When two or more blocks are placed one over the other on a horizontal ground, then normal reaction between two blocks will be equal to weight of the blocks over the common surface.
♦ The equipments which are used in measuring weight measure the normal reaction, not the actual weight. The normal reaction may be greater/equal/or less than actual weight.
♦ An isolated system is one in which no external force is acting.
♦ Action and reaction forces always act on different bodies. But in case of elastic bodies and springs, the action and reaction force act on same body.
♦ Action and reaction forces always act along the line joining the centres of two bodies.

- Impulse generally produces acceleration. But when the impulse is sharp, it produces velocity only.
- Kinetic friction is independent of velocity of the body.
- Centripetal force is not an independent force. It is governed by forces like gravitational force, tension, frictional force etc.
- If two masses m_1 and m_2 connected at the two ends of a string which is passing over a frictionless pulley, then

$$\text{Tension, T} = \frac{(2m_1 m_2)g}{m_1 + m_2} \text{ and Acceleration, a} = \left(\frac{m_1 - m_2}{m_1 + m_2}\right)g$$

- If w = weight of the body and θ = angle of friction then,

  Minimum pulling force, F of a block at an angle α from the horizontal, $F = \dfrac{w \sin \theta}{\cos(\alpha - \theta)}$.
- Minimum pushing force, F of a block at an angle α from the horizontal,

  $F = \dfrac{w \sin \theta}{\cos(\alpha + \theta)}$.
- Minimum pulling force, F of a block to move the body up on an inclined plane, $F = \dfrac{w \sin(\theta + \lambda)}{\cos(\alpha - \theta)}$; λ = angle of repose
- Minimum force, F to move a body in downward direction along the surface of inclined plane, $F = \dfrac{w \sin(\theta - \lambda)}{\cos(\alpha - \theta)}$.
- Minimum force, F of a block to avoid sliding of a body down on an inclined plane, $F = w\left[\dfrac{\sin(\lambda - \theta)}{\cos(\theta - \lambda)}\right]$.
- Force is not always in the direction of motion. Depending on the situation, **F** may be along **v**, opposite to **v**, normal to **v** or may make some other angle with **v**. In every case, it is parallel to acceleration.
- If **v** = 0 at an instant, i.e. if a body is momentarily at rest, it does not mean that force or acceleration are necessarily zero at that instant. For example, when a ball thrown upward reaches its maximum height, **v** = 0 but the force continues to be its weight *mg* and the acceleration is not zero but *g*.
- Force on a body at a given time is determined by the situation at the location of the body at that time. Force is not 'carried' by the body from its earlier history of motion. The moment after a stone is released out of an accelerated train, there is no horizontal force (or acceleration) on the stone, if the effects of the surrounding air are neglected. The stone then has only the vertical force of gravity.
- In the second law of motion $\mathbf{F} = m\,\mathbf{a}$, **F** stands for the net force due to all material agencies external to the body. **a** is the effect of the force. *m*a should not be regarded as yet another force, besides **F**.

Work, Energy and Power

Notions of Work and Kinetic Energy: The Work-energy Theorem

- Energy is our capacity to do work. In Physics too, the term 'energy' is related to work in this sense, but the term 'work' is defined much more precisely.
- Work is said to be done when a force applied on the body displaces the body through a certain distance in the direction of force.

The Scalar Product

- The scalar product or dot product of any two vectors **A** and **B**, denoted as **A·B** is defined as

$$\mathbf{A \cdot B} = A\,B \cos \theta$$

  where θ is the angle between the two vectors.

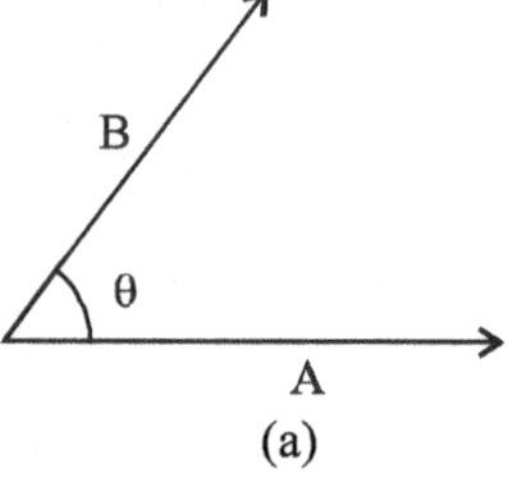

Fig.: (a) The scalar product of two vectors A and B is a scalar: A.B = AB cosθ.

- The dot product of **A** and **B** is a scalar quantity. Each vector, **A** and **B**, has a direction but their scalar product does not have a direction.
- **B** cos θ is the projection of **B** onto **A** and **A** cos θ is the projection of **A** onto **B**.

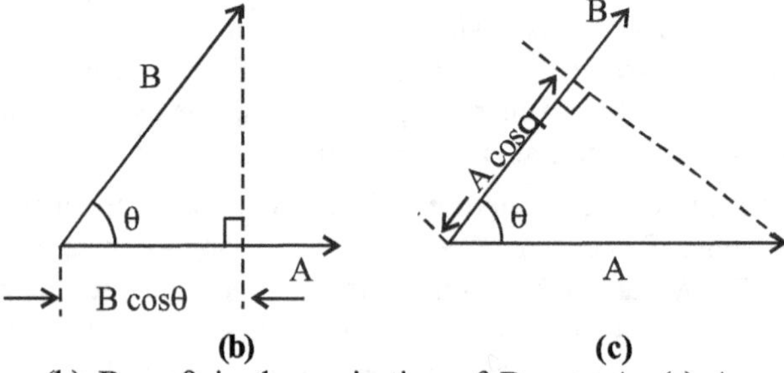

Fig.: (b) B cosθ is the projection of B onto A. (c) A cosθ is the projection of A onto B.

- The scalar product follows the **commutative law:**

$$\mathbf{A \cdot B = B \cdot A}$$

- Scalar product obeys the **distributive law:**

$$\mathbf{A \cdot (B + C) = A \cdot B + A \cdot C}$$

♦ For unit vectors $\hat{\mathbf{i}}, \hat{\mathbf{j}}, \hat{\mathbf{k}}$ we have

$$\hat{\mathbf{i}} \cdot \hat{\mathbf{i}} = \hat{\mathbf{j}} \cdot \hat{\mathbf{j}} = \hat{\mathbf{k}} \cdot \hat{\mathbf{k}} = 1$$

$$\hat{\mathbf{i}} \cdot \hat{\mathbf{j}} = \hat{\mathbf{j}} \cdot \hat{\mathbf{k}} = \hat{\mathbf{k}} \cdot \hat{\mathbf{i}} = 0$$

♦ The change in kinetic energy of a particle is equal to the work done on it by the net force.

$$K_f - K_i = w$$

$$\frac{1}{2}mv^2 - \frac{1}{2}mu^2 = \mathbf{ma.d} = \mathbf{F} \cdot \mathbf{d}$$

This is known as **work energy theorem**.

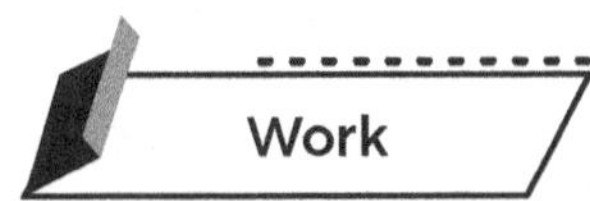
Work

♦ The **work** done by the force is defined to be the product of component of the force in the direction of the displacement and the magnitude of this displacement. Thus

$$W = (F \cos \theta)d = \mathbf{F} \cdot \mathbf{d}$$

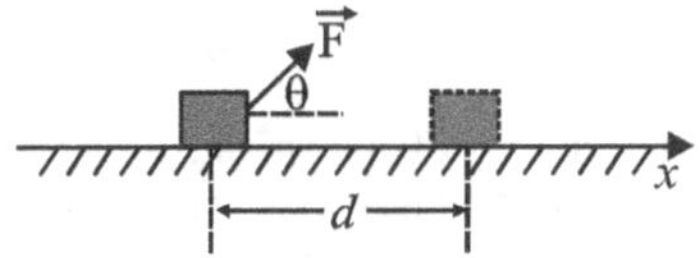

Fig.: An object undergoes a displacement d under the influence of the force F.

No work is done if :
- the displacement is zero. A weightlifter holding a 150kg mass steadily on his shoulder for 30 s does no work on the load during this time.
- the force is zero. A block moving on a smooth horizontal table is not acted upon by a horizontal force (since there is no friction), but may undergo a large displacement.
- the force and displacement are mutually perpendicular. This is so since, for $\theta = \pi/2$ rad $(= 90°)$, $\cos(\pi/2) = 0$.

♦ In many examples the frictional force opposes displacement and $\theta = 180°$. Then the work done by friction is negative $(\cos 180° = -1)$.

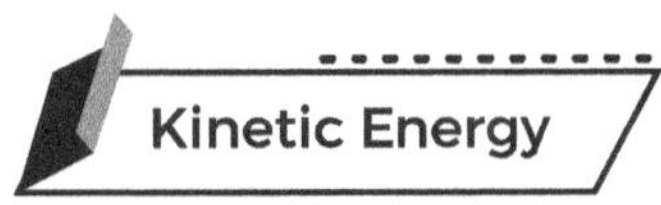
Kinetic Energy

♦ If an object of mass m has velocity $\mathbf{v}$, its kinetic energy K is

$$K = \frac{1}{2}m\,\mathbf{v} \cdot \mathbf{v} = \frac{1}{2}mv^2$$

♦ Kinetic energy is a scalar quantity. The kinetic energy of an object is a measure of the work an object can do by the virtue of its motion.

- The kinetic energy of a fast flowing stream has been used to grind corn. Sailing ships employ the kinetic energy of the wind.

Work Done by a Variable Force

- For a varying force the work done can be expressed as a definite integral of force over displacement.
- Then the work done by a variable force is

$$W = \int_{x_i}^{x_f} F(x)\,dx$$

The Work-Energy Theorem for a Variable Force

$$\text{or } K_f - K_i = \int_{x_i}^{x_f} F\,dx = W$$

The Concept of Potential Energy

- Potential energy is the 'stored energy' by virtue of the position or configuration of a body.
- Gravitational potential energy of an object, as a function of the height h, is denoted by V(h) and it is the negative of work done by the gravitational force in raising the object to that height.
$$V(h) = mgh$$
- If h is taken as a variable, the gravitational force F equals the negative of the derivative of $V(h)$ with respect to h.

$$F = -\frac{d}{dh}V(h) = mg$$

The negative sign indicates that the gravitational force is downward.
- Change in potential energy $(V_f - V_i) =$

$$\Delta V = V_f - V_i = \int_{x_i}^{x_f} F(x)\,dx = -W_{\text{conservative}}$$

- The work done by a **conservative force** such as gravity depends on the initial and final positions only.
- If the work done or the kinetic energy did depend on other factors such as the velocity or the particular path taken by the object, the force would be called **non-conservative**.

The Conservation of Mechanical Energy

- Suppose that a body undergoes displacement Δx under the action of a conservative force F. Then from the WE theorem we have,
$$\Delta K = F(x)\,\Delta x$$

- If the force is conservative, the potential energy function $V(x)$ can be defined such that
$$\Delta V = -F(x)\,\Delta x$$
The above equations imply that
$$\Delta K + \Delta V = 0$$
$$\Delta(K + V) = 0$$

- Individually the kinetic energy (K) and potential energy V(x) may vary from point to point but the sum is a constant.

- The work done by the **conservative force** depends only on the end points. This can be seen from the relation,
Work done $W = K_f - K_i = V(x_i) - V(x_f)$
which depends on the end points.

- Work done by this force in a closed path is zero.

- The total mechanical energy of a system is conserved if the forces, doing work on it, are conservative.

The Potential Energy of a Spring

- Force law for the spring is called Hooke's law and is mathematically stated as
$$F_s = -kx$$
The constant k is called the spring constant.

- The spring is said to be stiff if k is large and soft if k is small.

- If the extension is x_m, the work done by the spring force is

$$W_s = \int_0^{x_m} F_s \, dx = -\int_0^{x_m} kx \, dx = -\frac{k\,x_m^2}{2}$$

$$\Rightarrow V_f - V_i = -W = \frac{kx_m^2}{2}$$

$$\Rightarrow V = \frac{kx_m^2}{2} \qquad [\text{putting } V_i = 0 \ \& \ V_f = V]$$

$V = \dfrac{1}{2}kx_m^2$ is the potential energy stored in spring in extension or compression x_m.

♦ If the block is moved from an initial displacement x_i to a final displacement x_f, the work done by the spring force W_s is

$$W_s = -\int_{x_i}^{x_f} k\,x\,dx = \frac{k\,x_i^2}{2} - \frac{k\,x_f^2}{2}$$

♦ If the block is pulled from x_i and allowed to return to x_i;

$$W_s = -\int_{x_i}^{x_f} k\,x\,dx = \frac{k\,x_i^2}{2} - \frac{k\,x_i^2}{2} = 0$$

The **work done by the spring force in a cyclic process is zero.**

♦ Spring force (i) is position dependent only as first stated by Hooke ($F_s = -kx$); (ii) does work which only depends on the initial and final positions.

♦ The spring force is a **conservative force**.

♦ The kinetic energy (K) of spring gets converted to potential energy (V) and vice versa, however, the total mechanical energy remains constant.

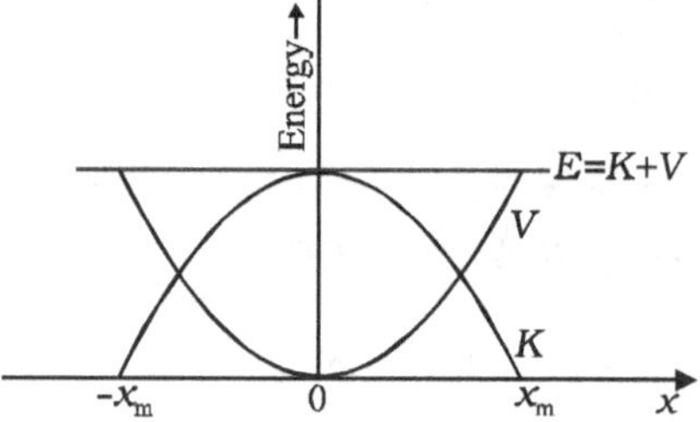

Various Forms of Energy : The Law of Conservation of Energy

Heat
♦ The form of energy which is exchanged among various bodies or system on account of temperature difference.

Chemical Energy
♦ A chemical reaction is basically a rearrangement of atoms. If the total energy of the reactants is more than the products of the reaction, heat is released and the reaction is said to be an **exothermic** reaction. If the reverse is true, heat is absorbed and the reaction is **endothermic**.

♦ The flow of electric current is associated with energy.

The Equivalence of Mass and Energy
♦ Albert Einstein (1879-1955) showed that mass and energy are equivalent and are related by the relation
$$E = m\,c^2$$

where c, the speed of light in vacuum is approximately 3×10^8 m s^{-1}. Thus, amount of energy associated with a kilogram of matter
$$E = 1 \times (3 \times 10^8)^2 \text{ J} = 9 \times 10^{16} \text{ J}.$$
This is equivalent to the annual electrical output of a large (3000 MW) power generating station.

Nuclear Energy

♦ In sun four light hydrogen nuclei fuse to form a helium nucleus whose mass is less than the sum of the masses of the reactants. This mass difference, called the **mass defect** Δm is the source of energy $(\Delta m)c^2$.
$\Delta m = \Delta E)/c^2$

♦ In **fission**, a heavy nucleus like uranium $^{235}_{92}$U, is split by a neutron into lighter nuclei. Once again the final mass is less than the initial mass and the mass difference translates into energy.

The Principle of Conservation of Energy

♦ The total mechanical energy of the system is conserved if the forces doing work on it are conservative. If some of the forces involved are non-conservative, part of the mechanical energy may get transformed into other forms such as heat, light and sound. However, the total energy of an isolated system does not change, as long as one accounts for all forms of energy.

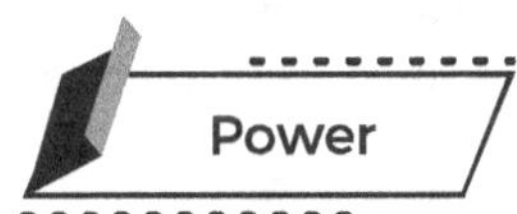

♦ **Power** is defined as the time rate at which work is done or energy is transferred.
♦ The **average power** of a force is defined as the ratio of the work, W, to the total time t taken

$$P_{av} = \frac{W}{t}$$

♦ The **instantaneous power** is defined as the limiting value of the average power as time interval approaches zero,

$$P = \frac{dW}{dt}$$

♦ The work dW done by a force F for a displacement dr is $dW = \mathbf{F} \cdot \mathbf{dr}$. The instantaneous power can also be expressed as

$$P = F \cdot \frac{\mathbf{dr}}{dt} = \mathbf{F} \cdot \mathbf{v}$$

where $\mathbf{v}$ is the instantaneous velocity when the force is $\mathbf{F}$.
♦ There is another unit of power, namely the **horse-power** (hp)
$$1 \text{ hp} = 746 \text{ W}$$
This unit is still used to describe the output of automobiles, motorbikes, etc.
♦ 1 kilowatt hour (kWh) of energy. $= 3.6 \times 10^6$ J

Our electricity bills carry the energy consumption in units of kWh.

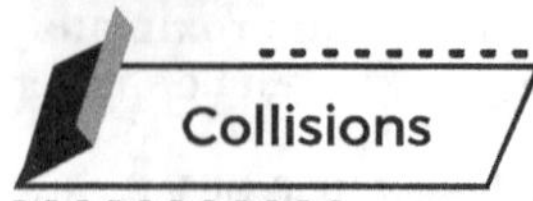

♦ In **collision** a strong force acts between two or more bodies for a short time as a result of which the energy and momentum of the interacting particles change.

Elastic and Inelastic Collisions

♦ In all collisions the total linear momentum is conserved; the initial momentum of the system is equal to the final momentum of the system.

♦ The total kinetic energy of the system is not necessarily conserved. The impact and deformation during collision may generate heat and sound. Part of the initial kinetic energy is transformed into other forms of energy.

♦ A useful way to visualise the deformation during collision is in terms of a 'compressed spring'. If the 'spring' connecting the two masses regains its original shape without loss in energy, then the initial kinetic energy is equal to the final kinetic energy but the kinetic energy during the collision time Δt is not constant. Such a collision is called an **elastic collision**.

♦ A collision in which the two particles move together after the collision is called a **completely inelastic collision.**

♦ The intermediate case where the deformation is partly relieved and some of the initial kinetic energy is lost is more common and is appropriately called an **inelastic collision.**

Collisions in One Dimension

♦ A **completely inelastic collision** in one dimension.

$\theta_1 = \theta_2 = 0$

$m_1 v_{1i} = (m_1 + m_2)v_f$ (momentum conservation)

$$v_f = \frac{m_1}{m_1 + m_2} v_{1i}$$

The loss in kinetic energy on collision is

$$\Delta K = \frac{1}{2}m_1 v_{1i}^2 - \frac{1}{2}(m_1 + m_2)v_f^2$$

$$= \frac{1}{2}m_1 v_{1i}^2 - \frac{1}{2}\frac{m_1^2}{m_1 + m_2}v_{1i}^2$$

$$= \frac{1}{2}\frac{m_1 m_2}{m_1 + m_2}v_{1i}^2$$

Fig.: Collision of mass m_1 with a stationary mass m_2.

the momentum and kinetic energy conservation equations are

$$m_1 v_{1i} = m_1 v_{1f} + m_2 v_{2f} \qquad \qquad \text{...(i)}$$

$$m_1 v_{1i}^2 = m_1 v_{1f}^2 + m_1 v_{2f}^2$$

$$\therefore v_{2f} = v_{1i} + v_{1f}$$

Substituting this in Eq. (i)

$$v_{1f} = \frac{(m_1 - m_2)}{m_1 + m_2} v_{1i}$$

and $v_{2f} = \dfrac{2m_1 v_{1i}}{m_1 + m_2}$

Case I: If the two masses are equal

$v_{1f} = 0$

$v_{2f} = v_{1i}$

Case II: If one mass dominates, e.g. $m_2 \gg m_1$

$v_{1f} \simeq -v_{1i} \; v_{2f} \simeq 0$

The heavier mass is undisturbed while the lighter mass reverses its velocity.

- If the initial velocities and final velocities of both the bodies are along the same straight line, then it is called a **one-dimensional collision**, or **head-on collision**.

Collisions in Two Dimensions

- Linear momentum is conserved. The x- and y-component equations are

$m_1 v_{1i} = m_1 v_{1f} \cos\theta_1 + m_2 v_{2f} \cos\theta_2$

$0 = m_1 v_{1f} \sin\theta_1 - m_2 v_{2f} \sin\theta_2$

If, the collision is elastic,

$$\frac{1}{2} m_1 v_{1i}^2 = \frac{1}{2} m_1 v_{1f}^2 + \frac{1}{2} m_2 v_{2f}^2$$

- In collision particles may or may not come in real touch.

  In scattering, the velocities and directions in which the two particles go away depend on their initial velocities as well as the type of interactions between them, their masses shapes and sizes.

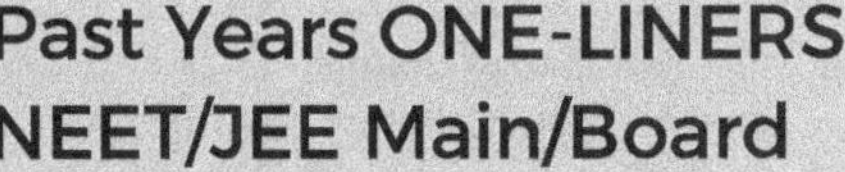

Past Years ONE-LINERS
NEET/JEE Main/Board

- Work done by a variable force $dw = \overline{F}.d\overline{r}$

- Change in potential energy due to extension of the wire, $\Delta E = \dfrac{1}{2} kx^2$

- Coefficient of restitution, $e = \dfrac{\text{velocity of seperation}}{\text{velacity of approach}}$

- For completing vertical circle $v_2 \geq \sqrt{5gR}$
- Work-energy theorem $k_f - k_i = w$

♦   Power, $P = F.V$
♦   Work-energy theorem $W = \Delta K.E$
♦   Power $P = FV$
♦   Work done to change in position = ΔU is change in PE
♦   Conservation of momentum & KE in Collisions, fractional loss of K.E in elastic collission
♦   Conservation of momentum & Velocity of seperation in inelastic collision
♦   Work-energy theorem $W = \Delta K.E$

♦   Efficiency $n = \dfrac{\text{work done}}{\text{input}}$

Tips/Tricks/Tecchniques ONE-LINERS
(Exam Sample)

- -

♦   If work is done on a body, its kinetic or potential energy increases. If work is done by the body, its potential or kinetic energy decreases.

♦   In the elastic collisions, the kinetic or mechanical energy is not converted into any other form of energy.

♦   The force involved in an inelastic collision is non-conservative in nature.

♦   If collision is head on the colliding bodies move along the same straight line before and after collision.

♦   If collision is oblique, the colliding bodies move at certain angles before and/or after the collisions.

♦   In static and dynamic equilibrium, work done is zero.

♦   Work done by a man holding the weight at fixed position is zero.

♦   Work done by a force depends on the frame of reference.

♦   Only tangential component of force is responsible for power dissipation. Power dissipated by radial component is zero. For example power dissipated by centripetal force is zero.

♦   In a perfectly elastic collision, in one dimension, when masses of the colliding particles are equal, their velocities get exchanged after collision.

♦   If a body starts rotating after collision, then both linear momentum and angular momentum are conserved.

♦   In the elastic collisions the forces involved are conservative.

♦   If the speed of water flowing through a pipe is v, then power is proportional to v^3.

♦   If n bullets are fired from a machine gun, each having kinetic energy k, then power of the machine gun will be nk.

♦   Work done by a body of mass m against friction on a rough horizontal surface of coefficient of friction μ is μmgx. Here, x is the distance moved by the body.

♦   Let h_1, h_2 .... h_n be the heights of the body to which the body rebounds again and again, then

$$e = \sqrt{\frac{h_1}{h}} = \sqrt{\frac{h_2}{h_1}} = \sqrt{\frac{h_3}{h_2}}$$

Clearly $h_1 = e^2h$; $h_2 = e^4h$ and similarly, after nth rebound $h_n = (e^{2n})h$

♦ The velocity of an object depends on the choice of reference frame. Thus, kinetic energy also depends on the choice of the reference frame.

♦ Potential energy depends on the reference level. In case of spring, it is advised to assume zero potential energy at the natural length of the spring. In case of gravity any convenient level can be chosen as reference frame.

♦ If a ball is dropped from a height h_0 on a horizontal floor, then time taken by the ball to stop bouncing is given by

$$T = \left(\frac{1+e}{1-e}\right)\sqrt{\frac{2h_0}{g}} \quad \text{(Here, } e = \text{coefficient of restitution)}$$

♦ An engine pulls a train of mass m with constant velocity. If the rails are on a plane surface and there is no friction, the power dissipated by the engine is zero.

♦ When the momentum of a body is made n times then its kinetic energy is increased by factor n^2.

♦ Slope of work time graph = power.

♦ Area under power time curve = work done by/on the body.

♦ If a chain of length L and mass M is held on a frictionless table with $(1/n)^{th}$ of its length is hanging over the edge, then work done in pulling the hanging portion on the table is given by

$$W = \frac{MgL}{2n^2}$$

♦ The phrase 'calculate the work done' is incomplete. We should refer to the work done by a specific force or a group of forces on a given body over a certain displacement.

♦ Work done is a scalar quantity. It can be positive or negative unlike mass and kinetic energy which are positive scalar quantities. The work done by the friction or viscous force on a moving body is negative.

♦ For two bodies, the sum of the mutual forces exerted between them is zero from Newton's Third Law,

$$\mathbf{F}_{12} + \mathbf{F}_{21} = 0$$

But the sum of the work done by the two forces need not *always cancel, i.e.*

$$W_{12} + W_{21} \neq 0$$

However, it may sometimes be true.

♦ The work done by a force can be calculated sometimes even if the exact nature of the force is not known.

♦ The WE theorem is not independent of Newton's Second Law. The WE theorem may be viewed as a scalar form of the Second Law. The principle of conservation of mechanical energy may be viewed as a consequence of the WE theorem for conservative forces.

System of Particles and Rotational Motion

Centre of Mass

- Ideally a **rigid body** is a body with a perfectly definite and unchanging shape. The distances between all pairs of particles of such a body do not change.

What kind of motion can a rigid body have?

- **Pure translational motion:** A rectangular block is sliding down an inclined plane. All the particles of the body have same velocity at any instant of time. The rigid body here is in pure translational motion.

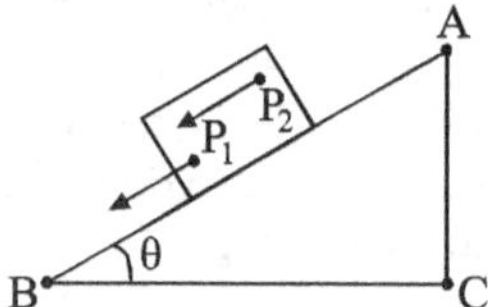

Fig.: Translational (sliding) motion of a block down an inclined plane.
(Any point like P_1 or P_2 of the block moves with the same velocity at any instant of time.)

- In pure translational motion at any instant of time, all particles of the body have the same velocity.
- **Pure rotational motion:** In rotation of a rigid body about a fixed axis, every particle of the body moves in a circle, which lies in a plane perpendicular to the axis and has its centre on the axis.
- For any particle on the axis like P_3, $r = 0$. Any such particle remains stationary while the body rotates.
- **Translational and rotational combined:** The motion of a rigid body which is not pivoted or fixed in some way is either a pure translation or a combination of translation and rotation. The motion of rigid body which is pivoted or fixed in some way is rotation.
- Let the distances of the two particles be x_1 and x_2 respectively from some origin O. Let m_1 and m_2 be respectively the masses of the two particles. The centre of mass of the system is point C at X from O, X is given by

$$X = \frac{m_1 x_1 + m_2 x_2}{m_1 + m_2}$$

If $m_1 = m_2 = m$, then $X = \dfrac{m x_1 + m x_2}{2m} = \dfrac{x_1 + x_2}{2}$

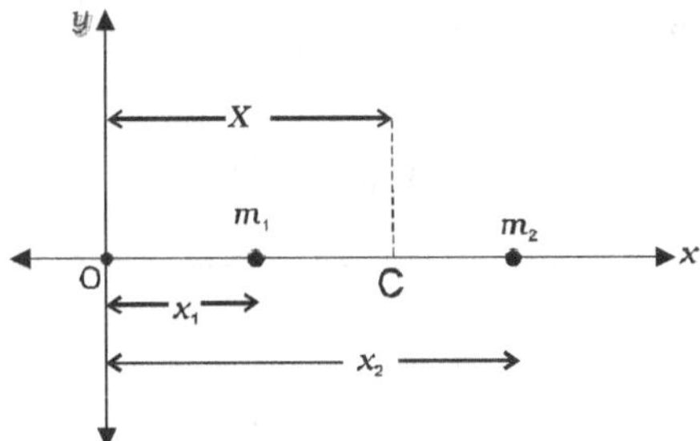

♦ If we have n particles of masses m_1, m_2,...m_n respectively, along a straight line taken as the x-axis, then the position of the centre of the mass is given by

$$X = \frac{m_1x_1 + m_2x_2 + ... + m_nx_n}{m_1 + m_2 + ... + m_n} = \frac{\sum_{i=1}^{n} m_ix_i}{\sum_{i=1}^{n} m_i} = \frac{\sum m_ix_i}{\sum m_i}$$

where x_1, x_2,...x_n are the distances of the particles from the origin.

♦ **A system of n particles in space:** The centre of mass of such a system is at (X, Y, Z), where

$$X = \frac{\sum m_ix_i}{M}, \ Y = \frac{\sum m_iy_i}{M} \text{ and } Z = \frac{\sum m_iz_i}{M}$$

$M = \sum m_i$ is the total mass of the system. m_i is the mass of the ith particle. The position of ith particle is given by (x_i, y_i, z_i).

♦ **Continuous distribution of mass:** The coordinates of the centre of mass are

$$X = \frac{1}{M}\int x\,dm, Y = \frac{1}{M}\int y\,dm \text{ and } Z = \frac{1}{M}\int z\,dm$$

♦ **Centre of mass of some symmetric bodies**

Rectangular plate (By symmetry) $$x_{CM} = \frac{b}{2}$$ $$y_{CM} = \frac{L}{2}$$	
Triangular plate At the centroid, $$y_{CM} = \frac{h}{3}$$ $$x_{CM} = 0$$	

Semi-circular ring $y_{CM} = \dfrac{2R}{\pi},\ x_{CM} = 0$	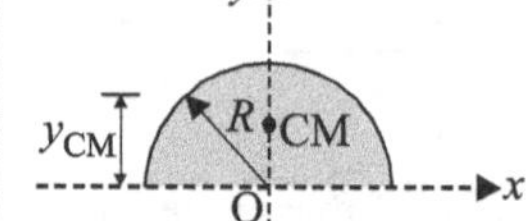
Semi-circular disc $y_{CM} = \dfrac{4R}{3\pi},\ x_{CM} = 0$	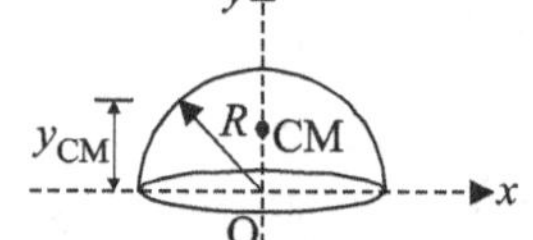
Hemispherical shell $y_{CM} = \dfrac{R}{2},\ x_{CM} = 0$	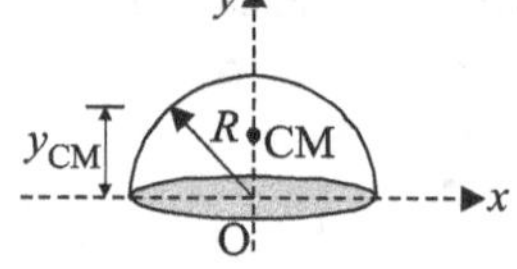
Solid hemisphere $y_{CM} = \dfrac{3R}{8},\ x_{CM} = 0$	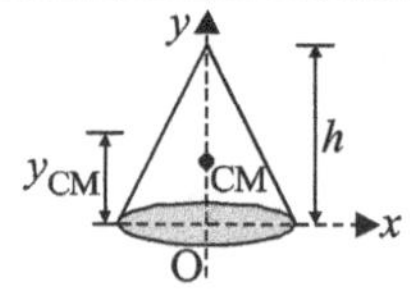
Circular cone (solid) $y_{CM} = \dfrac{h}{4},\ x_{CM} = 0$	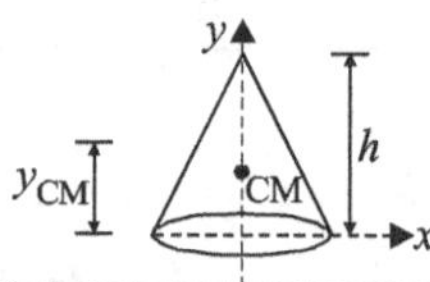
Circular cone (hollow) $y_{CM} = \dfrac{h}{3},\ x_{CM} = 0$	

Motion of Centre of Mass

- Consider a system of n particles.

$$M\mathbf{R} = \sum m_i \mathbf{r}_i = m_1 \mathbf{r}_1 + m_2 \mathbf{r}_2 + \ldots + m_n \mathbf{r}_n \qquad \ldots(i)$$

Differentiating the two sides with respect to time we get

$$M\mathbf{V} = m_1 \mathbf{v}_1 + m_2 \mathbf{v}_2 + \ldots + m_n \mathbf{v}_n \qquad \ldots(ii)$$

- Differentiating Eq. (ii) with respect to time, we obtain

$$M\frac{d\mathbf{V}}{dt} = m_1\frac{d\mathbf{v}_1}{dt} + m_2\frac{d\mathbf{v}_2}{dt} + \ldots + m_n\frac{d\mathbf{v}_n}{dt}$$

or $\quad M\mathbf{A} = m_1\mathbf{a}_1 + m_2\mathbf{a}_2 + \ldots + m_n\mathbf{a}_n \qquad \ldots(iii)$

- From Newton's second law, the force acting on the first particle is $\mathbf{F}_1 = m_1\mathbf{a}_1$. Likewise $\mathbf{F}_2 = m_2\mathbf{a}_2$ and so on. Eq. (iii) may be written as

$$M\mathbf{A} = \mathbf{F}_1 + \mathbf{F}_2 + \ldots + \mathbf{F}_n$$

$\mathbf{F}_1$ is sum of all the forces on the first particle. Among these forces there will be external and also internal forces. From Newton's third law internal forces occur in equal and opposite pairs, in the sum of forces their contribution is zero.

$$M\mathbf{A} = \mathbf{F}_{ext}$$

- The centre of mass of a system of particles moves as if all the mass of the system was concentrated at the centre of mass and all the external forces were applied at that point.

- Figure is a good illustration of Eq. $\vec{A} = \dfrac{\overline{F}_{ext}}{M}$. A projectile, explodes into fragments midway in air. Forces leading to the explosion are internal forces. The total external force, the force of gravity, the same before and after the explosion. The centre of mass continues, along the same parabolic trajectory.

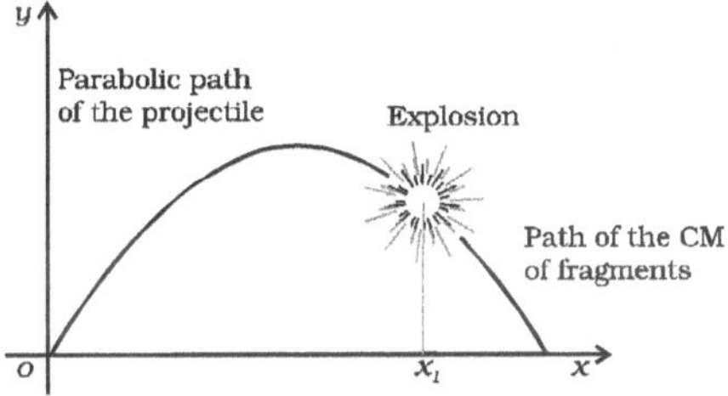

Linear Momentum of a System of Particles

- For the system of n particles, the linear momentum

$$\mathbf{P} = \mathbf{p}_1 + \mathbf{p}_2 + \ldots + \mathbf{p}_n$$
$$M\mathbf{V} = m_1\mathbf{v}_1 + m_2\mathbf{v}_2 + \ldots + m_n\mathbf{v}_n$$

Comparing this with Eq. (ii)

$$\mathbf{P} = M\mathbf{V} \qquad \ldots(iv)$$

- **The total momentum of a system of particles is equal to the product of the total mass of the system and velocity of its centre of mass.**
Differentiating Eq. (iv) with respect to time,

$$\frac{d\mathbf{P}}{dt} = M\frac{d\mathbf{V}}{dt} = M\mathbf{A}$$

$$\frac{d\mathbf{P}}{dt} = \mathbf{F}_{ext} \qquad \ldots(v)$$

This is the statement of **Newton's second law of motion extended to a system of particles.**

♦ Suppose now, that the sum of external forces acting on a system of particles is zero. Then from Eq.(v)

$$\frac{d\mathbf{P}}{dt} = 0 \quad \text{or} \quad \mathbf{P} = \text{Constant}$$

The total linear momentum of the system is constant.

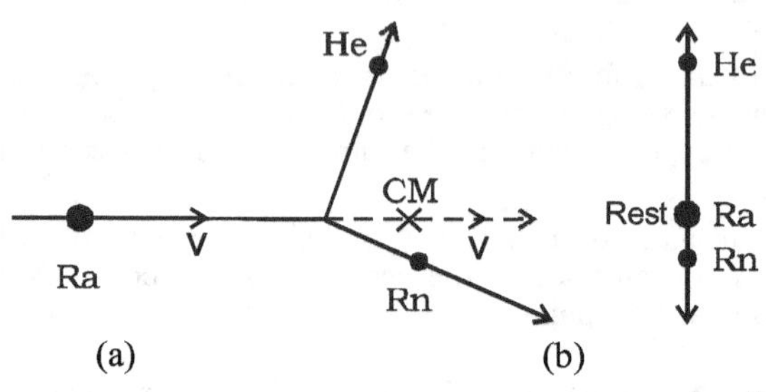

Angular Velocity and its Relation with Linear Velocity

♦ The average angular velocity of the particle over the interval Δt is $\Delta\theta/\Delta t$.
♦ Instantaneous angular velocity $= \omega = d\theta/dt$
♦ For a particle at a perpendicular distance r_i from the fixed axis, the linear velocity at a given instant v_i is given by

$$v_i = \omega r_i$$

i runs from 1 to n,
We refer to ω as the angular velocity of the whole body.

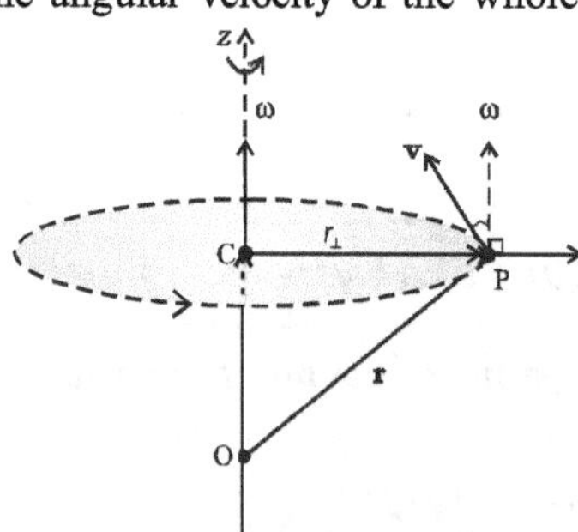

Fig.: The angular velocity vector ω is directed along the fixed axis as shown. The linear velocity of the particle at P is $\mathbf{v} = \omega \times \mathbf{r}$. It is perpendicular to both ω and r and is directed along the tangent to the circle described by the particle.

♦ The linear velocity vector **v** at P

$$\mathbf{v} = \omega \times \mathbf{r}$$

Angular acceleration

♦ We define angular acceleration α as the time rate of change of angular velocity;

$$\alpha = \frac{d\omega}{dt}$$

Torque and Angular Momentum

Moment of force (Torque)

♦ Rotational analogue of force is moment of force. It is also referred to as torque or couple.

♦ If a force acts on a single particle at a point P whose position with respect to the origin O is vector **r** the moment of the force acting on the particle with respect to the origin O is defined as

$$\tau = \mathbf{r} \times \mathbf{F}$$

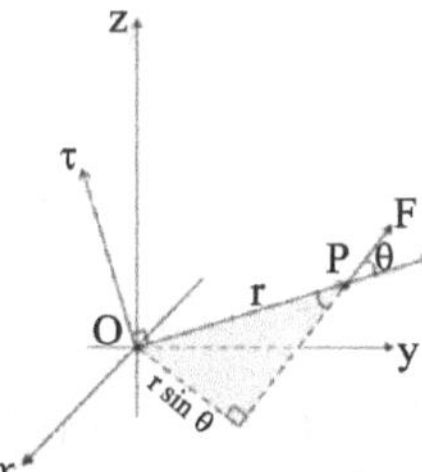

Fig.: $\tau = \mathbf{r} \times \mathbf{F}$, τ is perpendicular to the plane containing **r** and **F**, and its direction is given by the right handed screw rule.

♦ The magnitude of the moment of force may be written

$$\tau = (r \sin \theta)F = r_\perp F \text{ or } \tau = r F \sin \theta = rF_\perp$$

♦ $\tau = 0$ if $r = 0$, $F = 0$ or $\theta = 0°$ or $180°$.

♦ The moment of a force vanishes if either the magnitude of the force is zero, if the line of action of the force passes through the origin.

Angular momentum of a particle

♦ Angular momentum is the rotational analogue of linear momentum.

The angular momentum l of the particle with respect to the origin O is defined to be

$$\mathbf{l} = \mathbf{r} \times \mathbf{p}$$

The magnitude of the angular momentum vector is

$$l = r p \sin \theta ; l = r p_\perp \text{ or } r_\perp p$$

Torque and angular momentum for a system of particles

♦ For a system of n particles, $\mathbf{L} = l_1 + l_2 + ... + l_n = \sum_{i=1}^{n} l_i$

$$\mathbf{L} = \sum_i l_i = \sum_i \mathbf{r}_i \times \mathbf{p}_i$$

$$\frac{d\mathbf{L}}{dt} = \tau_{ext} \qquad\qquad ...(vi)$$

♦ The time rate of the total angular momentum of a system of particles about a point is equal to the sum of the external torques acting on the system taken about the same point.

Conservation of angular momentum

♦ The total external torque on a system of particles is zero, then the total angular momentum of the system is conserved, i.e. remains constant.

If $\tau_{ext} = 0$, Eq. (vi) reduces to

$$\frac{d\mathbf{L}}{dt} = 0 \text{ or } \mathbf{L} = \text{constant.}$$

Equilibrium of a Rigid Body

- A rigid body is said to be in mechanical equilibrium, if the body has neither linear acceleration nor angular acceleration. This means
  (1) the total force, on the rigid body is zero;

$$\mathbf{F}_1 + \mathbf{F}_2 + ... + \mathbf{F}_n = \sum_{i=1}^{n} \mathbf{F}_i = 0$$

  (2) The total torque, on the rigid body is zero,

$$\tau_1 + \tau_2 + ... + \tau_n = \sum_{i=1}^{n} \tau_i = 0$$

- A pair of forces of equal magnitude but acting in opposite directions with different lines of action is known as a **couple** or **torque**.

Principle of moments

- An ideal lever is essentially a light rod pivoted at a point along its length. This point is called the fulcrum.

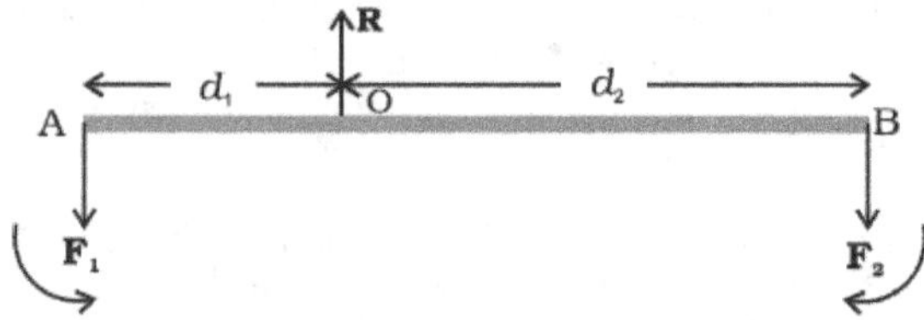

Fig. : Forces acting on lever are as shown.

- The lever is a system in mechanical equilibrium.
  For translational equilibrium,
  $$R - F_1 - F_2 = 0$$
  Considering rotational equilibrium we take the moments about the fulcrum; the sum of moments must be zero,
  $$d_1 F_1 - d_2 F_2 = 0$$
  or load arm × load = effort arm × effort

  F_1/F_2 is called the **Mechanical Advantage (M.A.)**; $\text{M.A.} = \dfrac{F_1}{F_2} = \dfrac{d_2}{d_1}$

Centre of gravity

- The centre of gravity (CG) of the cardboard (Fig.) is so located that the total torque on it due to the forces $m_1\mathbf{g}$, $m_2\mathbf{g}$....etc. is zero.

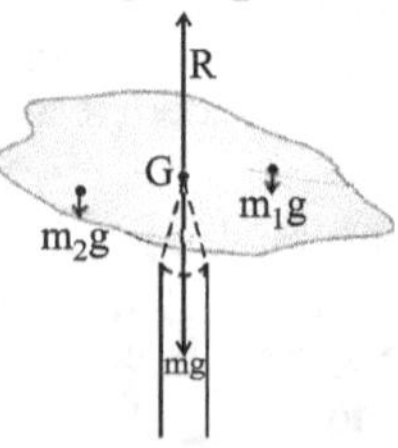

Fig.: Balancing a cardboard on the tip of a pencil.
The point of support, G, is the centre of gravity.

- The total gravitational torque about the CG is zero,

$$\tau_g = \sum \tau_i = \sum \mathbf{r}_i \times m_i\, \mathbf{g} = 0$$

- We may define the CG of a body as that point where the total gravitational torque on the body is zero.

Moment of Inertia

- It is analogue of mass in rotational motion?

  Moment of inertia I is given by $I = \sum_{i=1}^{n} m_i r_i^2$

- With this definition, expression for the kinetic energy of a rotating body.
- For a particle at a distance r_i from the axis, the linear velocity is $v_i = r_i \omega$.
- The kinetic energy of motion of this particle is

$$k_i = \frac{1}{2} m_i v_i^2 = \frac{1}{2} m_i r_i^2 \omega^2$$

The total kinetic energy K is

$$K = \sum_{i=1}^{n} k_i = \frac{1}{2} \sum_{i=1}^{n} (m_i r_i^2 \omega^2) = \frac{1}{2} \omega^2 \left(\sum_{i=1}^{n} m_i r_i^2 \right) \text{ or, } K = \frac{1}{2} I \omega^2$$

- The **radius of gyration** of a body about an axis may be defined as the distance from the axis of a mass point whose mass is equal to the mass of the whole body and whose moment of inertia is equal to the moment of inertia of the body about the axis.

  Radius of gyration, $K = \sqrt{\dfrac{I}{M}}$

- Flywheel, because of its large moment of inertia, resists the sudden increase or decrease of the speed of the vehicle. It allows a gradual change in the speed and prevents jerky motions.

Theorems of Perpendicular and Parallel Axes

Theorem of perpendicular axes

- The moment of inertia of a planar body (lamina) about an axis perpendicular to its plane is equal to the sum of its moments of inertia about two perpendicular axes concurrent with perpendicular axis and lying in the plane of the body.

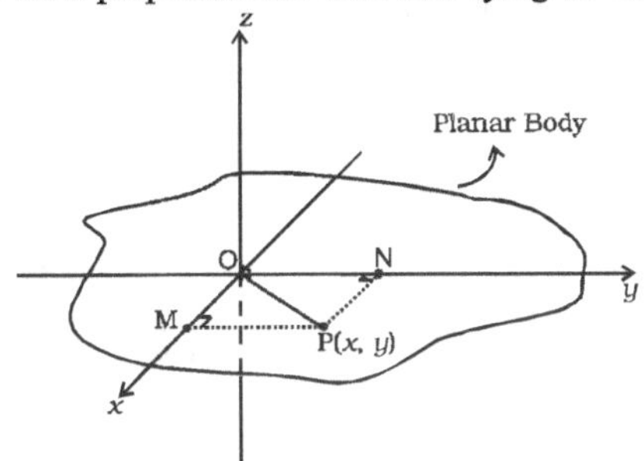

♦ The theorem states that
$$I_z = I_x + I_y$$

Theorem of parallel axes

♦ The moment of inertia about any axis is equal to the sum of the moment of inertia of the body about a parallel axis passing through its centre of mass and the product of its mass and the square of the distance between the two parallel axes. According to the theorem of parallel axes
$$I_{z'} = I_z + Ma^2$$

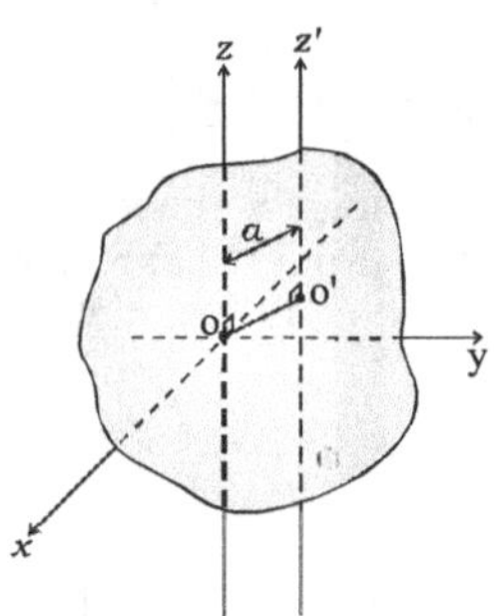

Table: Moments of inertia of some regular shaped bodies about specific axes

z	Body	Axis	Figure	I
(1)	Thin circular ring, radius R	Perpendicular to plane, at centre		$M R^2$
(2)	Thin circular ring, radius R	Diameter		$M R^2/2$
(3)	Thin rod, length L	Perpendicular to rod, at mid point		$M R^2/12$
(4)	Circular disc, radius R	Perpendicular to disc at centre		$M R^2/2$
(5)	Circular disc. radius R	Diameter		$M R^2/4$
(6)	Hollow cylinder, radius R	Axis of cylinder		$M R^2$

(7)	Solid cylinder, radius R	Axis of cylinder		$M R^2/2$
(8)	Solid sphere, radius R	Diameter		$2M R^2/5$

Kinematics of Rotational Motion about a Fixed Axis

- Angular velocity is the time rate of change of angular displacement, $\omega = d\theta/dt$.
- The angular acceleration, $\alpha = d\omega/dt$.
- The kinematic equations for rotational motion with uniform angular acceleration are:

$$\omega = \omega_0 + \alpha t$$
$$\theta = \theta_0 + \omega_0 t + \frac{1}{2}\alpha t^2$$
$$\omega^2 = \omega_0^2 + 2\alpha(\theta - \theta_0)$$

where θ_0 = initial angular displacement of the rotating body, and ω_0 = initial angular velocity of the body.

Dynamics of Rotational Motion About a Fixed Axis

Work done by a torque
- The work done by the force on the particle is
$$dW_1 = \mathbf{F}_1 \cdot \mathbf{ds}_1 = F_1 ds_1 \cos \phi_1 = F_1 (r_1\, d\theta) \sin \alpha_1$$

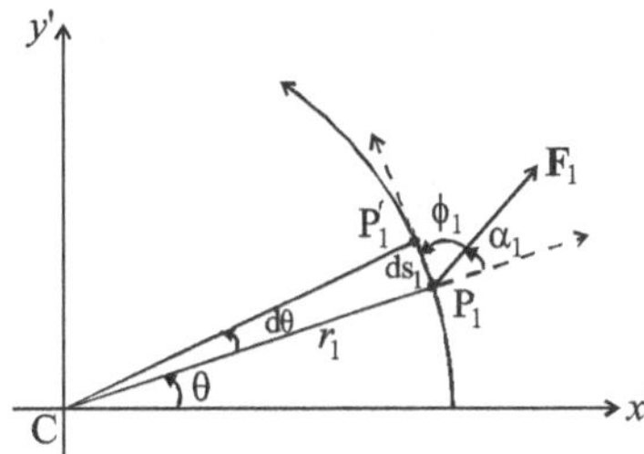

Fig.: Work done by a force $\mathbf{F}_1$ acting on a particle of a body otating about a fixed axis, arc describes a circular path with centre C on the axis arc; $P_1 P'_1 (ds_1)$ gives the displacement of the particle.

$\mathrm{d}W_1 = \tau_1 \mathrm{d}\theta$ $\qquad$ [As $\tau_1 = r_1 F_1 \sin\alpha$]

Total work done on the body. Denoting the magnitudes of the torques due to the different forces as τ_1, τ_2, ... etc,

$$\mathrm{d}W = (\tau_1 + \tau_2 + ...)\,\mathrm{d}\theta$$

$$\mathbf{dW = \tau d\theta} \qquad [\text{Where } \tau = \tau_1 + \tau_2 + ...]$$

Dividing both sides of Eq. by $\mathrm{d}t$ gives

♦ $\quad$ **Power** $P = \dfrac{dW}{\mathrm{d}t} = \tau \dfrac{\mathrm{d}\theta}{\mathrm{d}t} = \tau\omega$ or $\mathbf{P = \tau\omega}$

This is the instantaneous power.

The rate of increase of kinetic energy is

Since $\alpha = \mathrm{d}\omega/\mathrm{d}t$, we get

$$\frac{\mathrm{d}}{\mathrm{d}t}\left(\frac{I\omega^2}{2}\right) = I\omega\alpha$$

Equating rate of work done and of increase in kinetic energy

$$\tau\omega = I\,\omega\alpha \Rightarrow \tau = I\alpha$$

Table: Comparison of Translational and Rotational Motion

Linear Motion	Rotational Motion about a Fixed Axis
1 Displacement x	Angular displacement θ
2 Velocity $v = \mathrm{d}x/\mathrm{d}t$	Angular velocity $\omega = \mathrm{d}\theta/\mathrm{d}t$
3 Acceleration $a = \mathrm{d}v/\mathrm{d}t$	Angular acceleration $\alpha = \mathrm{d}\omega/\mathrm{d}t$
4 Mass M	Moment of inertia I
5 Force $F = Ma$	Torque $\tau = I\alpha$
6 Work $\mathrm{d}W = F\,\mathrm{d}s$	Work $W = \tau\,\mathrm{d}\theta$
7 Kinetic energy $K = Mv^2/2$	Kinetic energy $K = I\omega^2/2$
8 Power $P = Fv$	Power $P = \tau\omega$
9 Linear momentum $p = Mv$	Angular momentum $L = I\omega$

Angular Momentum in Case of Rotation About a Fixed Axis

♦ $\quad$ **Conservation of angular momentum**

$\quad$ If the external torque is zero, $L_z = I\omega = $ constant

♦ $\quad$ While the chair is rotating with considerable angular speed stretch your arms horizontally. Your angular speed is reduced. There is no external torque about the axis of rotation of the chair and hence $I\omega$ is constant.

♦ $\quad$ Stretching the arms increases I about the axis of rotation, resulting in decreasing the angular speed ω.

Rolling Motion

♦ $\quad$ All wheels used in gransportation have rolling motion. Disc rolls without slipping. This means the bottom of the disc is at rest on the surface.

Kinetic Energy of Rolling Motion

- The kinetic energy of a system of particles (K) can be separated into the kinetic energy of translational motion of the centre of mass ($MV^2/2$) and kinetic energy of rotational motion about the centre of mass of the system of particles (K').

$$K = K' + MV^2/2$$

- The kinetic energy of a rolling body, therefore, is given by

$$K = \frac{1}{2}I\omega^2 + \frac{1}{2}mv_{cm}^2$$

Substituting $I = mk^2$

$$K = \frac{1}{2}\frac{mk^2 v_{cm}^2}{R^2} + \frac{1}{2}mv_{cm}^2 \quad \text{or} \quad K = \frac{1}{2}mv_{cm}^2\left(1 + \frac{k^2}{R^2}\right)$$

- $$K_{translation} : K_{rotation} : K_{rolling} = 1 : \frac{K^2}{R^2} : \left(1 + \frac{K^2}{R^2}\right)$$

Past Years ONE-LINERS NEET/JEE Main/Board

- Moment of inertia of ring, (M.I.) $I_{ring} = \int R^2 dm = R^2 \int dm$ (M.I.) $I_{ring} = I_{remaining} + I_{removed}$

- In rotational equilibrium net torque $= 0$

- Position of centre of mass $x_{cm} = \dfrac{m_1 x_1 + m_2 x_2}{m_1 + m_2}$

- Torque $\overline{\tau} = \overline{r} \times \overline{F}$

- Kinetic energy in Rolling Motion $(K.E.) = \dfrac{1}{2}mv^2 + \dfrac{1}{2}I\omega^2$

- Total moment of inertia M.T. $(I) = I_1 + I_2 + I_3$
- Kinetic energy in Rolling K.E. $= K_t + K_R$
- (Torque = moment of inertia $\times$ angular acceleration) $\tau = I\alpha$

- Rotational kinetic energy, $(K.E.)R = \dfrac{1}{2}I\omega^2$

- Mechanical Advantage (M.A.) $= \dfrac{\text{Load}}{\text{Effort}}$

- Moment of inertia of whole part = M.I. of remaining part + M.I. of removed part $\quad$ M.I. (whole) $= I_{remaining} + I_{removed}$
- Torque = rate of change of angular momentum
- Comparision of MI of rigid bodies
- Total KE of rolling body will be converted into gravitational PE
- Work done = change in K.E.

$$\tau\, d\theta = dE \Rightarrow I\alpha = 2K\theta$$

- Centripetal force $\propto \dfrac{1}{R^n}$ $m\omega^2 R \propto \dfrac{1}{R^n}$

- Moment of inertia of whole disc = M.I. of remaining + M.I. of removed part (M.I.) $I_{whole} = I_{remaining} + I_{removed}$

- M.I. of cylinder about perpendicular by sector $= \dfrac{mR^2}{4} + \dfrac{ml^2}{12}$

- Torque $\tau = I\alpha$

- Angular momentum $L = mvR$

- From angular momentum censervation $I_1\omega_1 = I_2\omega_2$

Tips/Tricks/Tecchniques ONE-LINERS
(Exam Sample)

- A body's centre of mass lies exactly at the same position as its centre of gravity, provided the gravitational field strength does not vary within the body itself.
- In an isolated system, if external force on the system is zero, the centre of mass of a system moves with uniform velocity or be in rest.
- Centre of mass of a system may be inside or outside the system.
- The position of centre of mass does not depend on the choice of co-ordinate system.
- The position of the centre of mass does not change in rotatory motion while the position of the centre of mass changes in translatory motion.
- In case the body falling freely explodes into pieces, the centre of mass of the system still lies on the same vertical line and have downward acceleration = g.
- Theorem of perpendicular axis can be applied only to thin lamina like sheet, disc, ring etc.
- Parallel axes theorem can be applied to all type of bodies.
- Moment of inertia of a part of a rigid body (cut symmetrically from the whole mass) has the same value as that of whole body if whole mass is replaced with mass of that part.
- Moment of inertia of hollow bodies is more than that of solid bodies having same mass, same size and shape.
- For a cube, moment of inertia about its body diagonal is minimum.
- For a body to roll down the inclined plane without slipping the coefficient of limiting friction (μ) should follow the following relation

$$\mu \geq \left[\dfrac{K^2}{K^2 + R^2}\right] \tan\theta$$

- A body cannot roll down the inclined plane in the absence of friction. Accordingly, the relative values of μ of different bodies for rolling without slipping down the inclined plane are as follows :

$$\mu_{ring} > \mu_{shell} > \mu_{disc} > \mu_{solid\ sphere}$$

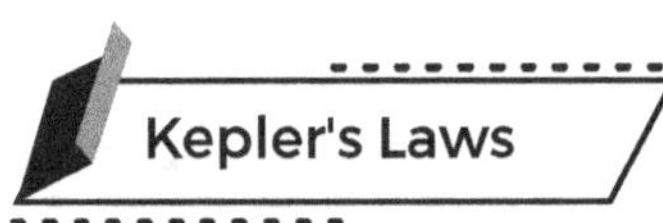

Kepler's Laws

♦ The earliest recorded model for planetary motions was a 'geocentric' model in which all celestial objects, stars, the sun and the planets, all revolved around the earth.

♦ **1. Law of orbits :** All planets move in elliptical orbits with the Sun situated at one of the foci of the ellipse.

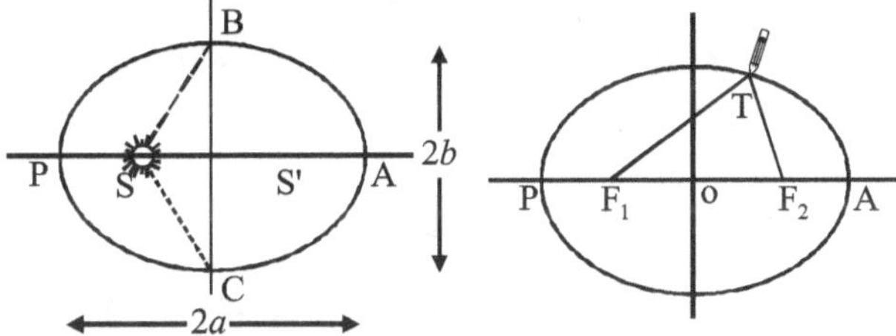

Point A = aphelion i.e., farthest point
Point P = perihelion i.e., closest point
and distance AP/2 = semi-major axis

♦ **2. Law of areas :** The line that joins any planet to the sun sweeps equal areas in equal intervals of time. This law comes from the observations that planets appear to move slower when they are farther from the sun than when they are nearer. The law of areas is a consequence of conservation of angular momentum.

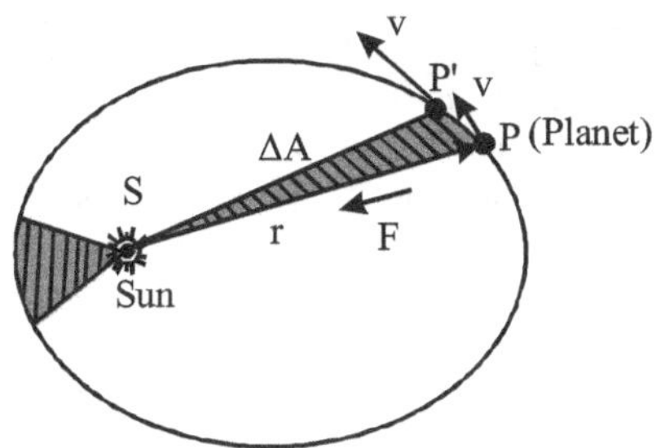

A central force is such that the force on the planet is along the vector joining the Sun and the planet. Then the area swept out by the planet of mass m in time interval Δt is $\Delta \mathbf{A}$ given by

$\Delta \mathbf{A} = \frac{1}{2}(\mathbf{r} \times \mathbf{v}\Delta t)$

$\Delta \mathbf{A}/\Delta t = \frac{1}{2}(\mathbf{r} \times \mathbf{p})/m, = \mathbf{L}/(2m)$

where $\mathbf{v}$ is the velocity, $\mathbf{L}$ is the angular momentum equal to $(\mathbf{r} \times \mathbf{p})$. For a central force, which is directed along $\mathbf{r}$, $\mathbf{L}$ is a constant. As torque of sun on planet is zero as $\vec{r}$ & $\vec{F}$ are in the same line. Hence, $\Delta \mathbf{A}/\Delta t$ is a constant.

♦ **3. Law of periods :** The square of the time period of revolution of a planet (T) is proportional to the cube of the semi-major axis (a) of the ellipse traced out by the planet.

i.e., $T^2 \propto a^3$

Universal Law of Gravitation

♦ Every body in the universe attracts every other body with a force which is directly proportional to the product of their masses and inversely proportional to the square of the distance between them.

$$\mathbf{F} = G\frac{m_1 m_2}{r^2}$$

♦ The force $\mathbf{F}$ on a point mass m_2 due to mass m_1 in vector form

$$\vec{\mathbf{F}} = G\frac{m_1 m_2}{r^2}(-\hat{r}) = -G\frac{m_1 m_2}{r^2}\hat{\mathbf{r}}$$

Where G is the universal gravitational constant, $\hat{r}$ is the unit vector from m_1 to m_2 and $\mathbf{r} = \mathbf{r}_2 - \mathbf{r}_1$.

♦ **The force of attraction between a hollow spherical shell of uniform density and a point mass situated outside is just as if the entire mass of the shell is concentrated at the centre of the shell.**

♦ **The force of attraction due to a hollow spherical shell of uniform density, on a point mass situated inside it is zero.**

The Gravitational Constant

♦ The value of the gravitational constant can be determined by Cavendish's experiment. S_1 and S_2 are large spheres which are kept on either side (shown shades) of the masses at A and B. When the big spheres are taken to the other side of the masses (shown by dotted circles), the bar AB rotates a little since the torque reverses direction. The angle of rotation can be measured experimentally.

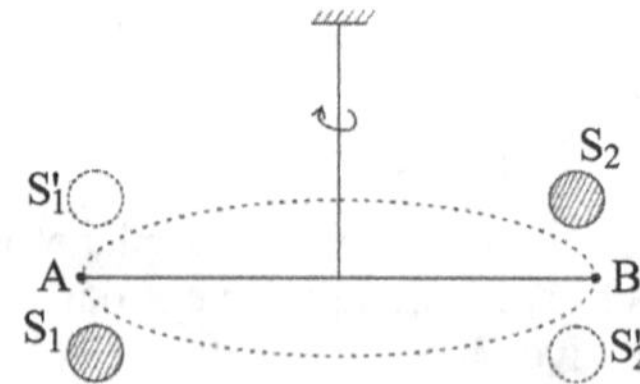

- The restoring torque on bar is proportional to θ, equal to $\tau\theta$. The gravitational force between the big sphere and its neighouring small ball is

$$F = \frac{GMm}{d^2}$$

If L is the length of the bar AB, then the torque arising out of F is F multiplied by L. At equilibrium, this is equal to the restoring torque and hence

$$G\frac{Mm}{d^2}L = \tau\theta$$

Substituting the values, we get, $G = 6.67 \times 10^{-11}$ N m^2/kg^2

Acceleration Due to Gravity of the Earth

- Consider the earth to be made up of concentric shells and a mass m situated at a distance r from the centre. For the shells of radius greater than r, the point P lies inside. Hence they exert no gravitational force on mass m kept at P. For shells of radius $\leq$ r, the point P lies on the surface.
  Force on the mass m at P has a magnitude

$$F = \frac{GmMr}{r^2}$$

- The acceleration experienced by the mass m, by Newton's 2$_{nd}$ law

$$g = \frac{F}{m} = \frac{GM_E}{R_E^2}$$

Acceleration due to Gravity below and above the Surface of Earth

Effect of Height

- Consider a point mass m at a height h above the surface of the earth

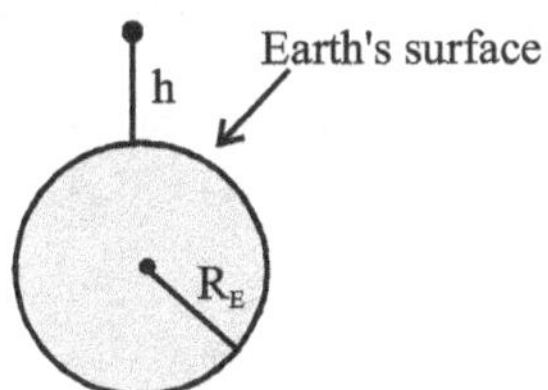

F (h) denoted the magnitude of the force on the point mass m , we get

$$F(\mathrm{h}) = \frac{GM_E m}{(R_E \mathrm{h})^2}$$

- The acceleration experienced by the point mass is

$$g(h) = \frac{F(\mathrm{h})}{m} = \frac{GM_E}{(R_E + h)^2}$$

♦ For $h \ll R_E$.

$$g(h) = \frac{GM_E}{R_E^2(1+h/R_E)^2} = g(1+h/R_E)^{-2}$$

For $\dfrac{h}{R_E} \ll 1$, using binominal expression,

$$g(h) \cong g\left(1-\frac{2h}{R_E}\right)$$

Clearly, the value of g at height h is less than the value of g on the surface of earth.

Effect of Depth

♦ A point mass m is situated at a depth d. M_s is the mass of the smaller sphere, $M_s/M_E = (R_E - d)^3/R_E^3$
The acceleration due to gravity

$$g(d) = \frac{F(d)}{m} = \frac{GM_E}{R_E^3}(R_E - d) = g\frac{R_E - d}{R_E} = g(1-d/R_E)$$

Gravitational Potential Energy

♦ The gravitational potential due to the gravitational force of the earth is defined as the potential energy of a particle of unit mass at that point.
♦ The gravitational potential energy associated with two particles of masses m_1 and m_2 separated by distance by a distance r is given by

$$V = -\frac{Gm_1m_2}{r} \text{ (if we choose } V = 0 \text{ as } r \to \infty)$$

Escape Speed

♦ Escape speed is the minimum speed required for an object to reach infinity (i.e. escape from the earth)
♦ If the object is thrown from the surface of the earth,

$$(V_i)_{\min} = \sqrt{\frac{2GM_E}{R_E}}$$

Using the relation $g = GM_E/R_E^2$, we get

$$(V_i)_{\min} = \sqrt{2gR_E}$$

♦ Using the value of g and R_E, numerically $(V_i)_{\min} \approx 11.2$ km/s. This is called the escape speed.
♦ Escape speed for the moon turns out to be 2.3 km/s, about five times smaller. This is the reason that moon has no atmosphere. Gas molecules if formed on the surface of the moon having velocities larger than this will escape the gravitational pull of the moon.

Earth Satellites

- Earth satellites are objects which revolve around the earth. Their motion is very similar to the motion of planets around the Sun and hence Kepler's laws of planetary motion are equally applicable to them.
- Consider a satellite in a circular orbit of a distance $(R_E + h)$ from the centre of the earth, where R_E = radius of the earth. If m is the mass of the satellite and V its speed, the centripetal force required for this orbit is

$$F_{(gravitation)} = \frac{mV^2}{(R_E + h)} \qquad \qquad ...(i)$$

(directed towards the centre.) This centripetal force is provided by the gravitational force, which is

$$F_{(gravitation)} = \frac{GmM_E}{(R_E + h)^2} \qquad \qquad ...(ii)$$

Equating Eqs. (i) and (ii), we get

$$V^2 = \frac{GM_E}{(R_E + h)} \Rightarrow V = \sqrt{\frac{GM_E}{R_E + h}}$$

For $h = 0$, speed is $V(h = 0) = \sqrt{GM / R_E} = \sqrt{gR_E}$

- Time period of satellite T is $T = \dfrac{2\pi(R_E + h)}{V} = \dfrac{2\pi(R_E + h)^{3/2}}{\sqrt{GM_E}}$

Energy of an Orbiting Satellite

- Kinetic energy of the satellite in a circular orbit with speed v is

$$K.E. = \frac{1}{2}mv^2 = \frac{GmM_E}{2(R_E + h)},$$

- The potential energy at distance $(R_e + h)$ is

$$P.E. = -\frac{GmM_E}{(R_E + h)}$$

- In magnitude the K.E. is half the P.E. The total energy E is

$$E = K.E. + P.E. = -\frac{GmM_E}{2(R_E + h)}$$

- When the orbit of a satellite becomes elliptic, both the K.E. and P.E. vary from point to point. The total energy which remains constant is negative as in the circular orbit case. If the total energy is positive or zero, the object escapes to infinity.

Geostationary and Polar Satellites

- Time period of satellite, $T = \dfrac{2\pi(R_E + h)^{3/2}}{\sqrt{GM_E}}$

$$\Rightarrow R_E + h = \left(\dfrac{T^2 GM_E}{4\pi^2}\right)^{1/3}$$

  for $T = 24$ hours, h works out to be 35800 km.

- Satellites in a circular orbits around the earth in the equatorial plane with $T = 24$ hours are called Geostationery Satellites. Since the earth rotates with the same period, the satellite would appear fixed from any point on earth.
- Polar satellites are low altitude ($h \approx 500$ to 800 km) satellites, but they go around the poles of the earth in a north-south direction whereas the earth rotates around its axis in east-west direction.

Uses:

- Remote sensing, meterology as well as for environmental studies of the earth.

Weightlessness

- In a satellite around the earth, every part and parcel of the satellite has an acceleration towards the centre of the earth which is exactly the value of earth's acceleration due to gravity at that position. Thus in the satellite everything inside it is in a state of free fall. Thus, in a manned satellite, people inside experience no gravity.

Past Years ONE-LINERS NEET/JEE Main/Board

- Escape velocity, $V_e = \sqrt{\dfrac{2GM}{R}}$

- Law of conservation of energy, $\dfrac{1}{2}mv^2 - \dfrac{GmM}{R} = -\dfrac{GmM}{(R+h)}$.

  Escape velocity, $V_e = \sqrt{\dfrac{2GM}{R}}$

- Orbital velocity, $V_0 = \sqrt{\dfrac{GM}{(R+h)}} = \sqrt{\dfrac{GM}{R^2} \cdot \dfrac{R^2}{(R+h)}}$

- Escape velocity, $V_e = \sqrt{\dfrac{2GM}{R}} = \sqrt{\dfrac{2G}{R} \cdot \left(\dfrac{4}{3}\pi R^3 \rho\right)} \propto R\sqrt{\rho}$

- Gravitational potential (V) and acceleration due to gravity (g) with height

$$V = \frac{-GM}{R+h} \text{ and } g = \frac{GM}{(R+h)^2}$$

- The orbital velocity is $\sqrt{gR}$. Escape velocity $= \sqrt{2gR}$

- Above earth surface. $g_h = g\left(1 - \frac{2h}{R_e}\right)$

- Below earth surface $g_d = g\left(1 - \frac{d}{R_e}\right)$

- Speed of the planet will be maximum when its distance from the sun is minimum as $mvr = $ constant.

- Acceleration due to gravity, $g = \dfrac{GM}{R^2}$

- Potential energy at the distance r from the surface of the earth $U_{\text{surface}} = \dfrac{-GMm}{r}$

- Acceleration due to gravity at a depth d from surface of earth $g' = g\left(1 - \dfrac{d}{R}\right)$

- Weight of a body on the surface of the earth, $W_S = mg$

- Acceleration due to gravity, g varies with height, $W_h = \dfrac{mg}{\left(1 + \dfrac{h}{R}\right)^2}$

- Weight at pole, $w = mg$
- Weight at equator, $w' = mg' = m(g - \omega^2 R)$
- Properties of satellite

- Gravitational force, $F = \dfrac{G(2\,\text{m})(\text{m})}{d^2}$

- Time period of satellite, $T = \dfrac{2\pi}{\omega}$

- Gravitational field, $E = \dfrac{GM}{r^2}$

- Gravitational potential, $V = -\dfrac{GM}{R}$

Tips/Tricks/Tecchniques ONE-LINERS
(Exam Sample)

- The gravitational force is much weaker than the electrical force because of small value of $G = 6.67 \times 10^{-11}\ \text{Nm}^2\,\text{kg}^{-2}$.
- If we connect two spheres of same material, mass and radius, then gravitational attraction between them is directly proportional to the fourth power of their radius.

- If we throw an ant or an elephant out of the gravitational field, we will require same velocity of projection.
- Gravitational force does not act on a particle due to a spherical shell if the particle is present inside the spherical shell.
- Intensity of gravitational field inside a hollow spherical shell is zero.
- The intensity of gravitational field at the centre of ring is zero.
- Moon has no atmosphere because escape velocity on the moon is less than the rms velocity of the gas molecules.
- Orbital velocity of a planet near the surface of the earth is about 7.92 kms^{-1}.
- The minimum increase in orbital velocity of a satellite revolving in a circular orbit at a height (h << R), so that it could escape from the earth's gravitational field $= V_{esc} - V_{orb} = \sqrt{2gR} - \sqrt{gR} = \sqrt{gR}(\sqrt{2}-1)$
- The centripetal acceleration of the satellite moving around the earth is equal to the acceleration due to gravity.
- From a solid sphere, if a spherical portion is removal as shown in the figure then the gravitational potential at the centre of cavity
$$V_{Remaining} = V_{Total} - V_{Cavity}$$
- If the altitude of the satellite is increased by n times the radius of the earth, then the orbital velocity will become $\left(1/\sqrt{1+n}\right)$ times the orbital velocity near the surface of the earth.
- If the radius of the orbit of a sattelite is increased by n times the radius of the earth, then its orbital velocity will be $\left(1/\sqrt{n}\right)$ times the orbital velocity near the surface of the earth.
- Escape velocity of a body at a height h above the surface of the earth is given by
$$v_{es} = \sqrt{2g(R+h)}$$

If the orbit of a satellite is elliptical, then

- The energy $E = -\dfrac{GMm}{2a} = $ const. with a as semi-major axis;
- KE will be maximum when the satellite is closest to the central body (at perigee) and minimum when it is farthest from the central body (at apogee) [as for a given orbit $L =$ const., *i.e.*, $mvr =$ const., *i.e.*, $v \propto 1/r$]
- PE $= (E - K)$ will be minimum when KE $=$ max, *i.e.*, the satellite is closest to the central body (at perigee) and maximum when KE $=$ min, *i.e.*, the satellite is farthest from the central body (at apogee).

Mechanical Properties of Solids

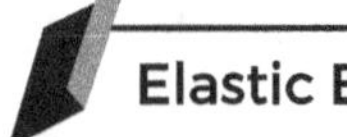

Elastic Behaviour of Solids

- Solid bodies are not perfectly rigid. In order to change (or deform) the shape or size of a body, a force is required.
- The property of a body, by virtue of which it tends to regain its original size and shape when the applied force is removed, is known as **elasticity**.
- If you apply force to a lump of putty or mud, they have no gross tendency to regain their previous shape, and they get permanently deformed. Such substances are called **plastic** and this property is called **plasticity**.
- The restoring mechanism can be visualised by taking a model of spring-ball system. Here the balls represent atoms and springs represent interatomic forces.
- When a solid is deformed, the atoms or molecules are displaced from their equilibrium positions causing a change in the interatomic (or intermolecular) distances. When the deforming force is removed, the interatomic forces tend to drive them back to their original positions.

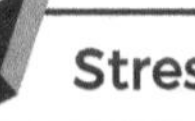

Stress and Strain

- When a body is subjected to a deforming force, a restoring force is developed in the body. This restoring force is equal in magnitude but opposite in direction to the applied force. The restoring force per unit area is known as **stress**.
- If F is the force applied normal to the cross–section and A is the area of cross section of the body,
  Magnitude of the stress $= F/A$
  The SI unit of stress is N m^{-2} or pascal (Pa).
- A cylinder is stretched by two equal forces applied normal to its cross-sectional area. The restoring force per unit area in this case is called **tensile stress**.
- If the cylinder is compressed under the action of applied forces, the restoring force per unit area is known as **compressive stress**.
- The change in the length ΔL to the original length L of the body is known as **longitudinal strain**.

  Longitudinal strain $\epsilon = \dfrac{\Delta L}{L}$

  It is a dimensionless physical quantity.

- The restoring force per unit area developed due to the applied tangential force is known as **tangential** or **shearing stress**.
- **Shearing strain** is defined as the ratio of relative displacement of the faces Δx to the length of the cylinder L.

$$\text{Shearing strain } = \frac{\Delta x}{L} = \tan\theta \approx \theta$$

- **Hydraulic stress** in magnitude is equal to the hydraulic pressure (applied force per unit area).
- **Volume strain** is the ratio of change in volume (ΔV) to the original volume (V).

$$\text{Volume strain } = \frac{\Delta V}{V}$$

Hooke's Law

- For small deformations the stress and strain are proportional to each other. This is known as Hooke's law.
- Stress $\propto$ strain $= \kappa \times$ strain
  where k is the proportionality constant and is known as modulus of elasticity.

Stress-Strain Curve

- A graph is plotted between the stress and the strain produced for a metal (Fig.). In the region between O to A, the curve is linear. Hooke's law is obeyed. The body regains its original dimensions when the applied force is removed.

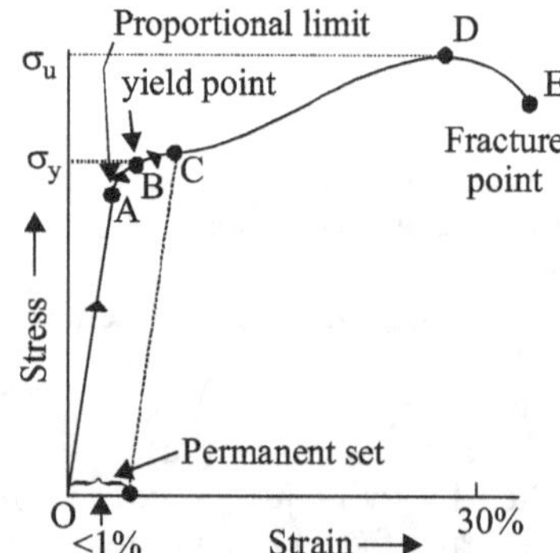

- In the region A to B, stress and strain are not proportional but the body still returns to its original dimension when the load is removed.
  The point B in the curve is known as **yield point** (also known as elastic limit) and the corresponding stress is known as **yield strength** (σ_y) of the material.
- Strain increases rapidly even for a small change in the stress. The portion of the curve between B and D shows this. When the load is removed, say at some point C between B and D, the body does not regain its original dimension.
  The point D on the graph is the **ultimate tensile strength** (σ_u) of the material. Beyond this point, additional strain is produced even by a reduced applied

♦ force and fracture occurs at point E. If the ultimate strength and fracture points D and E are close, the material is said to be **brittle**. If they are far apart, the material is said to be **ductile**.

♦ Substances like tissue of aorta, rubber etc. which can be stretched to cause large strains are called **elastomers**.

Elastic Modulii

♦ The ratio of stress and strain, called **modulus of elasticity**.

Young's Modulus

♦ The ratio of tensile (or compressive) stress (σ) to the longitudinal strain (ε) is defined as **Young's modulus** and is denoted by the symbol Y.

$$Y = \frac{\sigma}{\varepsilon} = (F/A)/(\Delta L/L) = (F \times L)/(A \times \Delta L)$$

Unit of Young's modulus is Nm^{-2} or Pascal (Pa).

Shear Modulus

♦ The ratio of shearing stress to the corresponding shearing strain is called the shear modulus of the material and is represented by G. It is also called the modulus of rigidity.

G = shearing stress (σ_s)/shearing strain

$G = (F/A)/(\Delta x/L) = (F \times L)/(A \times \Delta x) = (F/A)/\theta$ ... [as $\Delta x/L \approx \theta$]

Bulk Modulus

♦ The ratio of hydraulic stress to the corresponding hydraulic strain is called *bulk modulus*.

$B = -p/(\Delta V/V)$

The negative sign indicates the fact that with an increase in pressure, a decrease in volume occurs.

♦ SI unit of bulk modulus is the same as that of pressure i.e., $N\ m^{-2}$ or Pa.

♦ The reciprocal of the bulk modulus is called *compressibility* and is denoted by κ.

$\kappa = (1/B) = -(1/\Delta p) \times (\Delta V/V)$

Poisson's Ratio

♦ Within the elastic limit, lateral strain is directly proportional to the longitudinal strain. The ratio of the lateral strain to the longitudinal strain in a stretched wire is called **Poisson's ratio**.

Poisson's ratio is $(\Delta d/d)/(\Delta L/L)$ or $(\Delta d/\Delta L) \times (L/d)$. It is a pure number and has no dimensions or units. Its value depends only on the nature of material.

Elastic Potential Energy in a Stretched Wire

♦ When a wire is put under a tensile stress, work is done against the interatomic forces. This work is stored in the wire in the form of elastic potential energy.

let the length of the wire be elongated by l. Then $F = YA \times (l/L)$. for a further elongation of dl, dW is $F \times dl$ or $YAldl/L$.

♦ Work done (W) in increasing the length of the wire from L to $L + l$, that is from $l = 0$ to $l = l$ is

$$W = \int_0^1 \frac{YAl}{L} dl = \frac{YA}{2} \times \frac{l^2}{L} \; ; \; W = \frac{1}{2} \times Y \times \left(\frac{l}{L}\right)^2 \times AL$$

$$= \frac{1}{2} \times \text{Young's modulus} \times \text{strain}^2 \times \text{volume of the wire}$$

$$= \frac{1}{2} \times \text{stress} \times \text{strain} \times \text{volume of the wire}$$

- The elastic potential energy per unit volume of the wire (u) is

$$u = \frac{1}{2} \times \sigma\varepsilon$$

Applications of Elastic Behaviour of Materials

- Cranes have a thick metal rope to which the load is attached. How thick should the steel rope be? The area of cross-section (A)
  $A \geq W/\sigma_y = Mg/\sigma_y$
  where σ_y is yield strength of rope.
- A bar of length l, breadth b, and depth d when loaded at the centre by a load W sags by an amount given by
  $\delta = Wl^3/(4bd^3Y)$

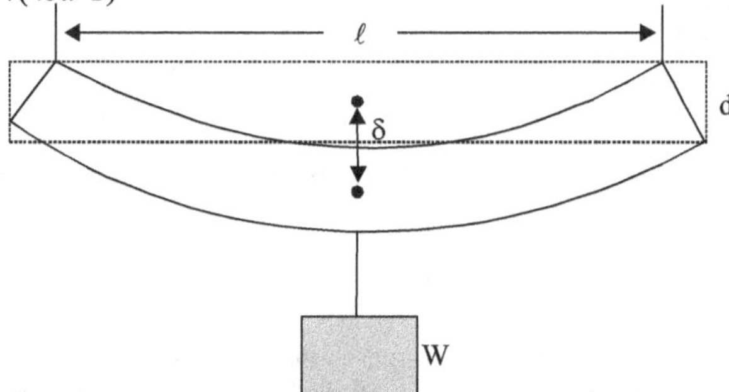

Past Years ONE-LINERS
NEET/JEE Main/Board

- Young's modulus, $Y = \dfrac{\text{Stress}}{\text{Strain}}$

- Bulk modulus, $B = \dfrac{P}{\dfrac{\Delta V}{V}}$

- Young's modulus, $Y = \dfrac{Wl}{A\Delta l}$

- Relation between Y, k, σ, η
  $Y = 3k\,(1 - 2\sigma)$ & $Y = 2\eta\,(1 + \sigma)$

- Energy density $= \dfrac{1}{2} \times \text{stress} \times \text{strain}$

- K.E. of stone = Energy stored in catapult

- Bulk modulus, $K = \dfrac{\text{Volumetric stress}}{\text{Volumetric strain}}$

Tips/Tricks/Tecchniques ONE-LINERS
(Exam Sample)

- Pressure is always normal to the surface but the stress may be parallel or perpendicular to the surface.
- When the applied deforming force is inclined with one of the surface, both the tangential as well as normal stress are produced.
- When a body is sheared by a force, two mutually perpendicular strains are produced. They are called longitudinal strain and compressional strain. Magnitude of these two strains is same.
- Hooke's law follows for small values of strain.
- The depression of a beam of radius r is inversely proportional to the fourth power of radius. *i.e.*, $\delta \propto \dfrac{1}{r^4}$.

- The weight of the wire Mg acts at the centre of gravity of the wire, so that length of wire stretched = L/2.
  The elongation l of the wire due to weight.

$$l = \frac{Mg(L/2)}{AY} = \frac{L^2 dg}{2Y}, \quad d = \text{density of wire}$$

- The area under stress-strain curve gives energy density of a wire *i.e.*,

$$\frac{U}{\text{volume}} = \frac{1}{2} \times \text{stress} \times \text{strain}$$

$$= \frac{1}{2} \times (\text{Young's modulus}) \times (\text{strain})^2$$

- If a spherical object of bulk modulus B is subjected to uniform pressure P, then fractional decrease in its radius, $\dfrac{\Delta R}{R} = \dfrac{P}{3B}$

- When copper wire of fixed volume v is drawn into wire of length ℓ. When this wire is subjected to a constant force F. The extension produced in the wire is $\Delta\ell$ then graph of $\Delta\ell$ versus ℓ^2 is a straight line.

Pressure

- Liquids and gases can flow and are therefore, called fluids.
- Unlike a solid, a fluid has no definite shape of its own. Solids and liquids have a fixed volume,
- Solids and liquids have much lower compressibility as compared to gases. **Pressure** P is defined as the normal force acting per unit area.

$$P_{av} = \frac{F}{A}$$

Pressure is a scalar quantity. The SI unit of pressure is Nm^{-2} or pascal.

Pascal's Law

- For a liquid in equilibrium the pressure is same at all points in a horizontal plane.

Variation of Pressure with Depth

- The pressure P, at depth h below the surface of a liquid open to the atmosphere is greater than atmospheric pressure by an amount ρgh. The excess of pressure, $P - P_a$, at depth h is called a **gauge pressure** at that point. atmospheric pressure (P_a)

$$P = P_a + \rho gh$$

- Consider three vessels A, B and C [Fig.] of different shapes. On filling with water, the level in the three vessels is the same, though they hold different amounts of water. This is so because water at the bottom has the same pressure below each section of the vessel.

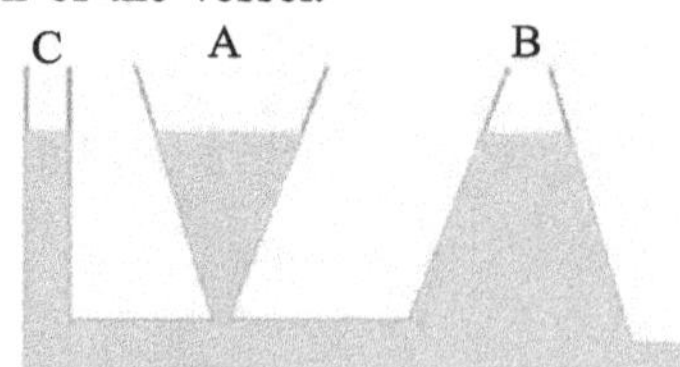

Atmospheric Pressure and Gauge Pressure

- The pressure of the atmosphere at any point is equal to the weight of a column of air of unit cross-sectional area extending from that point to the top of the atmosphere. At sea level, it is 1.013×10^5 Pa (1 atm). A long glass tube closed at one end and filled with mercury is inverted into a trough of mercury is known as 'mercury barometer'.

- The pressure at Point A = 0. The pressure inside the coloumn at Point B must be the same as the pressure at Point C, which is atmospheric pressure, P_a.

$P_a = \rho g h$

1 torr = 133 Pa & 1 bar = 10^5 Pa

♦ An open tube manometer is a useful instrument for measuring pressure differences. It consists of a U-tube containing a suitable liquid.

$P - P_a = \rho g h$

Hydraulic Machines

Pascal's Law

♦ If we push the piston, the fluid level rises in all the tubes, again reaching the same level in each one of them.

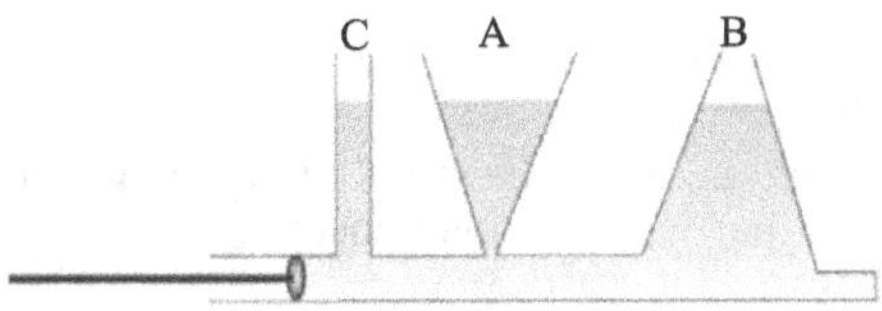

Fig. Whenever external pressure is applied on any part of a fluid in a vessel, it is equally transmitted in all directions.

♦ We can say **whenever external pressure is applied on any part of a fluid contained in a vessel, it is transmitted undiminished and equally in all directions. This is another form of the Pascal's law and it has many applications in daily life.**

♦ In a hydraulic lift, as shown in Fig., two pistons are separated by the space filled with a liquid. A piston of small cross-section A_1 is used to exert a force F_1 directly on the liquid. The pressure $P = \dfrac{F_1}{A_1}$ is transmitted throughout the liquid to the larger cylinder attached with a larger piston of area A_2,

$$F_2 = PA_2 = \frac{F_1 A_2}{A_1}$$

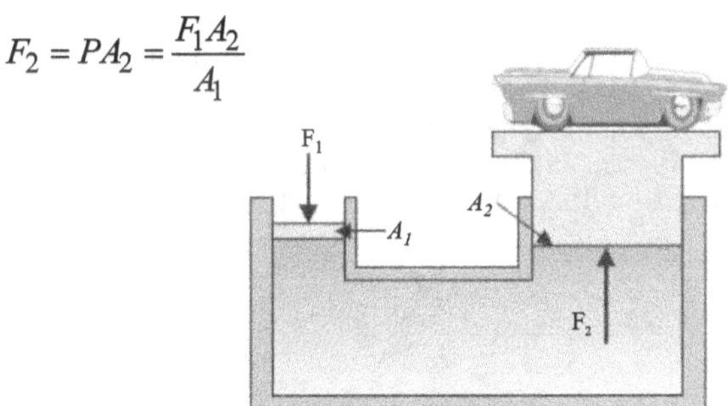

Fig. Schematic diagram illustrating the principle behind the hydraulic lift, a device used to lift heavy loads.

Archemedes's Principle

♦ When a body is wholly or partially immersed in a fluid at rest, the fluid exerts pressure on the surface of the body in contact with the fluid. The pressure is greater on lower surfaces of the body than on the upper surfaces as pressure in a fluid increases with depth. The resultant of all the forces is an upward force called buoyant force.

♦ The upward force exerted is equal to the weight of the displaced fluid = $\rho v g$ [ρ is density of fluid, v is volume of displaced fluid]

Laws of Floatation

♦ If the density of the immersed object is more than that of the fluid, the object will sink as the weight of the body is more than the upward thrust.

♦ If the density of the object is less than that of the fluid, it floats in the fluid partially submerged.

♦ Volume submerged : Total volume of the object is V_s and a part V_p of it is submerged, the upward force is $\rho_f g V_p$, which must equal to the weight of the body; $\rho_s g V_s = \rho_f g V_p$ or $\rho_s/\rho_f = V_p/V_s$

Streamline Flow

♦ The flow of the fluid is said to be **steady** if at any given point, the velocity of each passing fluid particle remains constant.

♦ The path taken by a fluid particle under a steady flow is a **streamline**. It is defined as a curve whose tangent at any point is in the direction of the fluid velocity at that point.

♦ **Equation of continuity :** It is a statement of conservation of mass in flow of incompressible fluids.

$Av = $ constant

$A_P v_P = A_R v_R = A_Q v_Q$

♦ Av gives the volume flux or flow rate and remains constant throughout the pipe of flow. At narrower portions velocity increases and its vice-versa. $A_R > A_Q$ or $v_R < v_Q$.

♦ Steady flow is achieved at low flow speeds. Beyond a limiting value, called critical speed, this flow loses steadiness and becomes turbulent.

♦ Figure displays streamlines for some typical flows. Fig. (a) describes a **laminar flow** where the velocities at different points in the fluid may have different magnitudes but their directions are parallel. Figure (b) gives a sketch of turbulent flow.

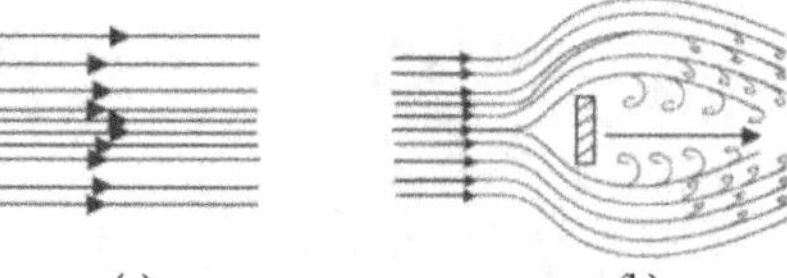

Fig. (a) Some streamlines laminar for fluid flow. (b) A jet of air striking a flat plate placed perpendicular to it. This is an example of turbulent flow.

Bernoulli's Principle

♦ As we move along a streamline the sum of the pressure (P), the kinetic energy per unit volume $\left(\dfrac{\rho v^2}{2}\right)$ and the potential energy per unit volume ($\rho g h$) remains a constant.

$$\Rightarrow P_1 + \left(\frac{1}{2}\right)\rho v_1^2 + \rho g h_1 = P_2 + \left(\frac{1}{2}\right)\rho v_2^2 + \rho g h_2$$

♦ This is Bernoulli's equation.

$$P + \left(\frac{1}{2}\right)\rho v^2 + \rho g h = \text{constant}$$

♦ When fluids flow, some energy does get lost due to internal friction. In a fluid flow, the different layers of the fluid flow with different velocities. These layers exert frictional forces on each other resulting in a loss of energy. This property of the fluid is called **viscosity**.

♦ When a fluid is at rest i.e., its velocity is zero everywhere, Bernoulli's equation becomes

$$P_1 + \rho g h_1 = P_2 + \rho g h_2$$
$$(P_1 - P_2) = \rho g (h_2 - h_1)$$

Speed of Efflux : Torricelli's Law

♦ The word efflux means fluid outflow. Torricelli discovered that the speed of efflux from an open tank is given by a formula identical to that of a freely falling body.

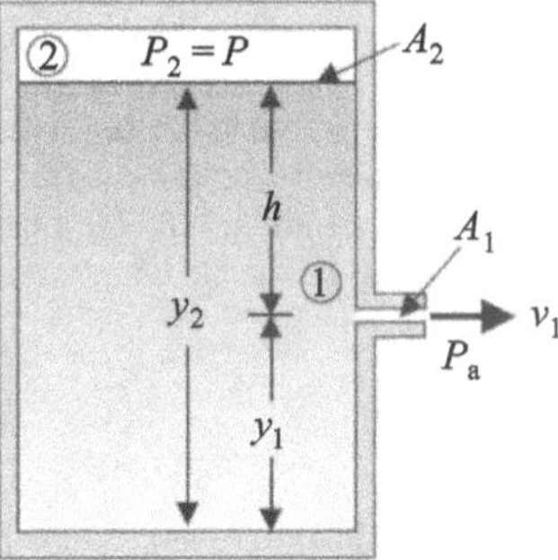

Fig. Torricelli's law. The speed of efflux, v_1, from the side of the container is given by the application of Bernoulli's equation. If the container is open at the top to the atmosphere then $v_1 = \sqrt{2gh}$.

♦ Applying the Bernoulli equation at points 1 and 2 and noting that at the hole $P_1 = P_a$, the atmospheric pressure,

$$P_a + \frac{1}{2}\rho v_1^2 + \rho g y_1 = P + \rho g y_2 \quad \left[\text{As } A_2 \gg A_1, V_2 = 0\right]$$
$$y_2 - y_1 = h$$

♦ If the tank is open to the atmosphere, then $P = P_a$ and Speed of efflux, $v_1 = \sqrt{2gh}$

Venturi-meter

♦ The Venturi-meter is a device to measure the flow speed of incompressible fluid.

♦ Using Bernoulli's equation

$$P_1 + \frac{1}{2}\rho v_1^2 = P_2 + \frac{1}{2}\rho v_1^2 (A/a)^2 \quad \left[\text{As } v_2 = \frac{A}{a} v_1\right]$$

$$P_1 - P_2 = \rho_m g h = \frac{1}{2}\rho v_1^2 \left[\left(\frac{A}{a}\right)^2 - 1\right]$$

$$v_1 = \sqrt{\left(\frac{2\rho_m g h}{\rho}\right)\left(\left(\frac{A}{a}\right)^2 - 1\right)^{-1/2}}$$

- The carburetor of automobile has a Venturi channel (nozzle) through which air flows with a high speed. The pressure is then lowered at the narrow neck and the petrol (gasoline) is sucked up in the chamber to provide the correct mixture of air to fuel necessary for combustion.
- Filter pumps or aspirators, Bunsen burner, atomisers and sprayers used for perfumes or to spray insecticides work on the same principle.

Blood Flow and Heart Attack

- The artery may get constricted due to the accumulation of plaque on its inner walls. In order to drive the blood through this constriction a greater demand is placed on the activity of the heart. The speed of the flow of the blood in this region is raised which lowers the pressure inside and the artery may collapse due to the external pressure.

Dynamic Lift

- Fig. (a) shows the streamlines around a non-spinning ball moving relative to a fluid. Velocity of fluid (air) above and below the ball at corresponding points is the same resulting in zero pressure difference.
- Fig. (b) shows the streamlines of air for a ball which is moving and spinning at the same time.
- The velocity of air above the ball relative to the ball is larger and below it is smaller.
- The stream lines, thus, get crowded above and rarified below.
- This difference in the velocities of air results in a net upward force on the ball. This dynamic lift due to spining is called **Magnus effect**.

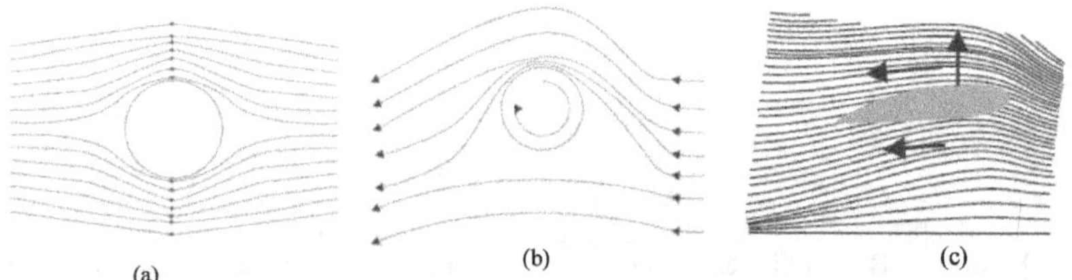

Fig. (a) Fluid streaming past a static sphere. (b) Streamlines for a fluid around a sphere spinning clockwise. (c) Air flowing past an aerofoil.

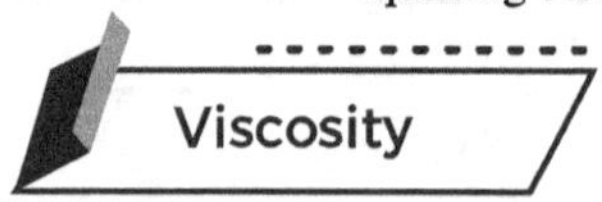

- Most of the fluids are not ideal ones and offer some resistance to motion. It is called **viscosity**. This force exists when there is relative motion between layers of the liquid. We consider a fluid enclosed between two glass plates.
- The layer of the liquid in contact with top surface moves with a velocity v and the layer of the liquid in contact with the fixed surface is stationary. For any layer of liquid, its upper layer pulls it forward while lower layer pulls it backward. This type of flow is known as laminar.

- When a fluid is flowing in a pipe or a tube, then velocity of the liquid layer along the axis of the tube is maximum and decreases gradually as we move towards the walls where it becomes zero, Fig. (b).

- Viscous force between layers is $F = -\eta A \dfrac{dv}{dy}$

  Where A is contact area of layers, η is coefficient of viscosity, $\dfrac{dv}{dy}$ is velocity gradient.

- The coefficient of viscosity for a fluid is defined as the ratio of shearing stress to the strain rate.

$$\eta = \frac{F/A}{v/l} = \frac{Fl}{vA}$$

The SI unit of viscosity is poiseuille (*Pl*). Its other units are Nsm^{-2} or Pa s.

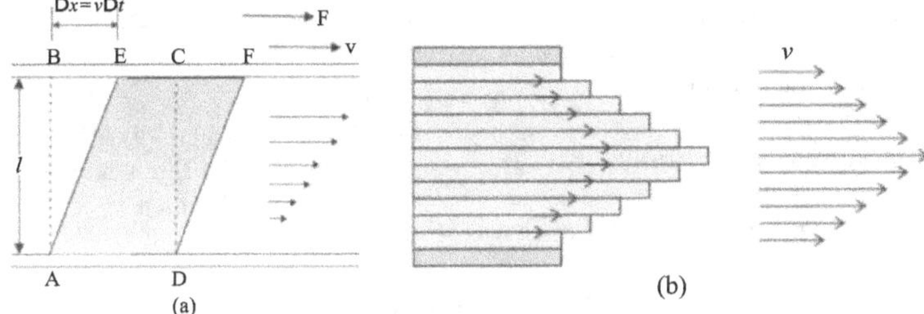

Fig. (a) A layer of liquid sandwiched between two parallel glass plates, in which the lower plate is fixed and the upper one is moving to the right with velocity v (b) velocity distribution for viscous flow in a pipe.

Stokes' Law

- Viscous or drag force due to different layers of the fluid, F depends on viscosity η of the fluid and radius a of the sphere.

  $F = 6\pi\eta \, av$

  where v = velocity of falling body

  This is known as Stokes' law.

- **Terminal velocity**

  $6\pi\eta av_t = (4\pi/3) \, a^3 \, (\rho-\sigma)g$

  ρ and σ are mass densities of sphere and the fluid, respectively.

  $v_t = 2a^2 \, (\rho-\sigma)g / (9\eta)$

  v_t depends on the square of the radius of the sphere and inversely on the viscosity of the medium.

Reynolds Number

- Reynold's number is a pure number which determines the nature of flow of liquid through a pipe.

- Reynold's number $N_R = \dfrac{\text{Inertial force per unit area}}{\text{Viscous force per unit area}}$

$$= \frac{v^2\rho}{nv/d} = \frac{v\rho d}{\eta}$$

- The flow of liquid is streamline or laminar if N_R lies between 0 to 2000.
- The flow of liquid is unstable and changing from streamline to turbulent flow if N_R lies between 2000 to 3000.
- The flow of liquid is definitely turbulent if $N_R > 3000$.

Surface Tension

- Liquids acquire a free surface when poured in a container. These surfaces possess some additional energy. This phenomenon is known as surface tension and it is concerned with only liquid.

Surface Energy and Surface Tension

- Consider a horizontal liquid film ending in bar free to slide over parallel guides (see figure).
- Move the bar by a small distance d. The work done by the applied force is $\mathbf{F.d} = Fd$.

  This is stored as additional energy in the film. If the surface energy of the film is S per unit area and a film has two sides.

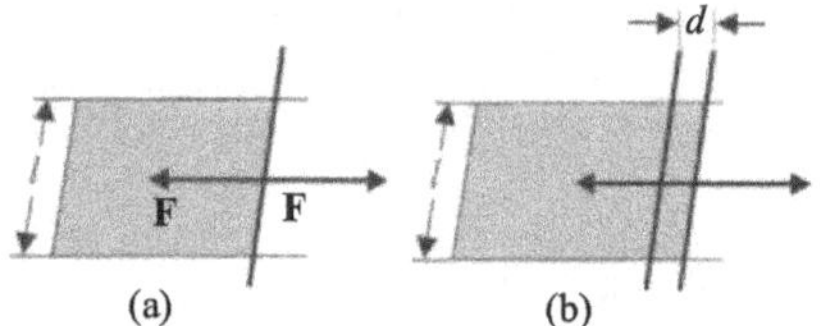

Fig. Stretching a film. (a) A film in equilibrium; (b) The film stretched an extra distance.

  So there are two surfaces and the extra energy is

  $S(2dl) = Fd$

  Or, $S = Fd/2dl = F/2l$

- *Quantity S is the magnitude of surface tension. It is equal to the surface energy per unit area of the liquid interface and is also equal to the force per unit length exerted by the fluid on the movable bar.*
- Like viscosity, the surface tension of a liquid usually falls with temperature.

Angle of Contact

- *The angle between tangent to the liquid surface at the point of contact and solid surface inside the liquid is termed as angle of contact.* Water forms droplets on lotus leaf while spreads over a clean plastic plate.

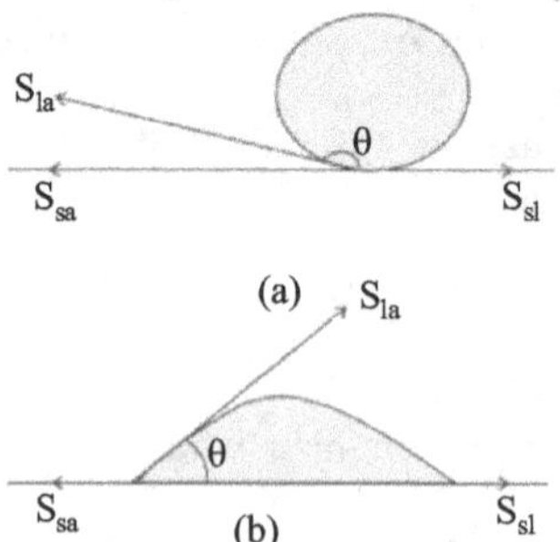

Fig. Different shapes of water drops with interfacial tensions (a) on a lotus leaf (b) on a clean plastic plate.

- The angle of contact is an obtuse angle if $S_{sl} > S_{la}$ as in the case of water-leaf interface while it is an acute angle if $S_{sl} < S_{la}$ as in the case of water-plastic interface.

Drops and Bubbles

♦ Why are drops and bubbles spherical?
A liquid-air interface has energy, so for a given volume the surface with minimum energy is the one with the least area. The sphere has this property.

Excess pressure inside soap bubble

♦ Another interesting consequence of surface tension is that the pressure inside a spherical drop Fig. (a) is more than the pressure outside. Suppose a spherical drop of radius r is in equilibrium. If its radius increase by Δr. The extra surface energy is

$$[4\pi(r+\Delta r)^2 - 4\pi r^2]S_{la} = 8\pi r\Delta r S_{la}$$

The work done due to $P_i - P_o$
$$W = (P_i - P_o)\, 4\pi r^2 \Delta r$$
so that
$$(P_i - P_o) = (2\, S_{la}/\, r)$$

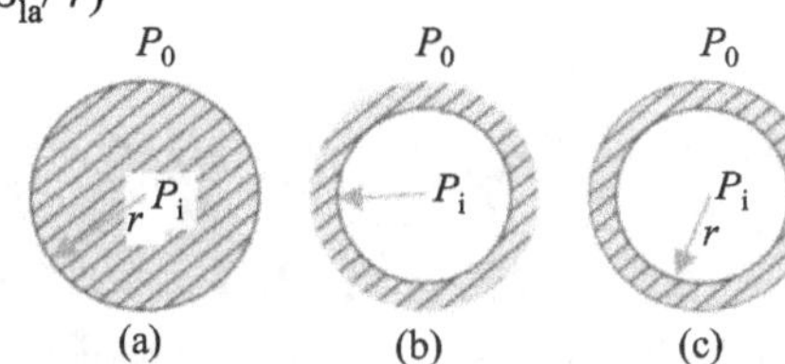

Fig. Drop, cavity and bubble of radius r.

♦ A bubble has two interfaces, so excess pressure
$$(P_i - P_o) = (4\, S_{la}/\, r)$$

Capillary Rise

♦ Consider a vertical capillary tube of circular cross section (radius a) inserted into an open vessel of water (Fig). The contact angle between water and glass is acute.

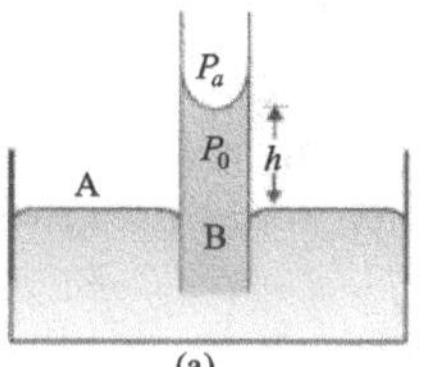

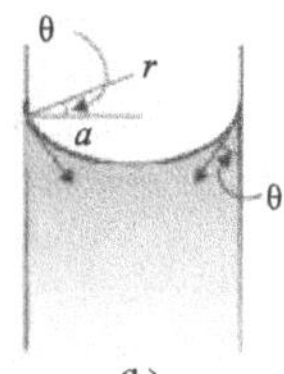

∴ **Capillary rise $h = (2S \cos \theta)/a\rho g$**

♦ If S, θ, ρ and g are constant then $h \propto \dfrac{1}{a}$
This is **Zurin's law**.

Past Years ONE-LINERS NEET/JEE Main/Board

♦ At terminal velocity, the body moves with constant velocity,
Viscous force = Weight − Buoyant force.

♦ Mass of water rise in capillary tube $\propto$ radius of capillary tube.

♦ Pressure inside the soap bubble $= P_0 + \dfrac{4T}{R}$

♦ Volume flow rate $= Av = A\sqrt{2gh}$

♦ Power, $P = Fv = 6\,\pi\eta r v v = 6\pi\eta r v^2$

- At same level in same liquid pressure is equal.
- For a floating body, weight = buoyant force
- Volumetric strain, $\dfrac{\Delta v}{v} = \dfrac{B}{P}$
- Equation of continuity $A_1 v_1 = A_2 v_2$
- According to Jurin's law, $h \propto \dfrac{1}{r}$
- From Pascal's law, pressure transferred is same everywhere in liquid.
- Equation of continuity $A_1 v_1 = A_2 v_2$
- Mass of water rise in capillary tube $\propto$ radius of capillary

Tips/Tricks/Tecchniques ONE-LINERS
(Exam Sample)

- For a fluid, the velocity increases at a point where pressure decreases and vice-versa.
- The pressure on the concave side of a curved surface is more than that on its convex side.
- Angle of contact do not depend on the angle of inclination of the solid in liquid.
- When a body of density (ρ) immersed in a liquid of density (σ) the apparent weight of the body = $V\rho g - V\sigma g$.
- When two soap bubbles of radii R_1 and R_2 combine to form a new bubble in vacuum under isothermal condition, then its new radius R is

$$R = \left(R_1^2 + R_2^2 \right)^{1/2}$$

- If two soap bubbles of radii R_1 and R_2 is combined to form a common surface, the radius of curvature (R) of the common surface is

$$R = \dfrac{R_1 R_2}{R_2 - R_1}$$

- In the absence of external force, the shape of a liquid drop is determined by the surface tension of the liquid.
- When the tank filled with fluid is closed and $P \gg P_a$ then velocity of efflux from the orifice $= \sqrt{\dfrac{2(P - P_a)}{\rho}}$.
- If n small drops of liquids, each of them having radius r and terminal velocity v combine together to form big drop of terminal velocity v' then value of v' is given by $v' = vn^{2/3}$
- Angle of contact between a liquid and a solid surface in contact increases with rise in temperature of the liquid and decreases with the addition of soluble impurities to the liquid.
- Power = rate of production of energy

$$P = \text{F.v.} = 6\pi\eta r V_T \cdot V_T = \dfrac{24}{81} \cdot \dfrac{\pi r^5 g^2 (\rho - \sigma)}{\eta}$$

# 11 Thermal Properties of Matter

- Temperature is a relative measure, or indication of hotness or coldness.
- An object that has a higher temperature than another object is said to be hotter. Hot and cold are relative terms, like tall and short.
- Heat transfer takes place between the system and the surrounding medium, until the body and the surrounding medium are at the same temperature.
- Heat is the form of energy transferred between two (or more) systems or a system and its surroundings by virtue of temperature difference.
- The SI unit of heat energy transferred is expressed in joule (J) while SI unit of temperature is Kelvin (K), and degree Celsius (°C) is a commonly used unit of temperature.

- In common liquid–in–glass thermometers, mercury, alcohol etc., are used whose volume varies linearly with temperature over a wide range.
- The ice point and the steam point of water are two convenient fixed points and are known as the freezing and boiling points, respectively.
- The ice and steam point have values 32°F and 212°F, respectively, on the Fahrenheit scale and 0°C and 100°C on the Celsius scale. On the Fahrenheit scale, there are 180 equal intervals between two reference points, and on the Celsius scale, there are 100.
- Relation between Fahrenheit and Celsius scales is $\dfrac{t_F - 32}{180} = \dfrac{t_c}{100}$

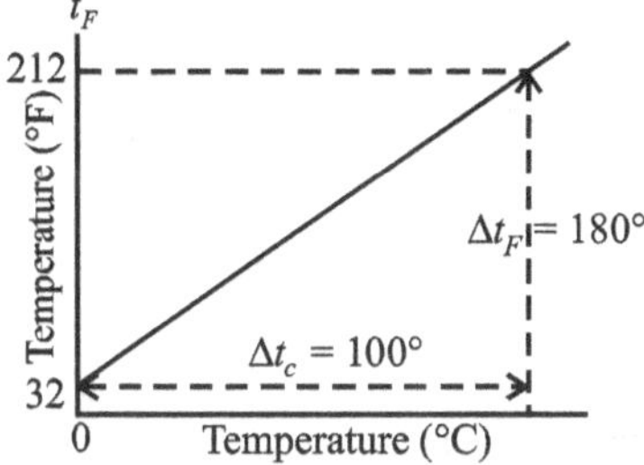

Fig.: *A plot of Fahrenheit temperature (t_F) versus Celsius temperature (t_c).*

Ideal-gas Equation and Absolute Temperature

- All gases at low densities exhibit same expansion behaviour.
- When temperature is held constant, the pressure and volume of a quantity of gas are related as PV = constant. This relationship is known as Boyle's law.
- When the pressure is held constant, the volume of a quantity of the gas is related to the temperature as V/T = constant. This relationship is known as Charles' law.

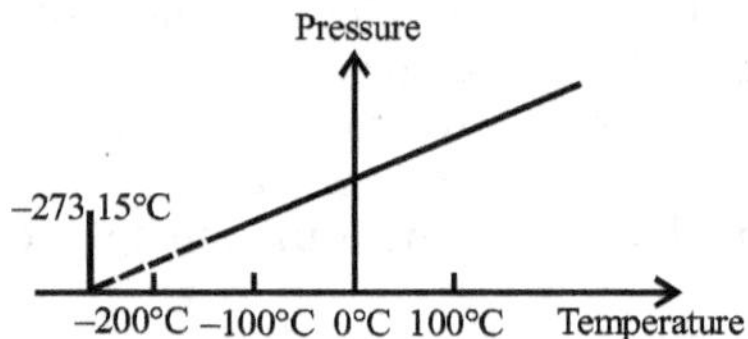

Fig.: *Pressure versus temperature of a low density gas kept at constant volume.*

- Since PV = constant and V/T = constant for a given quantity of gas, then PV/T should also be a constant. This relationship is known as ideal gas law.

- **Ideal-gas equation:** $\dfrac{PV}{T} = \mu R$ or PV = μRT

  where, μ is the number of moles in the sample of gas and R is called universal gas constant R = 8.31 J mol^{-1} K^{-1}

- PV $\propto$ T. This relationship allows a gas to be used to measure temperature in a constant volume gas thermometer. Holding the volume of a gas constant, it gives P $\propto$ T.

- The absolute minimum temperature for an ideal gas, therefore, inferred by extrapolating the straight line to the axis, as in Fig. This temperature is found to be –273.15°C and is designated as **absolute zero.**

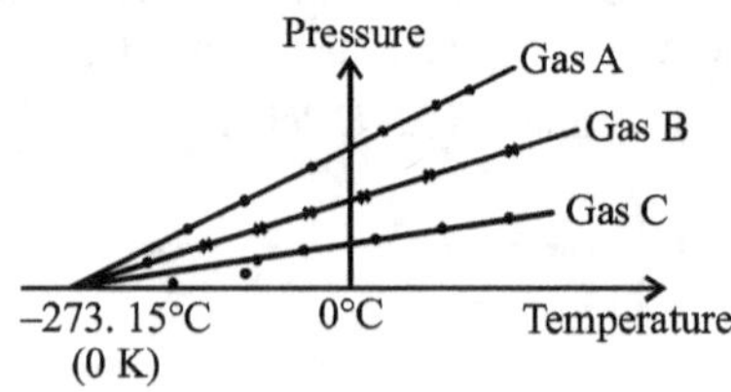

Fig.: *A plot of pressure versus temperature and extrapolation of lines for low density gases indicates the same absolute zero temperature.*

- The size of unit in Kelvin and Celsius temperature scales is the same. So, temperature on these scales are related by

  $T_K = t_C + 273.15$

Thermal Explansion

- The increase in the dimensions of a body due to the increase in its temperature is called thermal expansion.
- The expansion in length is called **linear expansion**. The expansion in area is called **area expansion**. The expansion in volume is called **volume expansion**.

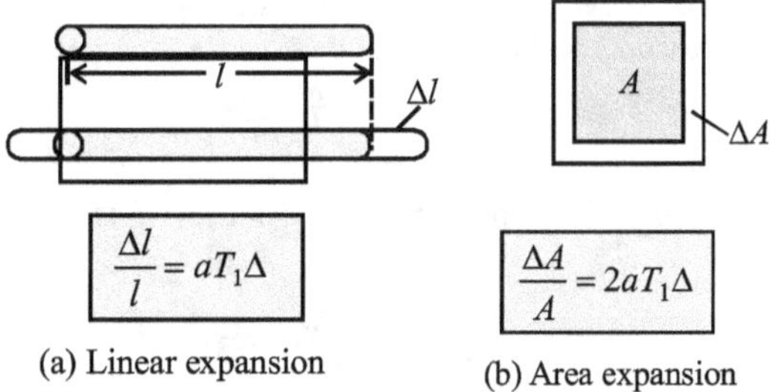

(a) Linear expansion

(b) Area expansion

Fig.: *Thermal Expansion.*

- If the substance is in the form of a long rod, then for small change in temperature, ΔT, the fractional change in length, $\Delta l/l$, is directly proportional to ΔT.

$$\frac{\Delta l}{l} = \alpha l \Delta T$$

where α_1 is known as the **coefficient of linear expansion**.

- The fractional change in volume, $\dfrac{\Delta V}{V}$, of a substance is proportional to temperature change ΔT.

Coefficient of volume expansion, $a_V = \left(\dfrac{\Delta V}{V}\right)\dfrac{1}{\Delta T}$

- Water exhibits an anomalous behaviour; it contracts on heating between 0°C and 4°C. The volume of a given amount of water decreases as it is cooled from room temperature, until its temperature reaches 4°C. Below 4°C, the volume increases, and therefore, the density decreases. This means that water has the maximum density at 4°C.

- Bodies of water, such as lakes and ponds, freeze at the top first. As a lake cools toward 4°C, water near the surface loses energy to the atmosphere, becomes denser, and sinks; the warmer, less dense water near the bottom rises. However, once the colder water on top reaches temperature below 4°C, it becomes less dense and remains at the surface, where it freezes.

- For an ideal gas, the coefficient of volume expansion at constant pressure can be found from the ideal gas equation:

$$PV = \mu RT$$

At constant pressure

$$P\Delta V = \mu R \, \Delta T$$

$$\frac{\Delta V}{V} = \frac{\Delta T}{T}$$

i.e., $\qquad \alpha_v = \dfrac{1}{T}$ for ideal gas

◆ **Relation between the coefficient of volume expansion (α_v) and coefficient of linear expansion (α_l).**

◆ Imagine a cube of length l, that expands equally in all directions, when its temperature increases by ΔT. We have

$$\Delta l = \alpha_1 \, l \, \Delta T$$

so, $\qquad \Delta V = (1 + \Delta l)^3 - l^3 \simeq 3l^2 \, \Delta l$

Terms $(\Delta l)^2$ and $(\Delta l)^3$ have been neglected since Δl is small compared to l. So

$$\Delta V = \frac{3V \, \Delta l}{l} = 3V\alpha_l \Delta T$$

which gives

$$\alpha_v = 3\alpha_1$$

Similarly, $\qquad \left(\dfrac{\Delta A}{A}\right)\dfrac{1}{\Delta T} \simeq 2\alpha$

◆ By preventing the thermal expansion of a rod by fixing its ends rigidly, the rod acquires a compressive strain due to the external forces provided by the rigid supports at the ends. The corresponding stress set up in the rod is called thermal stress. For example, consider a steel rail of length 5m and area of cross-section 40 cm^2 that is prevented from expanding while the temperature rises by 10°C.

◆ The coefficient of area expansion, $(\Delta A/A)/\Delta T$, of a rectangular sheet of the solid is twice its linear expansivity, α_1.

Specific Heat Capacity

◆ We define heat capacity, S of a substance as

$$S = \frac{\Delta Q}{\Delta T}$$

where ΔQ is the amount of heat supplied to the substance to change its temperature from T to $T + \Delta T$.

◆ Heat absorbed or given off to change the temperature of unit mass of substance by one unit. This quantity is referred to as the **specific heat capacity** of the substance.

Specific heat capacity, of that substance is given by

$$S = \frac{S}{m} = \frac{1}{m}\frac{\Delta Q}{\Delta T}$$

The SI unit of specific heat capacity is J kg^{-1} K^{-1}.

- If the amount of substance is specified in terms of moles μ, instead of mass m in kg, we can define heat capacity per mole of the substance by

$$C = \frac{S}{\mu} = \frac{1}{\mu}\frac{\Delta Q}{\Delta T}$$

where M = molar mass and C is known as **molar specific heat capacity**.
- The SI unit of molar specific heat capacity is J mol^{-1} K^{-1}.
- If the gas is held under constant pressure during the heat transfer, then it is called the **molar specific heat capacity at constant pressure C$_p$**.
- If the volume of the gas is maintained constant during the heat transfer, then the corresponding molar specific heat capacity is called **molar specific heat capacity at constant volume** and is denoted by C$_v$.
- Water has the highest specific heat capacity compared to other substances. For this reason water is also used as a **coolant in automobile radiators**, as well as, a heater in hot water bags. Owing to its high specific heat capacity, water warms up more slowly than land during summer, and consequently wind from the sea has a cooling effect.

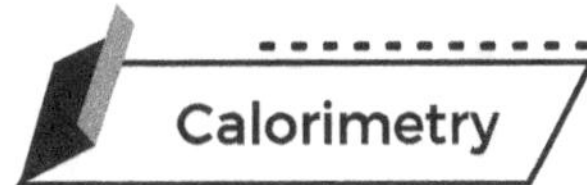

- A system is said to be isolated if no exchange or transfer of heat occurs between the system and its surroundings.
- Calorimetry means measurement of heat. When a body at higher temperature is brought in contact with another body at lower temperature, the **heat lost by the hot body is equal to the heat gained by the colder body**, provided no heat is allowed to escape to the surroundings. A device in which heat measurement can be done is called a **calorimeter**.

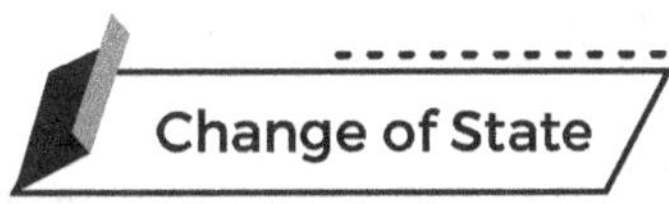

- Take some cubes of ice in a beaker. Start heating it slowly on a constant heat source. Note the temperature.
- Draw a graph between temperature and time. You will observe no change in the temperature as long as there is ice in the beaker. In the above process, the temperature of the system does not change even though heat is being continuously supplied. The heat supplied is being utilised in changing the state from solid (ice) to liquid (water).

◆ The change of state from solid to liquid is called melting and from liquid to solid is called **fusion**.

◆ The temperature at which the solid and the liquid states of the substance is in thermal equilibrium with each other is called its **melting point**.

◆ After the whole of ice gets converted into water and as we continue further heating, we shall see that temperature begins to rise. The temperature keeps on rising till it reaches nearly 100°C when it again becomes steady. The heat supplied is now being utilised to change water from liquid state to vapour or gaseous state.

◆ The change of state from liquid to vapour (or gas) is called **vaporisation**.

◆ The temperature at which the liquid and the vapour states of the substance coexist is called its **boiling point**.

Latent Heat

◆ The amount of heat per unit mass transferred during change of state of the substance is called **latent heat** of the substance for the process.

◆ If mass m of a substance undergoes a change from one state to the other, then the quantity of heat required is given by

$$Q = m L$$

or

$$L = Q/m$$

where L is known as latent heat. Its SI unit is J kg^{-1}.

◆ The latent heat for a solid-liquid state change is called the **latent heat of fusion** (L_f), and that for a liquid-gas state change is called the **latent heat of vaporisation** (L_v).

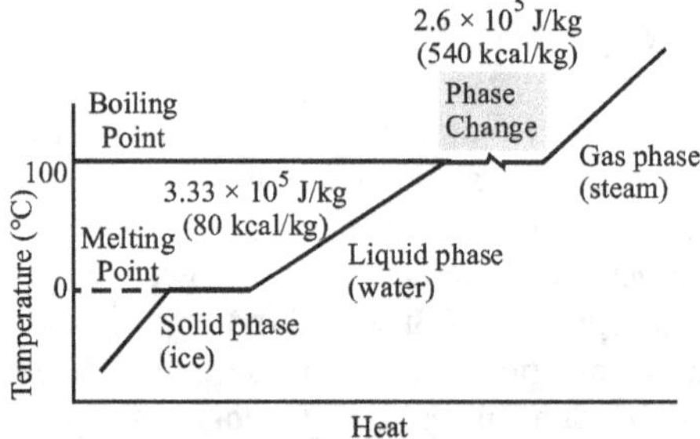

Fig.: *Temperature versus heat for water at 1 atm pressure (not to scale).*

Triple Point

◆ The temperature of a substance remains constant during its change of state (phase change). A graph between the temperature T and the pressure P of the substance is called a phase diagram or P – T diagram. The triple point of water is represented by the temperature 273.16 K and pressure 6.11×10^{-3} Pa.

◆ The change from solid state to vapour state without passing through the liquid state is called sublimation, and the substance is said to sublime. Dry ice (solid CO_2) sublimes, so also iodine. During the sublimation process both the solid and vapour states of a substance coexist in thermal equilibrium.

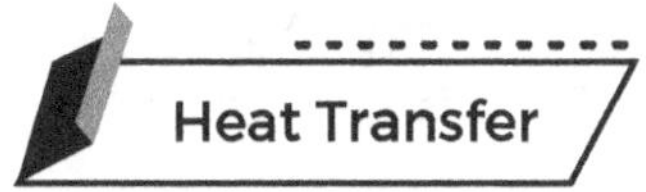

♦ There are three distinct modes of heat transfer: conduction, convection and radiation.

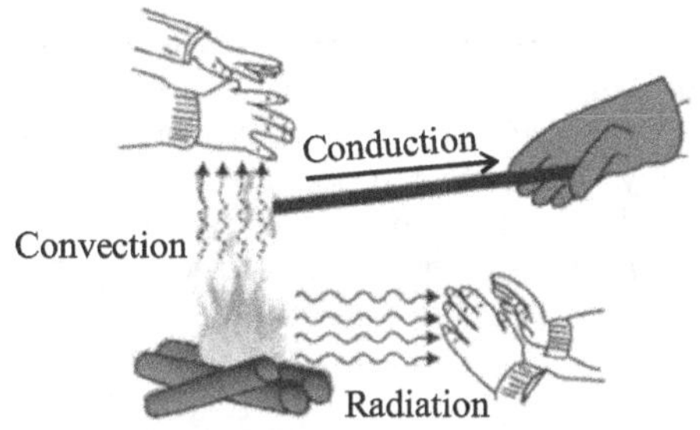

Fig.: *Heating by conduction, convection and radiation.*

Conduction

♦ Conduction is the mechanism of transfer of heat between two adjacent parts of a body because of their temperature difference.

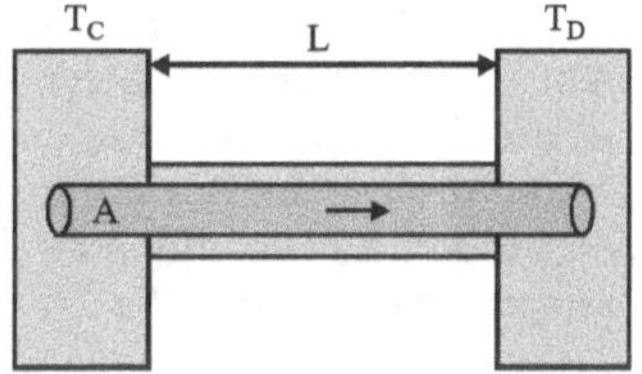

Fig.: *Steady state heat flow by conduction in a bar with its two ends maintained at temperatures T_C and T_D; ($T_C > T_D$).*

♦ The rate of flow of heat (or heat current) H is proportional to the temperature difference $(T_C - T_D)$ and the area of cross-section A and is inversely proportional to the length L :

$$H = KA \frac{T_C - T_D}{L}$$

♦ The constant of proportionality K is called the **thermal conductivity** of the material. The greater the value of K for a material, the more rapidly will it conduct heat. The SI unit of K is $J \ s^{-1} \ m^{-1} \ K^{-1}$ or $W \ m^{-1} \ K^{-1}$.

Equivalent Thermal Conductivity

(i) **Series combination :** If n slabs each of cross-sectional area A lengths l_1, l_2, l_3 .... l_n and conductivities k_1, k_2, k_3 ..... k_n respectively be connected in the series then

$$K_S = \frac{l_1 + l_2 + ... l_n}{\dfrac{l_1}{k_1} + \dfrac{l_2}{k_2} + \dfrac{l_3}{k_3} + ... \dfrac{l_n}{k_n}}$$

Physics

(ii) **Parallel combination :** If n slabs each of length l, areas A_1, A_2, A_3 ...... A_n and thermal conductivities k_1, k_2, k_3 ..... k_n respectively be connected in parallel then

$$K_p = \frac{K_1 A_1 + K_2 A_2 + K_3 A_3 + ...K_n A_n}{A_1 + A_2 + A_3 + ...A_n}$$

Convection

♦ Convection is a mode of heat transfer by actual motion of matter. It is possible only in fluids. Convection can be natural or forced.

♦ In natural convection, gravity plays an important part. When a fluid is heated from below, the hot part expands and, therefore, becomes less dense. Because of buoyancy, it rises and the upper colder part replaces it. This again gets heated, rises up and is replaced by the relative colder part of fluid. This process goes on.

♦ In forced convection, material is forced to move by a pump or by some other physical means. The common examples of forced convection systems are forced-air heating systems in home, the cooling system of an automobile engine.

♦ Natural convection is responsible for many familiar phenomena. During the day, the ground heats up more quickly than large bodies of water do. This occurs both because water has a greater specific heat capacity. The air in contact with the warm ground is heated by conduction. It expands, becoming less dense than the surrounding cooler air. As a result, the warm air rises (air currents) and the other air moves (winds) to fill the space-creating a **sea breeze** near a large body of water.

♦ Its opposite **sea breeze** at night, the ground loses its heat more quickly, and the water surface is warmer than the land. As a result, the cycle is reversed.

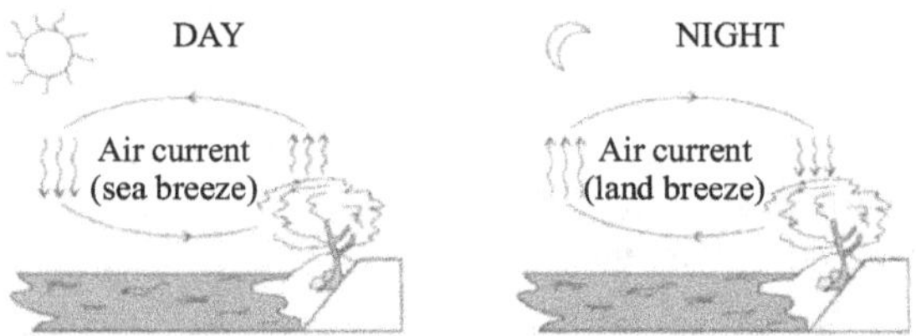

Fig.: Convection cycles.

Radiation

♦ The third mechanism for heat transfer needs no medium; it is called radiation and the energy so transferred by electromagnetic waves is called radiant energy.

♦ All bodies emit radiant energy, whether they are solid, liquid or gas. The electromagnetic radiation emitted by a body by virtue of its temperature, like radiation by a red hot iron or light from a filament lamp is called thermal radiation.

♦ Blackbodies absorb and emit radiant energy better than bodies of lighter colours.

♦ The bottoms of utensils for cooking food are blackened so that they absorb maximum heat from fire and transfer it to the vegetables to be cooked.

- A Dewar flask or thermos bottle is a device to minimise heat transfer between the contents of the bottle and outside. It consists of a double-walled glass vessel with the inner and outer walls coated with silver. Radiation from the inner wall is reflected back to the contents of the bottle.
- The outer wall similarly reflects back any incoming radiation. The space between the walls is evacuated to reduce conduction and convection losses and the flask is supported on an insulator, like cork.

Blackbody Radiation

- Thermal radiation at any temperature has a continuous spectrum from the small to the long wavelengths. The energy content of radiation, however, varies for different wavelengths.
- The following curve gives the experimental curves for radiation energy per unit area per unit wavelength emitted by a blackbody versus wavelength for different temperatures.

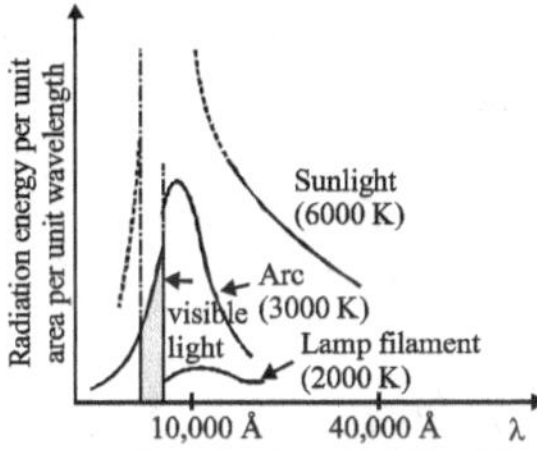

Fig.: *Energy emitted versus wavelength for a blackbody at different temperatures*

- The relation between λ_m and T known as **Wien's Displacement Law:**

$$\lambda_m\, T = \text{constant}$$

The value of the constant (Wien's constant) is

$$2.9 \times 10^{-3}\ \text{m K.}$$

- The total electromagnetic energy radiated by a body at absolute temperature T is proportional to its size, its ability to radiate (called emissivity) and most importantly to its temperature. For a body, which is a perfect radiator, the energy emitted per unit time (H) is given by

$$H = A\sigma T^4$$

This relation is known as **Stefan-Boltzmann law** and the constant σ is called Stefan-Boltzmann constant. Its value in SI units is $5.67 \times 10^{-8}\ \text{W m}^{-2}\ \text{K}^{-4}$.

Fraction e called *emissivity* and writes,

$$H = Ae\sigma T^4$$

$$e = 1 \text{ for a perfect radiator.}$$

- A body at temperature T, with surroundings at temperatures T_s, emits, as well as, receives energy. For a perfect radiator, the net rate of loss of radiant energy is

$$H = \sigma A\ (T^4 - T_s^{\,4})$$

For a body with emissivity e, the relation modifies to

$$H = e\sigma A\ (T^4 - T_s^{\,4})$$

Greenhouse Effect

- The earth's surface is a source of thermal radiation as it absorbs energy received from the Sun. But a large portion of this radiation is absorbed by greenhouse gases, namely, carbon dioxide (CO_2); methane (CH_4); nitrous oxide (N_2O); chlorofluorocarbon (CF_xCl_x); and tropospheric ozone (O_3). This heats up the atmosphere which, in turn, gives more energy to earth, resulting in warmer surface.

- The cycle of processes described above is repeated until no radiation is available for absorption. The net result is heating up of earth's surface and atmosphere. This is known as **Greenhouse Effect**. Without the Greenhouse Effect, the temperature of the earth would have been −18°C.

- Greenhouse gases has enhanced due to human activities, making the earth warmer. According to an estimate, average temperature of earth has increased by 0.3 to 0.6°C, since the beginning of this century.

- This global warming may cause problem for human life, plants and animals. Because of global warming, ice caps are melting faster, sea level is rising, and weather pattern is changing.

Newton's Law of Cooling

- From the graph you can infer how the cooling of hot water depends on the difference of its temperature from that of the surroundings. You will also notice that initially the rate of cooling is higher and decreases as the temperature of the body falls.

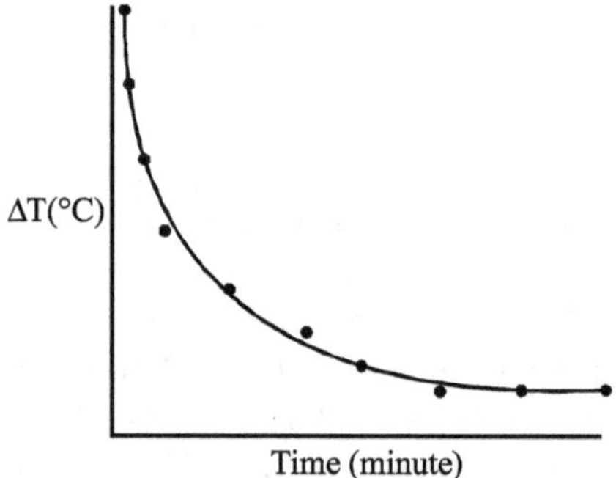

Fig.: *Curve showing cooling of hot water with time.*

- According to Newton's law of cooling, the rate of loss of heat, $-dQ/dt$ of the body is directly proportional to the difference of temperature $\Delta T = (T_2 - T_1)$ of the body and the surroundings. The law holds good only for small difference of temperature.

$$-\frac{dQ}{dt} = k(T_2 - T_1) \qquad \qquad \text{...(i)}$$

where k is a positive constant depending upon the area and nature of the surface of the body.

♦ Suppose a body of mass m and specific heat capacity s is at temperature T_2. Let T_1 be the temperature of the surroundings. If the temperature falls by a small amount dT_2 in time dt, then the amount of heat lost is

$$dQ = ms\, dT_2$$

∴ Rate of loss of heat is given by

$$-\frac{dQ}{dt} = ms\frac{dT_2}{dt} \qquad \text{...(ii)}$$

From Eqs. (i) and (ii), we have

$$-ms\frac{dT_2}{dt} = k\,(T_2 - T_1)$$

$$\frac{dT_2}{T_2 - T_1} = -\frac{k}{ms}dt = -Kdt$$

where $K = k/ms$

On integrating,

$$\log_e (T_2 - T_1) = -Kt + c$$

or
$$T_2 = T_1 + C'\, e^{-Kt}; \text{ where } C' = e^c$$

The above equation enables us to calculate the time of cooling of a body through a particular range of temperature.

Past Years ONE-LINERS
NEET/JEE Main/Board

♦ Rate of cooling ∝ mean temp. difference, $\dfrac{\theta_1 - \theta_2}{t} = k\left(\dfrac{\theta_1 + \theta_2}{2} - \theta_0\right)$

♦ Heat supplied, $\Delta Q = ms\Delta T$

♦ Final length, $l' = l(1 + \alpha\Delta T)$

♦ From Wein's law $\lambda_{max}\, T = $ constant

♦ Bulk modulus $K = \dfrac{\Delta P}{\left(\dfrac{-\Delta V}{V}\right)}$

♦ Rate of power loss $P \propto r^2 T^4$

♦ Heat current $H = H_1 + H_2 = \dfrac{K_1 A(T_1 - T_2)}{d} + \dfrac{K_2 A(T_1 - T_2)}{d}$

♦ Energy produced in falling of ice = energy absorbed in melting of ice $\dfrac{mgh}{4} = mL$

♦ According to wein's displacement law, maximum amount of emitted radiation corresponding to $\lambda_m = \dfrac{b}{T}$

♦ Coefficient of linear expansion $\alpha = \dfrac{\Delta l}{l_0 \Delta T}$.

♦ Density, $\rho = \rho_0(1 - \gamma \Delta t)$

Fractional change in density, $\dfrac{\Delta \rho}{\rho} = \gamma \Delta T$.

♦ Change in volume, $\Delta V = V_y \Delta T$
  $\because V = a^3$ and $y = 3\alpha$

♦ Volume, $V = lbh$

$$\therefore \gamma = \dfrac{\Delta V}{V} = \dfrac{\Delta \ell}{\ell} + \dfrac{\Delta b}{b} + \dfrac{\Delta h}{h} \qquad (\gamma = \text{coefficient of volume expansion})$$

♦ According to principle of calorimetry.
  Heat lost = Heat gain

Tips/Tricks/Tecchniques ONE-LINERS
(Exam Sample)

♦ At $-40°C$ temperature, readings of centigrade and Farhenheit scales are the same.
♦ Newton's law of cooling can be applied only if temperature difference between body and sorrounding is not very large *i.e.*, $20 - 30°C$.
♦ Radiant power, $P = \dfrac{Q}{t} = A\varepsilon\sigma T^4$.
♦ A pendulum clocks becomes slower in summer and faster in winter.
  Change in time period (ΔT) of a pendulum due to change in temperature $\Delta\theta$.

$$\Delta T = \dfrac{1}{2} \times (\Delta\theta) \cdot T$$

♦ Questions of calorimetry should perferably be done in CGS units. This method makes the calculations simpler.
♦ If temperature of a body changes from θ_1 to θ_2 in t time and it changes from θ_2 to θ_3 in next time then we can use $\dfrac{\theta_2 - \theta_0}{\theta_1 - \theta_0} = \dfrac{\theta_3 - \theta_0}{\theta_2 - \theta_0}$

  $(\theta_0 = \text{temperature of sorrounding})$

- If two liquids of equal mass and having same surface are allowed to cool from same initial temperature to same final temperature with same surrounding then $\dfrac{t_1}{t_2} = \dfrac{K_2}{K_1} = \dfrac{C_1}{C_2}$.

  Here, C_1 and C_2 are specific heat of two liquids.

- When temperature and phase both changes or only phase changes as in case of ice-water mixing

  $$\theta_{mix} = \dfrac{m_w \theta_w - \dfrac{m_i L_i}{cw}}{m_w + m_i}$$

  If $m_w = m_i$ then $\theta_{mix} = \dfrac{\theta_w - \dfrac{L_i}{c_w}}{2}$ and

  If $\theta_{mix} < \theta_i$ then take $\theta_{mix} = 0°C$

- As the temperature of the body increases, the wavelength at which the spectral intensity (E_λ) is maximum shifts towards left.

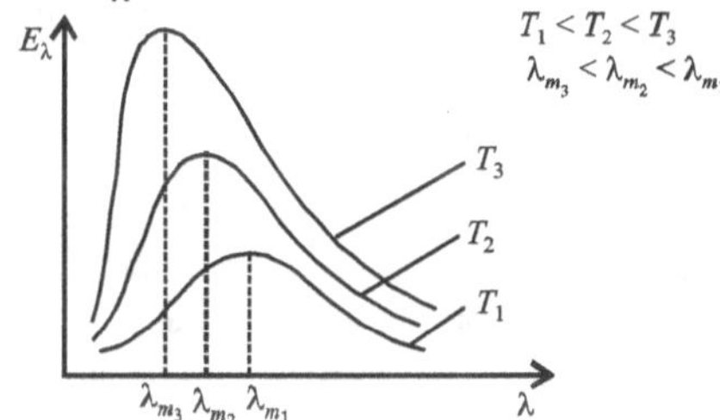

- The relation connecting Kelvin temperature (T) and the Celsius temperature t_c

  $T = t_c + 273.15$

  and the assignment $T = 273.16$ K for the triple point of water are exact relations (by choice). With this choice, the Celsius temperature of the melting point of water and boiling point of water (both at 1 atm pressure) are very close to, but not exactly equal to 0 °C and 100 °C respectively. In the original Celsius scale, these latter fixed points were exactly at 0 °C and 100 °C (by choice), but now the triple point of water is the preferred choice for the fixed point, because it has a unique temperature.

- A liquid in equilibrium with vapour has the same pressure and temperature throughout the system; the two phases in equilibrium differ in their molar volume (i.e. density). This is true for a system with any number of phases in equilibrium.

- Heat transfer always involves temperature difference between two systems or two parts of the same system. Any energy transfer that does not involve temperature difference in some way is not heat.

- Convection involves flow of matter *within a fluid* due to unequal temperatures of its parts. A hot bar placed under a running tap loses heat by conduction between the surface of the bar and water and not by convection within water.

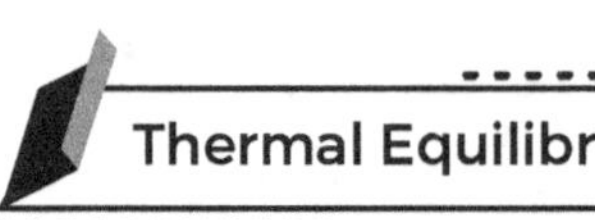

12. Thermodynamics

Thermal Equilibrium

- In winter, when we rub our palms together, we feel warmer; here work done in rubbing produces the 'heat'. Conversely, in a steam engine, the 'heat' of the steam is used to do useful work in moving the pistons.

- Thermodynamics is the branch of physics that deals with the concepts of heat and temperature and the inter-conversion of heat and other forms of energy. Thermodynamics is a macroscopic science. It deals with bulk systems and does not go into the molecular constitution of matter.

- The state of a gas in thermodynamics is specified by macroscopic variables such as pressure, volume, temperature, mass.

- The state of a system is an equilibrium state if the macroscopic variables that characterise the system do not change in time. For example, a gas inside a closed rigid container, completely insulated from its surroundings, with fixed values of pressure, volume, temperature, mass and composition that do not change with time, is in a state of thermodynamic equilibrium.

- **Adiabatic wall** – an insulating wall that does not allow flow of energy (heat)

- **diathermic wall** – a conducting wall that allows energy flow (heat) from one to another.

- There is no more energy flow from one to another. We then say that the system A is in thermal equilibrium with the system B.

  In thermal equilibrium, the temperatures of the two systems are equal.

Zeroth Law of Thermodynamics

- Imagine two systems A and B, separated by an adiabatic wall, while each is in contact with a third system C, **fig.** via a conducting wall. The states of the systems will change until both A and B come to thermal equilibrium with C. After this is achieved, suppose that the adiabatic wall between A and B is replaced by a conducting wall and C is insulated from A and B by an adiabatic wall. It is found that the states of A and B change.

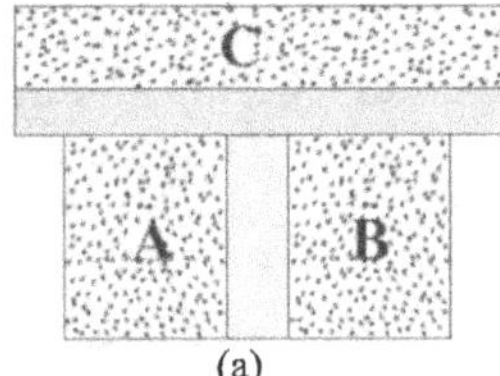
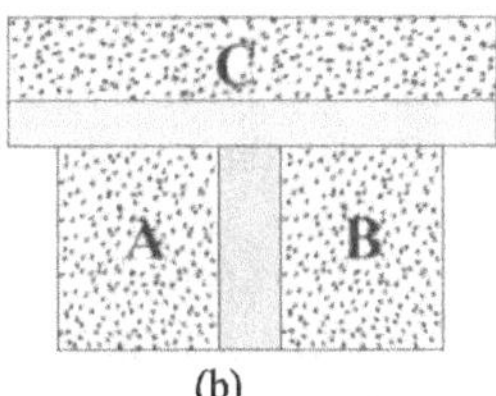

(a)   (b)

Fig.: *(a) Systems A and B are separated by an adiabatic wall, while each is in contact with a third system C via a conducting wall. (b) The adiabatic wall between A and B is replaced by a conducting wall, while C is insulated from A and B by an adiabatic wall.*

♦ **Zeroth Law of Thermodynamics**, states that '**two systems in thermal equilibrium with a third** system **separately are in thermal equilibrium with each other**.

♦ If A and B are separately in equilibrium with C, $T_A = T_C$ and $T_B = T_C$. This implies that $T_A = T_B$ i.e. the systems A and B are also in thermal equilibrium.

Heat, Internal Energy and Work

♦ Heat flows from the body at a higher temperature to the one at lower temperature. The flow stops when the temperatures equalise; the two bodies are then in thermal equilibrium.

♦ Every bulk system consists of a large number of molecules.

♦ **Internal energy** is simply the sum of the kinetic energies and potential energies of these molecules. The kinetic energy of the system, as a whole, is not relevant. Internal energy is thus, the sum of molecular kinetic and potential energies in the frame of centre of mass. It includes only the (disordered) energy associated with the random motion of molecules of the system.

♦ '**A gas in a given state has a certain amount of heat**' is as meaningless as the statement that '**a gas in a given state has a certain amount of work**'.

♦ '**A gas in a given state has a certain amount of internal energy**' is a perfectly meaningful statement. '**a certain amount of heat is supplied to the system**' or '**a certain amount of work was done by the system**' are perfectly meaningful.

♦ Heat and work in thermodynamics are not state variables. They are modes of energy transfer to a system resulting in change in its internal energy, which, is a state variable.

First Law of Thermodynamics

♦ **First law of thermodynamics** is simply the general law of conservation of energy applied to any system in which the energy transfer from or to the surroundings is taken into account.

The general principle of conservation of energy implies that

$$\Delta Q = \Delta U + \Delta W$$

Above equation is known as the **First Law of Thermodynamics**.

- If a system is taken through a process in which $\Delta U = 0$ (for example, isothermal expansion

$$\Delta Q = \Delta W$$

heat supplied to the system is used up entirely by the system in doing work on the environment.

- Work done by the system against a constant pressure P is $\Delta W = P \, \Delta V$

$$\therefore \qquad \Delta Q = \Delta U + P \, \Delta V$$

Specific Heat Capacity

- **Specific heat capacity** is the amount of heat energy required to raise the temperature of unit mass of a body through 1°C (or k)

- We define heat capacity of a substance

$$S = \frac{\Delta Q}{\Delta T} \quad \text{and } \textbf{specific heat capacity}$$

$$s = \frac{S}{m} = \left(\frac{1}{m}\right)\frac{\Delta Q}{\Delta T}$$

The unit of specific heat capacity is J kg^{-1} K^{-1}.

- If the amount of substance is specified in terms of moles μ (instead of mass m in kg), we can define heat capacity per mole of the substance **i.e., molar specific heat capacity** by

$$C = \frac{S}{\mu} = \frac{1}{\mu}\frac{\Delta Q}{\Delta T}$$

Specific heat capacity of water

- The specific heat capacity of water varies slightly with temperature. Specific heat of water is very high.

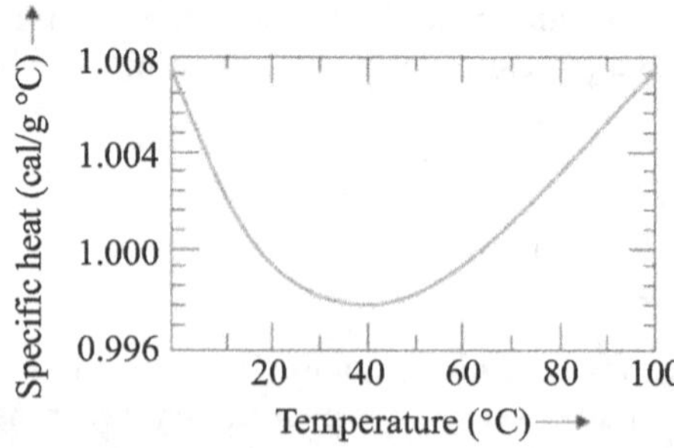

Fig.: *Variation of specific heat capacity of water with temperature.*

- The specific heat capacity depends on the process or the conditions under which heat capacity transfer takes place. For gases, we can define two specific heats : **specific heat capacity at constant volume (C_V) and specific heat capacity at constant pressure (C_p).**

- C_p and C_v are molar specific heat capacities of an ideal gas at constant pressure and volume respectively and R is the universal gas constant. For 1 mole of the gas:
$$\Delta Q = \Delta U + P\,\Delta V$$
If ΔQ is absorbed at constant volume, $\Delta V = 0$

$$C_V = \left(\frac{\Delta Q}{\Delta T}\right)_v = \left(\frac{\Delta U}{\Delta T}\right)_v = \left(\frac{\Delta U}{\Delta T}\right) \qquad \text{..... (i)}$$

If ΔQ is absorbed at constant pressure,

$$C_p = \left(\frac{\Delta Q}{\Delta T}\right)_p = \left(\frac{\Delta U}{\Delta T}\right)_p + P\left(\frac{\Delta V}{\Delta T}\right)_p$$

$$\Rightarrow\ C_p = \left(\frac{\Delta v}{\Delta t}\right) + P\left(\frac{\Delta V}{\Delta T}\right)_P \qquad \text{..... (ii)}$$

For a mole of an ideal gas
$$PV = RT \text{ which gives}$$

$$P\left(\frac{\Delta V}{\Delta T}\right)_p = R \qquad \text{..... (iii)}$$

Equations i, ii, iii give a simple relation.
$$\mathbf{C_p - C_v = R}$$

Thermodynamic State Variables and Equation of State

- An equilibrium state of a gas is completely specified by the values of pressure, volume, temperature, mass, no. of moles, etc. called thermodynamic variables.
- The connection between the state variables is called the equation of state. The equation of state is the ideal gas relation
$$PV = \mu RT$$
- The pressure-volume curve for a fixed temperature is called an **isotherm**.
- The thermodynamic state variables are of two kinds: **extensive** and **intensive**. Extensive variables indicate the 'size' of the system. Intensive variables such as pressure and temperature do not.
- In the equation $\Delta Q = \Delta u + P\Delta V$ quantities on both sides are extensive. The product of an intensive variable like P and an extensive quantity ΔV is extensive.

Thermodynamics Processes

Quasi-static process

♦ This process is, infinitely slow, hence the name quasi-static (meaning nearly static). The system changes its variables (P, T, V) so slowly that it remains in thermal and mechanical equilibrium with its surroundings throughout.

♦ A process in which the temperature of the system is kept fixed throughout is called an **isothermal process.**

♦ In **isobaric processes** the pressure is constant while in **isochoric processes** the volume is constant.

♦ If the system is insulated from the surroundings and no heat flows between the system and the surroundings, the process is **adiabatic.**

♦

Type of processes	Feature
Isothermal	Temperature (T) constant
Isobaric	Pressure (P) constant
Isochoric	Volume (v) constant
Adiabatic	No heat flow between the system and the surroundings ($\Delta Q = 0$)

Isothermal process

♦ For an isothermal process, the ideal gas equation

$$PV = \text{constant}$$

$$W = \int_{V_1}^{V_2} PdV = \mu RT \int_{V_1}^{V_2} \frac{dV}{V} = \mu RT = ln\frac{V_2}{V_1}$$

♦ There is no change in the internal energy of an ideal gas in an isothermal process i.e., $\Delta u = 0 \because \Delta T = 0$. Heat supplied to the gas equals the work done by the gas : $Q = W$. For $V_2 > V_1$, $W > 0$; and for $V_2 < V_1$, $W < 0$.

Adiabatic process

♦ In an adiabatic process, the system is insulated from the surroundings and heat absorbed or released is zero i.e., $\Delta Q = 0$.

♦ For an adiabatic process of an ideal gas.

$Pv^\gamma = \text{constant}$

γ is the ratio of specific heats at constant pressure and at constant volume.

$$\gamma = \frac{C_p}{C_v}$$

If an ideal gas undergoes a change in its state adiabatically from (P_1, V_1) to (P_2, V_2) :

$$P_1 V_1^\gamma = P_2 V_2^\gamma$$

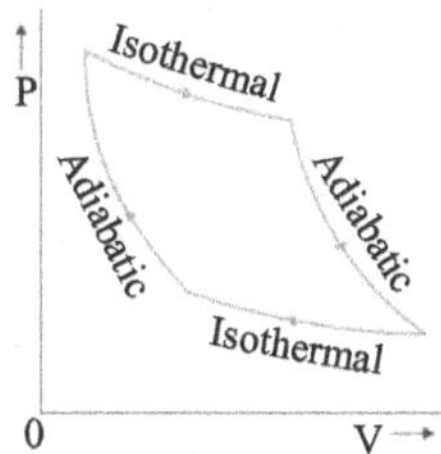

Fig.: *P-V curves for isothermal and adiabatic processes of an ideal gas.*

♦ The work done in an adiabatic change

$$W = \int_{V_1}^{V_2} P \, dV$$

$$W = \frac{1}{1-\gamma}\left[\frac{P_2 V_2^{\gamma}}{V_2^{\gamma-1}} - \frac{P_1 V_1^{\gamma}}{V_1^{\gamma-1}}\right]$$

$$= \frac{1}{1-\gamma}[P_2 V_2 - P_1 V_1] = \frac{\mu R(T_1 - T_2)}{\gamma - 1}$$

Isochoric process

♦ In an isochoric process, V is constant. No work is done on or by the gas. The heat absorbed by the gas goes entirely to change its internal energy and its temperature.

Isobaric process

♦ In an isobaric process, P is fixed. Work done by the gas is
$W = P(V_2 - V_1) = \mu R (T_2 - T_1)$
Temperature changes, so does internal energy. The heat absorbed goes partly to increase internal energy and partly to do work.

Cyclic process

♦ In a cyclic process, the system returns to its initial state. Internal energy is a state variable, $\Delta U = 0$ for a cyclic process. The total heat absorbed equals the work done by the system from $\Delta Q = \Delta u + \Delta W$.

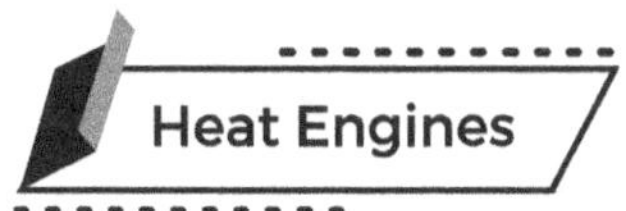

♦ Heat engine is a device by which a system is made to undergo a cyclic process that results in conversion of heat to work.

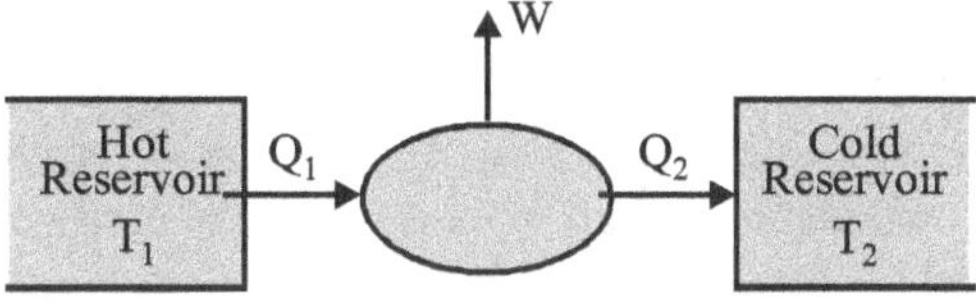

Fig.: *The engine takes heat Q_1 from a hot reservoir at temperature T_1, releases heat Q_2 to a cold reservoir at temperature T_2 and delivers work W to the surroundings.*

- The efficiency (η) of a heat engine is defined by

$$\eta = \frac{W}{Q_1}$$

- According to the First Law of Thermodynamics, over one complete cycle,

$$W = Q_1 - Q_2 \text{ and } \eta = 1 - \frac{Q_2}{Q_1}$$

- For $Q_2 = 0$, $\eta = 1$, i.e., the engine will have 100% efficiency in converting heat into work.

  Experience shows that such an ideal engine with $\eta = 1$ is never possible.

Refrigerators and Heat Pumps

- A refrigerator is the reverse of a heat engine. Here the working substance extracts heat Q_2 from the cold reservoir at temperature T_2, some external work W is done on it and heat Q_1 is released to the hot reservoir at temperature T_1.

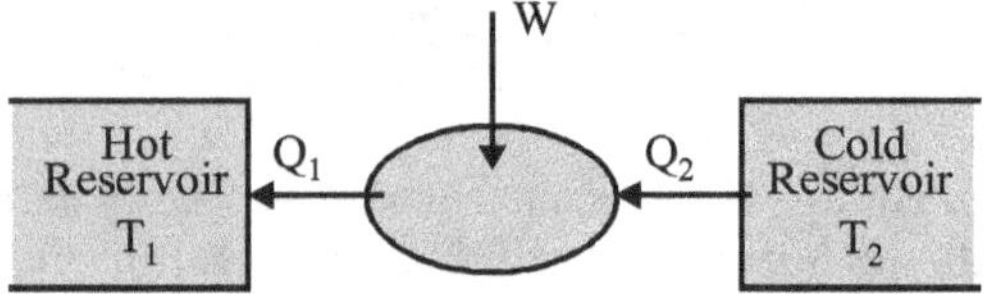

Fig.: *Schematic representation of a refrigerator or a heat pump, the reverse of a heat engine.*

- A heat pump is the same as a refrigerator.
- The coefficient of performance (α) of a refrigerator is given by

$$\alpha = \frac{Q_2}{W}$$

- By energy conservation, the heat released to the hot reservoir is

$$Q_1 = W + Q_2$$

$$\alpha = \frac{Q_2}{Q_1 - Q_2}$$

Second Law of Thermodynamics

- The Second Law of Thermodynamics says that efficiency of a heat engine can never be unity.
- The co-efficient of performance can never be infinite.

Kelvin-Planck statement

- No process is possible whose sole result is the absorption of heat from a reservoir and the complete conversion of the heat into work.

Clausius statement

- No process is possible whose sole result is the transfer of heat from a colder object to a hotter object.

Reversible and Irreversible Processes

- A thermodynamic process (state $i \to$ state f) is reversible if the process can be turned back such that both the system and the surroundings return to their original states.
- A process is reversible only if it is quasi-static and there are no dissipative effects.

Carnot Engine

- What is the maximum efficiency possible for a heat engine operating between the two reservoirs and what cycle of processes should be adopted to achieve the maximum efficiency? Sadi carnot a French engineer, first considered this question in 1824.
- A reversible heat engine operating between two temperatures is called a Carnot engine. Such an engine must have the following sequence of steps constituting one cycle, called the Carnot cycle.

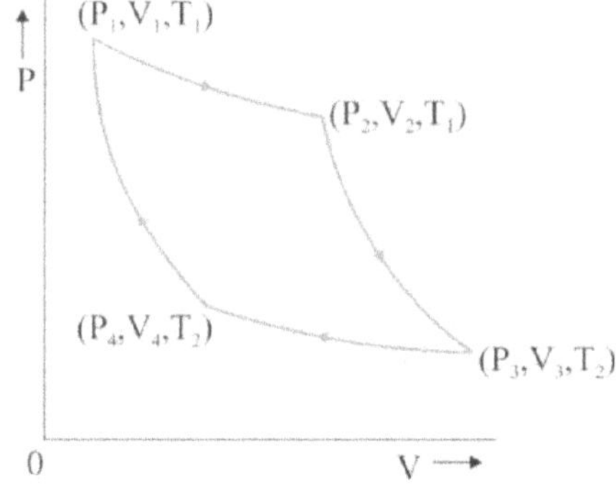

Fig.: *Carnot cycle for a heat engine with an ideal gas as the working substance.*

Efficiency $\quad \eta = 1 - \dfrac{T_2}{T_1}$

Past Years ONE-LINERS NEET/JEE Main/Board

- No heat encharge means adiabatic process.
- Heat neither absorbed nor released means adiabatic process.

- Efficiency of heat engine $(n) = 1 - \dfrac{T_2}{T}$

- In Isobaric process heat absorbed, $dQ = n\, C_p dT$

    work $dw = nRdT$

- From the first law of thermodynamics $\Delta Q = \Delta U + W$

- Coeficient of performance of refrigerator, $\beta = \dfrac{1-n}{n}$

- In isochoric process, volume is constant. In isobaric process, pressure is constant.

- Coeficient of performance of refrigerator, $\beta = \dfrac{Q_2}{W} = \dfrac{T_2}{T_1 - T_2}$

- Work done in adiabatic process > Work done in isothermal process

- Coeficient of performance of refrigerator, $\beta = \dfrac{T_2}{T_1 - T_2}$

- Area under P-V curve is maximum for adiabatic process.

- Work done in isothermal process, $W_{\text{isothermal}} = nRT\, \ell n \dfrac{V_2}{V_1}$

- In Isochoric process, volume is constant.

- Efficiency of heat engine $= 1 - \dfrac{T_2}{T_1}$

- If initial and final states are same $\Delta U_I = \Delta U_{II}$ (I and II paths)

- At maximum temperature $\dfrac{dT}{dV} = 0$

- For adiabatic expansion $d\theta = 0 \Rightarrow dU = -\, dW$

Tips/Tricks/Tecchniques ONE-LINERS
(Exam Sample)

- Internal energy of a system depend on the state of matter and also on temperature. It does not matter on how that state is attained.

- When a gas is allowed to expand, then work is done by the gas and thus work done is taken as positive.

- If a solid changes into liquid and then to vapour, internal energy of system increases as work is done against intermoleculer forces.

- No two isothermal curves can intersect each other.

♦ If an ideal gas is compressed to half of its initial volume by means of several processes, then the maximum work done on the gas in adiabatic process.

♦ In adiabatic process, specific heat of gas is zero. But in isothermal process, specific heat of gas is infinity.

♦ Among isothermal curves drawn at different temperatures, the one farthest from the origin has maximum temperature.

♦ According to second law of thermodynamics, efficiency of any heat engine cannot be 100%.

♦ Vaporisation of water, fusion of ice etc., are some example of reversible processes. Work done against friction, joule heating etc., are some examples of irreversible process.

♦ If relation between P and V is given by $PV^x = $ constant, where $x \neq 1$ or γ then the process is called a polytropic. In this process the molar heat capacity is,

$$C = C_V + \frac{R}{1-x} = \frac{R}{\gamma-1} + \frac{R}{1-x}$$

♦ Slope of adiabatic curve,

$$\left(\frac{dP}{dV}\right)_{adia} = -\frac{\gamma\, P}{V}$$

$$\left(\frac{dP}{dV}\right)_{adia} = \gamma\left(-\frac{P}{V}\right)$$

$$= \gamma\left(\frac{dP}{dV}\right)_{iso}$$

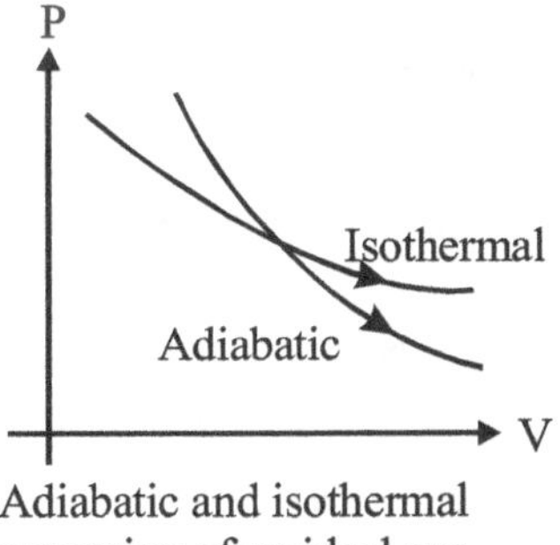

Adiabatic expansion of mono, dia and polyatomic gases

$$\frac{Slope\ of\ adiabatic\ changes}{Slope\ of\ isothermal\ changes} = \gamma$$

But γ is always greater than one.

Adiabatic and isothermal expansion of an ideal gas

So, slope of adiabatic is greater than the slope of isothermal.

13 Kinetic Theory

Molecular Nature of Matter

- Kinetic theory explains the behaviour of gases based on the idea that the gas consists of rapidly moving atoms or molecules. This is possible as the inter-atomic forces, that are important for solids and liquids, can be neglected for gases.
- Kinetic theory was developed in the nineteenth century by Maxwell, Boltzmann and others. It gives a molecular interpretation of pressure and temperature of a gas, and is consistent with gas laws and Avogadro's hypothesis. It explains specific heat capacities of many gases.
- Molecules (Made up of one or more atoms) constitute matter.
- The size of an atom is about an angstrom (10^{-10} m). In solids, atoms are spaced about a few angstroms (2 Å) apart.
- In gases the interatomic distances are in tens of angstroms.
- The average distance a molecule can travel without colliding is called the **mean free path**.
- The mean free path, in gases, is of the order of thousands of angstroms. The atoms are much freer in gases and can travel long distances without colliding.

Behaviour of Gases

- Gases at low pressures and high temperatures approximately satisfy a simple relation between their pressure, temperature and volume given by

$$PV = \kappa T$$
$$K = N\kappa$$

κ is same for all gases. It is called **Boltzmann constant** and is denoted by κ_B. $\kappa_B = 1.38 \times 10^{-23}$ Jk^{-1}.

$$As\ \frac{P_1 V_1}{N_1 T_1} = \frac{P_2 V_2}{N_2 T_2} = \text{constant} = \kappa_B$$

- If P, V and T are same, then N is also same for all gases. This is **Avogadro's hypothesis**.
- The number in 22.4 litres of any gas is 6.02×10^{23}. This is known as **Avogadro's number N_A**.

- The perfect gas equation can be written as
$$PV = \mu RT \qquad \text{...(i)}$$
where μ is the number of moles and $R = N_A \kappa_B$ is a universal gas constant, $R = 8.314 \text{ J mol}^{-1}\text{K}^{-1}$ and
$$\mu = \frac{M}{M_0} = \frac{N}{N_A} \qquad \text{...(ii)}$$
M_0 is the molar mass and N_A is the Avogadro's number, where M is the mass of the gas containing N molecules,
$$PV = K_B NT \quad \text{or,} \quad P = K_B nT$$

- Using equation (i) and (ii) we get
$$P = \left(\frac{M}{M_0}\right)\frac{RT}{V} = \frac{\rho RT}{M_0}$$

- A gas that satisfies Eq. (i) exactly at all pressures and temperatures is defined to be an ideal gas. All curves approach the ideal gas behaviour at low pressure and high temperature.

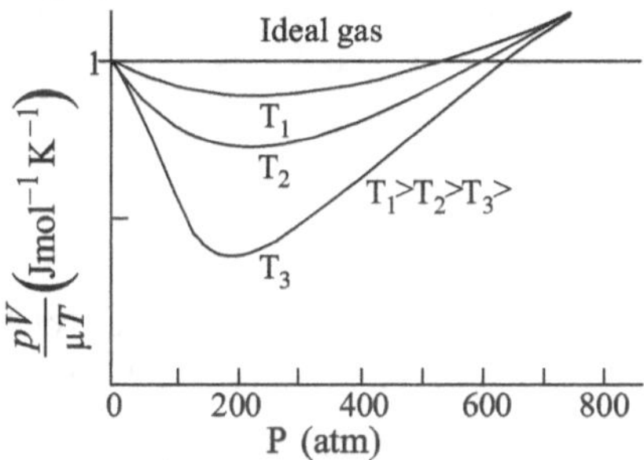

Fig.: *Real gases approach ideal gas behaviour at low pressures and high temperatures.*

- At low pressures or high temperatures the molecules are far apart and molecular interactions are negligible.
- If we fix μ and T in Eq. (i), we get
$$PV = \text{constant}$$
keeping temperature constant, pressure of a given mass of gas varies inversely with volume. This is the famous **Boyle's law**. Figure shows comparison between experimental P-V curves and the theoretical curves predicted by Boyle's law.

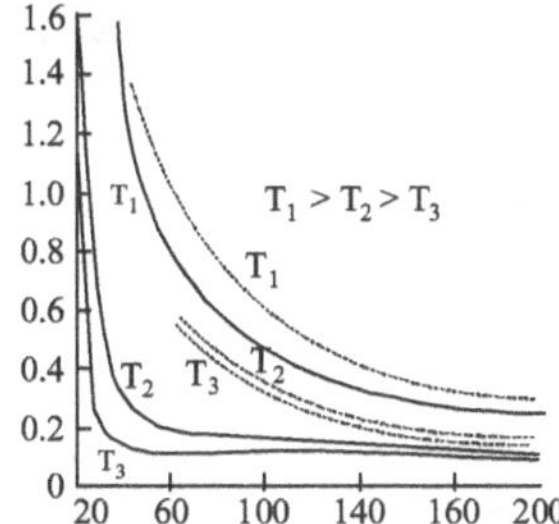

Fig.: *Experimental P-V curves (solid lines) for steam at three temperatures compared with Boyle's law (dotted lines). P is in units of 22 atm and V in units of 0.09 litres.*

If you fix P, Eq. (i) shows that $V \propto T$ i.e., for a fixed pressure, the volume of a gas is proportional to its absolute temperature T **Charles' law.**

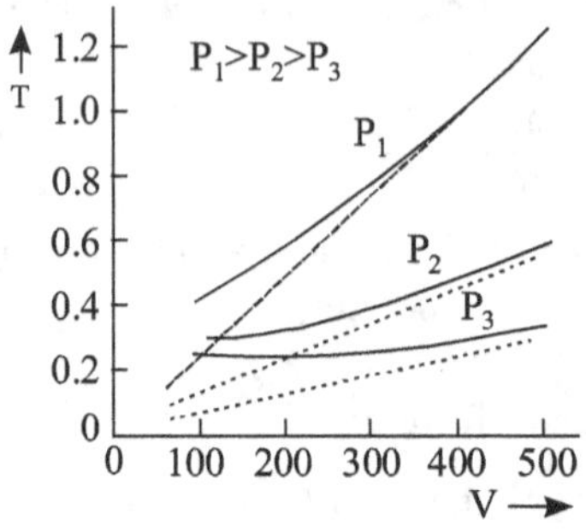

Fig.: *Experimental T-V curves (solid lines) for CO_2 at three pressures compared with Charles' law (dotted lines). T is in units of 300 K and V in units of 0.13 litres.*

♦ Consider a mixture of non-interacting ideal gases: μ_1 moles of gas 1, μ_2 moles of gas 2, etc. in a vessel of volume V at temperature T and pressure P. The equation of state of the mixture is :

$$PV = (\mu_1 + \mu_2 + \dots)RT$$

i.e.,
$$P = \mu_1 \frac{RT}{V} + \mu_2 \frac{RT}{V} + \dots$$

$$= P_1 + P_2 + \dots$$

♦ $P_1 = \mu_1 RT/V$ is called partial pressure of the gas. Total pressure of a mixture of ideal gases is the sum of partial pressures. This is **Dalton's law of partial pressures.**

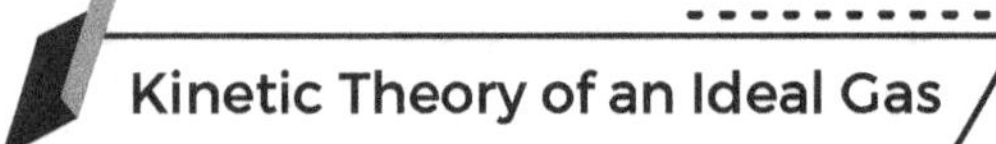

Kinetic Theory of an Ideal Gas

♦ A given amount of gas is a collection of a large number of molecules At ordinary pressure and temperature, the average distance between molecules is more than the typical size of a molecule (2Å).

♦ Interaction between molecules is negligible and we can assume that they move freely in straight lines according to Newton's first law.

♦ The molecules collide incessantly against each other or with the walls and change their velocities. The collisions are considered to be elastic.

Pressure of an Ideal Gas

♦ Consider a gas enclosed in a cube of side ℓ. A molecule with velocity (v_x, v_y, v_z) hits the planar wall parallel to yz plane of area A (= ℓ^2). Since the collision is elastic, the molecule rebounds with the same velocity; its y and z components of velocity do not change.

♦ The change in momentum of the molecule is: $-mv_x - (mv_x) = -2mv_x$. By the principle of conservation of momentum, the momentum imparted to the wall in the collision = $2mv_x$.

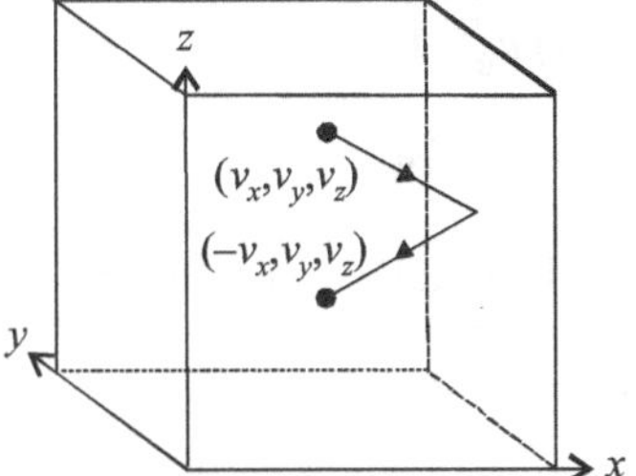

Fig.: *Elastic collision of a gas molecule with the wall of the container.*

- In a small time interval Δt, all molecules within the volume $Av_x\,\Delta t$ only can hit the wall in time Δt. Only half of these are moving towards the wall and the other half away from the wall. The number of molecules with hitting the wall in time Δt is $\frac{1}{2}A\,v_x\,\Delta t n$ where n is the number of molecules per unit volume. The total momentum transferred to the wall in time Δt is:

$$Q = (2mv_x)\,(\tfrac{1}{2}\,n\,A\,v_x\,\Delta t)$$

The force on the wall is the rate of momentum transfer $Q/\Delta t$ and pressure is force per unit area :

$$P = Q/(A\,\Delta t) = n\,m\,v_x^2$$

- Actually, all molecules in a gas do not have the same velocity.
- Total pressure is obtained by summing over the contribution due to all groups gas molecules (velocities)

$$P = nm\overline{v_x^2}$$

where $\overline{v_x^2}$ is the average of v_x^2.

By symmetry. $\overline{v_x^2} = \overline{v_y^2} = \overline{v_z^2}$

$$= (1/3)[\overline{v_x^2} + \overline{v_y^2} = \overline{v_z^2}] = (1/3)\overline{v^2}$$

where v is the speed and $\overline{v^2}$ denotes the mean of the squared speed. Thus **pressure**

$$P = (1/3)nm\overline{v^2}$$

Kinetic Interpretation of Temperature

- The above equation can also be written as

$$PV = (2/3)NVm\overline{v^2} \qquad \qquad \text{... (iii)}$$

where $N\,(= nV)$ is the number of molecules in the sample.

The quantity in the bracket is the average translational kinetic energy of the molecules in the gas. Since the internal energy E of an ideal gas is purely kinetic,

$$E = N \times (1/2\, m\, \overline{v^2})$$

Equation (iii) then gives:

$$PV = (2/3)\,E \qquad \qquad \text{... (iv)}$$

- Combining Eq. (iv) with the ideal gas Eq. (i), we get

$$E = (3/2)\,\kappa_B\,NT \qquad \qquad \text{... (v)}$$

or $\qquad E/N = \tfrac{1}{2}\,mv^2 = (3/2)\,\kappa_B T$

  The average kinetic energy of a molecule is proportional to the absolute temperature of the gas;

- Eq. (v) tells us that internal energy of an ideal gas depends only on temperature, not on pressure or volume.

- For a mixture of non-reactive ideal gases, the total pressure is

$$P = (1/3)[n_1 m_1 \overline{v_1^2} + n_2 m_2 \overline{v_2^2} + ...]$$

- In equilibrium, the average kinetic energy of the molecules of different gases will be equal. That is,

$$\tfrac{1}{2}\,m_1 \overline{v_1^2} = \tfrac{1}{2} m_2 \overline{v_2^2} = (3/2)\kappa_B T$$

  so that

$$P = (n_1 + n_2 + ...\,)\,\kappa_B T$$

  which is **Dalton's law of partial pressures**.

- $\sqrt{\overline{v^2}}$ is known as **root mean square speed**,

$$V_{rms} = \sqrt{\frac{3P}{\rho}} = \sqrt{\frac{3PV}{m}} = \sqrt{\frac{3RT}{M}} = \sqrt{\frac{3kT}{m}}$$

- $V_{av} = \dfrac{v_1 + v_2 + ... v_n}{N} = \sqrt{\dfrac{8P}{\pi\rho}} = \sqrt{\dfrac{8\,RT}{\pi\,M}} = \sqrt{\dfrac{8\,kT}{\pi\,m}}$ is **average speed** or **mean speed**.

- **Most probable speed,** $V_{MP} = \sqrt{\dfrac{2P}{\rho}} = \sqrt{\dfrac{2RT}{M}} = \sqrt{\dfrac{2kT}{m}}$

$$V_{rms} > V_{av} > V_{mp}.$$

Law of Equipartition of Energy

- The kinetic energy of a single molecule is

$$\varepsilon_t = \frac{1}{2}mv_x^2 + \frac{1}{2}mv_y^2 + \frac{1}{2}mv_z^2$$

- For a gas in thermal equilibrium at temperature T the average value of energy denoted by $< \varepsilon_t >$ is

$$\langle \varepsilon_t \rangle = \left\langle \frac{1}{2}mv_x^2 \right\rangle + \left\langle \frac{1}{2}mv_y^2 \right\rangle + \left\langle \frac{1}{2}mv_z^2 \right\rangle = \frac{3}{2}\kappa_B T$$

  Since there is no preferred direction implies

$$\left\langle \frac{1}{2}mv_x^2 \right\rangle = \frac{1}{2}\kappa_B T, \left\langle \frac{1}{2}mv_y^2 \right\rangle = \frac{1}{2}\kappa_B T,$$

$$\left\langle \frac{1}{2}mv_z^2 \right\rangle = \frac{1}{2}\kappa_B T$$

♦ In equilibrium, the total energy is equally distributed in all possible energy modes, with each mode having an average energy equal to $\frac{1}{2}\kappa_B T$. This is known as the **law of equipartition of energy**. each translational and rotational degree of freedom of a molecule contributes $\frac{1}{2}\kappa_B T$ to the energy, while each vibrational frequency contributes $2 \times \frac{1}{2}\kappa_B T = \kappa_B T$, since a vibrational mode has both kinetic and potential energy modes.

Specific Heat Capacity

Monatomic Gases

♦ The molecule of a monatomic gas has only three translational degrees of freedom. The average energy of a molecule at temperature T is $(3/2)\kappa_B T$. The total internal energy of a mole of such a gas is

$$U = \frac{3}{2}\kappa_B T \times N_A = \frac{3}{2}RT$$

The molar specific heat at constant volume,

$$C_v \text{ (monatomic gas) } = \frac{dU}{dT} = \frac{3}{2}R$$

♦ For an ideal gas, $C_P - C_v = R$

Thus, $$C_P = \frac{5}{2}R$$

♦ **The ratio of specific heats,** $\gamma = \dfrac{C_p}{C_v} = \dfrac{5}{3}$

Diatomic Gases

♦ Diatomic molecule treated as a rigid rotator, like a dumbbell, has 5 degrees of freedom: 3 translational and 2 rotational. The total internal energy of a mole of such a gas is

$$U = \frac{5}{2}\kappa_B T \times N_A = \frac{5}{2}RT$$

Molar specific heats are given by

$$C_v = \frac{5}{2}R, C_p = \frac{7}{2}R$$

$$\gamma \text{(rigid diatomic)} = \frac{7}{5}$$

$$U = \left(\frac{5}{2}\kappa_B T + \kappa_B T\right) N_A = \frac{7}{2}RT$$

If diatomic molecule is not rigid but has in addition a vibrational mode

$$C_v = \frac{7}{2}R, C_p = \frac{9}{2}R, \gamma = \frac{9}{7}R$$

Polyatomic Gases

♦ In general a polyatomic molecule has 3 translational, 3 rotational degrees of freedom and a certain number (f) of vibrational modes. One mole of such a gas has

$$U = \left(\frac{3}{2}\kappa_B T + \frac{3}{2}\kappa_B T + f\kappa_B T \right) N_A$$

i.e., $C_v = (3 + f)R, \ C_p = (4 + f)R,$

$$\gamma = \frac{(4+f)}{(3+f)}$$

Note that $C_p - C_v = R$ is true for any ideal gas, whether mono, di or polyatomic.

Specific Heat Capacity of Solids

♦ An oscillation in one dimension has average energy of $2 \times \frac{1}{2}\kappa_B T = \kappa_B T$. In three dimensions, the average energy is $3\kappa_B T$. For a mole of solid, $N = N_A$, and the total energy is $U = 3\kappa_B T \times N_A = 3RT$

At constant pressure $\Delta Q = \Delta U + P\Delta V = \Delta U$, since for a solid ΔV is negligible. Hence

$$C = \frac{\Delta Q}{\Delta T} = \frac{\Delta U}{\Delta T} = 3R$$

Specific Heat Capacity of Water

♦ We treat water like a solid. For each atom average energy is $3\kappa_B T$. Water molecule has three atoms, two hydrogen and one oxygen. So it has

$$U = 3 \times 3\kappa_B T \times N_A = 9RT$$

and $C = \Delta Q/\Delta T = \Delta U/\Delta T = 9R \sim 75 \ \text{J mol}^{-1} \text{k}^{-1}$

♦ The distance travelled by a gas molecule between two successive collision is known as **free path.**

♦ Suppose the molecules of a gas are spheres of diameter d. Focus on a single molecule with the average speed $<v>$. In time Δt, it sweeps volume $\pi d^2 <v> \Delta t$. If n is the number of molecules per unit volume, the molecule suffers $n\pi d^2 <v> \Delta t$ collisions in time Δt. Thus the rate of collisions is $n\pi d^2 <v>$ or the time between two successive collisions is on the average,

$$\tau = 1/(n\pi <v> d^2)$$

♦ The average distance between two successive collisions, called the mean free path l, is:

$$l = <v> \tau = 1/(n\pi d^2)$$

A more exact treatment gives

$$l = 1/(\sqrt{2}\,n\pi d^2)$$

Past Years ONE-LINERS
NEET/JEE Main/Board

- RMS speed, $V_{rms} = \sqrt{\dfrac{3RT}{m}}$,

  Pressure exerted by ideal gas, $P = \dfrac{1}{3} nm\overline{v^2}$

  Average kinetic energy of a molecule $= \dfrac{3}{2} k_B T$

  Total internal energy of 1 mole of diatomic gas, $U = \dfrac{5}{2} RT$

- Energy associated with each degree of freedom is $\dfrac{1}{2} kT$

  Average thermal energy for mono-atomic gas $KE_{avg} = 3 \times \dfrac{1}{2} k_B T = \dfrac{3}{2} k_B T$

- Mean free path for a gas $\lambda_m = \dfrac{1}{\sqrt{2} n\pi d^2}$

- Ideal gas equation, $PV = nRT$, $PM = \rho RT \Rightarrow \rho = \dfrac{PM}{RT}$

- Kinetic energy of a gas $U = \dfrac{f}{2} nRT$

- RMS speed = Escape speed, $V_{escape} = \sqrt{\dfrac{3k_B T}{m}}$

- Internal energy of the system is given by $U = \dfrac{f}{2} nRT$

- R.M.S. Velocity, $V \propto \sqrt{T}$
- From ideal gas equation, $PV = nRT$
- RMS speed, $V_{rms} = \sqrt{\dfrac{3RT}{m}}$
- Specific heat of mixture, $\gamma_{mixture} = \dfrac{n_1 C_{p_1} + n_2 C_{p_2}}{n_1 C_{v_1} + n_2 C_{v_2}}$

- RMS speed, $V_{rms} = \sqrt{\dfrac{3RT}{M}}$
- In an adiabatic process $TV^{\gamma-1} = $ Constant

  Change in internal energy, $\Delta U = n\dfrac{f}{2} R\Delta T$
- As we know, $C_p - C_v = R$ where C_p and C_v are molar specific heat capacities or,
  $C_p - C_v = \dfrac{R}{M}$
- From ideal gas equation number of molecules, $\Rightarrow N = \dfrac{PV}{RT}(N_0)$

- For a polytropic process $C = C_v + \dfrac{R}{1-n}$

♦ Mean free path, $\tau = \dfrac{1}{\sqrt{2}\pi d^2 \left(\dfrac{N}{V}\right)\sqrt{\dfrac{3RT}{M}}}$

Tips/Tricks/Tecchniques ONE-LINERS
(Exam Sample)

♦ The collisions of gas molecules among themselves as well as wall of the container is perfectly elastic.
♦ A real gas behaves like a perfect gas at low pressure and high temperature.
♦ On increasing the number of molecules in a gas, temperature, kinetic energy and pressure of the gas increases.
♦ At constant volume, with increase in temperature, RMS speed, pressure and collision frequency increases.
♦ RMS speed of gas molecules does not depend on the pressure of gas.
♦ A planet can have atmosphere only if $V_{rms} < V_e$.
♦ RMS speed of gas molecules is $\sqrt{\dfrac{3}{\gamma}}$ times of speed of sound in gas.
♦ Specific heat of an ideal/perfect gas does not depend upon temperature.
♦ Relation between degree of freedom of a gas (f) and ratio of specific heats (γ) is given by

$$\gamma = 1 + \frac{2}{f}$$

♦ The values of specific heats C_P and C_V of a gas is given by

$$C_P = \left(\frac{f}{2}+1\right)R, \quad C_V = \frac{f}{2}R \quad (f = \text{degree of freedom})$$

♦ If n_1 moles of one gas is mixed with n_2 moles of another gas. Then molar mass of mixture (M) is given by

$$M = \frac{n_1 M_1 + n_2 M_2}{n_1 + n_2}$$

Here, M_1 and M_2 are molar mass of gases to be mixed.
♦ Specific heat at constant volume for a mixture of gases is given by

$$C_v = \frac{n_1 C_{V_1} + n_2 C_{V_2}}{n_1 + n_2} \quad \text{Similarly at constant pressure}$$

$$C_p = \frac{n_1 C_{p_1} + n_2 C_{p_2}}{n_1 + n_2}$$

Here, n_1 and n_2 are number of moles of two gases.
♦ Force exerted by a single molecule on wall is equal to rate at which the momentum is transferred to the wall by this molecule, i.e.,

$$F_{Single\ molecule} = \frac{\Delta p}{\Delta t} = \frac{2mv_x}{(2L/v_x)} = \frac{mv_x^2}{L}$$

14. Oscillations

- In uniform circular motion and orbital motion of planets in the solar system, the motion is repeated after a certain interval of time, so it is **periodic motion**.
- In swinging on a swing, the object moves to and fro about a mean position. The pendulum of a wall clock executes a similar motion. Such a motion is termed as **oscillatory motion**.
- A motion that repeats itself at regular intervals of time is called **periodic motion**.
- The body undergoing periodic motion has an equilibrium position somewhere inside its path. When the body is at this position no net external force acts on it.
- If the body is given a small displacement from the position, a force comes into play which tries to bring the body back to the equilibrium point, giving rise to **oscillations** or **vibrations**.
- *Every oscillatory motion is periodic, but every periodic motion need not be oscillatory.* Circular motion is a periodic motion, but it is not oscillatory.
- When the frequency is small, we call it oscillation (like, the oscillation of a branch of a tree), while when the frequency is high, we call it vibration (like, the vibration of a string of a musical instrument).
- Simple harmonic motion is the simplest form of oscillatory motion. This motion arises when the force on the oscillating body is directly proportional to its displacement from the mean position, which is also the equilibrium position. Further, at any point in its oscillation, this force is directed towards the mean position i.e., $F \propto -x \Rightarrow F = -kx$ where k is known as force constant.

Period and Frequency

- The smallest interval of time after which the motion is repeated is called its **period** symbol T.
- The reciprocal of T gives the number of repetitions that occur per unit time. This quantity is called the **frequency of the periodic motion**. It is represented by the symbol v. The relation between v and T is $v = \dfrac{1}{T}$.

  Its S.I. unit is **hertz (Hz)**.

Displacement

- It refers to change with time of any physical property.

- The displacement can be represented by a mathematical function of time. One of the simplest periodic functions is given by
$$f(t) = A \cos \omega t$$

- The function $f(t)$ is then periodic and its period, T, is given by
$$T = \frac{2\pi}{\omega}$$

- The same result is obviously correct if we consider a sine function, $f(t) = A \sin \omega t$.
$$f(t) = A \sin \omega t + B \cos \omega t$$
is also a periodic function with the same period T.

- If $A = D \cos \phi$ and $B = D \sin \phi$ then
$$f(t) = D \sin (\omega t + \phi),$$
Here D and ϕ are constant given by
$$D = \sqrt{A^2 + B^2} \text{ and } \phi = \tan^{-1}\left(\frac{B}{A}\right)$$

- Any periodic function can be expressed as a superposition of sine and cosine functions of different time periods with suitable coefficients.

Simple Harmonic Motion

- Consider a particle oscillating back and forth about the origin of an x-axis between the limits +A and −A as shown in Fig. This oscillatory motion is said to be simple harmonic if the displacement x of the particle from the origin varies with time as :
$$x(t) = A \cos (\omega t + \phi) \qquad \qquad ..... (i)$$
where A, ω and ϕ are constants.

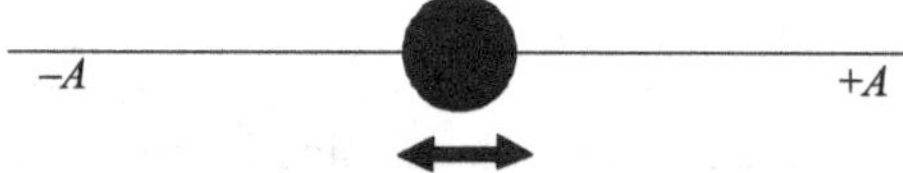

Fig.: *A particle vibrating back and forth about the origin of x-axis, between the limits +A and −A.*

$x(t)$	: displacement x as a function of time t
A	: amplitude
ω	: angular frequency
$\omega t + \phi$	: phase (time-dependent)
ϕ	: phase constant

Fig.: *The meaning of standard symbols in Eq. (i)*

- Fig. below shows the positions of a particle executing SHM, each interval of time being $T/4$,

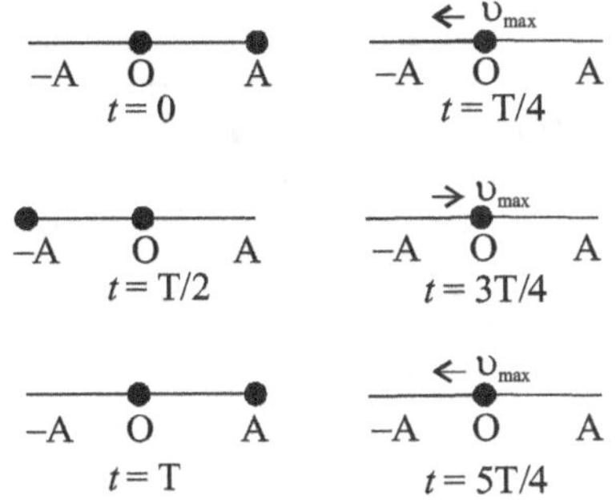

Fig.: *The location of the particle in SHM at t = 0, T/4, T/2, 3T/4, T, 5T/4. The speed is maximum for zero displacement (at x = 0) and zero at the extremes of motion.*

♦ Fig. the graph of x versus t, which gives the values of displacement as a continuous function of time. The quantities A, ω and f which characterize a given SHM have standard names, as summarised in Fig.

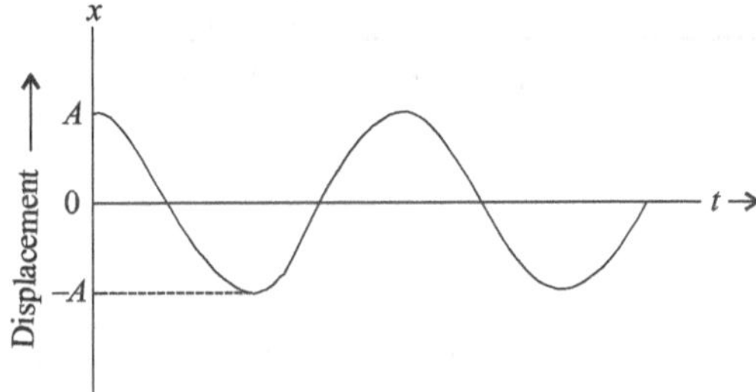

Fig.: *Displacement as a continuous function of time for simple harmonic motion.*

♦ The amplitutde A of SHM is the magnitude of maximum displacement of the particle.

♦ Two simple harmonic motions may have same ω and ϕ but different amplitudes A and B, as shown in Fig. (a).

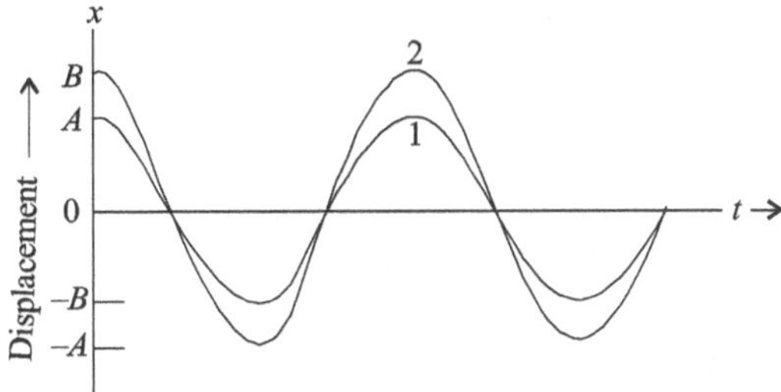

Fig.(a) : *A plot of displacement as a function of time as obtained from Eq. (i) with ϕ = 0. The curves 1 and 2 are for two different amplitudes A and B.*

♦ State of motion (position and velocity) at any time t is determined by ($\omega t + \phi$) in the cosine function. This time-dependent quantity, ($\omega t + \phi$) is called the phase. The value of phase at $t = 0$ is ϕ and is called the phase constant (or phase angle).

Velocity and Acceleration in Simple Harmonic Motion

- The speed of a particle v in uniform circular motion is its angular speed ω times the radius of the circle A.
$$v = \omega A$$

- We can, obtain velocity by differentiating
Eq. $x = A \cos(\omega t + \phi)$ with respect of t:
$$\upsilon(t) = \frac{d}{dt} x(t)$$
$$\upsilon(t) = -\omega A \sin(\omega t + \phi)$$

- Differentiating velocity with respect to time, we get acceleration
$$a(t) = \frac{d}{dt} \upsilon(t)$$
$$a(t) = -\omega^2 A \cos(\omega t + \phi) = -\omega^2 x(t)$$

- If $\phi = 0$; $x(t) = A \cos \omega t$, $\upsilon(t) = -\omega A \sin \omega t$, $a(t) = -\omega^2 A \cos \omega t$

Force Law for Simple Harmonic Motion

- Using Newton's second law of motion, the force acting on a particle of mass m in SHM is
$$F(t) = ma$$
$$= -m\omega^2 x(t)$$
i.e.,
$$F(t) = -k x(t)$$
where
$$k = m\omega^2$$
or
$$\omega = \sqrt{\frac{k}{m}}$$

- Like acceleration, force is always directed towards the mean position—hence it is sometimes called the **restoring force** in SHM.

Energy in Simple Harmonic Motion

- The **kinetic energy (K)** of a particle, defined as
$$K = \frac{1}{2} mv^2 = \frac{1}{2} m\omega^2 A^2 \sin^2(\omega t + \phi) = \frac{1}{2} k A^2 \sin^2(\omega t + \phi)$$
is also a periodic function of time, being zero when the displacement is maximum and maximum when the particle is at the mean position. The period of K is $T/2$.

- The spring force $F = -kx$ is a conservative force with associated potential energy,
$$\text{potential energy } U = \frac{1}{2} k x^2$$

- The *potential energy of a particle executing simple harmonic* motion is,

$$U(x) = \frac{1}{2}k\,x^2 = \frac{1}{2}k\,A^2\cos^2(\omega t + \phi)$$

- The potential energy of a particle executing simple harmonic motion is also periodic, with period $T/2$, being zero at the mean position and maximum at the extreme displacements.

- The total energy, E, of the system is,

$$E = U + K$$

$$= \frac{1}{2}k\,A^2\cos^2(\omega t + \phi) + \frac{1}{2}k\,A^2\sin^2(\omega t + \phi)$$

$$= \frac{1}{2}k\,A^2\left[\cos^2(\omega t + \phi) + \sin^2(\omega t + \phi)\right]$$

$$E = \frac{1}{2}k\,A^2$$

- The total mechanical energy of a harmonic oscillator is independent of time
- The time and displacement depends of the potential and kinetic energies of a linear simple harmonic oscillator are shown in the figure.

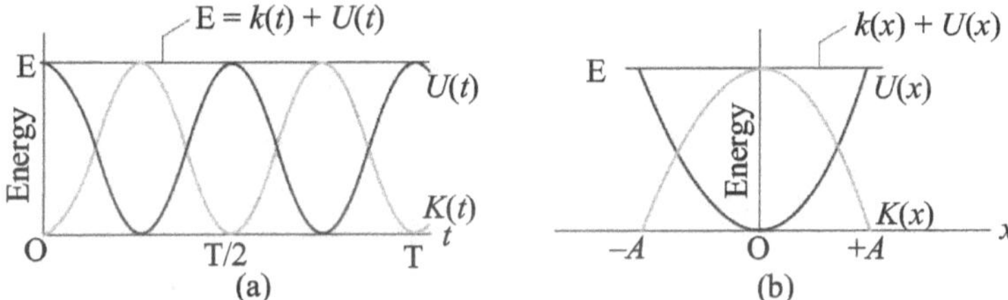

Some Systems Executing Simple Harmonic Motion

Oscillations due to a Spring

- The simplest example of simple harmonic motion is the small oscillations of a block of mass m fixed to a spring, which in turn is fixed to a rigid wall.
- The block is placed on a frictionless horizontal surface. If the block is pulled on one side and is released, it then executes a to and fro motion about the mean position. Let $x = 0$, indicate the position of the block when the spring is in equilibrium.

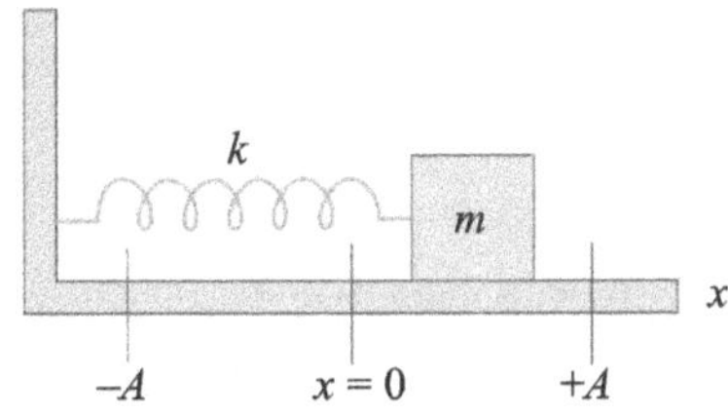

If the displacement of the block from its mean position is x, the restoring force F acting on the block is,

$$F(x) = -kx = -\omega^2 x$$

♦ A stiff spring has large k and a soft spring has small k.
From equation,

$$\omega = \sqrt{\frac{k}{m}}$$

The period, T, of the oscillator is given by,

$$T = 2\pi\sqrt{\frac{m}{k}}$$

The Simple Pendulum

♦ Consider simple pendulum — a small bob of mass m tied to an inextensible massless string of length L.

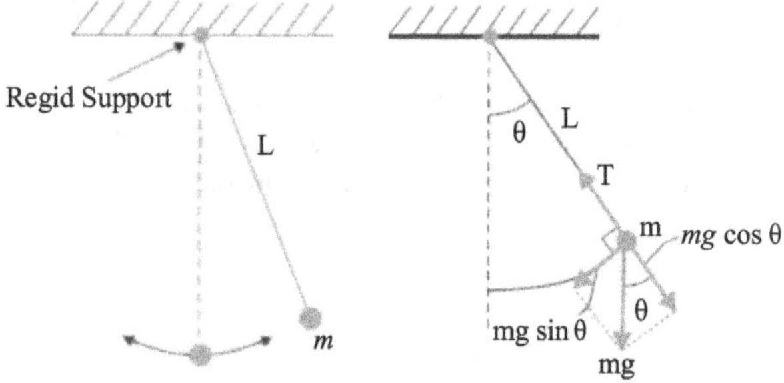

Fig.: *(a) A bob oscillating about its mean position.*
(b) The radial force T-mg cos θ provides centripetal force but no torque about the support.
The tangential force mg sin θ provides the restoring torque.

♦ Let θ be the angle made by the string with the vertical. When the bob is at the mean position, θ = 0.

♦ Torque τ about the support is $\tau = -L\,(mg \sin\theta)$
By Newton's law of rotational motion, $\tau = I\alpha$
Thus, $I\alpha = -mg \sin\theta\, L$

$$\alpha = \frac{mgL}{I}\sin\theta$$

If θ is small, sin θ can be approximated by θ

$$\alpha = \frac{mgL}{I}\theta = -\omega^2\theta$$

Motion of the bob is simple harmonic.

$$\Rightarrow \qquad \omega = \sqrt{\frac{mgL}{I}} \text{ and } T = 2\pi\sqrt{\frac{I}{mgL}}$$

Since the string of the simple pendulum is massless, the moment of inertia I is simply mL^2 then

$$T = 2\pi\sqrt{\frac{L}{g}}$$

Damped Simple Harmonic Motion

- In damped oscillations, the energy of the system is dissipated continuously; but, for small damping, the oscillations remain approximately periodic. The dissipating forces are generally the frictional forces.
- The damping force is generally proportional to velocity of the bob.
$$\mathbf{F}_d = -b\mathbf{v}$$
where the positive constant b depends on characteristics of the medium like viscosity and the size and shape of the block.

  This equation is valid only for small velocity.
- The total force acting on the mass at any time t, is
$$\mathbf{F} = -\mathbf{kx} - \mathbf{bv}.$$
If a(t) is the acceleration of mass at time t, by Newton's law of motion
$$m\,a(t) = -k\,x(t) - b\,v(t)$$
Using the first and second derivatives of x (t) for v(t) and a (t),

$$m\frac{d^2x}{dt^2} + b\frac{dx}{dt} + kx = 0$$

The solution is found to be of the form

$$x(t) = Ae^{-\frac{bt}{2m}}\cos(\omega't + \phi)$$

where A is the amplitude and ω' is the angular frequency of the damped oscillator given by,

$$\omega' = \sqrt{\frac{k}{m} - \frac{b^2}{4m^2}}$$

We can regard it as a cosine function whose amplitude, which is $Ae^{-bt/2m}$, gradually decreases with time.

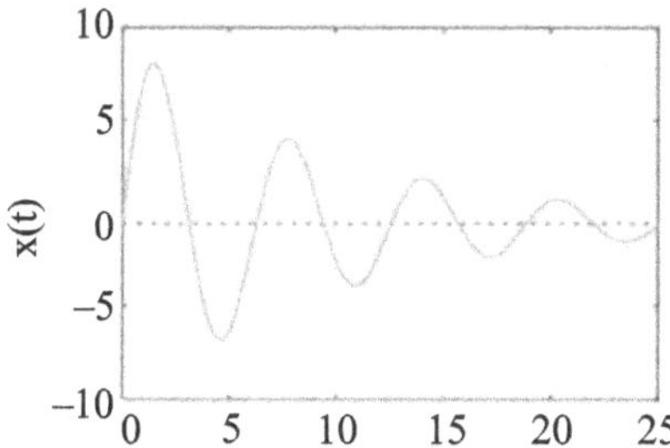

Fig. : *A damped oscillator is approximately periodic with decreasing amplitude of oscillation. With greater amping, oscillations die out faster.*

For a damped oscillator, total energy

$$E(t) = \frac{1}{2}kA^2\,e^{-bt/m}$$

♦ Small damping means that ratio $\left(\dfrac{b}{\sqrt{km}}\right)$ is much less than 1.

♦ If we put b = 0, all equations of a damped oscillator in this section reduce to the corresponding equations of an undamped oscillator.

Forced Oscillations and Resonance

♦ When a system is displaced from its equilibrium position and released, it oscillates with its natural frequency ω, and the oscillations are called **free oscillations**.

♦ All free oscillations eventually die out because of the ever present damping forces. An external agency can maintain these oscillations. These are called **forced** or **driven** oscillations. We consider the case when the external force is itself periodic, with a frequency ω_d called the driven frequency.
Suppose an external force F(t)
$$F(\text{t}) = F_o \cos \omega_d\text{t}$$

♦ The motion of a particle under the combined action of a linear restoring force, damping force and driving force is given by,
$$ma(\text{t}) = -kx(\text{t}) - bv(t) + F_o \cos \omega_d\text{t}$$
$$\Rightarrow \qquad m\frac{d^2x}{dt^2} + b\frac{dx}{dt} + kx = F_0 \cos\omega_d\text{t}$$
Its displacement, after the natural oscillations die out, is given by
$$x(t) = A \cos (\omega_d t + \phi)$$

♦ The amplitude is given by
$$A = \frac{F_0}{\left\{m^2\left(\omega^2 - \omega_d^2\right) + \omega_d^2 b^2\right\}^{1/2}}$$
$$\omega \rightarrow \text{natural frequency}$$
$$\omega_d \rightarrow \text{driving frequency}$$
and
$$\tan\phi = \frac{-v_0}{\omega_d x_0}$$

Consider two cases.

♦ Small damping, driving frequency far from natural frequency : In this case, $\omega_d b$ will be much smaller than $m(\omega^2 - \omega_d^2)$,
$$A = \frac{F_0}{m\left(\omega^2 - \omega_d^2\right)}$$

♦ The amplitude is the greatest at $\dfrac{\omega_d}{\omega} = 1$, the resonance condition. The three curves correspond to different extents of damping present in the system. The curves 1 and 3 correspond to minimum and maximum damping in the system.

- Driving Frequency Close to Natural Frequency : If ω_d is very close to ω, $m(\omega^2 - \omega_d^2)$ would be much less than $\omega_d b$,

$$A = \frac{F_0}{\omega_d b}$$

- The phenomenon of increase in amplitude when the driving force is close to the natural frequency of the oscillator is called **resonance**.

Past Years ONE-LINERS
NEET/JEE Main/Board

- In SHM, PE oscillates with twice the frequency of the body.

- Time period in SHM $= 2\pi\sqrt{\dfrac{m}{k}}$

- Phase difference between displacement & acceleration is π in S.H.M.

- Displacement $y = A_0 + A \sin \omega t + B \sin \omega t \Rightarrow y = \sqrt{A^2 + B^2}\,\sin(\omega t + \phi)$.

- Average velocity in a complete cycle is zero as displacement is zero.

- Acceleration in SHM $= -\omega^2 x$.

- Spring constant $(k) \propto \dfrac{1}{\text{length}(l)}$

- Velocity at displacement x in SHM is given by $v = \omega\sqrt{A^2 - x^2}$.

- In SHM maximum acceleration $= \omega^2 A$ & maximum velocity $= \omega A$

- When a mass is gentally placed at mean position on a body executing SHM total momentum of both bodies is conserved.

- A simple pendulum in liquid has time period $= 2\pi\sqrt{\dfrac{l}{g_{eff}}}$

  where $g_{eff} = g\left(1 - \dfrac{\rho_l}{\rho_0}\right)$, ρ_l & ρ_0 are density of liquid & object respectively.

- Frequency in SHM $= \dfrac{1}{2\pi}\sqrt{\dfrac{k}{m}}$.

- K.E. is maximum at centre in SHM.

- Time lost/gained per day $= \dfrac{1}{2}\alpha\Delta\theta \times 86400$.

- Speed in SHM, $v = \omega\sqrt{A^2 - x^2}$

- When PE $= \dfrac{1}{2}kd^2$, K.E. $= \dfrac{1}{2}kA^2 - \dfrac{1}{2}kd^2$ & total energy $= \dfrac{1}{2}kA^2$ in SHM.

Tips/Tricks/Tecchniques ONE-LINERS
(Exam Sample)

- In simple harmonic motion, the displacement and velocity may or may not be in the same phase.
- The acceleration and displacement are never in phase in simple harmonic motion.
- The potential energy in S.H.M. differ in phase with kinetic energy by $\pi/2$.
- If velocities of a particle performing S.H.M. at distance x_1 and x_2 from mean position are v_1 and v_2 respectively. Then

$$\omega = \sqrt{\frac{v_1^2 - v_2^2}{x_2^2 - x_1^2}}; \quad T = 2\pi\sqrt{\frac{x_2^2 - x_1^2}{v_1^2 - v_2^2}} \quad a = \sqrt{\frac{v_1^2 x_2^2 - v_2^2 x_1^2}{v_1^2 - v_2^2}}; \quad v_{\max} = \sqrt{\frac{v_1^2 x_2^2 - v_2^2 x_1^2}{x_2^2 - x_1^2}}$$

- Suppose a body of mass m is allowed to vibrate separately with two different springs having spring constants k_1 and k_2 respectively with time period T_1 and T_2 then $T_1 = 2\pi\sqrt{\dfrac{m}{k_1}}$ and $T_2 = 2\pi\sqrt{\dfrac{m}{k_2}}$.

    If the same body is connected with series combination of these two springs then time period for the system will be $T = \sqrt{T_1^2 + T_2^2}$.

    On connecting the same body with parallel combination of these two springs, time period of the system will be $T = \dfrac{T_1 T_2}{\sqrt{T_1^2 + T_2^2}}$.

- If infinite spring of force constant k, 2k, 4k, 8k........ respectively are connected in series. The effective force constant of the spring will become $\dfrac{k}{2}$.

- If g remains unchanged and length is changed by n%. Then % change in time period will be $\dfrac{\Delta T}{T} \times 100 = \dfrac{n}{2}\%$.

    If length remains unchanged and g is changed by n%. Then % change in time period will be $\dfrac{\Delta T}{T} \times 100 = -\dfrac{n}{2}\%$.

    (Valid only for percentage change less than 10%).

- If a spring of force constant k is divided into n equal parts then spring constant of each part will become nk and time period of oscillation of each part will become $\dfrac{T}{\sqrt{n}}$.

    If these n parts are in parallel then $k_{\text{eff}} = n^2 k$. So time period of the system becomes $T' = \dfrac{T}{n}$.

15 Waves

Transverse and Longitudinal Waves

- If you drop a little pebble in a pond of still water, the water surface gets disturbed. Disturbance does not remain confined to one place, propagates outward along a circle.
  The water mass does not flow outward with the circles, but rather a moving disturbance is created.
- Patterns, which move without the actual physical transfer or flow of matter as a whole, are called **waves.**
- Waves transport energy and the pattern of disturbance has information that propagate from one point to another.
- Not all waves require a medium for their propagation. Light waves or electromagnetic waves can travel through vacuum.
- Waves such as waves on a string, water waves, sound waves, seismic waves, etc. is the **mechanical waves**. These waves require a medium for propagation. They involve oscillations of constituent particles and depend on the elastic properties of the medium.
- If the constituents of the medium oscillate perpendicular to the direction of wave propagation, we call the wave a **transverse wave**.
- If they oscillate along the direction of wave propagation, we call the wave a **longitudinal wave**.
- Transverse or longitudinal waves are travelling or progressive waves since they travel from one part of the medium. The material medium as a whole does not move. In a water wave, it is the disturbance that moves, not water as a whole.
- Transverse waves can be propagated only in those media, which can sustain shearing stress, such as solids and not in fluids. Fluids, as well as, solids can sustain compressive strain; longitudinal waves can be propagated in all elastic media. For example, in medium like steel, both transverse and longitudinal waves can propagate, while air can sustain only longitudinal waves.
- Transverse and longitudinal waves travel with different speed in the same medium.

Displacement Relation in a Progressive Wave

- A sinusoidal travelling wave is described by:
$$y(x, t) = a \sin(kx - \omega t + \phi) \qquad \text{..... (i)}$$
Equation represents a sinusiodal (harmonic) wave travelling along the positive direction of the x-axis. On the other hand, a function.
$$y(x, t) = a \sin(kx + \omega t + \phi)$$
represents a wave travelling in the negative direction of x-axis.

The meaning of standard symbols in Eq. (i)

$y(x, t)$	:	displacement as a function of position x and time t
a	:	amplitude of a wave
ω	:	angular frequency of the wave
k	:	angular wave number
$kx - \omega t + \phi$	:	initial phase angle
		$(a + x = 0, t = 0)$

Amplitude and Phase

♦ In Eq. (i), a represents the maximum displacement of the constituents of the medium from their equilibrium position. It is called the **amplitude** of the wave.

♦ The quantity $(kx - \omega t + \phi)$ is called the **phase** of the wave. Clearly ϕ is the phase at x = 0 and t = 0. Hence, ϕ is called the initial phase angle.

Wavelength and Angular Wave Number

♦ The minimum distance between two points having the same phase is called the **wavelength** of the wave, denoted by λ.

$$k = \frac{2\pi}{\lambda}$$

k is the **angular wave number** or **propagation constant**; its SI unit is radian per metre or 1 rad m^{-1}

Period, Angular Frequency and Wave Number

♦ The **frequency** of the wave is the time it takes for an element to complete one full oscillation.

$$\omega = \frac{2\pi}{T}$$

ω is called the **angular frequency** of the wave.

Frequency $$\upsilon = \frac{1}{T} = \frac{\omega}{2\pi}$$

υ is usually measured in hertz.

The Speed of a Travelling Wave

♦ Fig. gives the shape of the wave at two instants of time, which differ by a small time internal Δt. The entire wave pattern is seen to shift to the right, by a distance Δx. The crest shown by a dot (•) moves a distance Δx in time Δt.

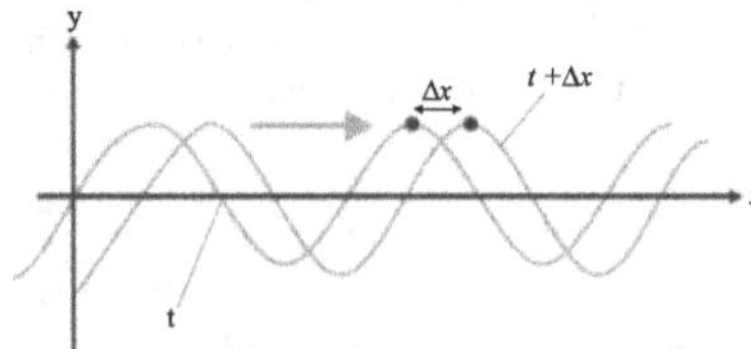

Fig. Progression of a harmonic wave from time t to t + Δt. Where Δt is a small interval. The wave pattern as a whole shifts to the right. The crest of the wave (or a point with any fixed phase) moves right by the distance Δx in time Δt.

♦ The speed of the wave is then $\Delta x/\Delta t$.
The motion of a fixed phase point on the wave is given by
$$kx - \omega t = \text{constant}$$

As time t changes, the position x of the fixed phase point must change so that the phase remains constant. Thus,

$$kx - \omega t = k(x+\Delta x) - \omega(t+\Delta t)$$

or $$k\,\Delta x - \omega\,\Delta t = 0$$

Taking Δx, Δt small,

$$\frac{dx}{dt} = \frac{\omega}{k} = \upsilon$$

$$\upsilon = \frac{2\pi v}{2\pi/\lambda} = \lambda v = \frac{\lambda}{T} \qquad \qquad ...(ii)$$

Equation (ii), shows that in the time required for one full oscillation by any constituent of the medium, the wave pattern travels a distance equal to the wavelength of the wave.

♦ The speed of a mechanical wave is determined by the inertial (linear mass density for strings, mass density in general) and elastic properties (Young's modulus for linear media/ shear modulus, bulk modulus) of the medium.

Speed of a Transverse Wave on Stretched String

♦ For waves on a string, the restoring force is provided by the tension T in the string. The inertial property will in this case be linear mass density μ, which is mass m of the string divided by its length L.

The speed of transverse waves on a stretched string is given by

$$v = \sqrt{\frac{T}{\mu}}$$

Speed of a Longitudinal Wave (Speed of Sound)

♦ The general formula for longitudinal waves in a medium is:

$$\upsilon = \sqrt{\frac{B}{\rho}}$$

♦ The speed of longitudinal waves in a solid bar is given by

$$\upsilon = \sqrt{\frac{Y}{\rho}}$$

♦ Liquids and solids generally have higher speed of sound than gases.

♦ Solids and liquids have higher mass densities (ρ) than gases. But the corresponding increase in both the modulus (B) of solids and liquids is much higher. This is the reason why the sound waves travel faster in solids and liquids than gases.

♦ Speed of sound in steel = 5941 ms^{-1}; water at 20°C = 1482 ms^{-1} and air 10°C = 331 ms^{-1}.

♦ Speed of sound in a gas in the ideal gas approximation.

$$PV = Nk_B T$$

For an isothermal change

$$V\Delta P + P\Delta V = 0$$

$$-\frac{\Delta P}{\Delta V/V} = P \quad \text{also } B = -\frac{\Delta P}{\Delta V/V}$$

So, we have B = P

♦ The speed of a longitudinal wave in an ideal gas is given by,

$$\upsilon = \sqrt{\frac{p}{\rho}} = \sqrt{\frac{B}{\rho}}$$

This relation was first given by Newton and is known as **Newton's formula.**

♦ Pressure variations in the propagation of sound waves are so fast that there is little time for the heat flow to maintain constant temperature.

♦ These variations are adiabatic not isothermal. For adiabatic processes the ideal gas satisfies the relation.

$$PV^\gamma = \text{constant}$$

i.e. $\quad\quad \Delta(PV^\gamma) = 0$

or $\quad\quad P\gamma\, V^{\gamma-1}\,\Delta V + V^\gamma\,\Delta P = 0$

♦ For an ideal gas the adiabatic bulk modulus is given by,

$$B_{ad} = -\frac{\Delta P}{\Delta V / V} = \gamma P$$

The **speed of sound**, is

$$\upsilon = \sqrt{\frac{\gamma P}{\rho}}$$

♦ This modification of Newton's formula is referred to as the **Laplace correction.** For air $\gamma = 7/5$. The speed of sound in air at STP, we get a value 331.3 ms^{-1}.

The Principle of Superposition of Waves

♦ When the pulses overlap, the resultant displacement is the algebraic sum of the displacement due to each pulse. This is known as the **principle of superposition of waves.**

♦ According to this principle, each pulse moves as if others are not present. The constituents of the medium, therefore, suffer displacments due to both and since the displacements can be positive and negative, the net displacement is an algebraic sum of the two.

♦ Let $y_1(x,t)$ and $y_2(x,t)$ be the displacements due to two wave disturbances in the medium. If the waves arrive in a region simultaneously, the net displacement $y(x,t)$ is given by

$$y(x, t) = y_1(x, t) + y_2(x, t)$$

♦ Consider two harmonic travelling waves on a stretched string.

$$y_1(x, t) = a \sin(kx - \omega t)$$

and $\quad\quad y_2(x, t) = a \sin(kx - \omega t + \phi)$

♦ The net displacement is

$$y(x, t) = a \sin(kx - \omega t) + a \sin(kx - \omega t + \phi)$$

$$y(x, t) = 2a \cos\frac{\phi}{2}\sin\left(kx - \omega t + \frac{\phi}{2}\right)$$

♦ Amplitude is

$$A(\phi) = 2a \cos\frac{\phi}{2}$$

♦ For $\phi = 0$, when the waves are in phase,

$$y(x, t) = 2a \sin(kx - \omega t)$$

the resultant wave has amplitude 2a,

♦ For $\phi = \pi$; waves are completely, out of phase and the resultant wave has zero displacement.

Reflection of Waves

- Fig. shows a pulse travelling along a stretched string and being reflected by the boundary.
- As the pulse arrives at the wall, it exerts a force on the wall. By Newton's Third Law, the wall exerts an equal and opposite force on the string generating a reflected pulse that differs by a phase of π.

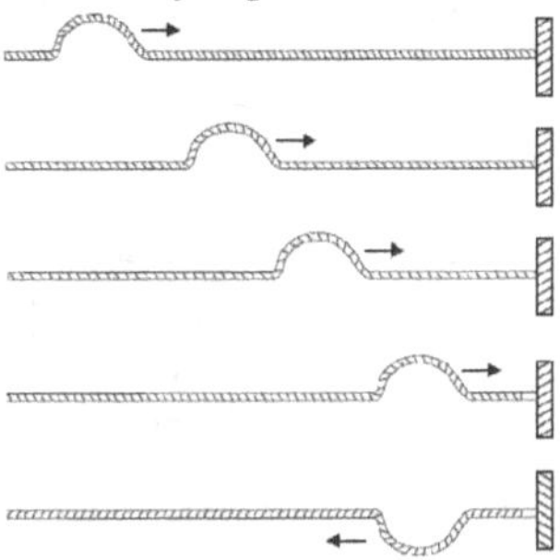

Fig.: *Reflection of a pulse meeting a rigid boundary.*

- A travelling wave or pulse suffers a phase change of π on reflection at a rigid boundary and no phase change on reflection at an open boundary.
- Let incident wave be
$$y_2 (x, t) = a \sin (kx - \omega t)$$
- At a rigid boundary, the reflected wave is given by
$$y_r(x, t) = a \sin (kx - \omega t + \pi).$$
$$= - a \sin (kx - \omega t)$$
- At an open boundary, the reflected wave is given by
$$y_r(x, t) = a \sin (kx - \omega t + 0).$$
$$= a \sin (kx - \omega t)$$
Clearly, at the rigid boundary, $y = y_2 + y_r = 0$ at all times.

Standing Waves and Normal Modes

- Consider a wave travelling along the positive direction of x-axis and a reflected wave of the same amplitude and wavelength in the negative direction of x-axis.
$$y_1(x, t) = a \sin (kx - \omega t) \ [\phi = 0]$$
$$y_2(x, t) = a \sin (kx + \omega t)$$
The resultant wave on the string is
$$y (x, t) = y_1(x, t) + y_2(x, t)$$
$$= a \left[\sin (kx - \omega t) + \sin (kx + \omega t)\right]$$
Using $\sin (A+B) + \sin (A-B) = 2 \sin A \cos B$ we get,
$$y (x, t) = 2a \sin kx \cos \omega t \qquad \qquad ...(i)$$
- The amplitude of this wave is $2a \sin kx$.
- There is no phase difference between oscillations of different elements of the wave. The string as a whole vibrates in phase with differing amplitudes at different points. *The wave pattern is neither moving to the right nor to the left. They are called* **standing** *or* **stationary waves**.
- The points at which the amplitude is zero (i.e., where there is no motion at all) are **nodes**; the points at which the amplitude is the largest are called **antinodes**.

- From Eq. (i), the positions of nodes (where the amplitude is zero) are given by $\sin kx = 0$.

$$kx = n\pi; n = 0, 1, 2, 3, ...$$

Since, $\quad k = 2\pi/\lambda$, we get

$$x = \frac{n\lambda}{2}; n = 0, 1, 2, 3, ...$$

 The distance between any two successive nodes is $\dfrac{\lambda}{2}$.

- Positions of antinodes (where the amplitude is the largest) are given by $|\sin kx| = 1$

$$kx = (n + \tfrac{1}{2})\,\frac{\lambda}{2}\;; n = 0, 1, 2, 3, ...$$

- The distance between any two consecutive antinodes is $\dfrac{\lambda}{2}$.

- **A stretched string of length L fixed at both ends**. Taking one end to be at $x = 0$, the boundary conditions are that $x = 0$ and $x = L$ are positions of nodes. The $x = 0$ condition is satisfied by equation (i). The $x = L$ node condition requires that the length L is related to λ by

$$L = n\,\frac{\lambda}{2}; \qquad n = 1, 2, 3, ...$$

- The possible wavelengths of stationary waves are

$$\lambda = \frac{2L}{n}; \qquad n = 1, 2, 3, ...$$

with corresponding frequencies

$$v = \frac{n\upsilon}{2L}, \text{ for } n = 1, 2, 3,$$

- The lowest possible natural frequency of a system is called its **fundamental mode** or the **first harmonic**. For the stretched string fixed at either end it is given by $\mathbf{v} = \dfrac{\upsilon}{2L}$, corresponding to $n = 1$. Here v is the speed of wave. The n = 2 frequency is called the **second harmonic**; n = 3 is the **third harmonic** and so on.

- Fig. shows the first six harmonics of a stretched string fixed at either end.

- **Consider normal modes of oscillation of an air column with one end closed and the other open.**
Taking the end in contact with water to be $x = 0$, the node condition is satisfied. If the other end $x = L$ is an antinode,

$$L = \left(n + \frac{1}{2}\right)\frac{\lambda}{2},$$

The possible wavelengths are:

$$\lambda = \frac{2L}{(n + 1/2)}, \text{ for } n = 0, 1, 2, 3,...$$

The normal modes – the natural frequencies – of the system are

$$v = \left(n + \frac{1}{2}\right)\frac{v}{2L}; \; n = 0, 1, 2, 3, ...$$

- The **fundamental frequency** corresponds to n = 0, and is given by $\dfrac{\upsilon}{4L}$. The higher frequencies are odd harmonics, i.e., odd multiples of the fundamental frequency :

$$3\frac{\upsilon}{4L},\ 5\frac{\upsilon}{4L},\ \text{etc.}$$

Fig. (b) shows the first six odd harmonics of air column with one end closed and the other open.

For a pipe open at both ends, each end is an antinode. It is then easily seen that an open air column at both ends generates all harmonics.

♦   If the external frequency is close to one of the natural frequencies, the system shows re

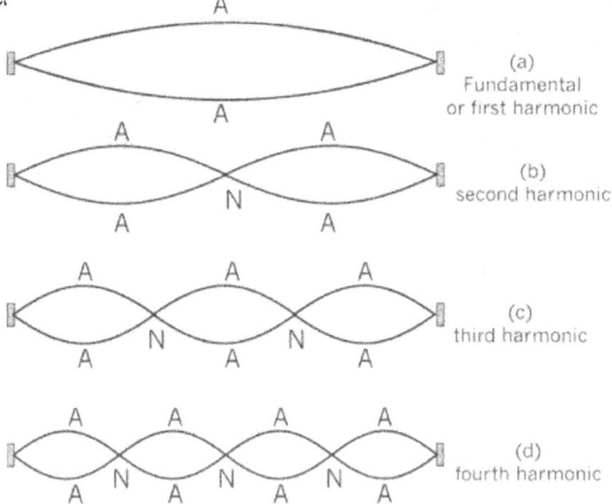

Fig.: *(a) The first six harmonics of vibrations of a stretched string fixed at both ends.*

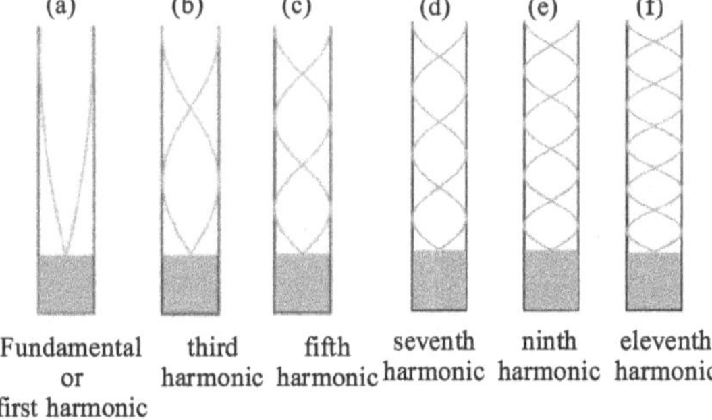

Fig.: *(b) Normal modes of an air column open at one end and closed at the other end. Only the odd harmonics are seen to be possible.*

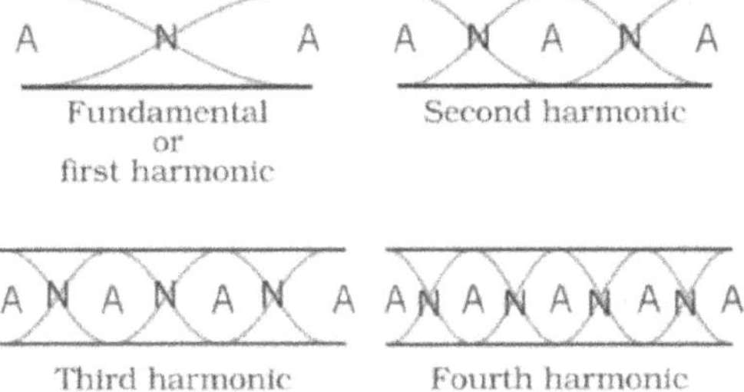

Fig.: *(c) Standing waves in an open pipe, first four harmonics are depicted.*

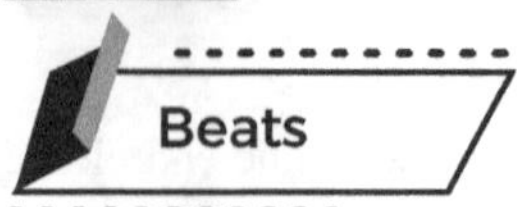

Beats

- 'Beats' is phenomenon arising from interference of waves. When two harmonic sound waves of close (but not equal) frequencies are heard at the same time, we hear a sound of similar frequency (the average of two close frequencies), but we hear something else also. We hear audibly distinct waxing and waning of the intensity of the sound, with a frequency equal to the difference in the two close frequencies.

- Consider two harmonic sound waves of nearly equal angular frequency ω_1 and ω_2 and fix the location to be x = 0 for convenience.

$$s_1 = a \cos \omega_1 t \text{ and } s_2 = a \cos \omega_2 t$$

$$s = s_1 + s_2 = a (\cos \omega_1 t + \cos \omega_2 t)$$

Using, cos A + cosB,

$$= 2 a \cos \frac{(\omega_1 - \omega_2)t}{2} \cos \frac{(\omega_1 + \omega_2)t}{2}$$

$$s = [2 a \cos \omega_b t] \cos \omega_a t \qquad \qquad ...(a)$$

If $|\omega_1 - \omega_2| << \omega_1, \omega_2, \omega_a >> \omega_b$, where

$$\omega_b = \frac{(\omega_1 - \omega_2)}{2} \text{ and } \omega_a = \frac{(\omega_1 + \omega_2)}{2}$$

- If we assume $|\omega_1 - \omega_2| << \omega_1$ which means $\omega_a >> \omega_b$ we can interpret eqn. (a) as follows. The resultant wave is oscillating with the average angular frequency ω_a; however its amplitude is **not** constant in time, the intensity of the resultant wave waxes and wanes with a frequency which is $2\omega_b = \omega_1 - \omega_2$. Since $\omega = 2\pi\nu$, the **beat frequency** ν_{beat}, is given by $\nu_{beat} = \nu_1 - \nu_2$.

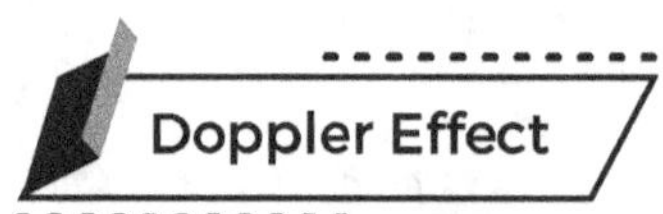

Doppler Effect

- It is an everyday experience that the pitch of the whistle of a fast moving train decreases as it recedes away. When we approach a stationary source of sound with high speed, the pitch of the sound heard appears to be higher than that of the source. As the observer recedes away from the source, the observed **pitch** (or frequency) becomes lower than that of the source. This motion-related frequency change is called **Doppler effect.**

Source Moving; Observer Stationary

- If $\qquad \nu_0$ = frequency emitted by source

$$v = \text{speed of sound in air}$$
$$v_s = \text{velocity of source.}$$
$$v_0 = \text{velocity of observer.}$$

- When source is moving away from observer, appanent frequency

$$v = v_0\left(\frac{v}{v + v_s}\right)$$

- When source is moving towards observer, apparent frequency

$$v = v_0\left(\frac{v}{v - v_s}\right)$$

Observer Moving; Source Stationary

- When observer is moving away from source, apparent frequency.

$$v = v_0\left(\frac{v - v_0}{v}\right)$$

- When observer is moving towards source, apparent frequency.

$$v = v_0\left(\frac{v + v_0}{v}\right)$$

Both Source and Observer Moving

- The frequency v observed by the observer is given by

$$v = v_0\left(\frac{v \pm v_0}{v \pm v_s}\right)$$

- When source & observer are moving towards each other apparent frequency

$$v = v_0\left(\frac{v + v_0}{v - v_s}\right)$$

- When source & observer are moving away from each other apparent frequency

$$v = v_0\left(\frac{v - v_0}{v + v_s}\right)$$

Past Years ONE-LINERS
NEET/JEE Main/Board

- Frequency of string $f \propto \sqrt{\text{Tension}}$

- For closed organ pipe n^{th} harmonic is $v = \left(n + \dfrac{1}{2}\right)\dfrac{v}{2L}$ $n = 0, 1, 2...$

- Successive resonances are produced at column length difference of $\dfrac{\lambda}{2}$ i.e.,

$$\dfrac{\lambda}{2} = \ell_1 - \ell_2$$

- When two cars approach each other apparent frequency $= f_0\left(\dfrac{v + v_0}{v - v_s}\right)$

- Difference between successive frequency in closed organ pipe $= \dfrac{2v}{4\ell}$

- Frequency reflected by a stationary wall, $n' = \left(\dfrac{v}{v - v_s}\right)v_0$

- For a closed organ pipe minimum resonating length $= \dfrac{\lambda}{4}$ and next resonating

  length $= \dfrac{3\lambda}{4}$

- For string fixed at both ends, difference between any successive frequencies = fundamental frequency

- Apparent frequency $= v_0\left(\dfrac{v}{v - v_s\cos\alpha}\right)$

- General form of wave equation is $y(x, t) = A \sin(kx - \omega t)$

- Velocity of wave on solid, $v = \sqrt{\dfrac{T\ell}{m}}$

- Frequency of string fixed at both ends has n^{th} harmonic, $v = n\dfrac{v}{2\ell}$

- Speed of sound $\propto \sqrt{\text{Temperature}}$

- Speed of wave in solids $= \sqrt{\dfrac{Y}{P}}$

- Fundamental frequency of open organ pipe, $f = \dfrac{v}{2l}$

- Velocity of sound in string $V = \sqrt{\dfrac{T}{\mu}}$

- When a train approach a person near track, apparent frequency $= v_0 \left(\dfrac{v}{v - v_s} \right)$

  When train recedes the person apparent frequency $= v_0 \left(\dfrac{v}{v + v_s} \right)$

Tips/Tricks/Tecchniques ONE-LINERS
(Exam Sample)

- Velocity of sound in a medium do not depend on wavelength or frequency.
- Two waves of unequal magnitude travelling in opposite directions produce standing waves.
- Diver inside the water cannot heard sound produced in air because most of the sound is reflected from the surface of water in comparison to the refraction.
- In an open pipe all harmonics are present whereas in a closed organ pipe, only alternate *i.e.*, odd harmonics of frequencies $|n_1, 3n_1, 5n_1,.....$ etc. are present.
- If the wire is divided into length in the ratio a : b : c, the ratio of frequencies of these lengths will be bc : ca : ab, for the same tension.
- Doppler effect gives information about change in frequency only. It says nothing about intensity of sound.
- Doppler effect in sound is asymmetric but in light it is symmetric. For example change in frequency depend on the fact whether the source is moving towards observer or observer is moving towards source.
- $n_{Last} = n_{First} + (N - 1)x : N =$ no. of tuning fork in series, $x =$ beat frequency between two successive forks.

♦ If the difference of the apparent frequency of a source of sound as perceived by an observer during it's approach and recession is x% of the natural frequency of source then speed of $v_S = \dfrac{v_{sound}}{200} x \quad (v^2 >> v_s^2)$.

♦ If an open pipe is kept half submerged in water, it becomes a closed organ pipe of length half that of a open pipe. Its fundamental frequency will become

$$n' = \dfrac{v}{4\left(\dfrac{l}{2}\right)} = \dfrac{v}{2l} = n_1 \quad i.e., \text{ equal to that of open pipe.}$$

♦ Frequency of vibration of clamped rod is same as that of organ pipes. For example If the rod is clamped at the middle, then

$$n_1 = \dfrac{v}{2l}\,;\ n_2 = 2n_1 \text{ and } n_3 = 3n_1$$

If the rod is clamped at the ends, then

$$n_1 = \dfrac{v}{4l}\,;\ n_2 = 2n_1 \text{ and } n_3 = 3n_1$$

♦ If three tuning forks having frequencies n, n + y and n + 2y are sounded together to produce waves of equal amplitude then these three wave produces beats with beat frequency = y beats/sec.

♦ If N tuning forks are arranged in such a way that every fork gives y beats per sec with the next then the frequency of last fork is given by

$$n_{Last} = n_{First} + (N - 1)\, y$$

♦ The velocity of transverse wave in a solid of modulus of rigidity n and density ρ is given by $v = \sqrt{\dfrac{n}{\rho}}$

♦ If a pressure wave is given by $P = A \sin[Bt = Cx]n - 2$ then ω = B and k = C

$$\therefore \qquad V = \dfrac{\omega}{k} = \dfrac{B}{C}$$

♦ If $y = A \sin(Bx) \cos(ct)$ then K = B and ω = C.

16 Electric Charges and Fields

Electric Charge

- Lightning that we see in the sky during thunderstorms, spark or hearing a crackle when we take off our synthetic clothes or sweater are the examples of electric discharge.
- Static means anything that does not move or change with time.
- *Electrostatics deals with the study of forces, fields and potentials arising from static charges.*
- Many materials on rubbing could attract light objects like straw, bits of papers.
- If two glass rods rubbed with wool or silk cloth are brought close to each other, they repel each other but glass rod and wool attract each other.
- Similarly, two plastic rods rubbed with cat's fur repelled each other but attracted the fur.

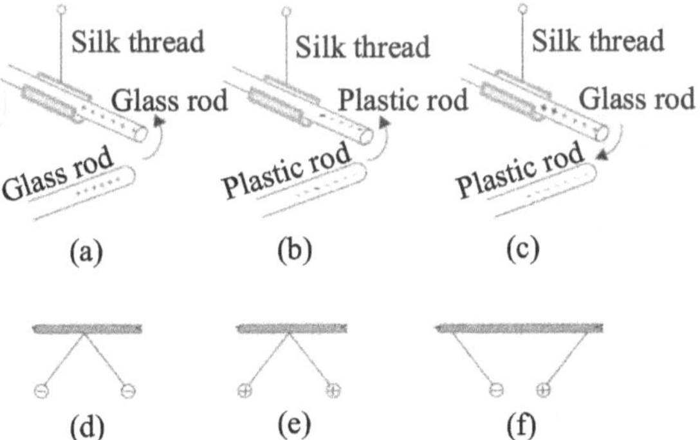

Fig.: Rods and pith balls: like charges repel
and unlike charges attract each other.

- We say that the bodies like glass or plastic rods, silk, fur and pith balls are electrified. They acquire an electric charge on rubbing.
- When a glass rod is rubbed with silk, the rod acquires one kind of charge and the silk acquires the second kind of charge. This is true for any pair.
- The experiments suggest that there are two kinds of electrification (i) like chrges repel (ii) unlike charges attract each other.

- By convention, the charge on glass rod or cat's fur is called positive and that on plastic rod or silk is termed negative.
- A simple apparatus to detect charge on a body is the *gold-leaf electroscope*

Conductors and Insulators

- Those substances which allow electricity to pass through them easily are called *conductors*. They have electric charges (electrons) that are comparatively free to move inside the material. Metals, human and animal bodies and earth are conductors.
- Most of the non-metals like glass, porcelain, plastic, nylon, wood offer high resistance to the passage of electricity through them. They are called *insulators*.
- When some charge is transferred to a conductor, it readily gets distributed over the entire surface of the conductor. In contrast, if some charge is put on an insulator, it stays at the same place.
- When we bring a charged body in contact with the earth, all the excess charge on the body disappears by causing a momentary current to pass to the ground through the connecting conductor (such as our body). This process of sharing the charges with the earth is called *grounding or earthing*.
- The electric wiring in our houses has three wires: live, neutral and earth. The first two carry electric current from the power station and the third is earthed by connecting it to the buried underground metal plate.
- Metallic bodies of the electric appliances are connected to the earth wire. When any fault occurs the charge flows to the earth.

Charging by Induction

- If charged body is brought near an uncharged body, one side of neutral body closer to charged body becomes oppositely charged while the other side becomes similarly charged.
- Remove the rod. Now, separate the spheres quite apart. The charges on them get uniformly distributed over them.
  This is *charging by induction*.

Basic Properties of Electric Charge

Additivity of Charges
- If a system contains n charges q_1, q_2, q_3, ..., q_n, then the total charge of the system is $q_1 + q_2 + q_3 + ... + q_n$.

Charges is Conserved
- *The total charge of the isolated system is always conserved.*

♦ A neutron turns into a proton and an electron. The proton and electron thus created have equal and opposite charges and the total charge is zero before and after the creation.

Quantisation of Charges

♦ All free charges are integral multiples of a basic unit of charge denoted by e. Thus charge q on a body is always given by

$$q = ne$$

where n is any integer, positive or negative. This basic unit of charge is the charge that an electron or proton carries. $e = 1.602192 \times 10^{-19}$ C

Coulomb's Law

♦ Coulomb measured the force between two point charges and found that *it varied inversely as the square of the distance between the charges and was directly proportional to the product of the magnitude of the two charges and acted along the line joining the two charges.*

♦ If two point charges q_1, q_2 are separated by a distance r in vacuum, the magnitude of the force (F) between them is given by

$$F = k\frac{|q_1\ q_2|}{r^2} \quad k = 1/4\pi\varepsilon_0$$

so Coulomb's Law is

$$F = \frac{1}{4\pi\varepsilon_0}\ \frac{|q_1\ q_2|}{r^2}$$

ε_0 is called the *permittivity of free space*. The value of ε_0 in SI units is $\varepsilon_0 = 8.854 \times 10^{-12}$ C^2 N^{-1}m^{-2}

Forces between Multiple Charges

♦ Force on any charge due to a number of other charges is the vector sum of all the forces on that charge due to the other charges. This is termed as the **principle of superposition**.

♦ Thus the total force F_1 on q_1 due to the two charges q_2 and q_3 is given as

$$\vec{F}_1 = \vec{F}_{12} + \vec{F}_{13} = \frac{1}{4\pi\varepsilon_0}\frac{q_1 q_2}{r_{12}^2}\hat{r}_{12} + \frac{1}{4\pi\varepsilon_0}\frac{q_1 q_3}{r_{13}^2}\hat{r}_{13}$$

♦ For a system of n charges, net force on charge q_1 is

$$\vec{F}_1 = \vec{F}_{12} + \vec{F}_{13} + \ldots\ldots + \vec{F}_{1n}$$

$$= \frac{1}{4\pi\varepsilon_0}\left[\frac{q_1 q_2}{r_{12}^2}\hat{r}_{12} + \frac{q_1 q_3}{r_{13}^2}\hat{r}_{13}\ldots\ldots + \frac{q_1 q_n}{r_{1n}^2}\hat{r}_{1n}\right] = \frac{q_1}{4\pi\varepsilon_0}\sum_{i=2}^{n}\frac{q_i}{r_{1i}^2}\hat{r}_{1i}$$

Electric Field

♦ The **electric field** due to a charge Q at a point in space may be defined as the force that a unit positive charge would experience if placed at that point. The charge Q which is producing the electric field is called a source charge and the charge q which tests the effect of source charge is called a test charge.

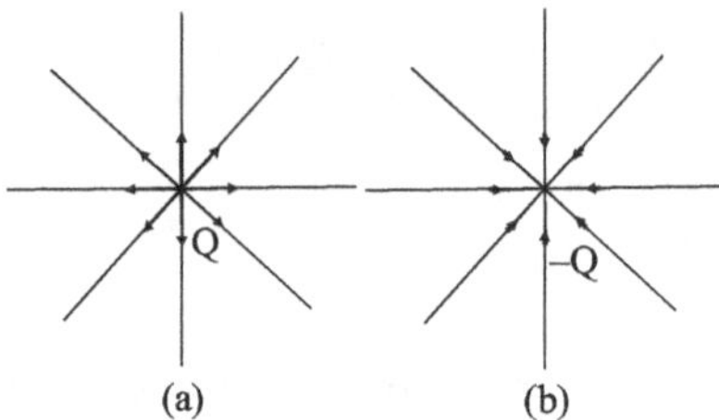

(a)   (b)

♦ Ratio F/q defines the electric field:

$$E = \lim_{q \to 0} \frac{F}{q}$$

Electric Field due to a System of Charges

♦ By the superposition principle electric field E at P. due to the system of charges is
$$E = E_1 + E_2 + \ldots + E_n$$

$$= \frac{1}{4\pi\varepsilon_0} \frac{q_1}{r_{1P}^2} \hat{r}_{1P} + \frac{1}{4\pi\varepsilon_0} \frac{q_2}{r_{2P}^2} \hat{r}_{2P} + \ldots + \frac{1}{4\pi\varepsilon_0} \frac{q_n}{r_{nP}^2} \hat{r}_{nP} = \frac{1}{4\pi\varepsilon_0} \sum_{i=1}^{n} \frac{q_i}{r_{iP}^2} \hat{r}_{iP}$$

Physical Significance of Electric Field

♦ Electric field is a characteristic of the system of charges. It is independent of the test charge placed at a point to find the field.

♦ Effect of any motion of q_1 on charge q_2 cannot arise instantaneously. The accelerated motion of charge q_1 produces electromagnetic waves, which then propagate with the speed of light C, reach q_2 and cause a force on q_2.

♦ Electric field can be detected only by its effects on charges.

♦ Electric field can also transport energy.

Electric Field Lines

♦ Electric field lines are pictorially mapping of the electric field around a configuration of charges.

♦ An **electric field line** is, in general, a curve drawn in such a way that the tangent to it at each point is in the direction of the net field at that point.

♦ The magnitude of the field is represented by the density of field lines. E is strong near the charge, so the density of field lines is more near the charge and the lines are closer. Away from the charge, the field gets weaker and the density of field lines is less, resulting in well-separated lines.

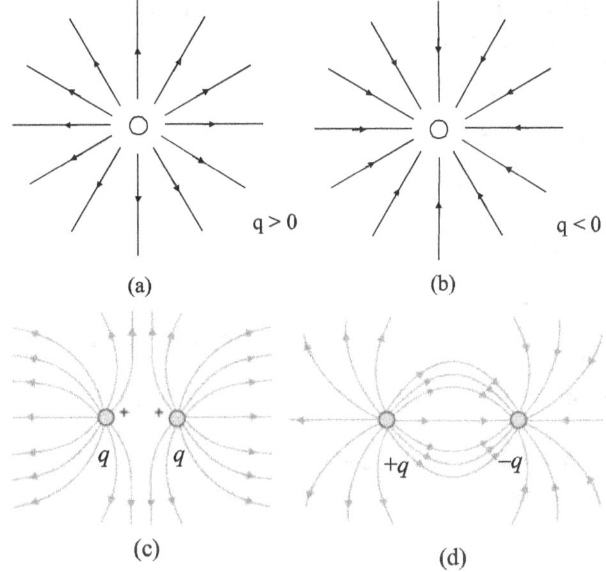

Fig.: Field lines due to some simple charge configuration

♦ The field lines follow some important general properties:

(i) Field lines start from positive charges and end at negative charges. If there is a single charge, they may start or end at infinity.

(ii) In a charge-free region, electric field lines can be taken to be continuous curves without any breaks.

(iii) Two field lines can never cross each other. (If they did, the field at the point of intersection will not have a unique direction, which is absurd.)

(iv) Electrostatic field lines do not form any closed loops. This follows from the conservative nature of electric field

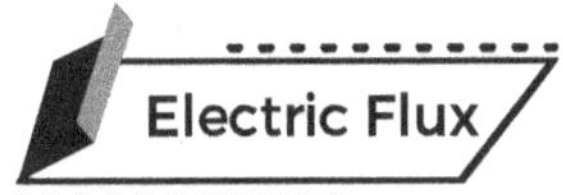

Electric Flux

♦ An area element should be treated as a vector. It has a magnitude and also a direction. The direction of a planar area vector is along its normal.

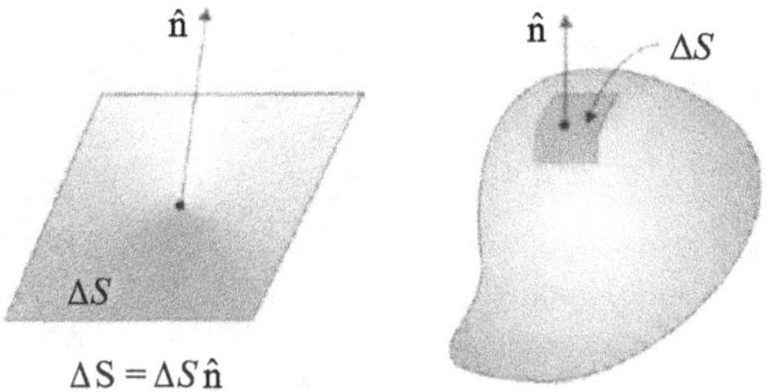

Fig.: Convention for defining normal n̂ and Δs.

- The vector associated with every area element of a closed surface is taken to be in the direction of the outward normal.
- **Electric flux** $\Delta\phi$ through an area element ΔS is defined by
  $$\Delta\phi = \mathbf{E}.\Delta\mathbf{S} = E\,\Delta S\,\cos\theta$$
  Thus, the total flux ϕ through a surface S is
  $$\phi = \int_S \vec{E}\cdot\vec{ds}$$

Electric Dipole

- An electric dipole is a pair of equal and opposite point charges q and $-q$, separated by a small distance $2a$.

  By convention, the direction from $-q$ to q is said to be the direction of the dipole.

The Field of an Electric Dipole

(i) For points on the axis

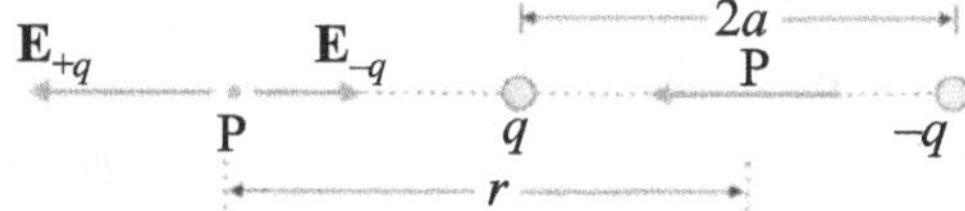

The total field at P is

$$\mathbf{E} = \mathbf{E}_{+q} + \mathbf{E}_{-q} = \frac{q}{4\pi\varepsilon_0}\left[\frac{1}{(r-a)^2} - \frac{1}{(r+a)^2}\right]\hat{\mathbf{P}}$$

$$= \frac{q}{4\pi\varepsilon_0}\frac{4ar}{\left(r^2-a^2\right)^2}\hat{\mathbf{P}}$$

- For $r \gg a$

$$\mathbf{E} = \frac{4qa}{4\pi\varepsilon_0 r^3}\hat{\mathbf{P}}$$

(ii) For points on the equatorial plane

- The total electric field is

$$\mathbf{E} = -\left(E_{+q} + E_{-q}\right)\cos\theta\,\hat{\mathbf{p}}$$

$$= -\frac{2qa}{4\pi\varepsilon_0\left(r^2+a^2\right)^{3/2}}\hat{\mathbf{p}}$$

At large distances $(r \gg a)$, this reduces to

$$\mathbf{E} = -\frac{2qa}{4\pi\varepsilon_0 r^3}\hat{\mathbf{p}}$$

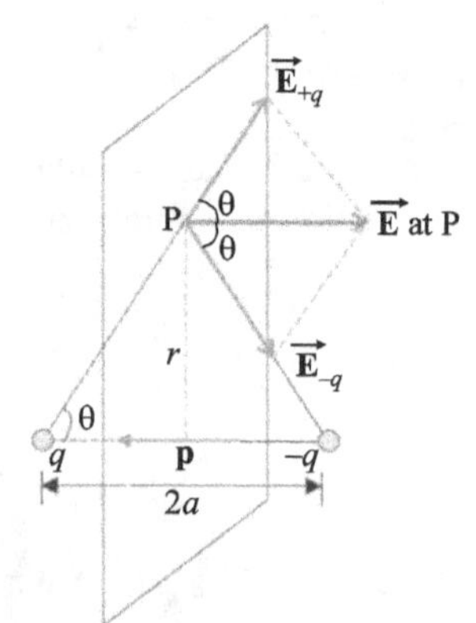

- The *dipole* moment *vector* $\vec{\mathbf{p}}$ of an electric dipole is defined by
  $$\vec{\mathbf{P}} = q \times 2a\,\hat{\mathbf{p}}$$

it is a vector whose magnitude is charge q times the separation and the direction is along the line from $-q$ to q.

Physical Significance of Dipole

♦ In most molecules, the centres of positive charges and that of negative charges exist at the same place. So, they have no dipole moment. For example CO_2, CH_4 etc.

♦ But in some molecules, the centres of negative charges and of positive charges do not coincide. Therefore they have a permanent electric dipole moment, even in the absence of an electric field. Such molecules are called polar molecules. Water molecules, H_2O, is an example of this type.

Dipole in a Uniform External Field

♦ There is a force qE on q and a force $-qE$ on $-q$. The net force on the dipole is zero, since **E** is uniform. However, the charges are separated, so the forces act at different points, resulting in a **torque on the dipole.**

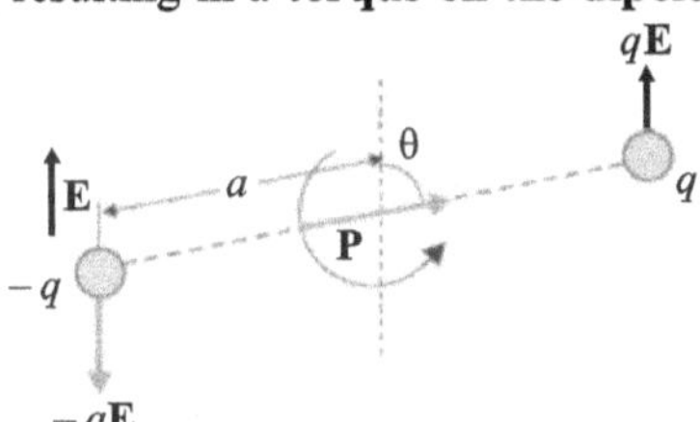

Fig.: Dipole in a uniform electric field.

$$\tau = \mathbf{p} \times \mathbf{E}$$

Magnitude of torque $= q\,E \times 2\,a\,\sin\theta$
$= 2\,q\,a\,E\,\sin\theta = pE\,\sin\theta$

Its direction is normal to the plane of the paper, coming out of it.

When **p** is aligned with **E**, the torque is zero.

♦ When **p** is parallel to **E** or antiparallel to **E**. In either case, the net torque is zero, but there is a net force on the dipole if **E** is not uniform.

Continuous Charge Distribution

♦ The *surface charge density* σ of the area element is defined by

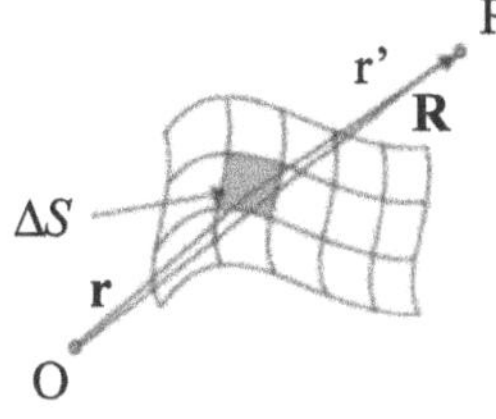

$$\sigma = \frac{\Delta Q}{\Delta S}$$

∴ Surface charge $\Delta Q = \sigma \Delta S$

- The *linear charge density* λ of a wire is defined by

$$\lambda = \frac{\Delta Q}{\Delta l}$$

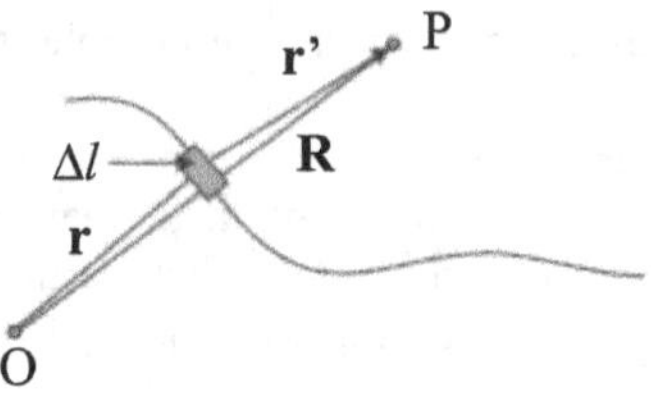

Line charge $\Delta Q = \lambda \Delta l$

- The *volume charge density* is defined by

$$\rho = \frac{\Delta Q}{\Delta V}$$

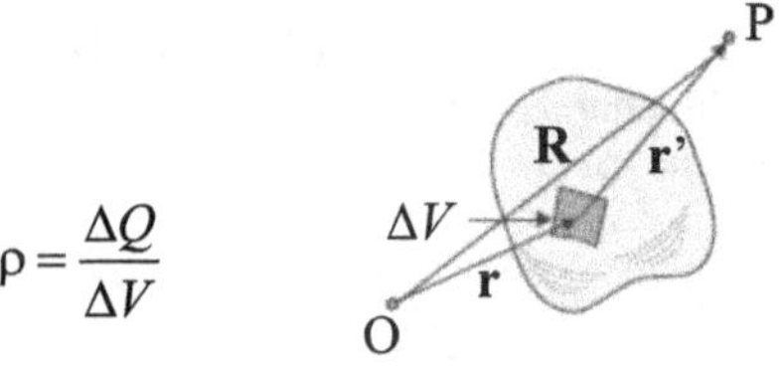

Volume charge $\Delta Q = \rho \Delta V$

- Electric field due to charge distribution.

$$\vec{E}_\lambda = \frac{1}{4\pi\varepsilon_0} \sum_{all\Delta\ell} \frac{\lambda\Delta\ell}{r'^2}\hat{r}' \quad \vec{E}_\sigma = \frac{1}{4\pi\varepsilon_0} \sum_{all\Delta s} \frac{\sigma\Delta s}{r'^2}\hat{r}', \vec{E}_\rho = \frac{1}{4\pi\varepsilon_0} \sum_{all\Delta V} \frac{\rho\Delta v}{r'^2}\hat{r}'$$

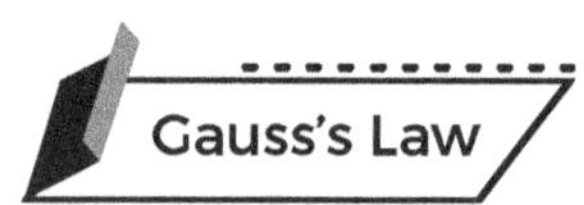

Gauss's Law

- Consider the total flux through a sphere of radius r, which encloses a point charge q at its centre. The flux through an area element $\Delta \mathbf{S}$ is

$$\Delta\phi = \vec{\mathbf{E}}\cdot\overrightarrow{\Delta\mathbf{S}} = \frac{q}{4\pi\varepsilon_0 r^2}\hat{r}\cdot\overrightarrow{\Delta\mathbf{S}} \quad \Rightarrow \quad \Delta\phi = \frac{q}{4\pi\varepsilon_0 r^2}\Delta S$$

The total flux

$$\phi = \sum_{all\ \Delta S} \frac{q}{4\pi\varepsilon_0 r^2}\Delta S$$

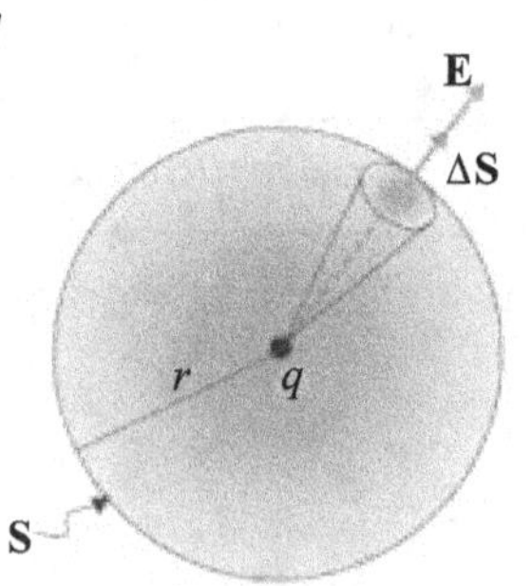

$$\Rightarrow \quad \phi = \frac{q}{4\pi\varepsilon_0 r^2} \sum_{all\ \Delta S} \Delta S = \frac{q}{4\pi\varepsilon_0 r^2}S$$

Total area equals $S = 4\pi r^2$. Thus,

$$\phi = \frac{q}{4\pi\varepsilon_0 r^2}\times 4\pi r^2 = \frac{q}{\varepsilon_0}$$

♦　***Gauss's law:*** *Electric flux through a closed surface S*

$$\phi = q/\varepsilon_0 \qquad\qquad ...(i)$$

q = total charge enclosed by S.

♦　The law implies that the total electric flux through a closed surface is zero if no charge is enclosed by the surface.

♦　Gauss's law is true for any closed surface, no matter what its shape or size.

♦　The term q on the right side of Gauss's law, Eq (i), includes the sum of all charges enclosed by the surface. The charges may be located anywhere inside the surface.

♦　In the situation when the surface is so chosen that there are some charges inside and some outside, the electric field [whose flux appears on the left side of Eq. (i)] is due to all the charges, both inside and outside S. The term q on the right side of Gauss's law, however, represents only the total charge inside S.

♦　Gauss's law is often useful *when the system has some symmetry.*

♦　Finally, Gauss's law is based on the inverse square dependence on distance

Applications of Gauss's Law

Gauss's law helps to determine the electric field intensity.

♦　**Electric field due to a linear charge distribution**

From Gauss's law

$$ES = \frac{q_{in}}{\varepsilon_0}$$

Here, S = area of

curved surface = $(2\pi r l)$

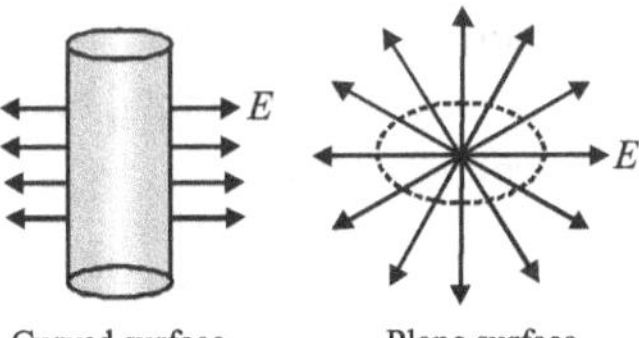

Curved surface　　　　Plane surface

and q_{in} = net charge enclosing

this cylinder = λl

$$\therefore\quad E(2\pi r l) = \frac{\lambda l}{\varepsilon_0}$$

$$\therefore\quad E = \frac{\lambda}{2\pi\varepsilon_0 r}$$

i.e., $E \propto \dfrac{1}{r}$

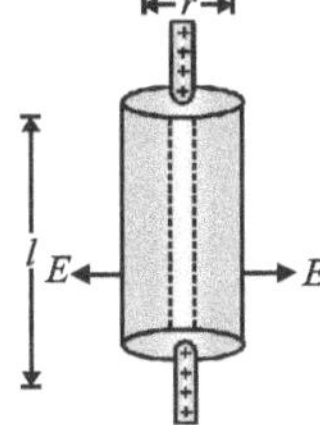

♦ **Electric field due to a plane sheet of charge**

From Gauss's law

$$ES = \frac{q_{in}}{\varepsilon_0}$$

$$\therefore \quad E(2S_0) = \frac{(\sigma)(S_0)}{\varepsilon_0}$$

or, $E = \dfrac{\sigma}{2\varepsilon_0}$

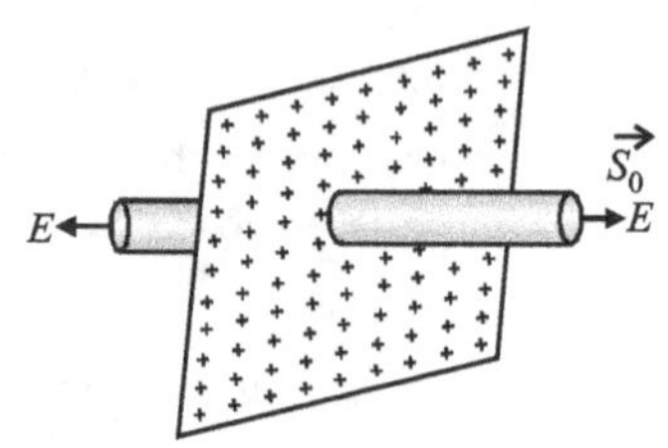

♦ **Electric field near a charged conducting surface**

This is similar to the previous one, the only difference is that this time charges are on both sides. Hence, applying

$$ES = \frac{q_{in}}{\varepsilon_0}$$

Here, $S = 2S_0$ and $q_{in} = (\sigma)(2S_0)$

$$E(2S_0) = \frac{(\sigma)(S_0)}{\varepsilon_0}$$

or, $\qquad E = \dfrac{\sigma}{\varepsilon_0}$

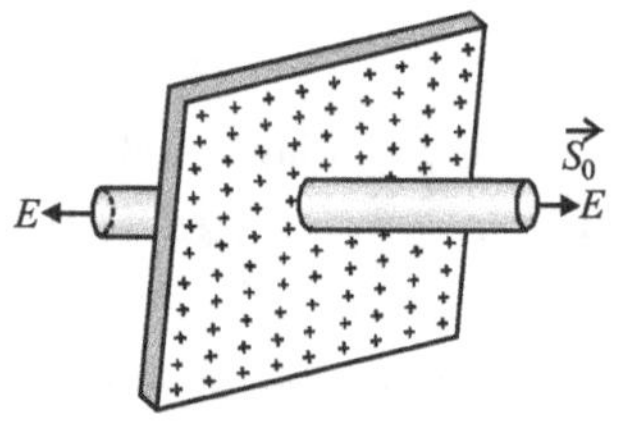

♦ **Electric field due to charged spherical shell or solid conducting sphere :**

Gaussian surface (a sphere) of radius $r > R$,

From Gauss's law $E(4\pi r^2) = \dfrac{q}{\varepsilon_0}$ or, $E = \dfrac{1}{4\pi\varepsilon_0} \dfrac{q}{R^2}$

Hence, the electric field at any external point is the same as if the total charge is concentrated at centre.

At the surface of sphere $r = R$,

$E = \dfrac{1}{4\pi\varepsilon_0} \dfrac{q}{R^2}$ Thus, we can write,

$E_{inside} = 0$

$E_{surface} = \dfrac{1}{4\pi\varepsilon_0} \dfrac{q}{R^2}$; $E_{outside}$

$= \dfrac{1}{4\pi\varepsilon_0} \dfrac{q}{r^2}$

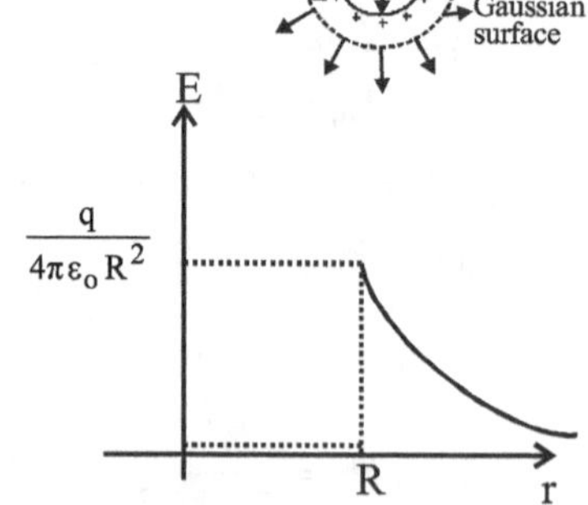

♦ **Electric field due to a uniformly non-conducting sphere:**

Applying Gauss's law, $ES = \dfrac{q_{in}}{\varepsilon_0}$ $\qquad$ ...(i)

Here, $S = 4\pi r^2$ and $q_{in} = (\rho) = \left(\dfrac{4}{3}\pi R^3\right)$

Here, $\rho = $ charge per unit volume $= \dfrac{q}{\dfrac{4}{3}\pi R^3}$

Substituting these values in eq. (i), we have $E = \dfrac{\rho}{\varepsilon_0}\dfrac{R^3}{3r^3}$

Thus, for a uniformly charged solid sphere, we have the following formulae for magnitude of electric field.

$$E_{\text{inside}} = \dfrac{\rho r}{3\varepsilon_0}(r < R)\,;\; E_{\text{surface}} = \dfrac{\rho R}{3\varepsilon_0}(r = R)$$

$$E_{\text{outside}} = \dfrac{\rho}{\varepsilon_0}\dfrac{R^3}{3r^2}(r > R)$$

♦ It shall be noted that due to symetrical charge distribution, direction of electric field is taken as along outword normal.

Also, if we put $r = R$ in the above for E_{inside} or E_{outside}, we get the same result

i.e., $E_{\text{surface}} = \dfrac{\rho}{3\varepsilon_0}.R$

Past Years ONE-LINERS
NEET/JEE Main/Board

♦ Polar molecules have a permanent electric dipole moment.

♦ Surface charge density, $\sigma = \dfrac{Q}{A}$

♦ If the charge on a spherical conductor of radius R is Q, then electric field at distance r from centre is
$E = 0$ (if $r \angle R$)
$$E = \dfrac{1}{4\pi\,\epsilon_0}\dfrac{Q}{r^2}\quad \text{(if } r \geq R)$$

♦ Electric field due to line charge $\vec{E}_1 = \dfrac{\lambda}{2\pi\varepsilon_0 R}\hat{i}\,\text{N/C}$

- From the Coulomb's law, $F = \dfrac{kq_1q_2}{r^2}$

- Time taken to fall a charge particle of mass m and charge q from rest through a vertical distance h in uniform electric field E is $t = \sqrt{\dfrac{2hm}{qE}}$

- The net electrostatic force $(F_E) = \dfrac{1}{4\pi\varepsilon_0}\dfrac{\Delta e^2}{d^2} = \dfrac{Gm^2}{d^2}$

- For two identical charged spheres suspended from a common point by two mass less strings of lengths l, $\tan\theta = \dfrac{F_e}{mg} \simeq \theta$

$$\Rightarrow \quad \frac{kq^2}{x^2 mg} = \frac{x}{2\ell}$$
$$\Rightarrow \quad x^3 \propto q^2$$
$$\Rightarrow \quad x^{3/2} \propto q$$

- Electric Field at the centre of cube
$$\vec{E} = \frac{\theta}{4\pi\varepsilon_0 r}\frac{(\hat{x}+\hat{y}+\hat{z})}{\sqrt{3}}$$

- Electric fields due to two infinite planes $\vec{E}_1 = \dfrac{\sigma}{2\varepsilon_0}\hat{y}$

$$\vec{E}_2 = \frac{\sigma}{2\varepsilon_0}(-\cos 60°\hat{x} - \sin 60°\hat{y})$$

- Force due to charge q and Q separated by a distance d
$$F_1 = \frac{KQQ}{d^2}$$

- Torque experienced by the dipole in an electric field, $\vec{\tau} = \vec{P} \times \vec{E}$

- From Gauss's law
$$\oint_S \vec{E} \cdot \vec{ds} = \frac{Q}{\epsilon_0}$$

- Field lines originate perpendicular from positive charge and terminate perpendicular at negative charge.

Tips/Tricks/Tecchniques ONE-LINERS
(Exam Sample)

- No point charge produces electric field at its own location.
- Electric field intensity at a point on the axial line of electric dipole is double the electric field intensity at a point on the equatorial line of electric dipole *i.e.*, $E_{axial} = 2E_{equatorial}$.
- Electric field always directs from higher potential to lower potential.
- A positive charge in electric field always moves from higher potential to lower potential while a negative charge moves from lower potential to higher potential.
- Coulombs law is valid for point charges and at a distance greater than 10^{-15} m.
- Electric field intensity inside a hollow conducting body is zero.
- Electric field is different at different points on the surface of an irregularly shaped charged conductor.
- It is a false that the path traced by a positive test charge is a field line but actually the path traced by a unit positive test charge represents a field line only when it moves along a straight line.
- Electric field at the centre of a charged ring of radius r is zero. Its value is maximum at a distance $\dfrac{r}{\sqrt{2}}$ on the axis of charged ring.
- The electric field at any point on the surface of a conductor is directly proportional to the surface charge density at that point *i.e*, $E \propto \sigma$.
- Electric field due to dipole $E \propto \dfrac{1}{r^3}$ decreases much rapidly as compared to the field due to point charge $\left(E \propto \dfrac{1}{r^2} \right)$.
- If two charged spheres of radii r_1 and r_2, have surface charege densities δ_1 and δ_2 respectively, then the ratio of electric field on their surfaces will be

$$\frac{E_1}{E_2} = \frac{\sigma_1}{\sigma_2} = \frac{r_2^2}{r_1^2} \quad \left\{ \sigma = \frac{Q}{4\pi r^2} \right\}.$$

- Let an electron of mass m and charge e is moving in a circular path of radius r about infinitely positively charged wire (charge density λ) then the velocity of electron in dynamic equilibrium is given by $v = \sqrt{\dfrac{e\lambda}{2\pi\varepsilon_0 m}}$.

- Electric field intensity due to a point charge q, at a distance $t_1 + t_2$ where t_1 is thickness of medium of dielectric constant K_1 and t_2 is thickness of medium of dielectric constant K_2 is

$$E = \frac{1}{4\pi\varepsilon_0} \frac{Q}{\left(t_1\sqrt{K_1} + t_2\sqrt{K_2}\right)} \, ;$$

- An infinite number of charges, each equal to q are placed along x-axis at x = 1, x = 2, x = 4, x = 8 --------- and so on. Electric field at the point x = 0 due to this set

of charges $\vec{E} = \dfrac{q}{3\pi\varepsilon_0}$

Electric field if in the above set up, the consecutive charges have opposite

sign $\vec{E} = \dfrac{q}{5\pi\varepsilon_0}$.

- Electric field(E) versus distance (r) graph for a charged conducting sphere or cell of charge.

$$E_{in} = 0 \text{ and } V_{in} = \text{constant} = V_s$$

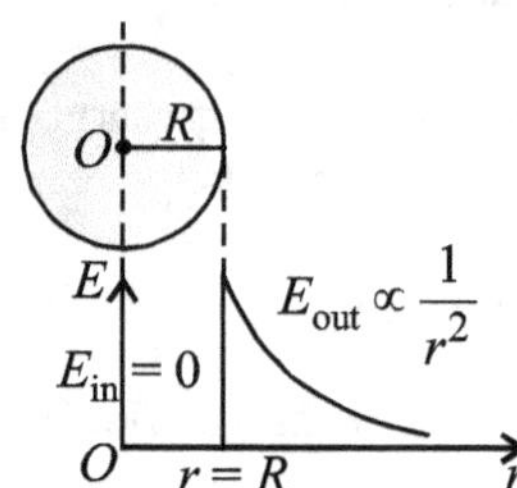

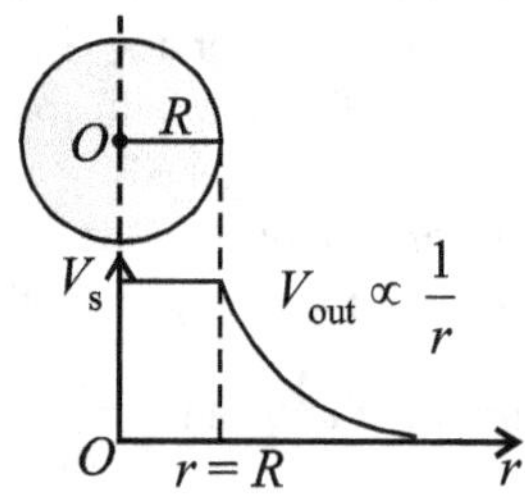

- Electric field (E) versus distance (r) graph for a uniformly charged non-conducting sphere.

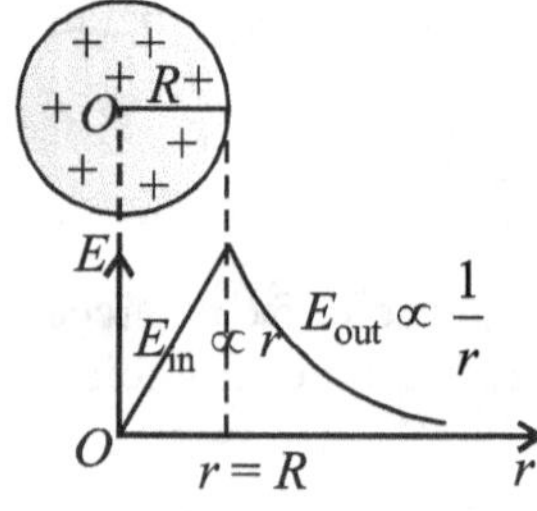

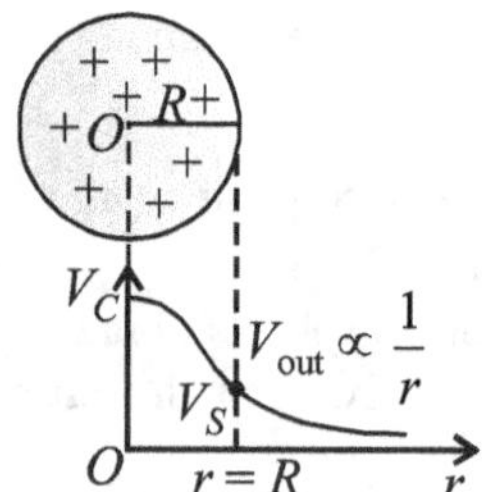

17 Electrostatic Potential and Capacitance

♦ When an external force does work in taking a body from a point to another against a force like spring force or gravitational force, that work gets stored as potential energy of the body.

♦ Consider the field E due to a charge Q placed at the origin. Now, imagine that we bring a test charge q from a point R to a point P.

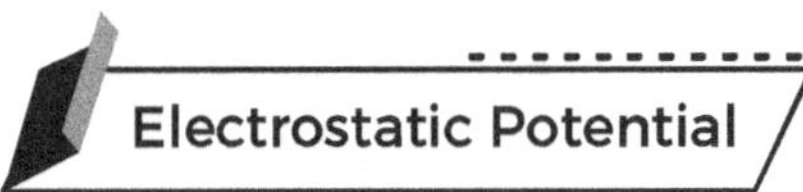

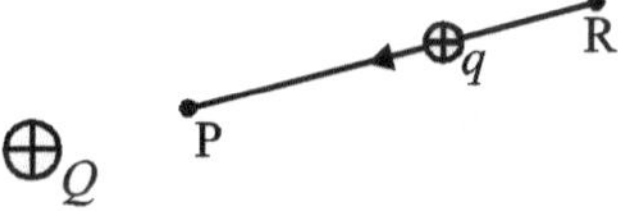

Fig.: A test charge q (> 0) is moved from the point R to the point P against the repulsive force on it by the charge Q (> 0) placed at the origin.

♦ Let us take Q, $q > 0$. We apply an external force F_{ext} just enough to counter the repulsive electric force F_E (i.e, $F_{ext} = -F_E$).

♦ Work done by external forces in moving a charge q from R to P is

$$W_{RP} = \int_R^P F_{ext} \cdot dr = -\int_R^P F_E \cdot dr$$

This work done is against electrostatic repulsive force and gets stored as potential energy.

♦ At every point on electric field, a particle with charge of possesses a certain electrostatic potential energy, this work done increases its potential energy by an amount equal to potential energy difference.

Thus, potential energy difference

$$\Delta U = U_P - U_R = W_{RP}$$

♦ Work done by an electrostatic field is independent of the path taken to go from one point to the other.

♦ If we take the point R at infinity,

$$W_{\infty P} = U_P - U_\infty = U_P$$

♦ Potential energy of charge q at a point is the work done by the external force (equal and opposite to the electric force) in bringing the charge q from infinity to that point.

♦ Work done by external force in bringing a unit positive charge from point R to P

$$= V_P - V_R = \frac{U_P - U_R}{q}$$

where V_P and V_R are the electrostatic potentials at P and R, respectively, we choose the potential to be zero at infinity.

♦ Work done by an external force in bringing a unit positive charge from infinity to a point = electrostatic potential (V) at that point.

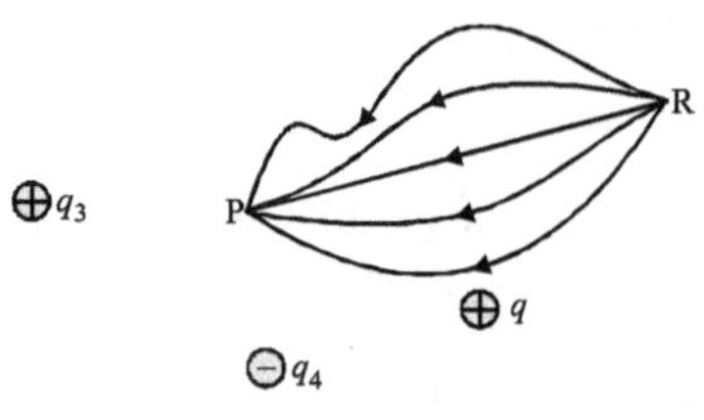

Fig.: Work done on a test charge q by the electrostatic field due to any given charge configuration is independent of the path, and depends only on its initial and final positions.

 **Potential due to a Point Charge**

♦ The potential at a distance r from charge Q due to the charge Q is given by

$$V(r) = \frac{Q}{4\pi\varepsilon_0 r}$$

♦ Figure shows how the electrostatic potential ($\propto 1/r$) and the electrostatic field ($\propto 1/r^2$) varies with r.

 **Potential due to an Electric Dipole**

♦ The electric potential of a dipole is given by

$$V = \frac{1}{4\pi\varepsilon_0}\frac{p \cdot \hat{r}}{r^2} = \frac{1}{4\pi\varepsilon_0}\frac{P\cos\theta}{r^2} \qquad [r >> a]$$

♦ From above Eq. potential on the dipole axis ($\theta = 0, \pi$) is given by

$$V = \pm\frac{1}{4\pi t_0}\frac{p}{r^2}$$

(Positive sign for $\theta = 0$, negative sign for $\theta = \pi$).

♦ The potential in the equatorial plane ($\theta = \pi/2$) is zero.

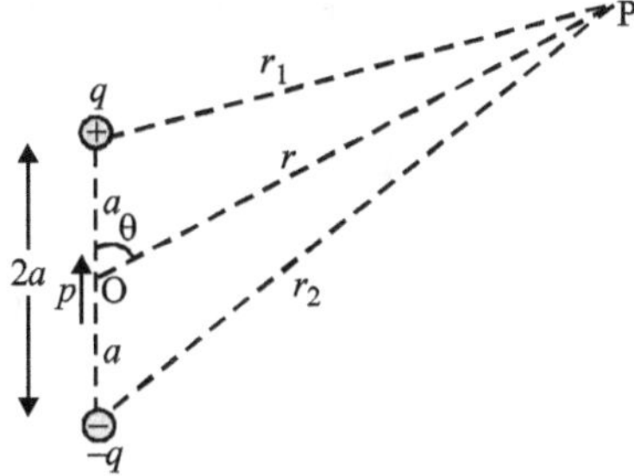

Fig.: Quantities involved in the calculation of potential due to a dipole.

Potential due to a System of Charges

♦ By the superposition principle, the potential V at P due to the total charge configuration is the algebraic sum of the potentials due to the individual charges

$$V = V_1 + V_2 + ... + V_n$$

$$= \frac{1}{4\pi\varepsilon_0}\left(\frac{q_1}{r_{1P}} + \frac{q_2}{r_{2P}} + ... + \frac{q_n}{r_{nP}}\right)$$

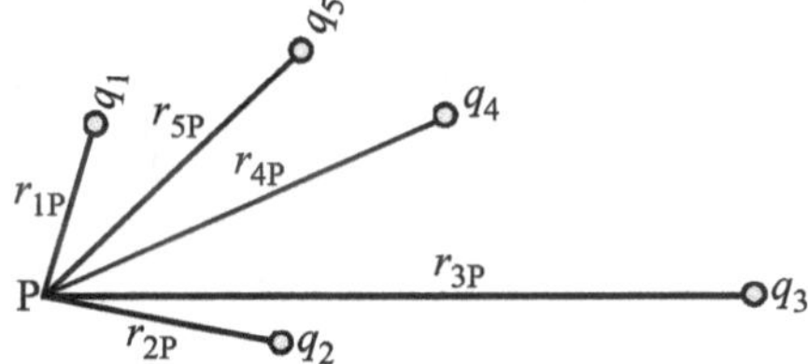

Fig.: Potential at a point due to a system of charges is
the sum of potentials due to individual charges.

Equipotential Surfaces

♦ An equipotential surface is a surface with a constant value of potential at all points on the surface.

♦ For a single charge q, the potential is given by

$$V = \frac{1}{4\pi\varepsilon_0}\frac{q}{r}$$

This shows that V is a constant if r is constant.

♦ The electric field at every point is normal to the equipotential surface passing through that point.

                                                    Physics

- There is no potential difference between any two points on the surface and no work is required to move a test charge on the equipotential surface.

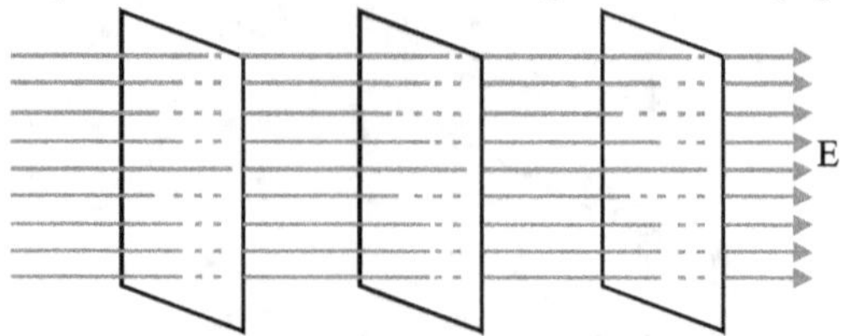

Fig.: Equipotential surfaces for a uniform electric field.

- For a uniform electric field **E**, say, along the x -axis, the equipotential surfaces are planes normal to the x -axis, i.e., planes parallel to the y-z plane.
- Equipotential surfaces for (a) a dipole and (b) two identical positive charges are shown in Fig.

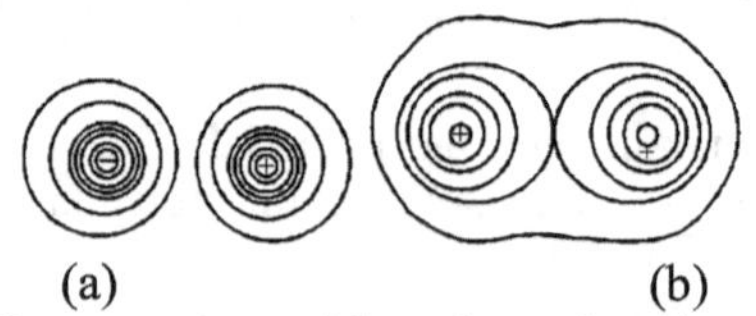

(a)   (b)

Fig.: Some equipotential surfaces for (a) a dipole, (b) two identical positive charges.

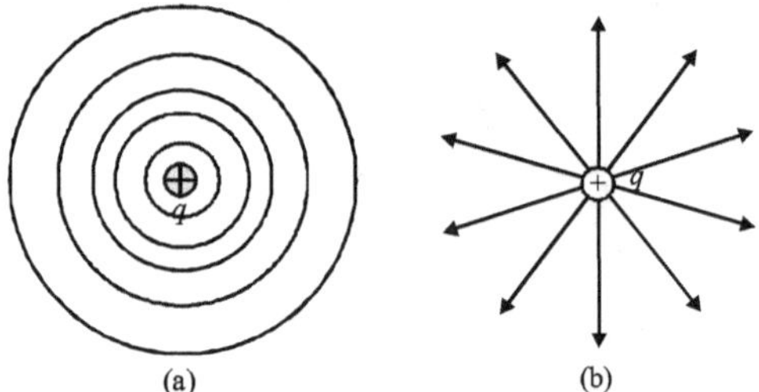

(a)   (b)

Fig.: For a single charge q (a) equipotential surfaces are spherical surfaces centred at the charge, and (b) electric field lines are radial, starting from the charge if $q > 0$.

Relation between Field and Potential

- Consider two closely spaced equipotential surfaces A and B.

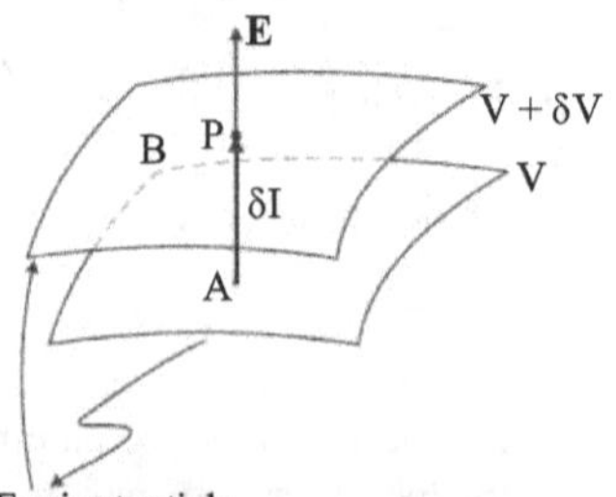

Fig.: From the potential to the field.

Unit positive charge is moved along this perpendicular from the surface B to surface A against the electric field. The work done in this process is $|E|\delta l$. This work equals the potential difference $V_A - V_B$.

Thus,

$$|E|\delta l = V - (V + \delta V) = -\delta V$$

i.e., $|E| = \dfrac{-\delta V}{\delta l}$

Since δV is negative, $\delta V = -|\delta V|$.

$$|E| = --\dfrac{\delta V}{\delta l} = +\dfrac{|\delta V|}{\delta l}$$

- Electric field is in the direction in which the potential decreases steepest.
- Its magnitude is given by the change in the magnitude of potential per unit displacement normal to the equipotential surface at the point.

Potential Energy of a System of Charges

- Consider the simple case of two charges q_1 and q_2 with position vector $\vec{r_1}$ and $\vec{r_2}$.

  We consider the charges q_1 and q_2 initially at infinity.

  Suppose, first the charge q_1 is brought from infinity to the point r_1. There is no external field against which work needs to be done, so work done in bringing q_1 from infinity to $\vec{r_1}$ is zero.

- q_1 produces potential at $\vec{r_2} = \dfrac{1}{4\pi\varepsilon_0}\dfrac{q_1}{r_{12}}$.

- Work done in bringing charge q_2 from infinity to the point $\vec{r_2}$ is q_2 times the potential at $\vec{r_2}$ due to q_1:

  work done on $q_2 = \dfrac{1}{4\pi\varepsilon_0}\dfrac{q_1 q_2}{r_{12}} = $ Potential energy of two point charge i.e.,

$$u = \dfrac{1}{4\pi\varepsilon_0}\dfrac{q_1 q_2}{r_{12}}$$

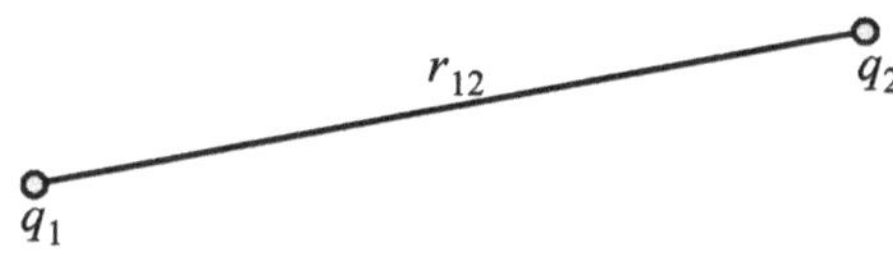

Fig.: Potential energy of a system of charges q_1 and q_2 is directly proportional to the product of charges and inversely to the distance between them.

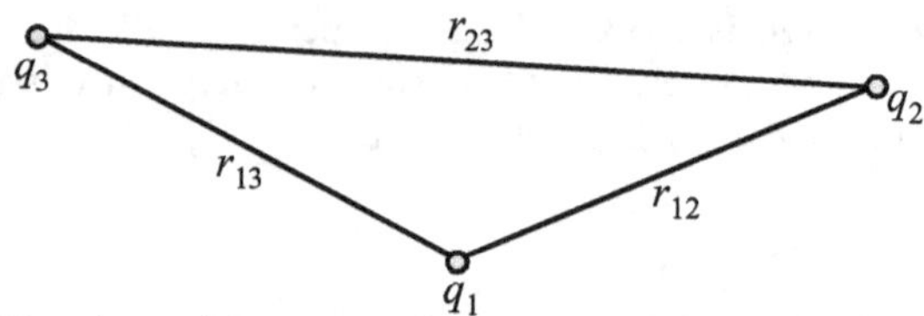

Fig.: Potential energy of a system of three charges is given by U with the notation given in the figure.

$$U = \frac{1}{4\pi\varepsilon_0}\left[\frac{q_1 q_3}{r_{12}} + \frac{q_1 q_2}{r_{12}} + \frac{q_2 q_3}{r_{23}}\right]$$

Potential Energy in an External Field

Potential Energy of a Single Charge

♦ Potential energy of q at $\vec{r}$ in an external field
$= qV(\vec{r})$ or U $= qV$
where $V(\vec{r})$ is the external potential at the point $\vec{r}$.

♦ If an electron with charge $q = e = 1.6 \times 10^{-19}$ C is accelerated by a potential difference of $\Delta V = 1$ volt, it would gain energy of $q\Delta V = 1.6 \times 10^{-19}$J. This unit of energy is defined as 1 **electron volt or 1eV, i.e., 1 eV = 1.6 × 10^{-19}J.** The units based on eV are most commonly used in atomic, nuclear and particle physics, (1 keV = 10^3eV = 1.6×10^{-16}J, 1 MeV = 106eV = 1.6×10^{-13}J.

Potential Energy of a System of Two Charges in an External Field

♦ Assume two charges q_1 and q_2 located at $\vec{r_1}$ and $\vec{r_2}$, respectively, in an external field. First, we calculate the work done in bringing the charge q_1 from infinity to $\vec{r_1}$.

Work done in this step is $q_1 V(\vec{r_1})$. Next, we consider the work done in bringing q_2 to $\vec{r_2}$. In this step, work is done not only against the external field E but also against the field due to q_1.

Work done on q_2 against the external field $= q_2\, V(\vec{r_2})$

Work done on q_2 against the field due to $q_1 = \dfrac{q_1 q_2}{4\pi\varepsilon_0 r_{12}}$

♦ Potential energy of the system = sum of all works

$$= q_1 V(\vec{r_1}) + p_2 V(\vec{r_2}) + \frac{q_1 q_2}{4\pi\varepsilon_0 r_{12}}$$

Potential Energy of a Dipole in an External Field

♦ In a uniform electric field the dipole experiences **no net force but experiences a torque.**

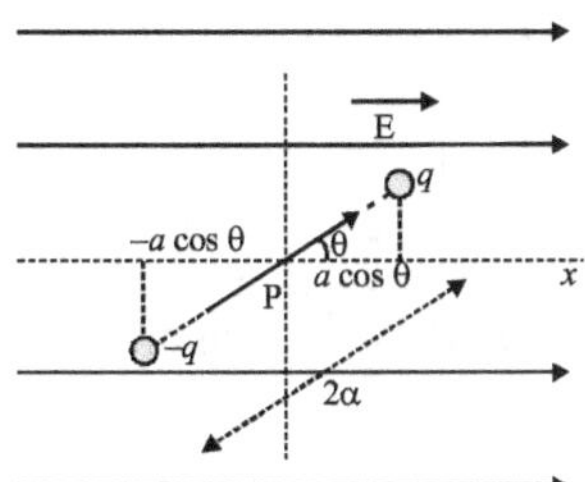

Fig.: Potential energy of a dipole in a uniform external field.

- Torque τ on dipole

$$\vec{\tau} = \vec{P} \times \vec{E}$$

- Work done to rotate from θ_0 to θ_1 is

$$W = \int_{\theta_0}^{\theta_1} \tau_{ext} \, (\theta)d\theta = \int_{\theta_0}^{\theta_1} pE \sin\theta \, d\theta$$
$$= pE \, (\cos\theta_0 - \cos\theta_1)$$

- This work is stored as the potential energy U is taken to be zero at $\theta_0 = \pi/2$.

- $U(\theta) = pE \left[\cos\dfrac{\pi}{2} - \cos\theta\right] = -pE \cos\theta = -\mathbf{p.E}$

Electrostatics of Conductors

- In a metal, the outer shell electrons are free to move within the metal.
- **Inside a conductor, electrostatic field is zero.**
  As long as electric field is not zero, the free charge carriers would experience force and drift.
- In the static situation, the free charges have so distributed themselves that the electric field is zero everywhere inside.
- **At the surface of a charged conductor, electrostatic field must be normal to the surface at every point.**
- If E were not normal to the surface, it would have some non-zero component along the surface. Free charges on the surface of the conductor would then experience force and move.
- In the static situation, therefore, E should have no tangential component.
- **The interior of a conductor can have no excess charge in the static situation.**
  This follows from the Gauss's law. Consider any arbitrary volume element v inside a conductor. On the closed surface S bounding the volume element v, electrostatic field is zero. Thus the total electric flux through S is zero. there is no net charge at any point inside the conductor, and any excess charge must reside at the surface.
- **Electrostatic potential is constant throughout the volume of the conductor and has the same value (as inside) on its surface**
  Since $\mathbf{E} = 0$ inside the conductor and has no tangential component on the surface, no work is done in moving a small test charge. That is, there is no potential difference between any two points inside or on the surface of the conductor.

♦ **Electric field at the surface of a charged conductor**

$$\vec{E} = \frac{\sigma}{\varepsilon_0}\hat{n}$$

where σ is the surface charge density choose a pill box (a short cylinder) as the Gaussian surface as shown in Fig. The pill box is partly inside and partly outside the surface. It has a small area of cross section δS and negligible height.

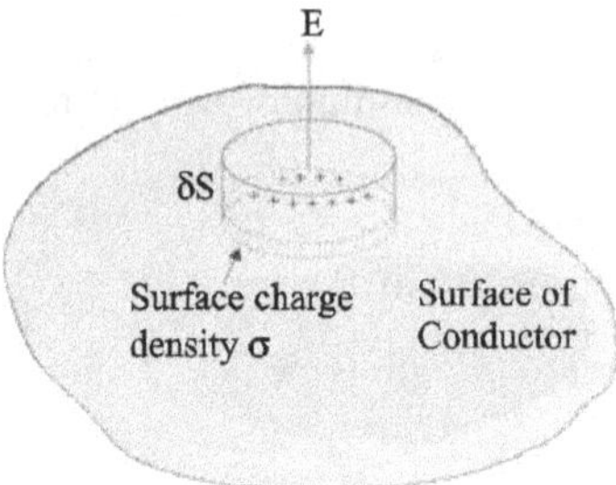

Fig.: The Gaussian surface (a pill box) chosen to derive for electric field at the surface of a charged conductor.

♦ By Gauss's law

$$E\delta S = \frac{|\sigma|\,\delta S}{\varepsilon_0}$$

$$E = \frac{|\sigma|}{\varepsilon_0}$$

♦ For $\sigma > 0$, electric field E is normal to the surface outward. For $\sigma < 0$, E is normal to the surface inward.

Electrostatic shielding

♦ If the conductor is charged or charges are induced on a neutral conductor by an external field, all charges reside only on the outer surface of a conductor with cavity.

♦ Whatever be the charge and field configuration outside, any cavity in a conductor remains shielded from outside electric influence: *the field inside the cavity is always zero.* This is known as *electrostatic shielding.* The effect can be made use of in protecting sensitive instruments from outside electrical influence.

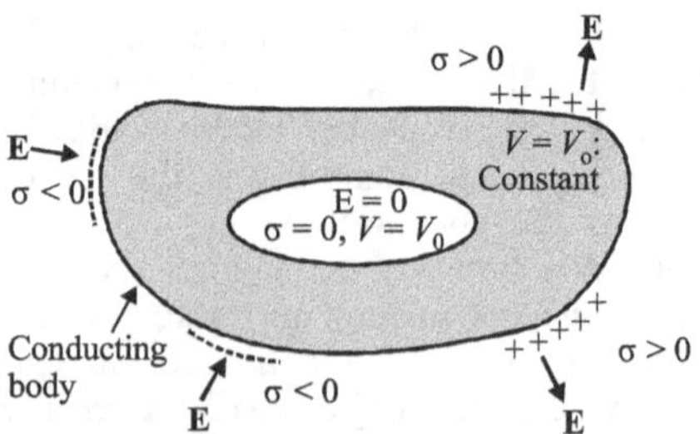

Fig.: The electric field inside a cavity of any conductor is zero.

All charges reside only on the outer surface of a conductor with cavity. (There are no charges placed in the cavity.)

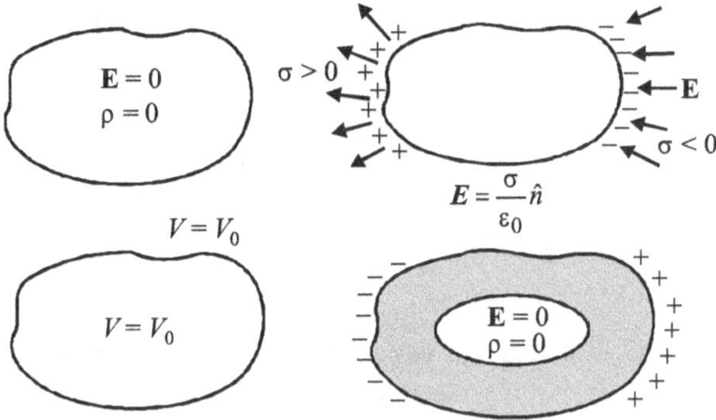

Fig.: Some important electrostatic properties of a conductor.

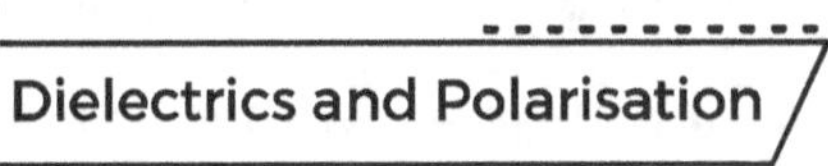

Dielectrics and Polarisation

♦ **Dielectrics** are non-conducting substances. They have no (or negligible number of) charge carriers.

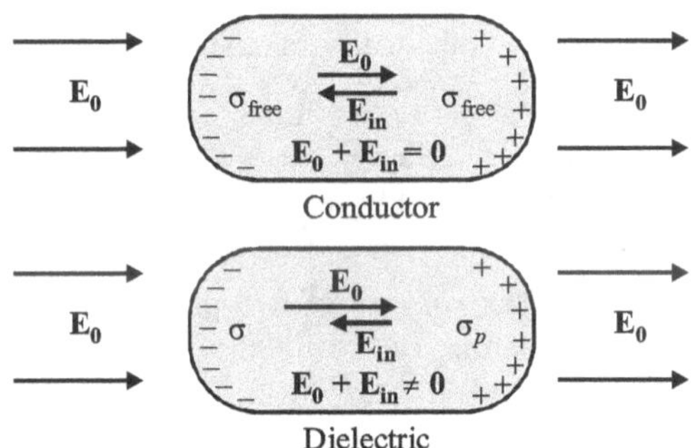

Fig.: Difference in behaviour of a conductor and a dielectric in an external electric field.

♦ In a dielectric, free movement of charges is not possible. The external field induces dipole moment by stretching or re-orienting molecules of the dielectric.

Capacitors and Capacitance

♦ A capacitor is a system of two conductors separated by an insulator. The conductors have charges, say Q_1 and Q_2, and potentials V_1 and V_2. Usually, in practice, the two conductors have charges Q and $-Q$, with potential difference $V = V_1 - V_2$ between them. A single conductor can be used as a capacitor by assuming the other at infinity.

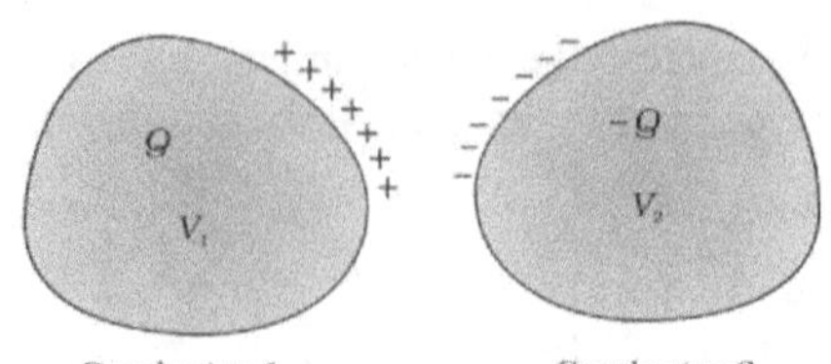

Fig.: A system of two conductors
separated by an insulator forms a capacitor.

◆ V is proportional to Q, and the ratio Q/V is a constant:

$$C = \frac{Q}{V}$$

◆ The constant C is called the **capacitance of the capacitor** is independent of Q or V.

◆ The capacitance C depends only on the geometrical configuration (shape, size, separation) of the system of two conductors.

◆ It also depends on the nature of the insulator (dielectric) separating the two conductors.

The SI unit of capacitance is 1 **farad** ($=1$ coulomb volt^{-1})

◆ The maximum electric field that a dielectric medium can withstand without break-down (of its insulating property) is called its *dielectric strength*; for air it is about 3×10^6 Vm^{-1}.

◆ Capacitance (fixed) is symbolically shownn as ─┤├─ and ─╫─ variable capacitance.

The Parallel Plate Capacitor

◆ A **parallel plate capacitor** consists of two plane parallel conducting plates separated by a small distance. The two plates have charges Q and $-Q$. Plate 1 has surface charge density $\sigma = Q/A$.

◆ The electric field in the inner region between the plates 1 and 2,

$$E = \frac{\sigma}{2\varepsilon_0} + \frac{\sigma}{2\varepsilon_0} = \frac{\sigma}{\varepsilon_0} = \frac{Q}{\varepsilon_0 A}$$

Fig.: The parallel plate capacitor

- The direction of electric field is from the positive to the negative plate.
- Potential difference is

$$V = Ed = \frac{1}{\varepsilon_0}\frac{Qd}{A}$$

- The capacitance C is

$$C = \frac{Q}{V} = \frac{\varepsilon_0 A}{d}$$

Effect of Dielectric on Capacitance

- When there is vacuum between the plates,

$$E_0 = \frac{\sigma}{\varepsilon_0}$$

and the potential difference V_0 is

$$V_0 = E_0 d$$

The capacitance C_0 in this case is

$$C_0 = \frac{Q}{V_0} = \varepsilon_0 \frac{A}{d} \qquad \dots (1)$$

- Consider next a dielectric inserted between the plates. The effect is equivalent two charged sheets with surface charge densities σ_p and $-\sigma_p$. The electric field in the dielectric

$$E = \frac{\sigma - \sigma_p}{\varepsilon_0}$$

so the potential difference across the plates is

$$V = Ed = \frac{\sigma - \sigma_p}{\varepsilon_0}d$$

$$\sigma - \sigma_p = \frac{\sigma}{K}$$

K is a constant of the dielectric. Clearly $K > 1$. We then have

$$V = \frac{\sigma d}{\varepsilon_0 K} = \frac{Qd}{A\varepsilon_0 K}$$

- The capacitance C, is then

$$C = \frac{Q}{V} = \frac{\varepsilon_0 KA}{d} \qquad \dots (2)$$

- The product $\varepsilon_0 K$ is called the permittivity of the medium denoted by E

$$\varepsilon = \varepsilon_0 K$$

For vacuum $K = 1$ and $\varepsilon = \varepsilon_0$; ε_0 is the permittivity of the vacuum.

- The dimensionless ratio

$$K = \frac{\varepsilon}{\varepsilon_0}$$

is called the dielectric constant of the substance. From Eqs. (1) and (2)

$$K = \frac{C}{C_0}$$

Combination of Capacitors

Capacitors in series

♦   In the series combination, charges on the two plates ($\pm Q$) are the same on each capacitor.

♦   The total potential drop V across the combination is the sum of the potential drops V_1 and V_2 across C_1 and C_2, respectively.

♦ $V = V_1 + V_2 = \dfrac{Q}{C_1} + \dfrac{Q}{C_2}$

i.e., $\dfrac{V}{Q} = \dfrac{1}{C_1} + \dfrac{1}{C_2},$ ..... (3)

♦   The effective capacitance of the combination is

$$C = \frac{Q}{V} \qquad ..... (4)$$

♦   We compare Eq. (3) with Eq. (4), and obtain

$$\frac{1}{C} = \frac{1}{C_1} + \frac{1}{C_2}$$

♦   **Effective capacitance of a series combination of n capacitors:**

$$\frac{1}{C} = \frac{1}{C_1} + \frac{1}{C_2} + \frac{1}{C_3} + ... + \frac{1}{C_n}$$

Capacitors in Parallel

♦   The same potential difference is applied across both the capacitors. The plate charges ($\pm Q_1$) on capacitor 1 and the plate charges ($\pm Q_2$) on the capacitor 2 are not necessarily the same:

$Q_1 = C_1 V, Q_2 = C_2 V$

The equivalent capacitor is one with charge

$Q = Q_1 + Q_2$

and potential difference V.

$Q = CV = C_1 V + C_2 V \qquad ..... (5)$

The effective capacitance C is, from Eq. (5),

$C = C_1 + C_2$

- **Effective capacitance C for parallel combination** of n capacitors
$C = C_1 + C_2 + \dots C_n$

Energy Stored in a Capacitor

- Consider the intermediate situation when the conductors 1 and 2 have charges Q' and $-Q'$ respectively. At this stage, the potential difference V' between conductors 1 to 2 is Q'/C. Next imagine that a small charge d Q' is transferred from conductor 2 to 1.

- The total work done (W) is

$$W = \int_0^Q \frac{Q'}{C} \delta Q' = \frac{1}{C} \frac{Q'^2}{2} \Big|_0^Q = \frac{Q^2}{2C}$$

- We can write the final result, in different ways

$$W = \frac{Q^2}{2C} = \frac{1}{2}CV^2 = \frac{1}{2}QV$$

- Consider a parallel plate capacitor. Energy stored in the capacitor

$$= \frac{1}{2}\frac{Q^2}{C} = \frac{(A\sigma)^2}{2} \times \frac{d}{\varepsilon_0 A} \qquad \dots (6)$$

- Also, between plates

$$E = \frac{\sigma}{\varepsilon_0} \qquad \dots (7)$$

- From Eqs. (6) and (7), we get
Energy stored in the capacitor
$U = (1/2)\ \varepsilon_0 E^2 \times Ad$

- Energy density defined as energy stored per unit volume of space,
Energy density of electric field
$u = (1/2)\varepsilon_0 E^2$

Past Years ONE-LINERS NEET/JEE Main/Board

- Energy stored in parallel capacitor $= \dfrac{1}{2}\varepsilon_0 E^2 \times Ad$

- Dipole released from rest moves in the direction of net force.

- Capacitor having same potential on both plates can form the equivalent circuit.

- Potential of a spherical drop $= \dfrac{1}{4\pi\varepsilon_0 R}$.

- Capacitance of a parallel plate capacitor with a dielectric $= \dfrac{K\varepsilon_0 A}{d}$.

- Potential due to dipole at an angle θ, $V = \dfrac{KP\cos\theta}{r^2}$.

- Electric field $(\bar{E}) = -\dfrac{dV}{dr}$, V is potential.

- Charge, $q = CV$

- Force on plates of capacitors is $F = \dfrac{Q^2}{2A}$.

- When a charged isolated capacitor is connected across uncharged identical capacitor, charge is equally shared.

- Work done to move charge q across potential difference V is $W = q\Delta V$.

- When terminals of 2 capacitors are connected charge on capacitors will be proportional to capacitor.

- Final energy in capacitor, $u_f = \dfrac{1}{2}(C_1 + C_2)V_f^{\,2}$.

- $\bar{E} = -\left(\dfrac{\partial V}{\partial x}\hat{i} + \dfrac{\partial V}{\partial y}\hat{j} + \dfrac{\partial V}{\partial z}\hat{k} \right)$.

- Equivalent capacitance in series $\dfrac{1}{C_{eq}} = \dfrac{1}{C_1} + \dfrac{1}{C_2}$.

- Capacitance of an element of thickness $dx = \dfrac{K\varepsilon_0 A}{dx}$.

- Potential energy (U) of q_1, q_2, & q_3 is $\dfrac{Kq_1 q_2}{r_{12}} + \dfrac{Kq_2 q_3}{r_{23}} + \dfrac{Kq_3 q_1}{r_{31}}$.

Tips/Tricks/Tecchniques ONE-LINERS
(Exam Sample)

- The value of electric potential at the centre of the line joining two equal and opposite charge is zero. But, at the centre of the line joining two equal and similar charge, potential is not zero.

- The relation between electric field and potential is given by $E = -\dfrac{dv}{dr}$. This equation suggest that electric potential can exist at a point where the electric field is zero and its vice versa.

- No work is done in moving a charge over any equipotential surface. But work will be done if a charge moves from one equipotential surface to other.

- Capacitance of a parallel plate capacitor does not depend upon the charge given, potential raised or nature of metals and thickness of plates.

- If plates of a parallel plate capacitor (initial seperation d) is moved away with some velocity. Then the rate of change of capacitance with time is proportional to $\dfrac{1}{d^2}$.

- Force of attraction between the plates of a parallel plate capacitor is independent of separation between the plates but varies inversely with area of plates.

- Electrostatic force between the metal plates of an isolated parallel plate capacitor $F_{\text{plate}} = \dfrac{Q^2}{2A\varepsilon_0}$

- Spherical conductor is equivalent to a spherical capacitor if its outer sphere has infinite radius.

- A spherical capacitor behaves as a parallel plate capacitor if its spherical surfaces have large radii and are close to each other.

- Electric field intensity is a vector quantity. Therefore, vector algebra is used for finding resultant electric field intensity. But, electric potential and electric potential energy both are scalar quantity. Therefore, they should be added algebraically only.

- If two spheres having radii R_1 and R_2 and charges Q_1 and Q_2 are joined by a wire, then

  Common potential $V = \dfrac{Q_1 + Q_2}{4\pi\varepsilon_0(R_1 + R_2)}$

  After joining the two spheres with a conducting wire, charges left are

  $Q_1' = \dfrac{(Q_1 + Q_2)R_1}{(R_1 + R_2)}$ and $Q_2' = \dfrac{(Q_1 + Q_2)R_2}{(R_1 + R_2)}$

- If n identical capacitors, each of capacitance C are connected in parallel which are charged to a potential V. If these are separated and connected in series then potential difference of combination will be nV.

- Let n charged drops, each of capacitance C and charge q is charged to potential V. If they are coalesce to form a single drop, then, Total charge = nq, Total capacity = $n^{1/3}C$

♦ A capacitor of capacity C_1 charged to potential V_1 is connected to another capacitor of capacity C_2 and potential V_2. Now if batteries are connected to each other with reverse polarity i.e., positive plate of a capacitor connected to negative plate of other. Then common potential is given by

For numerical calculation we may assume as

$$V = \frac{Q_1 + Q_2}{C_1 + C_2} = \frac{C_1 V_1 - C_2 V_2}{C_1 + C_2}$$

♦ Two plates having unequal area can form capacitor. But, in this case effective overlapping area should be considered.

♦ When a dielectric is placed between the plates of a parallel plate capacitor then it's capacitance increases but potential difference decreases. To maintain the same capacitance and potential difference of capacitor, separation between the plates has to be increased say by 'd'. In such case

$$K = \frac{t}{t - d'}$$

♦ If a parallel plate capacitor area of plate $= A$ separation between the plates $= d$, filled with a dielectric of dielectric constant varies as $k(x) = k(1 + dx)$ then

the capacitance, $C = \dfrac{Ak \in_0}{d}\left(1 + \dfrac{\alpha d}{2}\right)$

18

Current Electricity

Electric Current

♦ Charges in motion constitute an **electric current**. Such currents occur naturally in many situations.

♦ Lightning is one such phenomenon in which charges flow from the clouds to the earth through the atmosphere, sometimes with disastrous results. The flow of charges in lightning is not steady.

♦ The current at time t across the cross-section of the conductor is defined as the value of the ratio of ΔQ to Δt in the limit of Δt tending to zero,

$$I(t) \equiv \lim_{\Delta t \to 0} \frac{\Delta q}{\Delta t}$$

♦ In SI units, the unit of current is **ampere (A)**.

Electric Currents in Conductors

♦ In atoms and molecules, the negatively charged electrons and the positively charged nuclei are bound to each other and are thus not free to move.

♦ In solid conductors, the atoms are tightly bound to each other so that the current is carried by the negatively charged electrons.

♦ In electrolytic solutions positive and negative charges both can move.

♦ When no electric field is present, the electrons will be moving due to thermal motion during which they collide with the fixed ions. An electron colliding with an ion emerges with the same speed as before the collision.

♦ The direction of its velocity after the collision is completely random. At a given time, there is no preferential direction for the velocities of the electrons. Thus on the average, the number of electrons travelling in any direction will be equal to the number of electrons travelling in the opposite direction. So, there will be no net electric current.

♦ When charges $+Q$ and $-Q$ put at the ends of a metallic conductor of radius R. Electric drift takes place to neutralise the charge. So, there will be current due to motion of electrons. The supply of charges is done by cells or batteries.

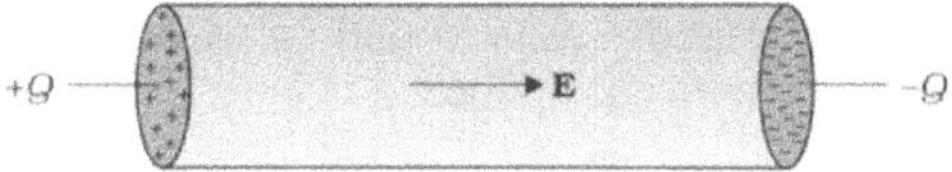

Fig.: Charges $+Q$ and $-Q$ put at the ends of a metallic cylinder.

The electrons will drift because of the electric field created to neutralise the charges. The current thus will stop after a while unless the charges $+Q$ and $-Q$ are continuously replenished.

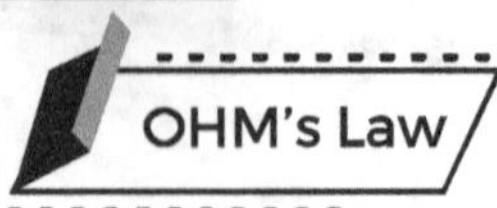

OHM's Law

- Imagine a conductor through which a current I is flowing and V be the potential difference between the ends of the conductor. Then **Ohm's law** states that
$$V \propto I$$
or, $V = R I$
where the constant of proportionality R is called the **resistance** of the conductor.

- The SI units of resistance is **ohm**, and is denoted by the symbol Ω. The *resistance R* not only *depends on the material of the conductor* but *also on the dimensions of the conductor.*

- Doubling the length of a conductor doubles the resistance. In general resistance is proportional to length,
$R \propto l$

- Halving the area of the cross-section of a conductor doubles the resistance. In general, then the resistance R is inversely proportional to the cross-sectional area,
$$R \propto \frac{1}{A}$$

- For a given conductor
$$R = \rho \frac{l}{A}$$
where the constant of proportionality ρ depends on the material of the conductor but not on its dimensions. ρ is called **resistivity or specific resistance**.

- Current per unit area (taken normal to the current), I/A, is called **current density** and is denoted by j.
$$j = \frac{I}{A}$$
or, $E = j \rho$

- The current density, (which we have defined as the current through unit area **normal** to the current) is also directed along $\mathbf{E}$, and is also a vector $\mathbf{j}$ ($\equiv j\,\mathbf{E}/E$).
$$\mathbf{E} = \mathbf{j}\rho$$
or, $\mathbf{j} = \sigma \mathbf{E}$
where $\sigma \equiv 1/\rho$ is called the **conductivity**.

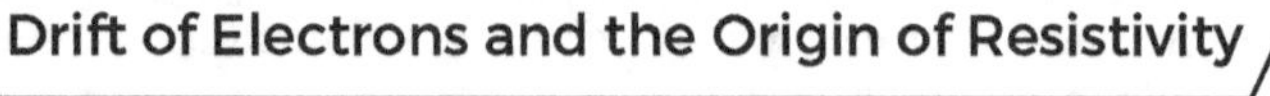

Drift of Electrons and the Origin of Resistivity

- An electron will suffer collisions with the heavy fixed ions, but after collision, it will emerge with the same speed but in random directions. If we consider all the electrons, their average velocity will be zero since their directions are random. Thus, if there are N electrons and the velocity of the ith electron ($i = 1, 2, 3, \ldots N$) at a given time is v_i, then
$$(v_i)_{\text{average}} = \frac{1}{N}\sum_{i=1}^{N} V_i = 0$$

- Average time between two successive collisions is called **relaxation time** τ. Using $v = u + t$ at over the N-electrons at any given time t gives the average velocity $\mathbf{v_d}$ called **drift velocity**.

$$v_d = (v_i)_{\text{average}} - \frac{eE}{m}(t_i)_{\text{average}} \qquad \left(\because a = \frac{-eE}{m} \right)$$

$$= 0 - \frac{eE}{m}\tau = -\frac{eE}{m}\tau$$

- By definition $\mathbf{I}$ is related to the magnitude $|\mathbf{j}|$ of the current density by $I = |\mathbf{j}|A$

$$|\mathbf{j}| = \frac{\mathbf{ne}^2}{\mathbf{m}}\tau|\mathbf{E}|$$

$$\because \mathbf{j} = \sigma\mathbf{E} \qquad \therefore \sigma = \frac{ne^2}{m}\tau$$

Mobility

- Mobility μ defined as the magnitude of the drift velocity per unit electric field:

$$\mu = \frac{|\mathbf{v}_d|}{E}$$

$$\because \quad v_d = \frac{e\tau E}{m}$$

$$\therefore \quad \mu = \frac{v_d}{E} = \frac{e\tau}{m}$$

where τ is the average collision time for electrons.

- The SI unit of mobility is m^2/Vs and practical unit is $cm^2V^{-1}s^{-1}$. Mobility is positive.

Limitations of OHM's Law

- There do exist materials and devices used in electric circuits where the proportionality of V and I does not hold. The deviations broadly are one or more of the following types:

(a) V ceases to be proportional to I.

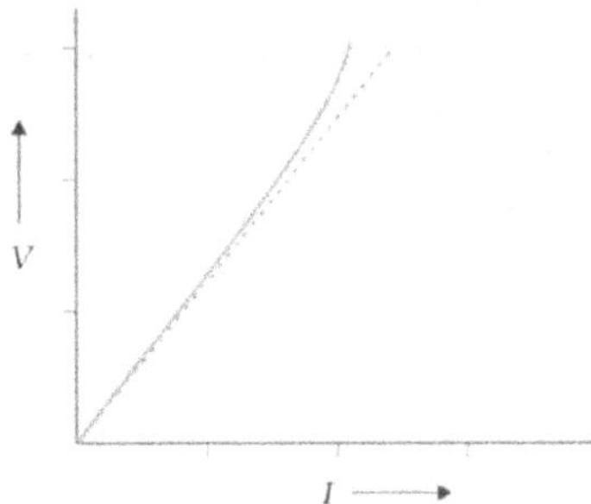

Fig.: The dashed line represents the linear Ohm's law. The solid line is the voltage V versus current I for a good conductor.

(b) The relation between V and I depends on the sign of V. This happens in a diode.

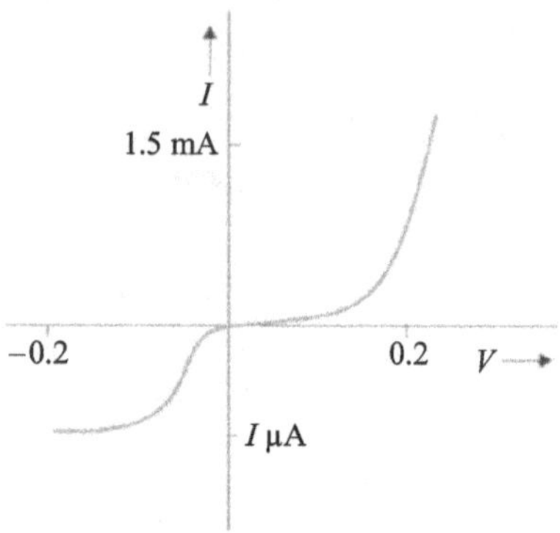

Fig.: Characteristic curve of a diode. Note the different scales for negative and positive values of the voltage and current.

(c) The relation between V and I is not unique, i.e., there is more than one value of V for the same current I. A material exhibiting such behaviour is GaAs.

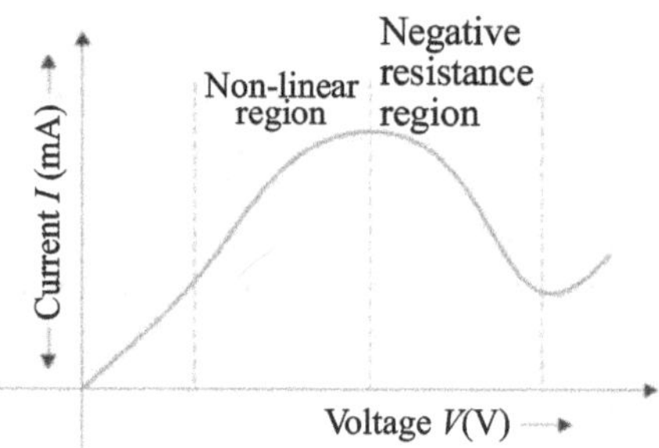

Fig.: Variation of current versus voltage for GaAs.

Resistivity of Various Materials

- The materials are classified as conductors, semiconductors and insulators depending on their resistivities, in an increasing order of their values.
- Metals have low resistivities in the **range of 10^{-8} Ωm to 10^{-6} Ωm**.
- Insulators like ceramic, rubber and plastics having resistivities 10^{18} times greater than metals or more.
- Semiconductors have resistivities characteristically decreasing with a rise in temperature. The resistivities of semiconductors can be decreased by adding small amount of suitable impurities.
- Commercially produced resistors for domestic use or in laboratories are of two major types: wire bound resistors and carbon resistors.
- **Wire bound** resistors are made by winding the wires of an alloy, viz., manganin, constantan, nichrome or similar ones.
- The choice of these materials is dictated mostly by the fact that their resistivities are relatively insensitive to temperature.

♦ Resistors in the higher range are made mostly from carbon. **Carbon resistors** are compact, inexpensive and thus find extensive use in electronic circuits. Carbon resistors are small in size and hence their values are given using a colour code.

Table: Resistor Colour Codes

Colour	Number	Multiplier	Tolerance (%)
Black	0	1	
Brown	1	10^1	
Red	2	10^2	
Orange	3	10^3	
Yellow	4	10^4	
Green	5	10^5	
Blue	6	10^6	
Violet	7	10^7	
Gray	8	10^8	
White	9	10^9	
Gold		10^{-1}	5
Silver		10^{-2}	10
No colour			20

♦ The first two bands from the end indicate the first two significant figures of the resistance in ohms. The third band indicates the decimal multiplier.

♦ The last band stands for tolerance or possible variation in percentage about the indicated values. Sometimes, this last band is absent and that indicates a tolerance of 20%.

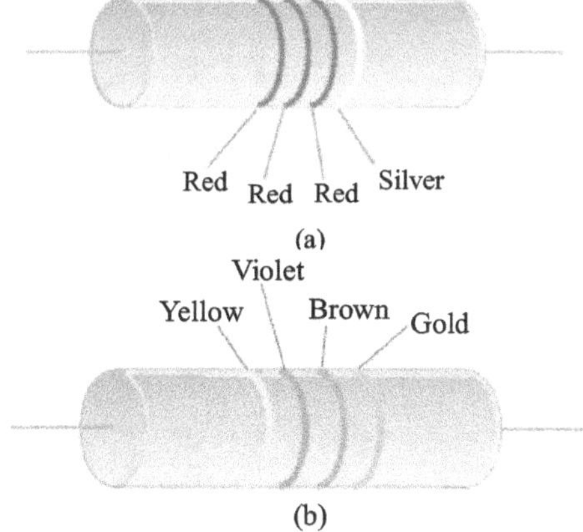

Fig.: Colour coded resistors
(a) $(22 \times 10^2 \text{ W}) \pm 10\%$, (b) $(47 \times 10 \text{ W}) \pm 5\%$.

♦ For example, if the four colours are orange, blue, yellow and gold, the resistance value is $36 \times 10^4 \ \Omega$, with a tolerence value of 5%.

Temperature Dependence of Resistivity

- The resistivity of a material is found to be dependent on the temperature. Different materials do not exhibit the same dependence on temperatures.

- The resistivity of a metallic conductor is approximately given by,

$$\rho_T = \rho_0 \left[1 + \alpha (T - T_0)\right]$$

where ρ_T is the resistivity at a temperature T and ρ_0 is the same at a reference temperature T_0. α is called the temperature co-efficient of resistivity.

- For metals, α is positive.

- Graph of ρ_T plotted against T would be a straight line. At temperatures much lower than 0°C, the graph, however, deviates considerably from a straight line.

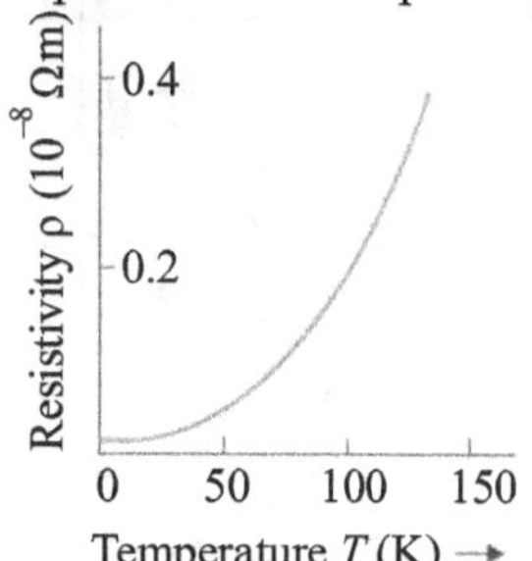

Fig.: Resistivity ρ_T of copper as a function of temperature T.

- Some materials like Nichrome (which is an alloy of nickel, iron and chromium) exhibit a very weak dependence of resistivity with temperature. Manganin and constantan have similar properties. These materials are thus widely used in wire bound standard resistors since their resistance values would change very little with temperatures.

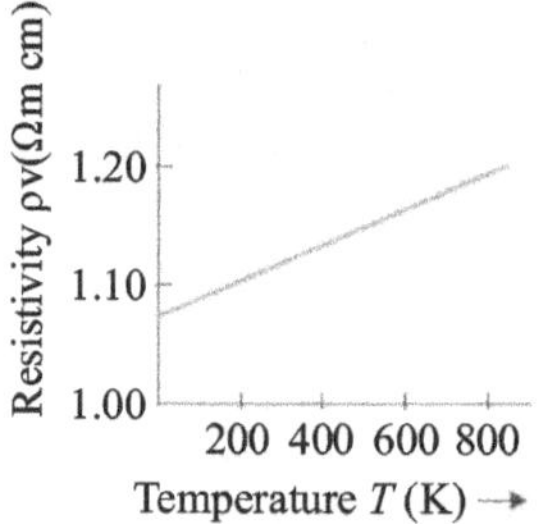

Fig.: Resistivity ρ_T of nichrome as a function of absolute temperature T.

- Unlike metals, the resistivities of semiconductors decrease with increasing temperatures.

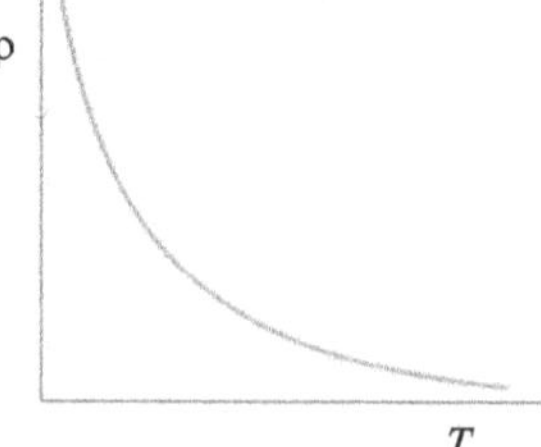

Fig.: Temperature dependence of resistivity for a typical semiconductor.

- Resistivity of a material is given by

$$\rho = \frac{1}{\sigma} = \frac{m}{ne^2\tau}$$

ρ thus depends inversely both on the number n of free electrons per unit volume and on the average time τ between collisions. As we increase temperature, average speed of the electrons, which act as the carriers of current, increases resulting in more frequent collisions. The average time of collisions τ, thus decreases with temperature.

♦ In a metal, n is not dependent on temperature to any appreciable extent and thus the decrease in the value of τ with rise in temperature causes ρ to increase as we have observed.

♦ For insulators and semiconductors, however, n increases with temperature. This increase more than compensates any decrease in τ, so that for such materials, ρ decreases with temperature.

Electrical Energy, Power

♦ The energy dissipated per unit time is the power dissipated $P = \Delta W/\Delta t = P = IV$

♦ $P = I^2 R = V^2/R$ is called the power loss in a conductor of resistance R carrying a current I.
Since, $V = IR$ **OHM's law.**

Combination of Resistors – Series and Parallel

♦ Two **resistors** are said to be **in series** if only one of their end points is joined. If a third resistor is joined with the series combination of the two, then all three are said to be in series. Clearly, we can extend this definition to series combination of any number of resistors.

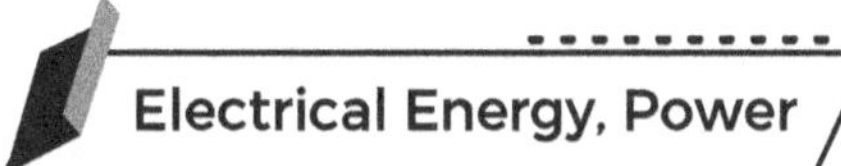

Fig.: A series combination of three resistors R_1, R_2, R_3.

♦ Two or more **resistors** are said to be **in parallel** if one end of all the resistors is joined together and similarly the other ends joined together

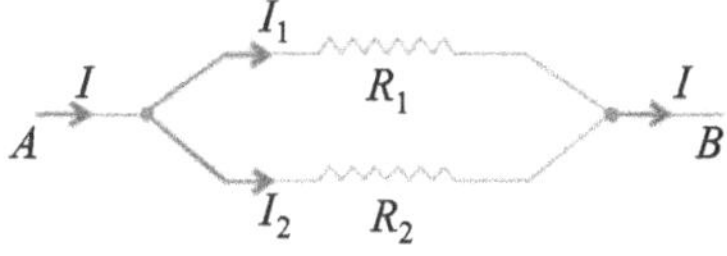

Fig.: Two resistors R_1 and R_2 connected in parallel.

♦ The equivalent resistance of series combination of any number n of resistors $R_1, R_2 ....., R_n$ is $R_{eq} = R_1 + R_2 + ... + R_n$

♦ The equivalent resistance of n resistors $R_1, R_2 . . ., R_n$ in parallel combination is

$$\frac{1}{R_{eq}} = \frac{1}{R_1} + \frac{1}{R_2} + ... + \frac{1}{R_n}$$

Cells, EMF, Internal Resistance

- Simple device to maintain a steady current in an electric circuit is the electrolytic cell.
- The electrolyte through which a current flows has a finite resistance r, called the *internal resistance*.
- emf ε is the potential difference between the positive and negative electrodes in an open circuit, i.e., when no current is flowing through the cell.

$$V = \varepsilon - Ir$$

  From OHM's law

$$V = IR$$

$$\therefore \quad IR = \varepsilon - Ir$$

$$\Rightarrow \quad I = \frac{\varepsilon}{R + r}$$

- The actual values of the internal resistances of cells vary from cell to cell. The internal resistance of dry cells, however, is much higher than the common electrolytic cells.
- The maximum current that can be drawn from a cell is for $R = 0$ and it is $I_{max} = \varepsilon/r$. However, in most cells the maximum allowed current is much lower than this to prevent permanent damage to the cell.

Cells in Series and in Parallel

- Two cells are said to be in series where one terminal of the two cells is joined together leaving the other terminal in either cell free. ε_1, ε_2 are the emf's of the two cells and r_1, r_2 their internal resistances, respectively.

$$\varepsilon_{eq} = \varepsilon_1 + \varepsilon_2$$
$$\text{and } r_{eq} = r_1 + r_2$$

Fig.: Two cells of emf's ε_1 and ε_2 in the series r_1, r_2 are their internal resistances. For connections across A and C, the combination can be considered as one cell of emf ε_{eq} and an internal resistance r_{eq}.

- If two cells of emf ε_1 and ε_2 and of internal resistances r_1 and r_2 respectively, connected in parallel, the combination is equivalent to a single cell of emf ε_{eq} and internal resistance r_{eq}, such that

$$\frac{1}{r_{eq}} = \frac{1}{r_1} + \frac{1}{r_2}$$

$$\frac{\varepsilon_{eq}}{r_{eq}} = \frac{\varepsilon_1}{r_1} + \frac{\varepsilon_2}{r_2}$$

Fig.: Two cells in parallel. For connections across A and C, the combination can be replaced by one cell of emf ε_{eq} and internal resistances r_{eq}.

Kirchhoff's Rules

- **Kirchhoff's rules**, are very useful for analysis of electric circuits.
- **Junction rule:** *At any junction, the sum of the currents entering the junction is equal to the sum of currents leaving the junction.*
- This rule is based on conservation of change.
- **Loop rule:** *The algebraic sum of charges in potential around any closed loop involving resistors and cells in the loop is zero.*
- This rule is based on conservation of energy.

Wheatstone Bridge

- **Wheatstone Bridge** is an application of Kirchhoff's rules. The circuit shown in fig. is called the Wheatstone bridge. The bridge has four resistors R_1, R_2, R_3 and R_4 then

- The equation relating the four resistors is called the balance condition for the galvanometer to give zero or null deflection.

$$\frac{R_2}{R_1} = \frac{R_4}{R_3}$$

- The Wheatstone bridge and its balance condition provide a practical method for determination of an unknown resistance.

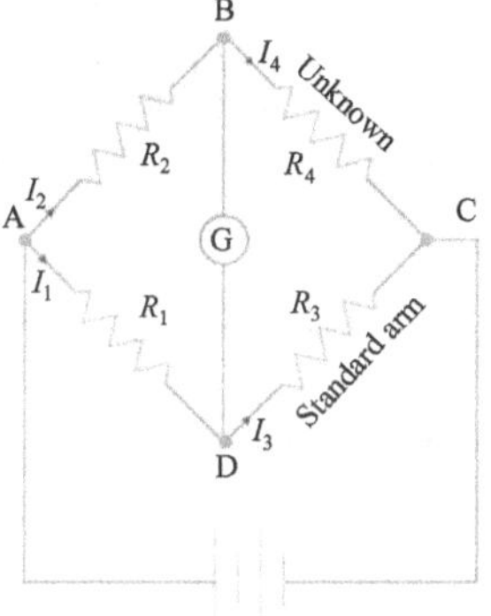

Fig.: Wheatstone Bridge

Meter Bridge

- A practical device using the principle of wheatstone bridge is called **meter bridge**.
- Meter bridge consists of a wire of length 1 m and of uniform cross sectional area stretched taut and clamped between two thick metallic strips bent at right angles, as shown.

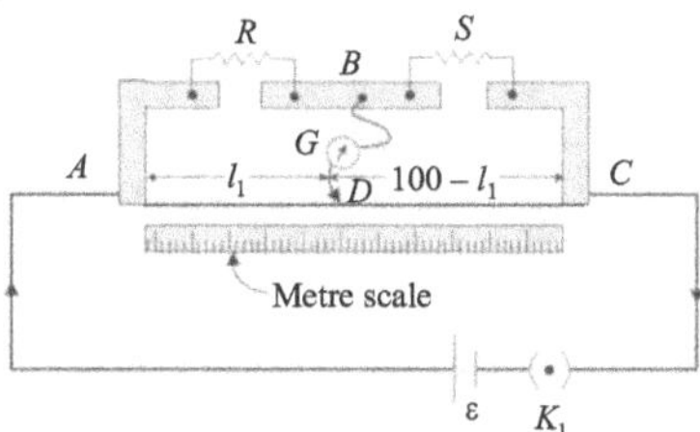

Fig.: A meter bridge. Wire AC is 1 m long. R is a resistance to be measured and S is a standard resistance.

♦ The balance condition of meter bridge gives

$$\frac{R}{S} = \frac{R_{cm}l_1}{R_{cm}(100-l_1)} = \frac{l_1}{100-l_1}$$

Thus, once we have found out l_1, the unknown resistance R is known in terms of the standard known resistance S by

$$R = S\frac{l_1}{100-l_1}$$

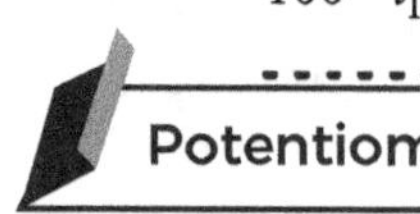

Potentiometer

♦ This is a versatile instrument. It is basically a long piece of uniform wire, sometimes a few meters in length across which a standard cell (B) is connected.

♦ In actual design, the wire is sometimes cut in several pieces placed side by side and connected at the ends by thick metal strip.

♦ Since the wire is uniform, the potential difference between A and any point at a distance l from A is

$$\varepsilon(l) = \phi l$$

where ϕ is the potential drop per unit length.

Application of Potentiometer

♦ An application of the potentiometer is to compare the emf of two cells of emf ε_1 and ε_2.

$$\frac{\varepsilon_1}{\varepsilon_2} = \frac{l_1}{l_2}$$

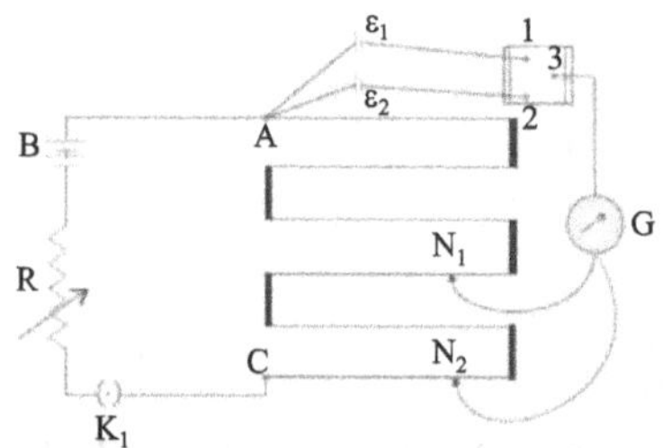

Fig.: Circuit for comparing emfs of two cells

Internal resistance, $r = \dfrac{\varepsilon - v}{I} = \left(\dfrac{\varepsilon - v}{v}\right)R \Rightarrow r = R\left(\dfrac{l_1}{l_2} - 1\right)$

NEET/JEE Main ONE-LINERS
(Past Years NEET/JEE Main Questions)

♦ Drift velocity, $V_d = \dfrac{eE\tau}{m}$, Electrical resistivity $= \dfrac{m}{ne^2\rho}$

♦ Equivalent resistance of four wire of resistance R in parallel combination, $R_{eq} = \dfrac{R}{4}$

- In potentiometer circuit, for comparing emf of two cells, $\dfrac{E_1}{E_2} = \dfrac{\ell_1}{\ell_2}$

- In parallel combination, potential across each resistors is same.

- According to colour coding -

Yellow	Violet	Brown	Gold
4	7	1	5%

- For metals like copper, at temperature much lower than $0°C$, graph deviates considerably from a straight line.

- For metals temperature coefficient of resistance is positive while for insulators and semiconductors, temperature coefficient of resistance is negative.

- Mobility, $\mu = \dfrac{V_d}{E}$

  From the balancing condition of metre bridge $\dfrac{R_1}{R_2} = \dfrac{l_1}{l_2}$

- Fuse is a circuit protection device

- Resistance for ideal voltmeter $= \infty$ resistance for ideal ammeter $= 0$

- Power in parallel combination, $P = \dfrac{V^2}{R}$

- In series grouping equivalent resistance $R_{series} = nR$

  In parallel grouping equivalent resistance $R_{parallel} = \dfrac{R}{n}$

- Short circuited current, $I = \dfrac{n\varepsilon}{nr} = \dfrac{\varepsilon}{r}$

  $(47 \pm 4.7)\, k\Omega = 47 \times 10^3 \pm 10\%$

  $\therefore$ Yellow - Violet - Orange - Silver

- Reading of potentiometer is accurate because during taking reading it does not draw any current from the circuit.

- Resistance, $R = \dfrac{\rho\ell}{A} \Rightarrow R = \dfrac{\rho\ell^2}{\text{Volume}} \Rightarrow R \propto \ell^2$

- For potentrometer circuit, $\dfrac{E_1 + E_2}{E_1 - E_2} = \dfrac{\ell_1}{\ell_2}$

- Heat, $H = \int\limits_0^t i^2 R\, dt$

- EMF, $E = Kl$ where $K = \dfrac{V}{L}$ potential gradient

- Potential difference, $V = E - Ir$

  Current, $I = \dfrac{V}{Req}$

- Resistance in parallel combination, $\dfrac{1}{R_p} = \dfrac{1}{R_1} + \dfrac{1}{R_2} + \cdots$

- Resistance in series combination, $R_{eq} = R_1 + R_2 + \ldots$

- Charge, $q = CV$

- Using formula, internal resistance, $r = \left(\dfrac{l_1 - l_2}{l_2}\right) s$

Tips/Tricks/Tecchniques ONE-LINERS
(Exam Sample)

- The drift velocity of electrons is small due to frequent collisions suffered by electrons.
- Electric field is zero inside a charged conductor, but it is non zero inside a current carrying conductor and is given by $E = \dfrac{V}{l}$ where V = potential difference across the conductor.
- Fuse acts as a circuits protection device.
- If length of wire is increased by n times then resistance will increase by n^2 times *i.e.*, $|R_2 = n^2 R_1|$. Similarly if radius of wire is reduced to $\dfrac{1}{n}$ times then area of cross-section will decrease $\dfrac{1}{n^2}$ times so the resistance becomes n^4 times *i.e.*, $R_2 = n^4 R_1$.
- If length of a conductor increases by x% then resistance will increase by 2x % (valid only if 2x < 10%) but its resistivity remains unchanged.
- If we have n conductor, each of equal resistance, the number of possible combinations is 2^{n-1}.
- If we have n conductors, each of different resistance then the number of possible combinations will be 2^n.
- If a wire of resistance R, is cut into n equal parts and then these parts are collected to form a bundle then resistance of combination formed will be $\dfrac{R}{n^2}$.
- If two resistance of R_1 and R_2 are connected first in series and then in parallel. If R_s and R_p are their equivalent resistance in series and parallel combination respectively then

$$R_1 = \frac{1}{2}\left[R_s + \sqrt{R_s^2 - 4R_s R_p} \right] \text{ and}$$

$$R_2 = \frac{1}{2}\left[R_s + \sqrt{R_s^2 - 4R_s R_p} \right]$$

- If in the series combination of n identical cells (each having emf E and internal resistance r) if x cells are wrongly connected then equivalent emf will be $E_{eq} = (n - 2x)E$ and equivalent internal resistance will be $r_{eq} = nr$.
- Consider the parallel combination of two cells having emf E_1 and E_2 respectively, if they are connected with reversed polarity then equivalent emf is given by

$$E_{eq} = \frac{E_1 r_2 - E_2 r_1}{r_1 + r_2}$$

- Thus, power consumed by a n equal resistors in parallel combination is n^2 times that of power consumed in series combination if V remains same.
- Short circuited current, $I = \dfrac{n\varepsilon}{nr} = \dfrac{\varepsilon}{R}$ *i.e.*, I is independent of n $I\|n$.
- Kirchhoff's junction rule is based on conservation of charge and the outgoing currents add up and are equal to incoming current at a junction. Bending or reorienting the wire does not change the validity of Kirchhoff's junction rule.

19 Moving Charges and Magnetism

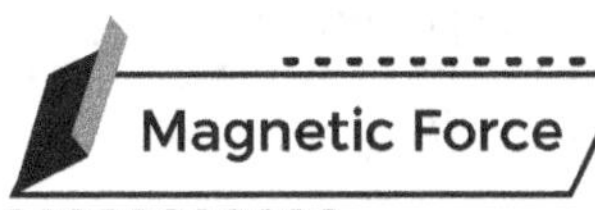

Magnetic Force

- Hans Christian Oersted noticed that a current in a straight wire caused a noticeable deflection in a nearby magnetic compass needle. He found that the alignment of the needle is tangential to an imaginary circle which has the straight wire as its centre and has its plane perpendicular to the wire.
- A current or a field (electric or magnetic) emerging out of the plane of the paper is depicted by a dot (•). A current or a field going into the plane of the paper is depicted by a cross ($\otimes$).

Magnetic Field, Lorentz Force

- A point charge q (moving with a velocity **v** and, located at **r** at a given time t) in presence of both the electric field **E (r)** and the magnetic field **B(r)**. The force on an electric charge q due to both of them can be written as
$$\mathbf{F} = q\,[\mathbf{E(r)} + \mathbf{v} \times \mathbf{B(r)}] \equiv \mathbf{F}_{electric} + \mathbf{F}_{magnetic}$$
This force is called **Lorentz force**.
- It depends on q, **v** and **B** (charge of the particle, the velocity and the magnetic field). *Force on a negative charge is opposite to that on a positive charge.*
- The force acts in a (sideways) direction perpendicular to both the velocity and the magnetic field. Its direction is given by the **screw rule** or **right hand rule** for vector (or cross) product.

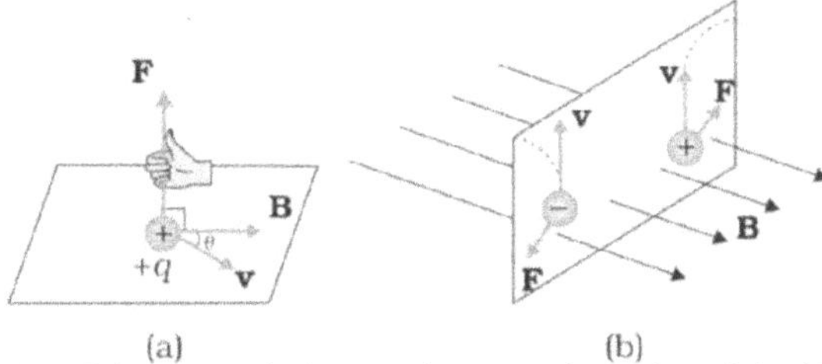

Fig.: The direction of the magnetic force acting on a charged particle. (a) The force on a positively charged particle with velocity **v** and making an angle θ with the magnetic field **B** is given by the right-hand rule. (b) A moving charged particle q is deflected in an opposite sense to $-q$ in the presence of magnetic field.

- $[B] = [F/qv]$ and the unit of **B** are Newton second / (coulomb metre). This unit is called tesla (T).

Magnetic Force on a Current-carrying Conductor

Force on current carrying conductor
$$\mathbf{F} = [(nq\,\mathbf{v}_d)lA] \times \mathbf{B} = [\,\mathbf{j}Al] \times \mathbf{B}$$
$$= I\mathbf{l} \times \mathbf{B}$$

Motion in a Magnetic Field

- In the case of motion of a charge in a magnetic field, the magnetic force is perpendicular to the velocity of the particle. So no work is done and no change in the magnitude of the velocity is produced.
- **Motion of a charged particle in a uniform magnetic field:**
  First consider the case of **v** perpendicular to **B**. The perpendicular force, q **v** × **B**, acts as a centripetal force and produces a circular motion perpendicular to the magnetic field. *The particle will describe a circle if* **v** *and* **B** *are perpendicular to each other.*

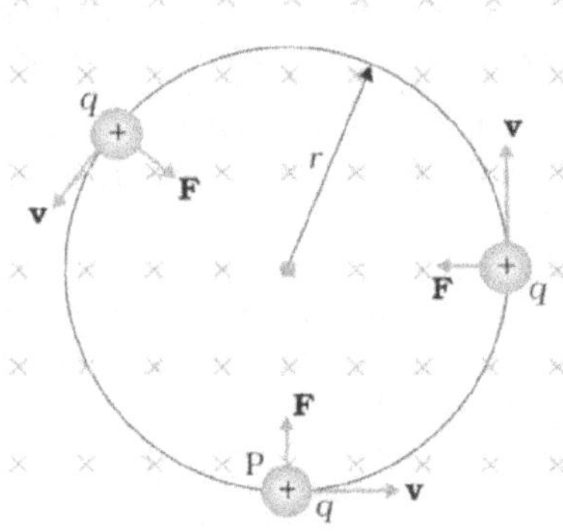

Fig.: Circular motion

- If velocity has a component along **B**, this component remains unchanged as the motion along the magnetic field will not be affected by the magnetic field. The motion in a plane perpendicular to **B** is as before a circular one, thereby producing a *helical motion*.

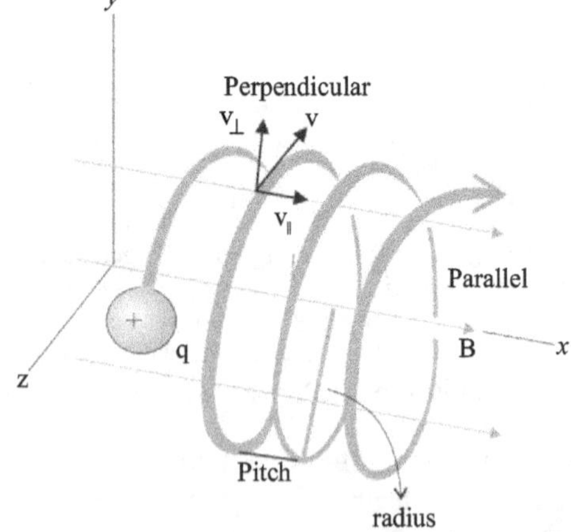

Fig.: Helical motion

- If the velocity **v** is perpendicular to the magnetic field **B,** the magnetic force is perpendicular to both **v** and **B** and acts like a centripetal force. It has a magnitude $q\,v\,B$. Equating the two expressions for centripetal force,

$$\frac{mv^2}{r} = qvB$$

$$\Rightarrow \quad r = m\,v\,/\,qB \qquad\qquad ..... \text{(i)}$$

- The larger the momentum, the larger is the radius and bigger the circle described.

- If ω is the angular frequency, then
$v = \omega\,r.$ So,
$\omega = 2\pi\,v = q\,B/\,m$
which is independent of the velocity or energy .

- The time taken for one revolution is $T = 2\pi/\omega = 1/n$.

- If there is a component of the velocity parallel to the magnetic field (denoted by $v_{\parallel}$), it will make the particle move along the field and the path of the particle would be a helical one.

- The distance moved along the magnetic field in one rotation is called pitch p.
$p = v_{\parallel}T = 2\pi m\,v_{\parallel}\,/\,qB$
The radius of the circular component of motion is called the *radius of the helix.*

Motion in Combined Electric and Magnetic Fields

Velocity Selector

- Consider the case when $\overline{E}, \overline{B}\ \&\ \overline{v}$ are perpendicular to each other as shown in figure.
When the value of **E** and **B** such that magnitudes of the two forces are equal. Then, total force on the charge is zero and the charge will move in the fields undeflected. This happens when,

$$qE = qvB \text{ or } v = \frac{E}{B}$$

- This condition can be used to select charged particles of a particular velocity out of a beam containing charges moving with different speeds (irrespective of their charge and mass). The crossed E and B fields, therefore, serve as a **velocity selector.**

Cyclotron

- The **cyclotron** is a machine to accelerate charged particles or ions to high energies. It was invented by E.O. Lawrence and M.S. Livingston in 1934 to investigate nuclear structure.

♦ The cyclotron uses both electric and magnetic fields in combination to increase the energy of charged particles. As the fields are perpendicular to each other they are called *crossed fields*.

♦ Cyclotron uses the fact that the frequency of revolution of the charged particle in a magnetic field is independent of its energy.

♦ The period of revolution, is given by

$$T = \frac{1}{v_c} = \frac{2\pi m}{qB} \text{ or } v_c = \frac{qB}{2\pi m}$$

This frequency is called the *cyclotron frequency* for obvious reasons and is denoted by v_c.

♦ Radius of circular path, $R = \dfrac{mv}{qB}$

♦ The frequency v_a of the applied voltage is adjusted so that the polarity of the dees is reversed in the same time that it takes the ions to complete one half of the revolution. The requirement $v_a = v_c$ is called the *resonance condition*.

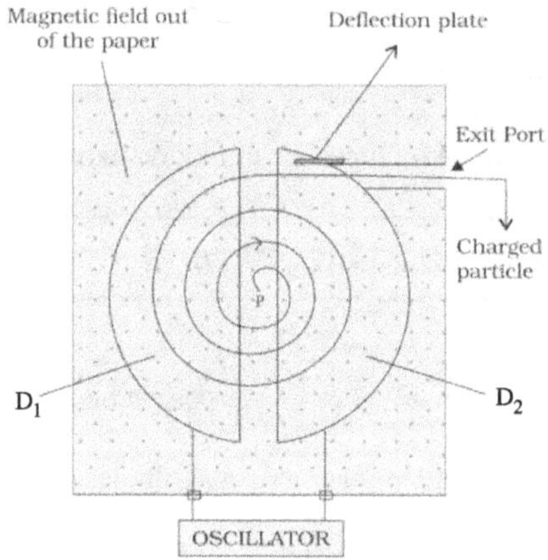

Fig.: A schematic sketch of the cyclotron. There is a source of charged particles or ions at P which move in a circular fashion in the dees, D_1 and D_2, on account of a uniform perpendicular magnetic field B. An alternating voltage source accelerates these ions to high speeds. The ions are eventually 'extracted' at the exit port.

♦ The kinetic energy of the ions is,

$$\frac{1}{2}mv^2 = \frac{q^2B^2R^2}{2m}$$

♦ The operation of the cyclotron is based on the fact that the time for one revolution of an ion is independent of its speed or radius of its orbit. The cyclotron is used to bombard nuclei with energetic particles.

Magnetic Field due to a Current Element, Biot-Savart's Law

♦ According to **Biot-Savart's law**, the magnitude of the magnetic field dB is proportional to the current I, the element length |dl|, and inversely proportional to the square of the distance r. Its direction is perpendicular to the plane containing dl and **r**. Thus, in vector notation,

$$\overrightarrow{dB} \propto \frac{I\,d\,\boldsymbol{l}\times\boldsymbol{r}}{r^3} = \frac{\mu_0}{4\pi}\frac{I\,d\,\boldsymbol{l}\times\boldsymbol{r}}{r^3}$$

where $\mu_0/4\pi$ is a constant of proportionality. The above expression holds when the medium is vacuum. The magnitude of this field is,

$$|dB| = \frac{\mu_0}{4\pi}\frac{I\,dl\,\sin\theta}{r^2}$$

- The proportionality constant in SI units has the exact value,

$$\frac{\mu_0}{4\pi} = 10^{-7}\ \text{Tm/A}$$

We call μ_0 the *permeability* of free space (or vacuum).

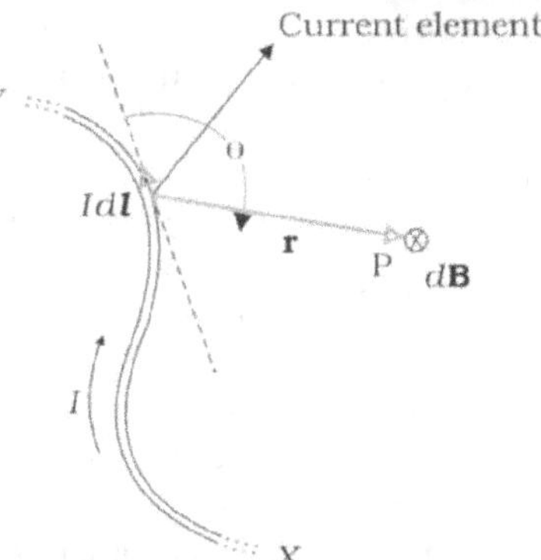

Fig.: Illustration of the Biot-Savart law. The current element I dl produces a field dB at a distance r. The $\otimes$ sign indicates that the field is perpendicular to the plane of this page and directed into it.

Magnetic Field on the Axis of a Circular Current Loop

- The magnetic field on the axis at a point P due to entire current carrying circular loop is

$$\mathbf{B} = B_x\,\hat{i} = \frac{\mu_0 I\,R^2}{2(x^2 + R^2)^{3/2}}\,i$$

At the centre of the loop $x = 0$, and we obtain,

$$\mathbf{B}_0 = \frac{m_0 I}{2R}\,i$$

where, $m = IA$

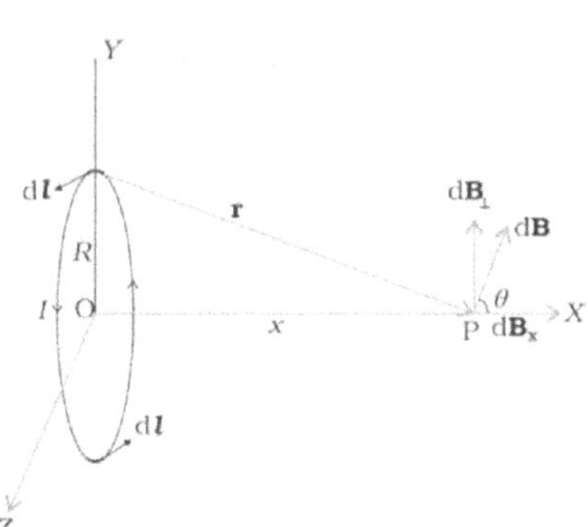

Fig.: Magnetic field on the axis of a current carrying circular loop of radius R. Shown are the magnetic field dB (due to a line element dl) and its components along and perpendicular to the axis.

- The magnetic field lines due to a circular wire form closed loops. The direction of the magnetic field is given by (another) **right-hand thumb rule** stated below:

Curl the palm of your right hand around the circular wire with the fingers pointing in the direction of the current. The right-hand thumb gives the direction of the magnetic field.

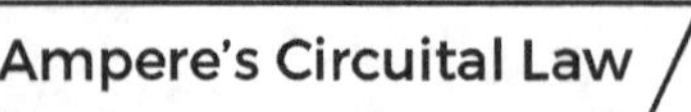

Ampere's Circuital Law

- It gives another method to calculate the magnetic field due to a given current distribution.
- Line integral of the magnetic field $\vec{B}$ around any close curve is μ_0 times the net current I through the area enclosed by the curve.

$$\oint \mathbf{B}.dl = \mu_0 I$$

where I is the total current through the surface. The integral is taken over the closed loop coinciding with the boundary C of the surface. The relation above involves a sign-convention, given by the right-hand rule.

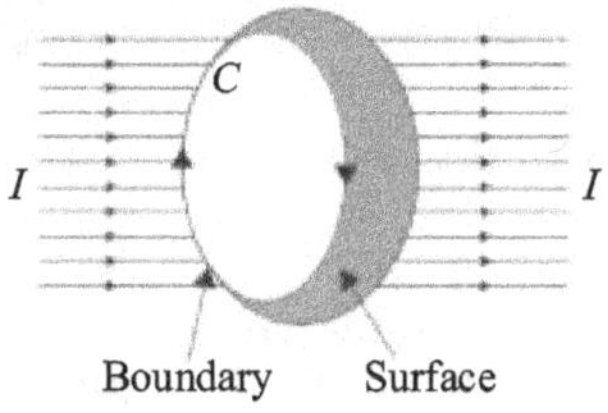

The Solenoid and the Toroid

The Solenoid

- By long **solenoid** we mean that the solenoid's length is large compared to its radius.
- It consists of a long wire wound in the form of a helix where the neighbouring turns are closely spaced. So each turn can be regarded as a circular loop.
- The net magnetic field is the vector sum of the fields due to all the turns. Enamelled wires are used for winding so that turns are insulated from each other.

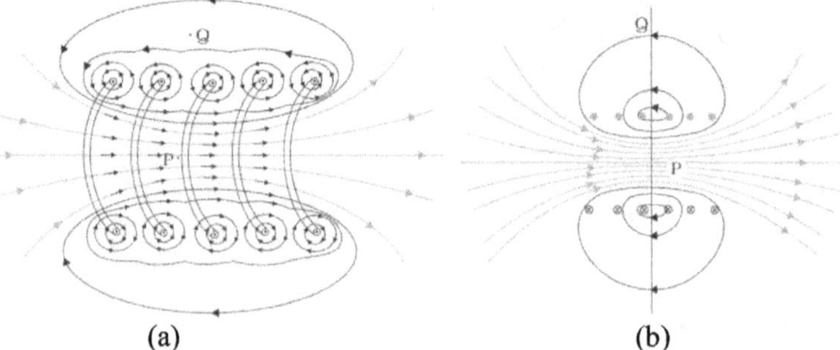

Fig.: (a) The magnetic field due to a section of the solenoid which has been stretched out for clarity. Only the exterior semi-circular part is shown. Notice how the circular loops between neighbouring turns tend to cancel. (b) The magnetic field of a finite solenoid.

- **Magnetic field due to solenoid :** Let n be the number of turns per unit length, then the total number of turns is nh. In loop abcd, the enclosed current is, $I_e = I\,(n\,h)$, where I is the current in the solenoid. From Ampere's circuital law

$$BL = \mu_0 I_e, \quad B h = \mu_0 I (n h)$$
$$B = \mu_0 n I$$

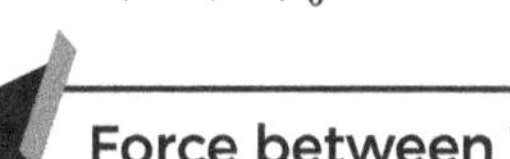

Fig.: The magnetic field of a very long solenoid. We consider a rectangular Amperian loop abcd to determine the field.

♦ The direction of the field is given by the right-hand rule.

The Toroid

♦ The **toroid** is a hollow circular ring on which a large number of turns of a wire are closely wound. It can be viewed as a solenoid which has been bent into a circular shape to close on itself.

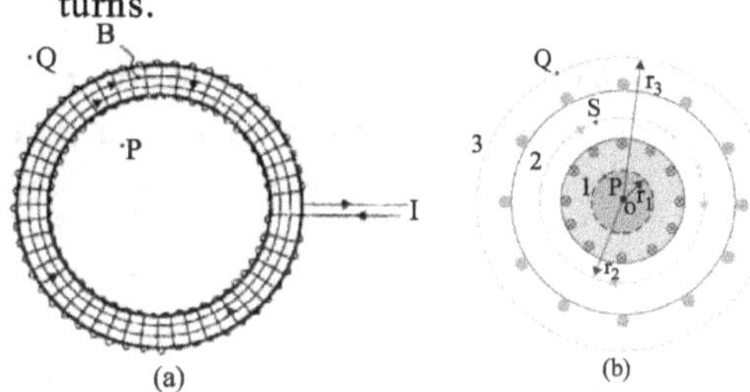

♦ The field **B** inside the toroid is constant in magnitude for the ideal toroid of closely wound turns.

Fig.: (a) A toroid carrying a current I. (b) A sectional view of the toroid. The magnetic field can be obtained at an arbitrary distance r from the centre O of the toroid by Ampere's circuital law. The dashed lines labelled 1, 2 and 3 are three circular Amperian loops.

♦ **Magnetic field due to toroid :** Applying Ampere's law a long S we find, $L = 2\pi r$. The current enclosed I_e is (for N turns of toroidal coil) $N I$.

$$B (2\pi r) = \mu_0 NI \Rightarrow B = \frac{\mu_0 NI}{2\pi r}$$

Force between Two Parallel Currents, the Ampere

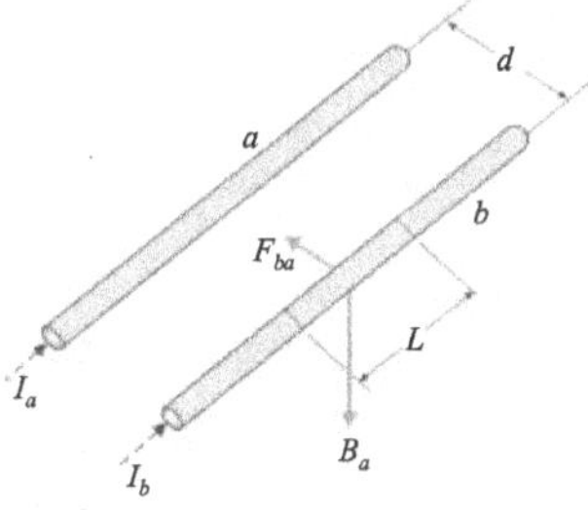

Fig.: Two long straight parallel conductors carrying steady currents I_a and I_b and separated by a distance d. B_a is the magnetic field set up by conductor 'a' at conductor 'b'.

♦ Force $\mathbf{F}_{ab}$, on a segment of length L of 'a' due to the current in 'b' is equal in magnitude to $\mathbf{F}_{ba}$, and directed towards 'b'. Thus,
$$\mathbf{F}_{ba} = -\mathbf{F}_{ab}$$

♦ *Parallel currents attract, and antiparallel currents repel.*

♦ Let f_{ba} represent the magnitude of the force $\mathbf{F}_{ba}$ per unit length. Then,
$$f_{ba} = \frac{\mu_0 I_a I_b}{2\pi d}$$

♦ The *ampere* is the value of that steady current which, when maintained in each of the two very long, straight, parallel conductors of negligible cross-section, and placed one metre apart in vacuum, would produce on each of these conductors a force equal to 2×10^{-7} newtons per metre of length.

Torque on Current Loop, Magnetic Dipole

Torque on a Rectangular Current Loop in a Uniform Magnetic Field

♦ A rectangular loop carrying a steady current I and placed in a uniform magnetic field experiences a torque. It does not experience a net force.

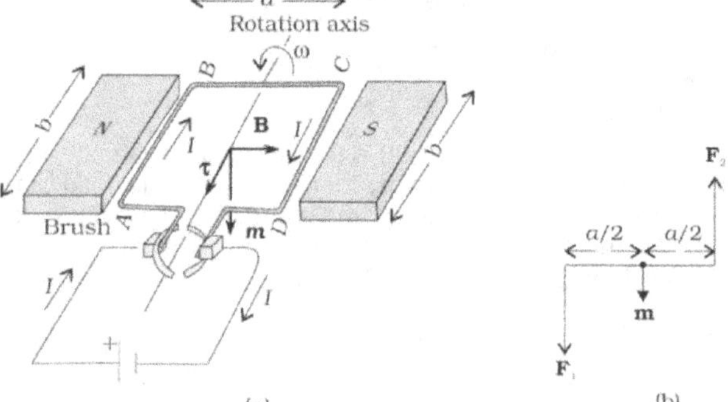

Fig.: (a) A rectangular current-carrying coil in uniform magnetic field. The magnetic moment **m** points downwards. The torque τ is along the axis and tends to rotate the coil anticlockwise. (b) The couple acting on the coil.

♦ The magnetic moment of the current loop is
$$\mathbf{m} = I\mathbf{A}$$
where the direction of the area vector **A** is given by the right-hand thumb rule and is directed into the plane of the paper. Then as the angle between **m** and **B** is θ,
$$\boldsymbol{\tau} = \mathbf{m} \times \mathbf{B}$$
This is analogous to the electrostatic case $\boldsymbol{\tau} = \mathbf{P}_e \times \mathbf{E}$

♦ If the loop has N closely wound turns, the expression for torque, still holds, with
$$\mathbf{m} = NI\mathbf{A}$$

The Magnetic Dipole Moment of a Revolving Electron

♦ In the Bohr model of hydrogen-like atoms, the negatively charged electron is revolving with uniform speed around a centrally placed positively charged $(+Z\,e)$ nucleus. The uniform circular motion of the electron constitutes a current. The direction of the magnetic moment is into the plane of the paper and is indicated separately by $\otimes$.

$$\mu_1 = \frac{e}{2m_e}(m_e vr) = \frac{e}{2m_e}l$$

Magnetic moment of electron,
Here, l is the magnitude of the angular momentum of the electron about the central nucleus ("orbital" angular momentum). Vectorially,

$$\mu_1 = -\frac{e}{2m_e}l.$$

- The negative sign indicates that the angular momentum of the electron is opposite in direction to the magnetic moment.

- Instead of electron with charge ($-e$), if we had taken a particle with charge ($+q$), the angular momentum and magnetic moment would be in the same direction. The ratio

$$\frac{\mu_1}{l} = \frac{e}{2m_e}$$

is called the *gyromagnetic ratio* and is a constant. Its value is 8.8×10^{10} C/kg for an electron, which has been verified by experiments.

The Moving Coil Galvanometer

- The galvanometer consists of a coil with many turns free to rotate about a fixed axis. There is a cylindrical soft iron core which not only makes the field radial but also increases the strength of the magnetic field.

- The deflection ϕ is indicated on the scale by a pointer attached to the spring. We have

$$\phi = \left(\frac{NAB}{k}\right)I$$

The quantity in brackets is a constant for a given galvanometer.

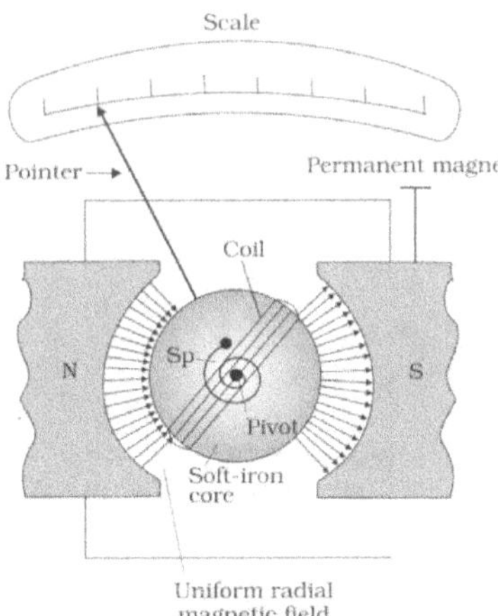

Fig.: The moving coil galvanometer. Depending on the requirement, this device can be used as a current detector or for measuring the value of the current (ammeter) or voltage (voltmeter).

- The galvanometer cannot as such be used as an ammeter to measure the value of the current in a given circuit. This is for two reasons: (i) Galvanometer is a very sensitive device, it gives a full-scale deflection for a current of the order of μA. (ii) For measuring currents, the galvanometer has to be connected in series, and as it has a large resistance, this will change the value of the current in the circuit.

- To overcome these difficulties, one attaches a small resistance r_s, called *shunt resistance,* in parallel with the galvanometer coil; so that most of the current passes through the shunt. The resistance of this arrangement is,
$$R_G\, r_s\,/\,(R_G + r_s) = r_s \ \ \text{if } R_G \gg r_s$$

- We define the *current sensitivity of the galvanometer as the deflection per unit current.*
$$\frac{\phi}{I} = \frac{NAB}{k}$$

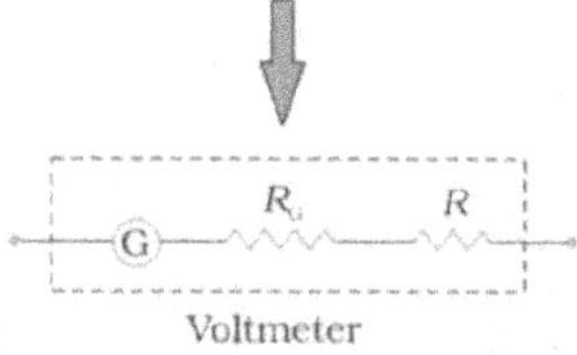

Ammeter

Fig.: Conversion of a galvanometer (G) to an ammeter by the introduction of a shunt resistance r_s of very small value in parallel.

- Resistance of voltmeter is $R_G + R$ R : large
Voltage sensitivity is defined as the deflection per unit voltage.
$$\frac{\phi}{v} = \left(\frac{NAB}{k}\right)\frac{I}{v} = \left(\frac{NAB}{k}\right)\frac{1}{R}$$

Voltmeter

Fig.: Conversion of a galvanometer (G) to a voltmeter by the introduction of a resistance R of large value in series.

Past Years ONE-LINERS
NEET/JEE Main/Board

- Magnetic dipole moment $= IA$.
- Lorentz force $= q(\overline{v}\times \overline{B})$.

- Magnetic field inside a thick wire $\propto r$ where r is distance from centre.

- Magnetic field at r distance from wire $= \dfrac{\mu_0 i}{2\pi r}$.

- Magnetic field inside solenoid is $\mu_0 ni$.
- Magnetic field inside thick wire $B_{in} \propto r$.

  Magnetic field outside thick wire $B_{out} \propto \dfrac{1}{r}$

- Force per unit length between two parallel wire $= \dfrac{\mu_0 i_1 i_2}{2\pi d}$.

- Magnetic field inside thick wire is $\dfrac{\mu_0 ir}{2\pi a^2}$ & outside wire is $\dfrac{\mu_0 i}{2\pi r}$.

- Radius of charged particle in a uniform magnetic field $= \dfrac{mv}{qB} = \dfrac{\sqrt{2KEm}}{qB}$ where KE is kinetic energy.

- Magnetic field inside thick wire is $\dfrac{\mu_0 ir}{2\pi a^2}$ while outside wire is $\dfrac{\mu_0 i}{2\pi r}$.

- Voltage across voltmeter $V = i_G(G + R)$.

- Torque on a current carrying wire in a magnetic field $\overline{\tau} = \overline{M} \times \overline{B}$.

- Dipole moment of a circular loop $= i\pi R^2$

- Radius of a particle in uniform magnetic field $= \dfrac{mv}{qB}$.

- Magnetic field at the centre of loop, $B = \dfrac{\mu_0 I}{2R}$.

Tips/Tricks/Tecchniques ONE-LINERS
(Exam Sample)

- When charged particle is moving perpendicular to the direction of magnetic field, the path of particle will be circular. In this motion, the magnitude of momentum of the particle remain constant but its direction keeps changing. Also, KE of particle in magnetic field is constant.

- Magnetic force depends on velocity, while electric force is independent of the state of rest or motion of the charged particle.

- A radial magnetic field used in moving coil galvanometer to make the scale of galvanometer linear.

- Magnetic field inside a conductor $B = kd$ *i.e.*, straight line passing through origin.

  At surface $(d = R)$ $B = \dfrac{\mu_0 I}{2\pi d}$

- Same $B = \dfrac{\mu_0 I}{2\pi d}$ outside the conductor *i.e.*, Hyperbolic.

- If a current carrying circular loop $(n = 1)$ is bent sharply so as to convert into a coil having n identical turns then magnetic field at the centre of the coil becomes n^2 times the previous field *i.e.*, $B_{(n\ turn)} = n^2 B_{(single\ turn)}$.

- If an electron moves in a circular path of radius r with speed v then magnetic field produced at the centre of circular path will be

  $$B = \frac{\mu_0}{4\pi} \cdot \frac{ev}{r^2} \Rightarrow r \propto \sqrt{\frac{v}{B}}$$

- If two coils of radius r_1 and r_2 are connected in series to the source of direct current, then the ratio of magnetic field inductions at their centres is given by

  $$\frac{B_1}{B_2} = \frac{r_2}{r_1}$$

  If the same coil is connected in parallel combination, then

  $$\frac{B_1}{B_2} = \frac{r_2^2}{r_1^2}$$

- Magnetic field induction at one end of solenoid is given by

  $$B = \frac{\mu_0 NI}{2\ell}$$

- If a current i_2 carrying conductor AB is placed transverse to another long wire CD carrying current i_1 then force experienced by wire AB is given by

  $$F = \frac{\mu_0 i_1 i_2}{2\pi} \log_e\left(\frac{x+l}{x}\right)$$

- To increase the range of voltmeter having resistance G from V to $\dfrac{V}{n}$, a shunt of resistance nG should be connect in parallel to it.

- Ampere's Circuital law is not independent of the Biot-Savart law. It can be derived from the Biot-Savart law. Its relationship to the Biot-Savart law is similar to the relationship between Gauss's law and Coulomb's law.

20 Magnetism and Matter

The Bar Magnet

- Magnetic phenomena are universal in nature.
- The directional property of magnets was known since ancient times. A thin long piece of a magnet, when suspended freely, pointed in the north-south direction.
- The earth behaves as a magnet with the magnetic field pointing approximately from the geographic south to the north.
- When a bar magnet is freely suspended, it points in the north-south direction. The tip which points to the geographic north is called the *north pole* and the tip which points to the geographic south is called the *south pole* of the magnet.
- There is a repulsive force when north poles (or south poles) of two magnets are brought close together. Conversely, there is an attractive force between the north pole of one magnet and the south pole of the other.
- We cannot isolate the north, or south pole of a magnet. If a bar magnet is broken into two halves, we get two similar bar magnets with somewhat weaker properties. Unlike electric charges, isolated magnetic north and south poles known as *magnetic monopoles* do not exist.

The magnetic field lines

- The magnetic field lines of a magnet (or a solenoid) form continuous closed loops. This is unlike the electric dipole where these field lines begin from a positive charge and end on the negative charge or escape to infinity.
- The tangent to the field line at a given point represents the direction of the net magnetic field B at that point.

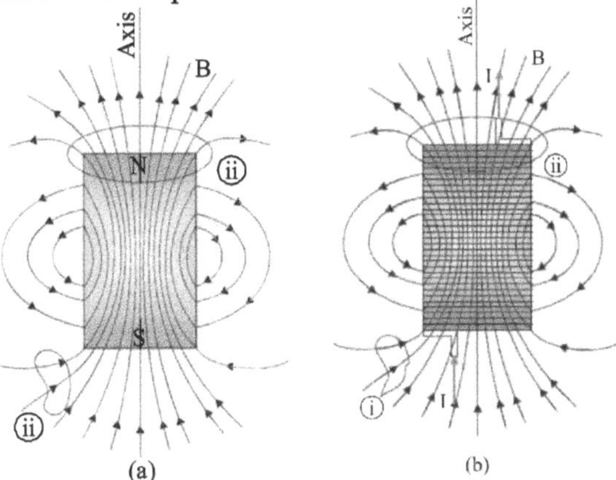

Fig.: The field lines of (a) a bar magnet, (b) a current-carrying finite solenoid

- The larger the number of field lines crossing per unit area, the stronger is the magnitude of the magnetic field B. In Fig. (a), B is larger around region (ii) than in region (i).
- The magnetic field lines do not intersect, for if they did, the direction of the magnetic field would not be unique at the point of intersection.

Bar magnet as an equivalent solenoid

- Magnetic dipole moment m associated with a current loop was defined to be m = NI A where N is the number of turns in the loop, I the current and A the area vector.
- The resemblance of magnetic field lines for a bar magnet and a solenoid suggest that a bar magnet may be thought of as a large number of circulating currents in analogy with a solenoid.
- A bar magnet and a solenoid produce similar magnetic fields. The magnetic moment of a bar magnet is thus equal to the magnetic moment of an equivalent solenoid that produces the same magnetic field.

The dipole in a uniform magnetic field

- The torque on the magnetic dipole is.

$$\tau = m \times B$$

In magnitude $\tau = mB \sin\theta$

Here T is restoring torque and θ is the angle between m and B.

The magnetic potential energy U_m is given by

$$U_m = \int \tau(\theta)d\theta$$

$$= \int mB \sin\theta \, d\theta = -mB \cos\theta = -m.B$$

- Potential energy is minimum (= –mB) at $\theta = 0°$ (most stable position) and maximum (= +mB) at $\theta = 180°$ (most unstable position).

Magnetism and Gauss's Law

- The number of magnetic field lines leaving the surface is balanced by the number of lines entering it. The net magnetic flux is zero for both the surfaces. This is true for any closed surface.

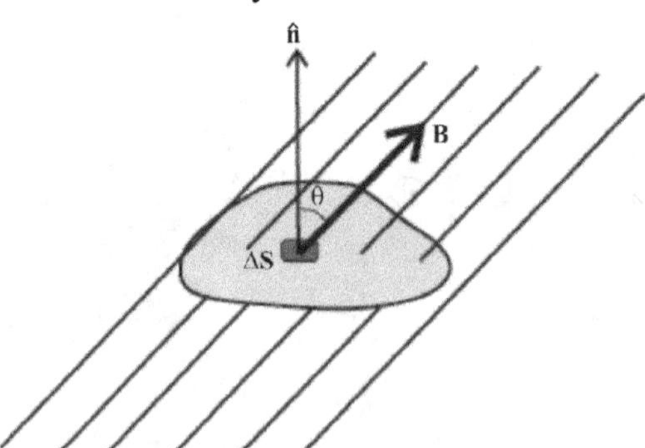

- The net flux ϕ_B is,

$$\phi_B = \sum_{'all'} \Delta\phi_B = \sum_{'all'} B.\Delta S = 0$$

where 'all' stands for 'all area elements ΔS'.

- Thus, Gauss's law for magnetism is:
  The net magnetic flux through any closed surface is zero.

The Earth's Magnetism

- The strength of the earth's magnetic field varies from place to place on the earth's surface, its value being of the order of 10^{-5} T.
- The magnetic field is now thought to arise due to electrical currents produced by convective motion of metallic fluids (consisting mostly of molten iron and nickel) in the outer core of the earth. This is known as the **dynamo effect**.

- The magnetic field lines of the earth resemble that of a (hypothetical) magnetic dipole located at the centre of the earth. The axis of the dipole does not coincide with the axis of rotation of the earth but is presently titled by approximately $11.3°$ with respect to the later.
- The location of the north magnetic pole is at a latitude of $79.74°$ N and a longitude of $71.8°$ W, a place somewhere in north Canada. The magnetic south pole is at $79.74°$ S, $108.22°$ E in the Antarctica.

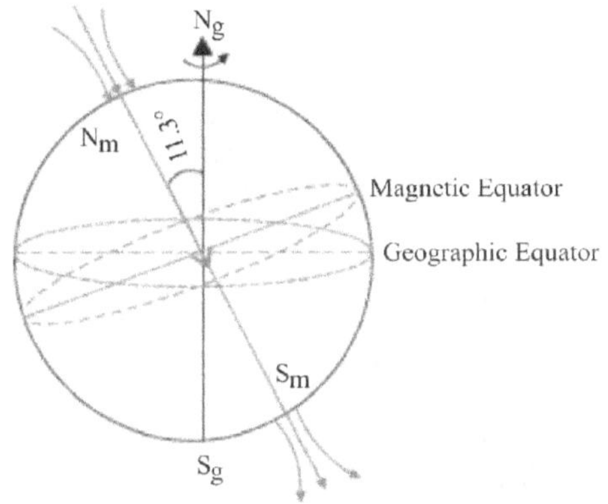

Fig.: The earth as a giant magnetic dipole.

- The pole near the geographic north pole of the earth is called the north magnetic pole. Likewise, the pole near the geographic south pole is called the south magnetic pole.
- Unlike in the case of a bar magnet, the field lines go into the earth at the north magnetic pole (N_m) and come out from the south magnetic pole (S_m).

Magnetic declination and dip

- The vertical plane containing the longitude circle and the axis of rotation of the earth is called the **geographic meridian.**
- Magnetic meridian of a place is the vertical plane which passes through the imaginary line joining the magnetic north and the south poles.
- A magnetic needle, which is free to swing horizontally, would then lie in the magnetic meridian and the north pole of the needle would point towards the magnetic north pole.
- Since the line joining the magnetic poles is titled with respect to the geographic axis of the earth, the magnetic meridian at a point makes angle with the geographic meridian. This angle is called the **magnetic declination or simply declination**.
- The declination is greater at higher latitudes and smaller near the equator.

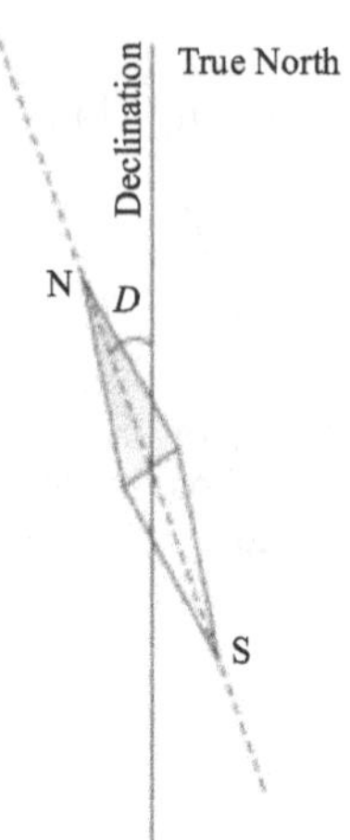

Fig.: A magnetic needle free to move in horizontal plane, points toward the magnetic north-south direction.

♦ The declination in India is small, it being 0°41′ E at Delhi and 0°58′ W at Mumbai.

♦ If a magnetic needle is perfectly balanced about a horizontal axis so that it can swing in a plane of the magnetic meridian, the needle would make an angle with the horizontal. This is known as **the angle of dip (also known as inclination)**. Thus, dip is the angle that the total magnetic field B_E of the earth makes with the surface of the earth.

The angle between B_E and the horizontal component H_E is the angle of dip.

♦ The magnetic field of the earth at a point on its surface, can be described by three quantities, the declination D, the angle of dip or the inclination I and the horizontal component of the earth's field H_E. These are known as the element of the earth's magnetic field. Representing the verticle component by Z_E, we have

$$Z_E = B_E \sin I$$
$$H_E = B_E \cos I$$

which gives, $\tan I = \dfrac{Z_E}{H_E}$

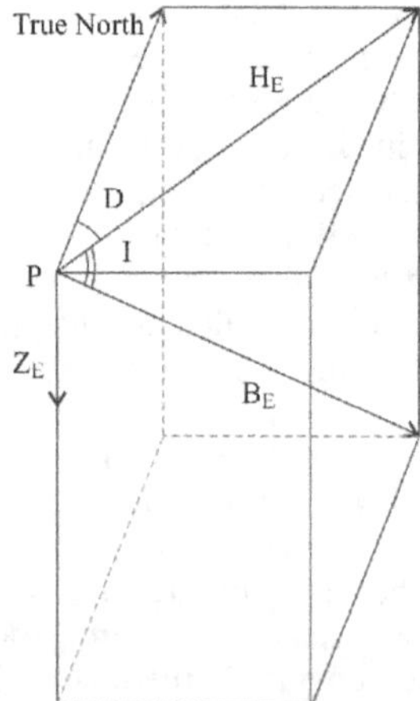

Fig.: The earth's magnetic field B_E, its horizontal and vertical components, H_E and Z_E. Also shown are the inclination or angle of dip, I.

Magnetisation and Magnetic Intensity

- **Magnetisation M** of a sample to be equal to its net magnetic moment per unit volume:

$$M = \frac{m_{net}}{V}$$

M is a vector with dimensions L^{-1} A and is measured in a units of A m^{-1}.

- **Magnetic intensity**, H is defined by

$$H = \frac{B}{\mu_0} - M$$

where H has the same dimensions as M and is measured in units of A m^{-1}.
- Magnetisation, M = χH
  where χ, a dimensionless quantity, is called the magnetic susceptibility. It is a measure of how a magnetic material responds to an external field.
  Total magnetic field, B = μ (1 + χ)H
  = $\mu_0 \mu_r$ H = μH
  where μ_r = 1 + χ, is a dimensionless quantity called the relative magnetic permeability of the substance. It is the analog of the dielectric constant in electrostatics.
- The **magnetic permeability** of the substance is μ and it has the same dimensions and units as μ_0;
  $\mu = \mu_0 \mu_r = \mu_0 (1 + \chi)$.

Magnetic Properties of Materials

- In terms of the susceptibility χ, a material is diamagnetic if χ is negative, para- if χ is positive and small, and ferro- if χ is large and positive.

Diamagnetism
- Diamagnetic substances are those which have tendency to move from stronger to the weaker part of the external magnetic field. In other words, unlike the way a magnet attracts metals like iron, it would repel a diamagnetic substance.

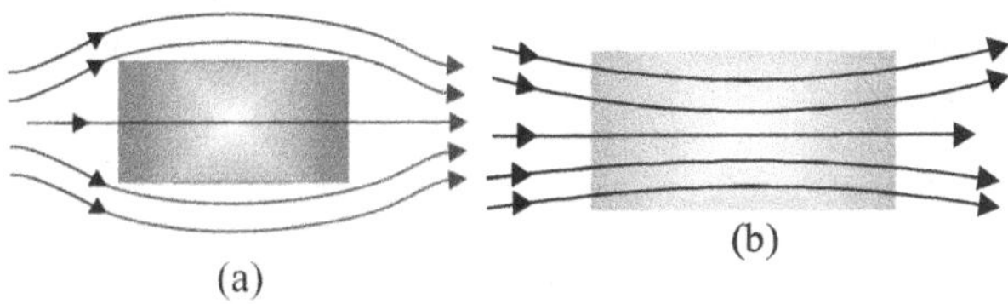

Fig.: Behaviour of magnetic field lines near a (a) diamagnetic, (b) Paramagnetic substance.
- Figure (a) shows a bar of diamagnetic material placed in an external magnetic field. The field lines are repelled or expelled and the field inside the material is reduced.
- When placed in a non-uniform magnetic field, the bar will tend to move from high to low field.

♦ Some diamagnetic materials are bismuth, copper, lead, silicon, nitrogen (at STP), water and sodium chloride. Diamagnetism is present in all the substances. However, the effect is so weak in most cases that it gets shifted by other effects like paramagnetism, ferromagnetism, etc.

Paramagnetism

♦ Paramagnetic substances are those which get weakly magnetised when placed in an external magnetic field.

♦ They have tendency to move from a region of weak magnetic field to strong magnetic field, i.e., they get weakly attracted to a magnet.

♦ The field lines gets concentrated inside the material, and the field inside is enhanced.

♦ When placed in a non-uniform magnetic field, the bar will tend to move from weak field to strong. Some paramagnetic materials are aluminium, sodium, calcium, oxygen (at STP) and copper chloride.

♦ Experimentally, one finds that the magnetisation of a paramagnetic material is inversely proportional to the absolute temperature T,

$$M = C\frac{B_0}{T}$$

or equivalently, $\chi = C\dfrac{\mu_0}{T}$

♦ This is known as Curie's law, the constant C is called Curie's constant.

Ferromagnetism

♦ Ferromagnetic substances are those which gets strongly magnetised when placed in an external magnetic field. They have strong tendency to move from a region of weak magnetic field to strong magnetic field, i.e., they get strongly attracted to a magnet.

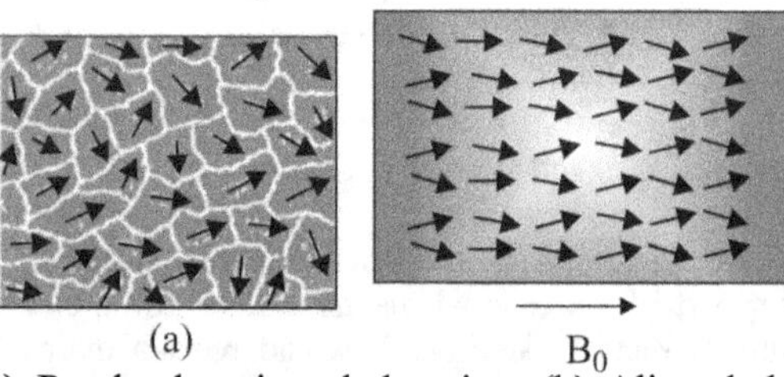

Fig.: (a) Randomly oriented domains, (b) Aligned domains

♦ In a ferromagnetic material the field lines are highly concentrated. In non-uniform magnetic field, the sample tends to move towards the region of high field. When the external field is removed, in some ferromagnetic materials the magnetisation persists. Such materials are called hard magnetic materials or hard ferromagnets. Alnico, an alloy of iron, aluminium, nickel, cobalt and copper, are such material.

♦ In some ferromagnetic materials magnetisation disappears on removal of the external field. Soft iron is one such material. Such materials are called soft ferromagnetic materials. There are a number of elements, which are ferromagnetic: iron, cobalt, nickel, gadolinium, etc. The relative magnetic permeability is > 1000!

♦ The ferromagnetic property depends on temperature. At high enough temperature, a ferromagnet becomes a paramagnet.

- The susceptibility above the Curie temperature, i.e., in the paramagnetic phase is described by,

$$\chi = \frac{C}{T - T} \quad (T > T)$$

- At H = 0, B ≠ 0. This is represented by the curve ab. The value of B at H = 0 is called **retentivity or remanence**.
- The value of H at c is called **coercivity**.
- Next, the current is reduced (curve de) and reversed (curve ea). The cycle repeats itself. This phenomenon is called **hysterisis**.

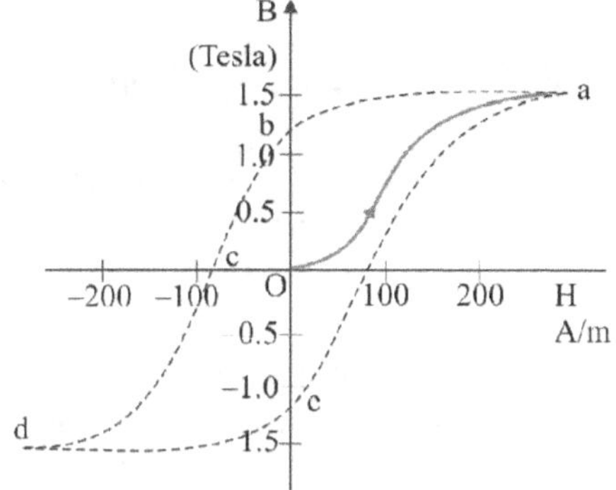

Fig.: The magnetic hysteresis loop is the B-H curve for ferromagnetic materials.

Permanent Magnets and Electromagnets

- Substances which at room temperature retain their ferromagnetic property for a long period of time are called permanent magnets.
- An efficient way to make a permanent magnet is to place a ferromagnetic rod in a solenoid and pass a current. The magnetic field of the solenoid magnetises the rod.
- The hysteresis curve allows us to select suitable materials for permanent magnets.
- Steel is one-favoured choice. It has a slightly smaller retentivity than soft iron but this is outweighed by the much smaller coercivity of soft iron. Other suitable materials for permanent magnets are alnico, cobalt steel and ticonal.
- Core of electromagnets are made of ferromagnetic materials which have high permeability and low retentivity. Soft iron is a suitable material for electromagnets.
- On placing a soft iron rod in a solenoid and passing a current, we increase the magnetism of the solenoid by a thousand fold. When we switch off the solenoid current, the magnetism is effectively switched off since the soft iron core has a low retentivity.

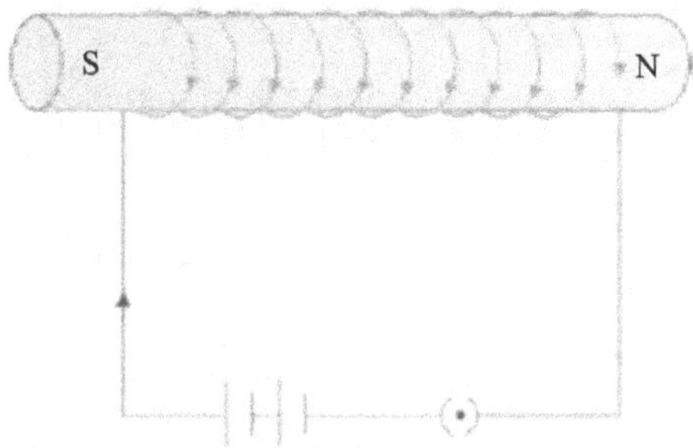

Fig.: A soft iron core in solenoid acts as an electromagnet

Past Years ONE-LINERS
NEET/JEE Main/Board

- Relative permeability, $\mu_r = 1 + \chi_m$
- At equator, dip is zero. At northern hemisphere, dip is positive. At southern hemisphere, dip is negative.
- Gravitational potential energy gain = Energy of current source.
- Time period of oscillations of magnetic needle, $T = 2\pi\sqrt{\dfrac{I}{MB}}$.
- True angle of dip, $\cot^2\theta = \cot^2\theta_1 + \cot^2\theta_2$.
- Magnetic susceptibility is negative for diamagnetic material.
- Minimum work required to rotate bar magnet from stable to unstable equilibrium position, $W = 2MB$.
- Materials used for making permanent magnets should have high coercivity.

Tips/Tricks/Tecchniques ONE-LINERS
(Exam Sample)

- For a straight current carrying wire, magnetic moment is zero.
- Horizontal component of earth's magnetic field is zero at poles. Vertical component of earth's magnetic field is zero at equator.
- Angle of dip and declination change from place to place and time to time.
- Angle of dip at magnetic equator is $0°$ and at magnetic poles, it is $90°$.
- Magnetic susceptibility is independent of temperature for diamagnetic substances.
- Material used for making soft iron should have high retentivity and low coercivity.
- The origin of diamagnetism is due to orbital motion of electrons. But, the origin of paramagnetism and ferromagnetism is due to magnetic moment of spinning of electrons.
- In a vibration magnetometer, the reference line of vibration of suspended magnet must be in magnetic meridian.
- Time period of oscillation in difference position is always greater than that in sum position $T_d > T_s$.
- Intensity of magnetisation (I) is produced due to spin motion of electrons.

- To protect a magnetic material from the external magnetic field it should be placed inside a soft iron case. This phenomenon is called magnetic screening or shielding.

- Consider a vertical plane inclined at an angle β to the magnetic meridian. In such plane vertical component of earth's magnetic field will remain unchanged while in the new inclined plane, horizontal component of magnetic field is given by $B'_H = B_H \cos \beta$

  $\phi' =$ apparent angle of dip

  and $\tan \phi' = \dfrac{B_V}{B_H} = \dfrac{B_V}{B_H \cos\beta}$

  $\Rightarrow \quad \tan \phi' = \dfrac{\tan \phi}{\cos \beta}$

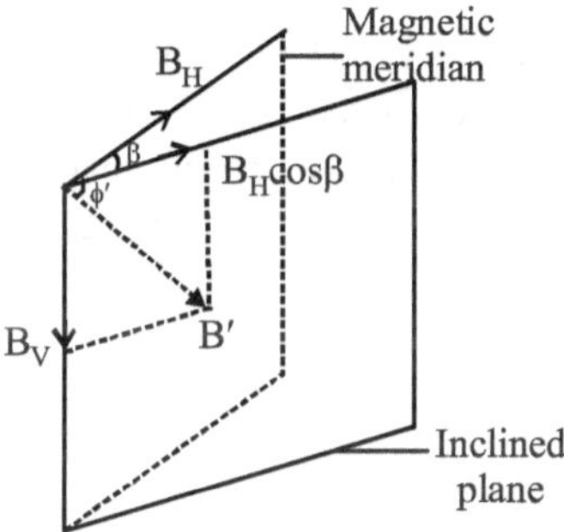

- If θ is angle of dip at a place and magnetic latitude is λ then $\tan \theta = 2 \tan \lambda$

- If two bar magnets of magnetic moment M_1 and M_2 are lying at an angle to each other, then net magnetic moment, $M = \sqrt{M_1^2 + M_2^2 + 2M_1M_2 \cos\theta}$

- The area of hysteresis loop for soft iron is much smaller than for steel so energy loss per unit volume per cycle of soft iron is smaller than steel.

- If a bar magnet requires a magnetic intensity H to become demagnetised inside a long solenoid having n turns per unit length, then

  $H = nI$

  Here, $I =$ current passing through the solenoid.

- A consequence of the fact that magnetic monopoles do not exist is that the magnetic field lines are continuous and form closed loops. In contrast, the electrostatic lines of force begin on a positive charge and terminate on the negative charge (or fade out at infinity).

- Magnetic field at an axial point of bar magnet, $\vec{B}_{axial} = \dfrac{\mu_0}{4\pi} \dfrac{2\vec{m}}{r^3}$

- Magnetic field at an equatorial point of bar magnet $\vec{B}_{equatorial} = \dfrac{-\mu_0}{4\pi} \dfrac{\vec{M}}{r^3}$

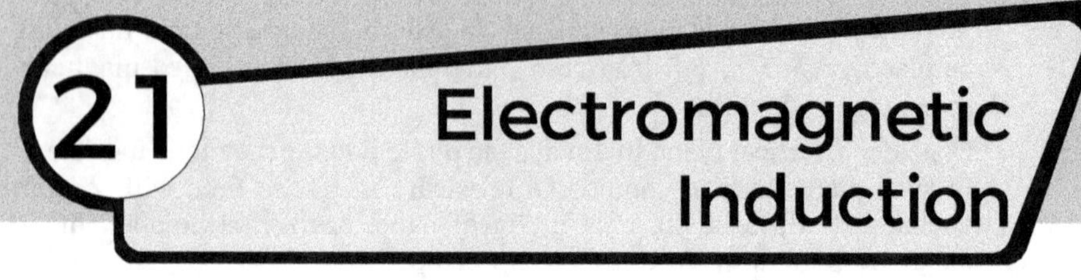

21 Electromagnetic Induction

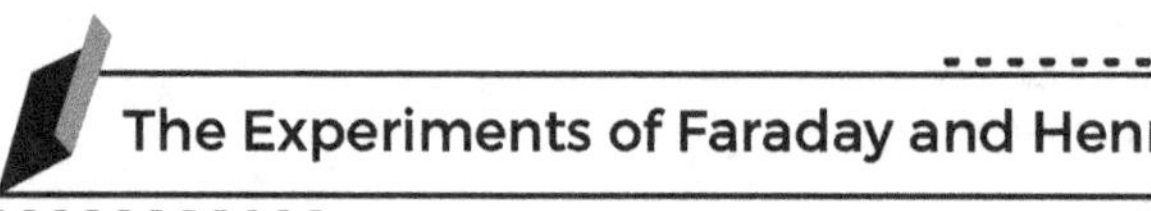

The Experiments of Faraday and Henry

- The phenomenon in which electric current is generated by varying magnetic fields is called *electromagnetic induction.*
- When the North-pole of a bar magnet is pushed towards the coil, the pointer in the galvanometer deflects, indicating the presence of electric current in the coil. The deflection lasts as long as the bar magnet is in motion.
- The galvanometer does not show any deflection when the magnet is held stationary.

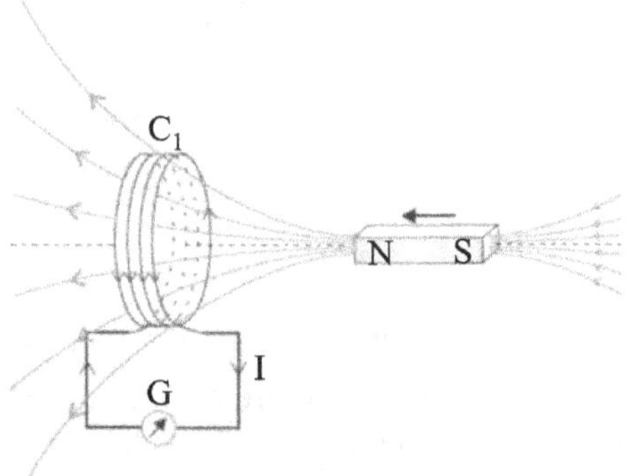

Fig.: When the bar magnet is pushed towards the coil,
the pointer in the galvanometer G deflects.

- *It is the relative motion between the magnet and the coil that is responsible for generation (induction) of electric current in the coil.*
- Replacing the bar magnet by a second coil C_2 connected to a battery and Coil C_2 is moved towards the coil C_1, the galvanometer shows a deflection. This indicates that electric current is induced in coil C_1. When C_2 is moved away, the galvanometer shows a deflection again, but this time in the opposite direction. The deflection lasts as long as coil C_2 is in motion.

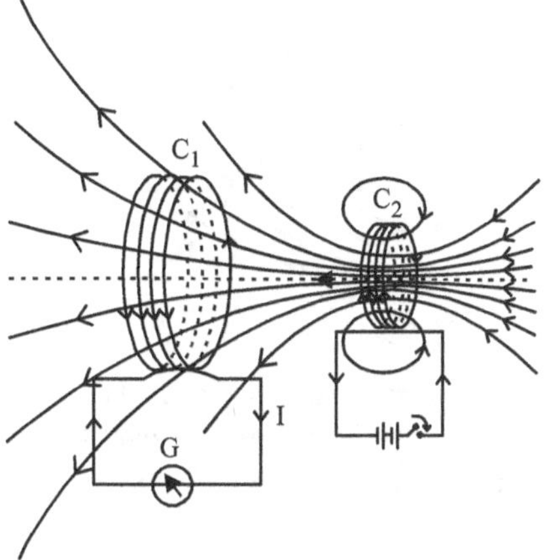

Fig.: Current is induced in coil C_1 due to
motion of the current carrying coil C_2.

- *It is the relative motion between the coils that induces the electric current.*
- It is also observed that the deflection increases dramatically when an iron rod is inserted into the coils along their axis.

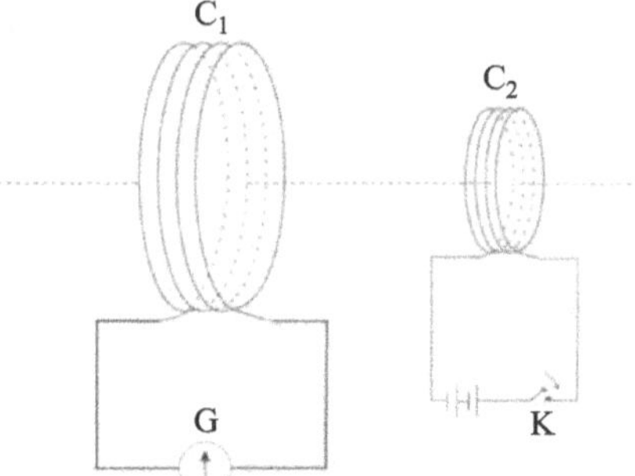

Fig.: Experimental set-up

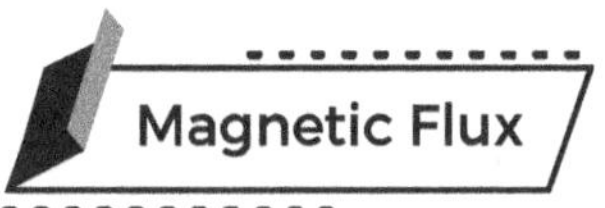

Magnetic Flux

- Magnetic flux through a plane of area A placed in a uniform magnetic field B can be written as

$$\Phi_B = \mathbf{B} \cdot \mathbf{A} = BA \cos \theta$$

where θ is angle between $\mathbf{B}$ and $\mathbf{A}$.

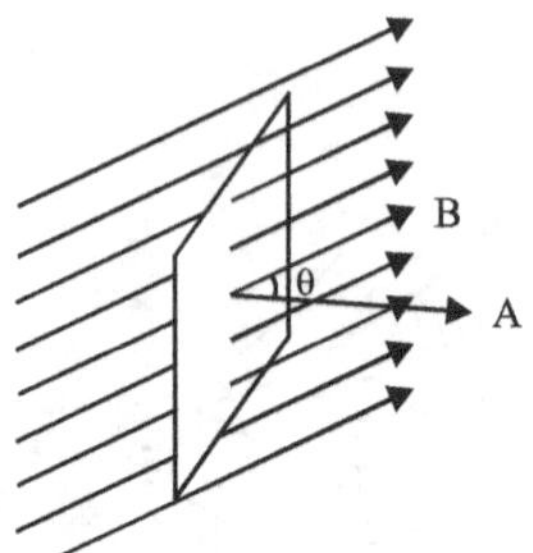

Fig.: A plane of surface area A placed in a
uniform magnetic field B.

♦ The SI unit of magnetic flux is weber (Wb) or tesla meter Magnetic flux is a
scalar quantity.

Faraday's Law of Induction

♦ Faraday stated experimental observations in the form of a law called *Faraday's
law of electromagnetic induction*. The law is stated below.
*The magnitude of the induced emf in a circuit is equal to the time rate of
change of magnetic flux through the circuit.*
Mathematically, the induced emf is given by

$$\varepsilon = -\frac{d\Phi_B}{dt}$$

♦ The negative sign indicates the direction of ε and hence the direction of
current in a closed loop.

Lenz's Law and Conservation of Energy

♦ *The polarity of induced emf is such that it tends to produce a current which
opposes the change in magnetic flux that produced it.*

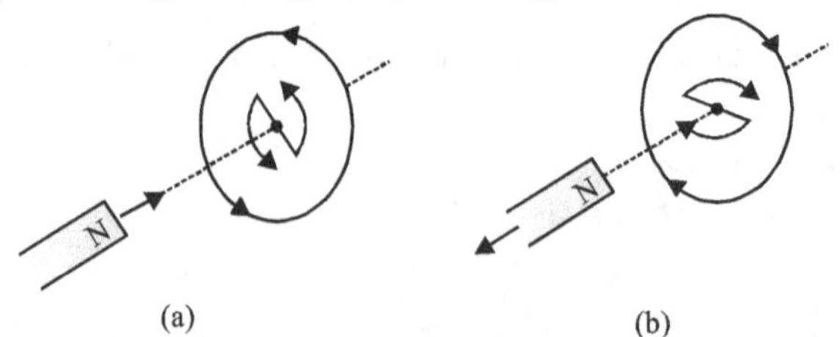

Fig.: Illustration of Lenz's law.

♦ The North-pole of a bar magnet is being pushed towards the closed coil. As the North-pole of the bar magnet moves towards the coil, the magnetic flux through the coil increases. Hence current is induced in the coil in such a direction that it opposes the increase in flux. This is possible only if the current in the coil is in a counter-clockwise direction with respect to an observer situated on the side of the magnet.

♦ If the North-pole of the magnet is being withdrawn from the coil, the magnetic flux through the coil will decrease. To counter this decrease in magnetic flux, the induced current in the coil flows in clockwise direction and its Southpole faces the receding North-pole of the bar magnet. This would result in an attractive force which opposes the motion of the magnet and the corresponding decrease in flux.

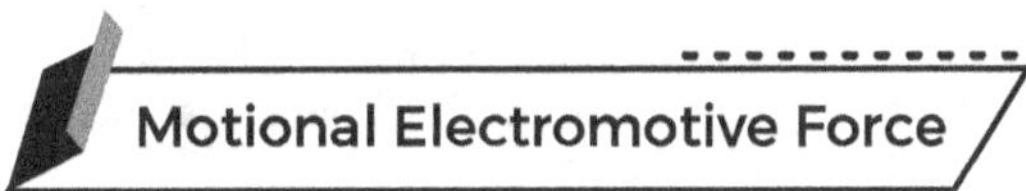

Motional Electromotive Force

♦ The magnetic flux Φ_B enclosed by the loop PQRS will be
$$\Phi_B = Blx$$
Since x is changing with time, the rate of change of flux Φ_B will induce an emf given by:

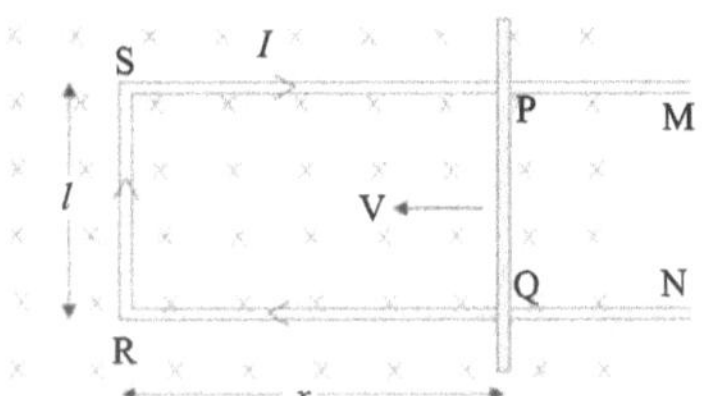

Fig.1: The arm PQ is moved to the left side, thus decreasing the area of the rectangular loop. This movement induces a current I as shown.

$$\varepsilon = \frac{-\mathrm{d}\Phi_B}{\mathrm{d}t} = -\frac{\mathrm{d}}{\mathrm{d}t}(Blx) = -Bl\frac{\mathrm{d}x}{\mathrm{d}t} = Blv$$

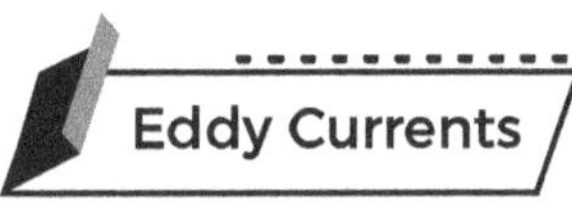

Eddy Currents

♦ When bulk pieces of conductors are subjected to changing magnetic flux, induced currents are produced in them.
These currents are called **eddy currents**.

♦ A copper plate is allowed to swing like a simple pendulum between the pole pieces of a strong magnet. It is found that the motion is damped and in a little while the plate comes to a halt in the magnetic field.

♦ Eddy currents are used to advantage in certain applications like:
(i) Magnetic braking in trains
(ii) Electromagnetic damping

(iii) Induction furnace: Induction furnace can be used to produce high temperatures and can be utilised to prepare alloys, by melting the constituent metals.

(iv) Electric power meters: The shiny metal disc in the electric power meter (analogue type) rotates due to the eddy currents. Electric currents are induced in the disc by magnetic fields produced by sinusoidally varying currents in a coil.

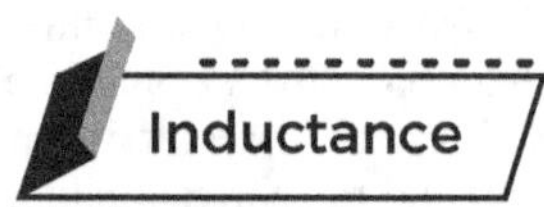

Inductance

- Flux through a coil is proportion to current $\Phi_B \propto I$
- When the flux Φ_B through the coil changes, each turn contributes to the induced emf. Therefore, a term called flux linkage is used which is equal to $N\Phi_B$ for a closely wound coil and in such a case
  $N\Phi_B \propto I$
- The constant of proportionality, in this relation, is called *inductance*.
- Inductance depends only on the geometry of the coil and intrinsic material properties.

Mutual inductance

- When a current I_2 is set up through S_2, it in turn sets up a magnetic flux through S_1. Let us denote it by Φ_1. The corresponding flux linkage with solenoid S_1 is
  $$N_1\Phi_1 = M_{12}I_2 \qquad \qquad ...(i)$$
- M_{12} is called the *mutual inductance* of solenoid S_1 with respect to solenoid S_2. It is also referred to as the *coefficient of mutual induction*.
  $$M_{12} = \mu_0 n_1 n_2 \pi r_1^2 l$$

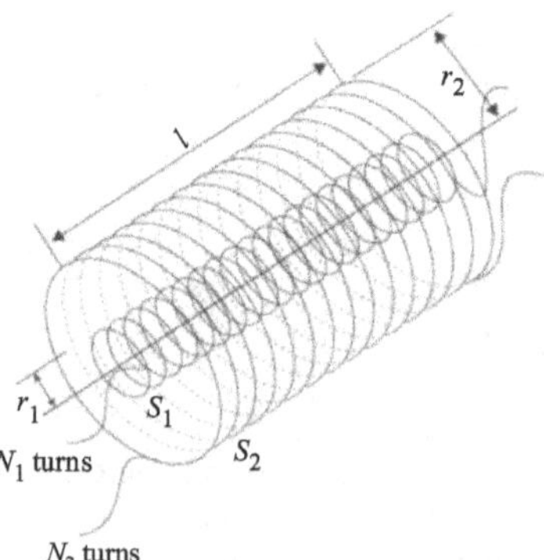

Fig.: Two long co-axial solenoids of same length l.

- In above case $M_{12} = M_{21} = M$ (say)
- We calculated mutual inductance above with air as the medium within the solenoids. Instead, if a medium of relative permeability μ_r had been present, the mutual inductance would be
  $$M = \mu_r \mu_0 n_1 n_2 \pi r_1^2 l$$

Self-inductance

- Emf is induced in a single isolated coil due to change of flux through the coil by means of varying the current through the same coil. This phenomenon is called *self-induction*.

- In this case, flux linkage through a coil of N turns is proportional to the current through the coil and is expressed as $N\Phi_B \propto I$ or, $N\Phi_B = L\,I$

  Where constant of proportionality L is called *self-inductance* of the coil. It is also called the *coefficient of self-induction* of the coil.

- The total flux linked with the solenoid is

  $N\Phi_B = (nl)(\mu_0 n\,I)\,(A) = \mu_0 n^2 A l I$

  Where nl is the total number of turns. Thus, the self-inductance is,

  $$L = \frac{N\Phi_B}{I} = \mu_0 n^2 A l$$

- The self-inductance of the coil depends on its geometry and on the permeability of the medium.

- Work needs to be done against the back emf (e) in establishing the current. This work done is stored as magnetic potential energy.

  $$W = \frac{1}{2}LI^2$$

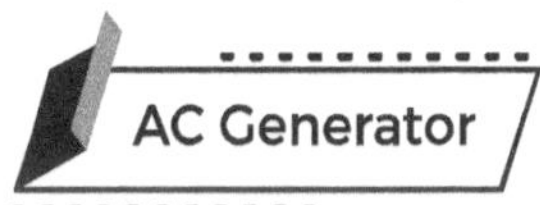

AC Generator

- The method of producing a flux change is the principle of operation of a simple ac generator. An **ac generator converts mechanical energy into electrical energy**.

- Thus, the instantaneous value of the emf is

  $\varepsilon = NBA\,\omega \sin \omega t$

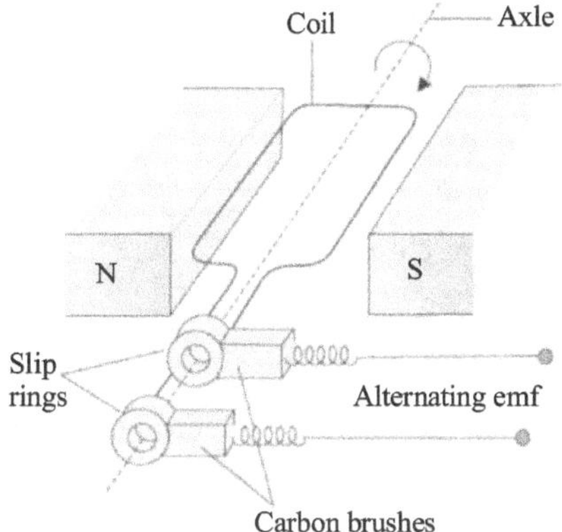

Fig.: AC Generator

- $NBA\omega$ is the maximum value of the emf, which occurs when $\sin \omega t = \pm 1$. If we denote $NBA\omega$ as ε_0, then
  $\varepsilon = \varepsilon_0 \sin \omega t$
- The direction of the current changes periodically and therefore the current is called *alternating current* (ac). Since $\omega = 2\pi v$,
  $\varepsilon = \varepsilon_0 \sin 2\pi v\, t$
  where v is the frequency of revolution of the generator's coil.

- The frequency of rotation is 50 Hz in India. In certain countries such as USA it is 60 HZ.

Past Years ONE-LINERS
NEET/JEE Main/Board

- Magnetic flux = Mi where M is mutual inductance

  Mutual inductance, $M \propto \dfrac{R_2^2}{R_1}$

- Induced emf in a coil'e $= -\dfrac{\Delta\phi}{\Delta t}$ where $\Delta\phi$ is change in flux

- Magnetic potential energy stored in inductor, $U = \dfrac{1}{2}Li^2$

- Current, $I = \dfrac{e}{R} = \dfrac{-\Delta\phi}{R\Delta t}$

- Total flux, $\phi = Li$

  where total flux = no. of turns × flux linked through each coil

- Current flows opposite to motion of electrons

- Magnetic flux through an area, $\phi = \vec{B}.\vec{A}$

- Induced current, $I = -\dfrac{d\phi}{Rdt}$

- Magnetic field lines form closed loop.

- Self inductance of a solenoid $= \dfrac{\mu_0 N^2 A}{L}$

- Change in flux $(d\phi)$ = R × area under current-time graph]

Tips/Tricks/Tecchniques ONE-LINERS
(Exam Sample)

- When a conducting rod is allowed to fall freely in earth's magnetic field in such a way that its length lies along East-West direction then induced emf continuously increases w.r.t. time and induced current flows from West - East.

- Inductance of a solenoid at its end is half of its inductance at the centre.

$$\left(L_{end} = \frac{1}{2} L_{centre} \right)$$

- If current varies as a function of time then the induced e.m.f. produced in the inductor due to rate of current change through it is given by

$$e = -L\frac{dI}{dt}$$

- If two coils are connected in series having currents in the same direction, then we can calculate equivalent induction, $L = L_1 + L_2 + 2M$ Here, L_1 and L_2 are the self induction of two coils.
  If the direction of currents in the two coils is in opposite direction, then $L = L_1 + L_2 - 2M$

- If two solenoids have different area of cross-section, then $M = k\sqrt{L_1 L_2}$

  Here, k is coefficient of coupling between the two coils.

- If two coils are connected in parallel combination, then

$$\frac{1}{L} = \frac{1}{(L_1 + M)} + \frac{1}{(L_2 + M)}$$

$$\Rightarrow \quad L = \frac{L_1 L_2 M^2 + M(L_1 + L_2)}{L_1 + L_2 + 2M}$$

$$\text{If } M = 0, L = \frac{L_1 L_2}{L_1 + L_2}$$

- Mutual induction between two concentric coils having radii r_p and r_s and respective number of turns n_p and n_s is

$$M = \frac{\pi \mu_0 n_p n_s r_s^2}{2r_p}$$

22. Alternating Current

AC Voltage Applied to a Resistor

- The electric mains supply in our homes and offices is a voltage that varies like a sine function with time. Such a voltage is called alternating voltage (ac voltage) and the current driven by it in a circuit is called the alternating current (ac current)
- Alternating currents change direction with time.
- The main reason for preferring use of ac voltage over dc voltage is that ac voltages can be easily and efficiently converted from one voltage to the other by means of transformers.

- For a source voltage, given by

$$v = v_m \sin\omega t \qquad \qquad ...(i)$$

v_m is the amplitude of the potential difference ω is its angular frequency.

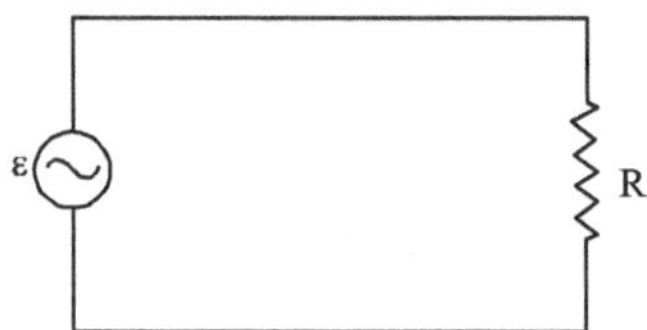

Fig.: AC voltage applied to a resistor

Current amplitude i_m is given by

$$i_m = \frac{v_m}{R}$$

The above equation works for both ac and dc voltages.

- Eqs. (i) and (ii) are plotted as a function of time as shown in Fig.

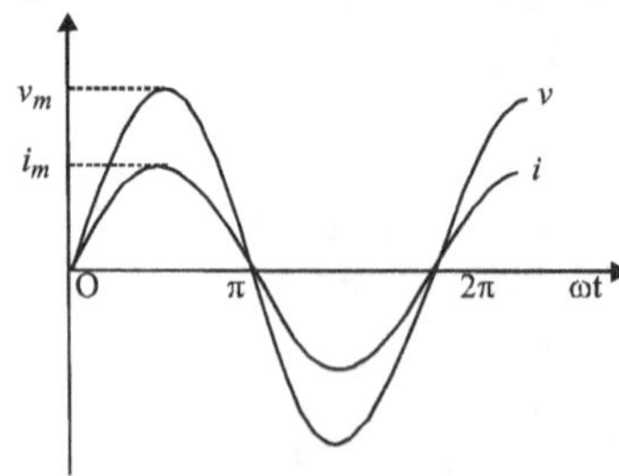

Fig.: In a pure resistor, the voltage and current are in phase. The minima, zero and maxima occur at the same respective times.

Figure shows v and i reach zero, minimum and maximum values at the same time. The voltage and current are in phase with each other.

Average Power Over a Cycle

♦ The **instantaneous power** dissipated in the resistor is

$$p = i^2 R = i_m^2 R \sin^2 \omega t$$

The average value of p over a cycle is*

$$\bar{p} = <i_m^2 R> \Rightarrow \bar{p} = \frac{1}{2} i_m^2 R \quad \left(\because <\sin^2 \omega t> = \frac{1}{2} \right)$$

♦ To express ac power in the same form as dc power $(P = I^2 R)$, a special value of current is defined and used. It is called, root mean square (rms) or effective current denoted by I_{rms} or I.

♦ **Root mean square (rms)** value of current is defined by

$$I = \frac{i_m}{\sqrt{2}} = 0.707\, i_m$$

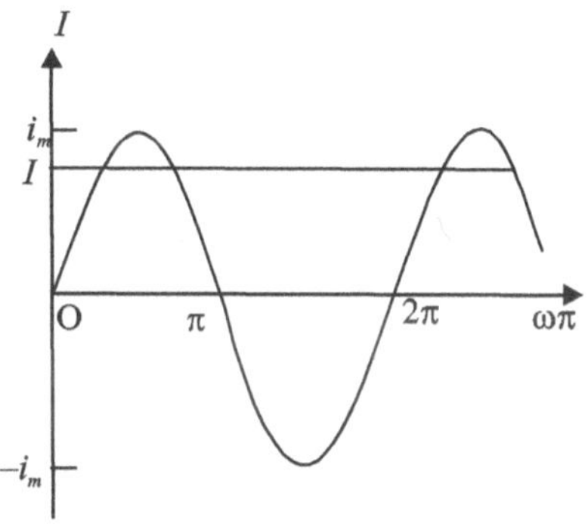

Fig.: The rms current I is related to the peak current

$$I = i_m / \sqrt{2} = 0.707\, i_m$$

♦ In terms of I, the **average power**, denoted by P is

$$P = \bar{p} = \frac{1}{2} i_m^2 R = I^2 R \quad \left[\text{As} \quad I = \frac{i_m}{\sqrt{2}} \right]$$

♦ The **rms voltage or effective voltage** is given by $V = \dfrac{v_m}{\sqrt{2}} = 0.707\, v_m$

♦ The household line voltage of 220 V is an rms value with a peak voltage of

$$v_m = \sqrt{2}\, V = (1.414)(220\,V) = 311\,V$$

Representation of AC Current and Voltage by Rotating Vectors–Phasors

♦ In order to show phase relationship between voltage and current in an ac circuit, we use phasors.

♦ A phasor is a vector which rotates about the origin with angular speed ω, as shown in Fig. The vertical components of phasors V and I represent the sinusoidally varying quantities v and i. The magnitudes of phasors V and I represent the amplitudes or the peak values v_m and i_m

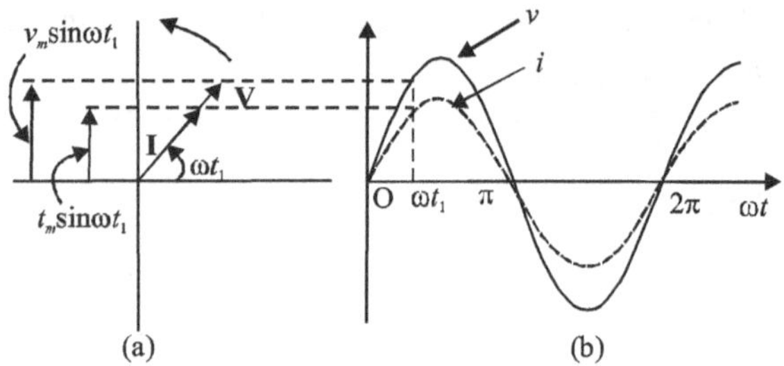

Fig.: (a) A phasor diagram for the circuit in containing resistor
(b) Graph of v and i versus ωt.

♦ From Fig. (a) we see phasors V and I of a resistor are in the same direction. This means the phase angle between the voltage and the current is zero.

AC Voltage Applied to an Inductor

♦ Let voltage $v = v_m \sin\omega t$ be applied across a circuit containing inductor.

Fig.: An ac source connected to an inductor.

Current $i_m = \dfrac{v_m}{\omega L}$. The quantity ωL is analogous to the resistance and is called inductive reactance, denoted by X_L:

$X_L = \omega L$

The amplitude of the current is, then

$$i_m = \frac{v_m}{X_L}$$

♦ Figure (a) shows the voltage and the current phasors in the present case at instant t_1.

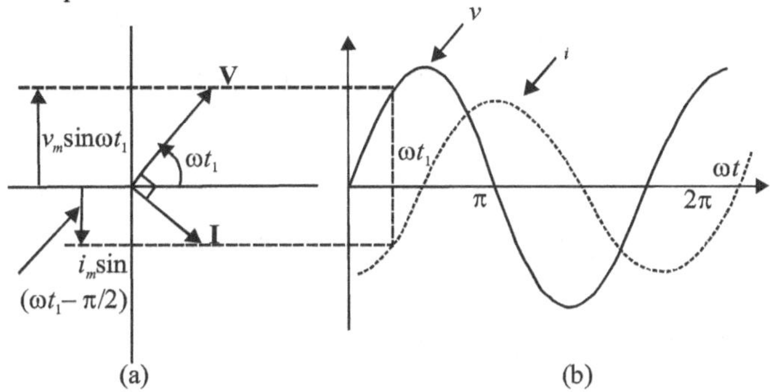

Fig.: (a) A Phasor diagram for the circuit in
Fig (b) Graph of v and i versus ωt.

♦ The instantaneous power supplied to the inductor is

$$p_L = iv = i_m \sin\left(\omega t - \frac{\pi}{2}\right) \times v_m \sin(\omega t) = -\frac{t_m v_m}{2}\sin(2\omega t)$$

So, the average power over a complete cycle is

$$P_L = \left\langle -\frac{t_m v_m}{2}\sin(2\omega t)\right\rangle = -\frac{t_m v_m}{2}\left\langle \sin(2\omega t)\right\rangle = 0$$

AC Voltage Applied to a Capacitor

♦ Shows an ac source e generating ac voltage $v = v_m \sin\omega$t connected to a capacitor only, a purely capacitive ac circuit.

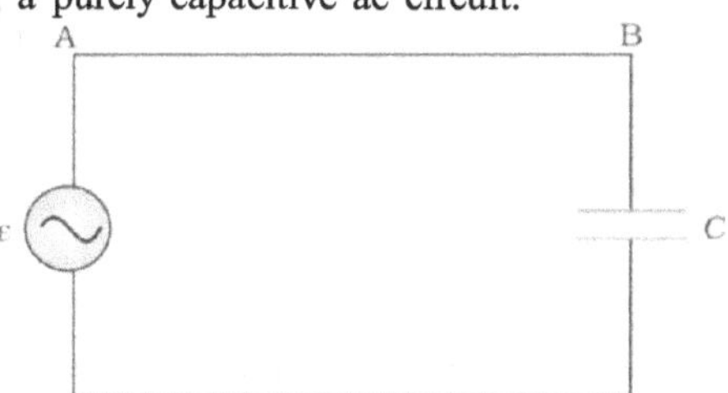

Fig.: An ac source connected to a capacitor.

♦ The instantaneous voltage v across the capacitor is $v = \dfrac{q}{C}$

Amplitude of current,

$i_m = \dfrac{v_m}{X_C}$ Here, X_C = Capacitive reactance

♦ The current is $\pi/2$ ahead of voltage. Figure (a) shows the phasor diagram at an instant t_1.

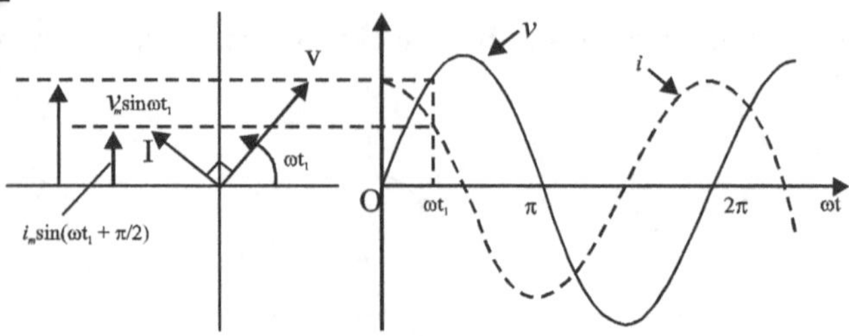

Fig.: (a) A Phasor diagram for the circuit in Fig. (b) Graph of v and i versus ωt.

♦ Average power, $p_c = iv = i_m \cos(\omega t) v_m \sin(\omega t)$

$$= i_m v_m \cos(\omega t) \sin(\omega t) = \frac{i_m v_m}{2} \sin(2\omega t)$$

♦ In the case of an inductor, the average power

$$P_C = \left\langle \frac{i_m v_m}{2} \sin(2\omega t) \right\rangle = \frac{i_m v_m}{2} \left\langle \sin(2\omega t) \right\rangle = 0$$

since $<\sin(2\omega t)> = 0$ over a complete cycle.

AC Voltage Applied to a Series LCR Circuit

♦ Let voltage of the source to be $v = v_m \sin \omega t$ be applied across a series LCR circuit.

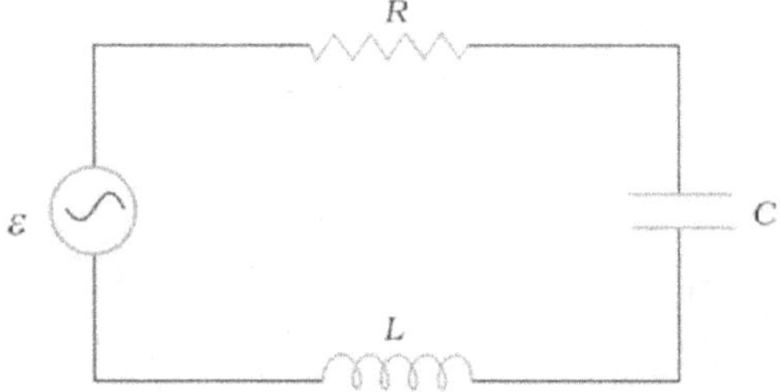

Fig.: A series *LCR* circuit connected to an ac source.

Phasor-diagram solution

♦ Current in each element of LCR circuit, $i = i_m \sin(\omega t + \phi)$ where ϕ is the phase difference between the voltage across the source and the current in the circuit.

♦ The length of these phasors or the amplitude of $\mathbf{V_R}$, $\mathbf{V_C}$ and $\mathbf{V_L}$ are:

$$v_{Rm} = i_m R, \; v_{Cm} = i_m X_C, \; v_{Lm} = i_m X_L$$

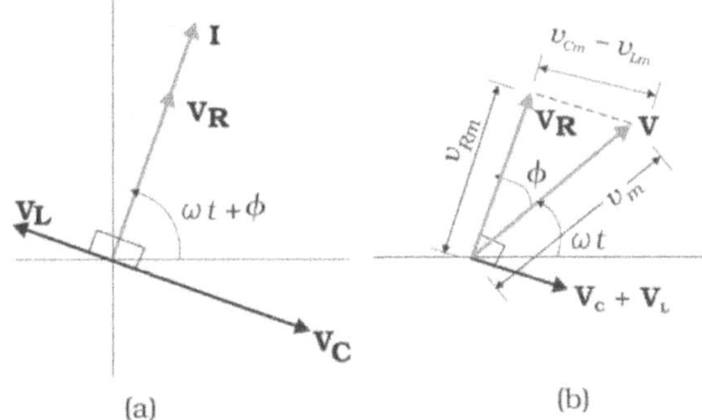

Fig.: (a) Relation between the phasors V_L, V_R, V_C, and I,
(b) Relation between the phasors V_L, V_R, and
$(V_L + V_C)$ for the circuit

Current, $i_m = \dfrac{v_m}{Z}$

where $Z = \sqrt{R^2 + (X_C - X_L)^2}$

♦ Since phasor **I** is always parallel to phasor V_R, the phase angle ϕ is the angle between V_R and **V** and can be determined from Fig.:

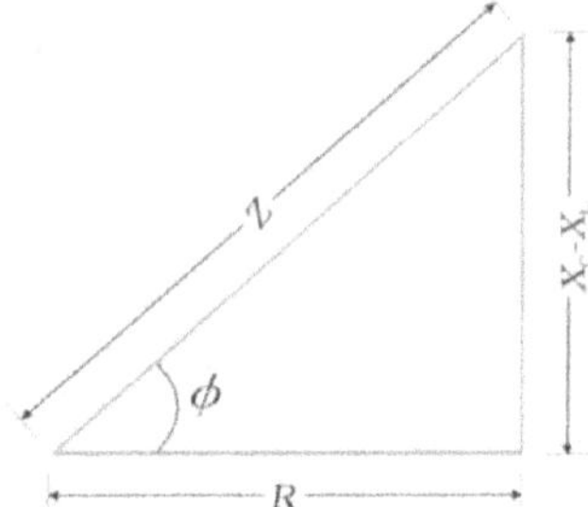

Fig.: Impedance diagram.

$$\tan \phi = \frac{v_{Cm} - v_{Lm}}{v_{Rm}}$$

Substituting the values we have

$$\tan \phi = \frac{X_C - X_L}{R}$$

This is called Impedance diagram which is a right-triangle with Z as its hypotenuse.

♦ The following diagram shows the variation of v and i with ωt for the case $X_C > X_L$.

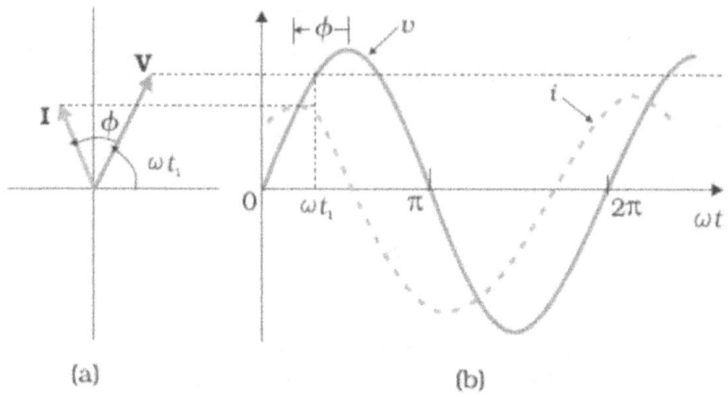

Fig.: (a) Phasor diagram of V and I. (b) Graphs of v and i
versus w t for a series LCR circuit where $X_C > X_L$.

Resonance

♦ The phenomenon of resonance is common among systems that have a tendency to oscillate at a particular frequency. This frequency is called the system's natural frequency. If such a system is driven by an energy source at a frequency that is near the natural frequency, amplitude of oscillation is found to be large.

♦ For an RLC circuit driven current amplitude is given by

$$i_m = \frac{v_m}{Z} = \frac{v_m}{\sqrt{R^2 + (X_C - X_L)^2}}$$ with $X_c = 1/\omega C$ and $X_L = \omega L$. If ω is varied, at a particular frequency ω_0, $X_c = X_L$, and the impedance is minimum. This frequency is called the *resonant frequency*:

$$X_c = X_L \text{ or } \frac{1}{\omega_0 C} = \omega_0 L \text{ or } \omega_0 = \frac{1}{\sqrt{LC}}$$

Sharpness of resonance

♦ The sharpness of resonance is given by,

$$\frac{\omega_0}{2\Delta\omega} = \frac{\omega_0 L}{R}$$

The ratio $\frac{\omega_0 L}{R}$ is also called the quality factor, Q of the circuit.

Power in AC Circuit: The Power Factor

♦ A voltage $v = v_m \sin\omega t$ applied to a series RLC circuit and drives current in the circuit given by $i = i_m \sin(\omega t + \phi)$ the instantaneous power p supplied by the

source $p = vi = (v_m \sin\omega t) \times [i_m \sin(\omega t + \phi)] = \frac{v_m i_m}{2}[\cos\phi - \cos(2\omega t + \phi)]$

♦ The average power over a cycle is given by

$$P = \frac{v_m i_m}{2}\cos\phi = \frac{v_m}{\sqrt{2}}\frac{i_m}{\sqrt{2}}\cos\phi$$
$$= V\,I\,\cos\phi = I^2 Z\cos\phi$$

The quantity $\cos\phi$ is called the power factor.

♦ **Case (i)** *Resistive circuit*: In that case $\phi = 0$, $\cos\phi = 1$. There is maximum power dissipation.

♦ **Case (ii)** *Purely inductive or capacitive circuit*: If the circuit contains only an inductor or capacitor, we know that the phase difference between voltage and current is $\pi/2$. Therefore, $\cos\phi = 0$, and no power is dissipated even though a current is flowing in the circuit. This current is sometimes referred to as wattless current.

♦ **Case (iii)** *LCR series circuit*: power dissipated is given by $P = VI\cos\phi$ where $\phi = \tan^{-1}(X_c - X_L)/R$. So, ϕ may be non-zero in a *RL* or *RC* or *RCL* circuit. Even in such cases, power is dissipated only in the resistor.

♦ **Case (iv)** *Power dissipated at resonance in LCR circuit*: At resonance $X_c - X_L = 0$, and $\phi = 0$. Therefore, $\cos\phi = 1$ and $P = I^2Z = I^2 R$. That is, maximum power is dissipated in a circuit (through R) at resonance.

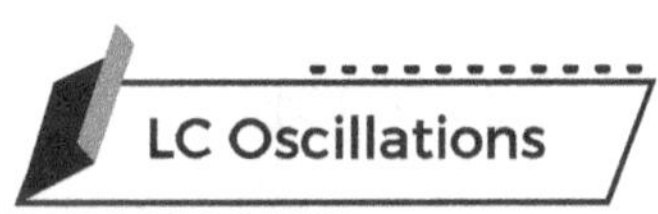

LC Oscillations

♦ A capacitor and an inductor can store electrical and magnetic energy, respectively. When a capacitor (initially charged) is connected to an inductor, the charge on the capacitor and the current in the circuit exhibit the phenomenon of electrical oscillations similar to oscillations in mechanical systems.

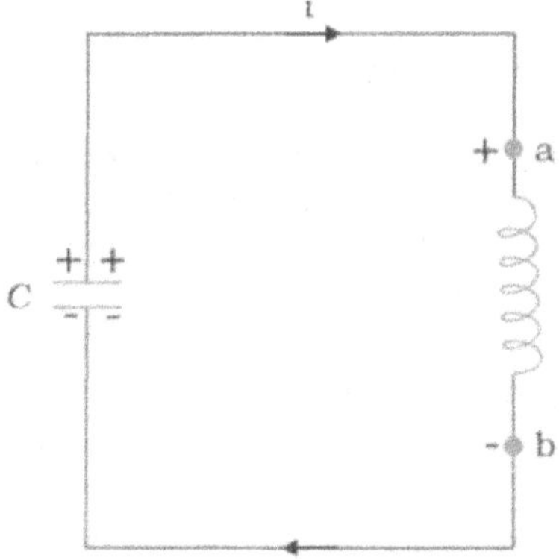

Fig.: At the instant shown, the current is increasing; so the polarity of induced emf in the inductor is as shown.

♦ This equation has the form $\dfrac{d^2x}{dt^2} + \omega_0^2 x = 0$ for a simple harmonic oscillator.

The charge therefore, oscillates with a natural frequency $\omega_0 = \dfrac{1}{\sqrt{LC}}$ and varies sinusoidally with time as $q = q_m\cos(\omega t + \phi)$

♦ The total energy of LC circuit is, $U = U_E = \dfrac{1}{2}\dfrac{q_m^2}{C}$

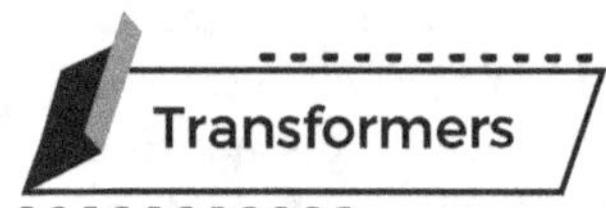

Transformers

♦ For many purposes, it is necessary to change (or transform) an alternating voltage from one to another of greater or smaller value. This is done with a device called transformer using the principle of mutual induction.

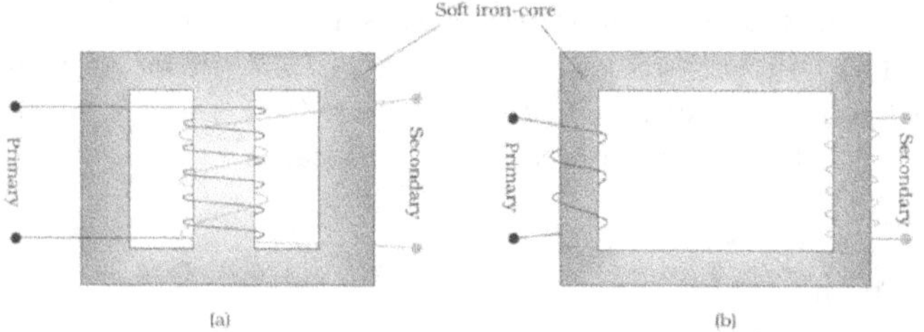

Fig.: Two arrangements for winding of primary and secondary
coil in a transformer: (a) two coils on top of each other,
(b) two coils on separate limbs of the core.

♦ For ideal transformer, $\dfrac{v_s}{v_p} = \dfrac{N_s}{N_p}$

♦ Above relation has been obtained using three assumptions: (i) the primary resistance and current are small; (ii) the same flux links both the primary and the secondary as very little flux escapes from the core, and (iii) the secondary current is small.

♦ If the secondary coil has a greater number of turns than the primary ($N_s > N_p$), the voltage is stepped up ($V_s > V_p$). This type of arrangement is called a **step-up transformer**. However, in this arrangement, there is less current in the secondary than in the primary ($N_p/N_s < 1$ and $I_s < I_p$).

♦ If the secondary coil has less turns than the primary ($N_s < N_p$), we have a **step-down transformer**. In this case, $V_s < V_p$ and $I_s > I_p$. That is, the voltage is stepped down, or reduced, and the current is increased.

♦ In actual transformers, small energy losses do occur due to the following reasons:

(i) *Flux Leakage*: There is always some flux leakage; that is, not all of the flux due to primary passes through the secondary due to poor design of the core or the air gaps in the core. It can be reduced by winding the primary and secondary coils one over the other.

(ii) ***Resistance of the windings***: The wire used for the windings has some resistance and so, energy is lost due to heat produced in the wire (I^2R). In high current, low voltage windings, these are minimised by using thick wire.
(iii) ***Eddy currents***: The alternating magnetic flux induces eddy currents in the iron core and causes heating. The effect is reduced by using a laminated core.
(iv) ***Hysteresis***: The magnetisation of the core is repeatedly reversed by the alternating magnetic field. The resulting expenditure of energy in the core appears as heat and is kept to a minimum by using a magnetic material which has a low hysteresis loss.

Past Years ONE-LINERS
NEET/JEE Main/Board

- For LCR series circuit resonance frequency $\omega_0 = \dfrac{1}{\sqrt{LC}}$

- For an ideal transformer Input power = Output power

- Voltage across LCR circuit, $V_{RMS} = \sqrt{V_R^2 + (V_L - V_C)^2}$

- RMS value of current for circuit containing capacitor only. $I_{rms} = \dfrac{\varepsilon_{rms}}{X_C} = \dfrac{\varepsilon_{rms}}{\dfrac{1}{C\omega}}$

- In LCR circuit, When L is removed, Phase difference $\tan\phi = \dfrac{|X_C|}{R}$

  When C is removed, Phase difference $\tan\phi = \dfrac{|X_L|}{R} = \therefore$ Power factor, $\cos\phi = \dfrac{R}{Z} = 1$.

- Power dissipated in an LCR series circuit connected to an a.c. source of emf E

  $$P = E_{rms}\, i_{rms}\, \cos\phi = \dfrac{E_{rms}^2 R}{Z^2} = \dfrac{E_{rms}^2 R}{R^2 + \left(\omega L - \dfrac{1}{C\omega}\right)^2}$$

- Inductor offer infinite resistance to DC current.

- Impedance, $Z = \sqrt{R^2 + (X_C - X_L)^2}$ Power loss in A.C. circuit, $P = i_{rms}^2 R = \left(\dfrac{V_{rms}}{Z}\right)^2 R$

- Power $P = V_{rms} \cdot I_{rms} \cos\phi$

- For series R – C circuit, reactance, $Z = \sqrt{R^2 + \left(\dfrac{1}{C\omega}\right)^2}$ Current $i = \dfrac{V}{Z_c}$

- LCR circuit is in resonance condition behaves as resistive circuit.

- In damped harmonic oscillation, $\dfrac{md^2x}{dt^2} = -kx - bv \Rightarrow \dfrac{md^2x}{dt^2} + b\dfrac{dx}{dt} + kx = 0$

- Quality factor $Q = \dfrac{\omega_0}{2\Delta\omega} = \dfrac{\omega_0 L}{R}$

- Average power $P_{avg} = V_{rms}\, I_{rms}\, \cos\theta = \left(\dfrac{V_0}{\sqrt{2}}\right)\left(\dfrac{I_0}{\sqrt{2}}\right)\cos\theta$

- Current in R.L circuit, $I = \dfrac{e}{\sqrt{R^2 + X_L^2}}$

- The equation for growth of current in R-L circuit $I = I_0(1 - e^{-\frac{Rt}{L}})$ Here $\dfrac{L}{R} = \tau =$ time constant

Tips/Tricks/Tecchniques ONE-LINERS
(Exam Sample)

- Alternating current in electric wires, bulbs etc., flows 50 times in one direction and 50 times in the opposite direction in 1 second.
- A direct current flows over the cross-section of the conductor. But an alternating current flows mainly along the surface of the conductor.
- AC equipments such as electric motors are more durable as compared to DC equipments.
- AC ammeter and AC voltmeter always measure r.m.s. value.
- AC is more dangerous than DC. It is because peak value of AC for 220 V AC is $220\sqrt{2} = 311\,V$. Thus, 311 V can cause more harm to the human body than 220 V DC.
- Average value of AC over a complete cycle is zero.
- All AC measuring instruments is based on heating effect of current.
- The AC supply in our country is 220 volt, 50 c/s.
- While drawing phasor diagram for combination of elements the quantity which is constant should be plotted along X-axis.
    (i)   In series circuit, current should be plotted along X-axis.
    (ii) In parallel circuit, voltage should be plotted along X-axis.

♦ The equation for growth and decay of current in R-L circuit is given by
$$I = I_0(1 - e^{-Rt/L})$$

Here, $\dfrac{L}{R} = \tau = $ time constant of the circuit.

♦ The equation for charging and discharing of a condenser through resistance R is given by
$$q = q_0(1 - e^{-t/RL})$$
Here, $RC = \tau = $ time constant of the circuit.

♦ The inductor and capacitor have different behaviour in ac and dc circuit.
For DC supply, $v = 0$. Therefore, $X_L = 2\pi v L = 0$
Thus, we can say an inductor act as conductor for DC current.

$$X_C = \frac{1}{2\pi v C} = \frac{1}{0} = \infty$$

Thus, condenser just block dc and allows ac current to pass through.

♦ In RLC circuit, impedance is infinite for $\omega = 0$ and also for $\omega = \infty$. The impedance is minimum $(Z = R)$, when $\omega L = \dfrac{1}{\omega C}$ or $\omega = \dfrac{1}{\sqrt{LC}}$. At this frequency, resonance occur.

♦ When a value is given for ac voltage or current, it is ordinarily the rms value. The voltage across the terminals of an outlet in your room is normally 240 V. This refers to the *rms* value of the voltage. The amplitude of this voltage is

$$v_m = \sqrt{2}\, V = \sqrt{2}\,(240) = 340V$$

♦ The power rating of an element used in ac circuits refers to its average power rating.

Displacement Current

- Does an electric field changing with time give rise to a magnetic field? Maxwell (1831-1879), argued that this was indeed the case – not only an electric current but also a time-varying electric field generates magnetic field.

- Maxwell formulated a set of equations involving electric and magnetic fields, and their sources, the charge and current densities. These equations are known as Maxwell's equations.

- If the plates of the capacitor have an area A, and a total charge Q, the *electric flux* ϕ_E through the surfaces.

$$\phi_E = |\mathbf{E}|A = \frac{1}{\varepsilon_0}\frac{Q}{A}A = \frac{Q}{\varepsilon_0}$$

- Current $i = (dQ/dt)$, using Eq., we have

$$\frac{d\phi_E}{dt} = \frac{d}{dt}\left(\frac{Q}{\varepsilon_0}\right) = \frac{1}{\varepsilon_0}\frac{dQ}{dt}$$

This implies that for consistency $\varepsilon_0\left(\dfrac{d\phi_E}{dt}\right) = i$ ..... (i)

- The current carried by conductors due to flow of charges is called **conduction current**. The current, is due to changing electric field. It is, therefore, called *displacement current*

- The source of a magnetic field is not just the conduction electric current due to flowing charges, but also the time rate of change of electric field. The total current i is the sum of the conduction current denoted by i_c, and the displacement current denoted by $i_d = (\varepsilon_0\,(d\phi_E/dt))$.

$$i = i_c + i_d = i_c + \varepsilon_0\frac{d\phi_E}{dt}$$

- "The total current passing through any surface of which the closed loop is the perimeter" is the sum of the conduction current and the displacement current.

$$\oint \mathbf{B}\cdot d\mathbf{l} = \mu_0\,i_c + \mu_0\,\varepsilon_0\frac{d\phi_E}{dt}$$

and is known as **Ampere-Maxwell law**.

Maxwell's Equations

1. $\oint \mathbf{E} \cdot d\mathbf{A} = Q / \varepsilon_0$ (Gauss's Law for electricity)

2. $\oint \mathbf{B} \cdot d\mathbf{A} = 0$ (Gauss's Law for magnetism)

3. $\oint \mathbf{E} \cdot d\mathbf{l} = \dfrac{-d\phi_B}{dt}$ (Faraday's Law)

4. $\oint \mathbf{B} \cdot d\mathbf{l} = \mu_0 \, i_c + \varepsilon_0 \dfrac{d\phi_E}{dt}$ (Ampere – Maxwell Law)

Electromagnetic Waves

Sources of Electromagnetics Waves

- Neither stationary charges nor charges in uniform motion (steady currents) can be sources of electromagnetic waves. The former produces only electrostatic fields, while the latter produces magnetic fields that, however, do not vary with time. It is an important result of Maxwell's theory that accelerated charges radiate electromagnetic waves.

- Consider a charge oscillating with some frequency. This produces an oscillating electric field in space, which produces an oscillating magnetic field, and so on. The oscillating electric and magnetic fields thus regenerate each other.

Nature of Electromagnetics Waves

- It can be shown from Maxwell's equations that electric and magnetic fields in an electromagnetic wave are perpendicular to each other, and to the direction of propagation.

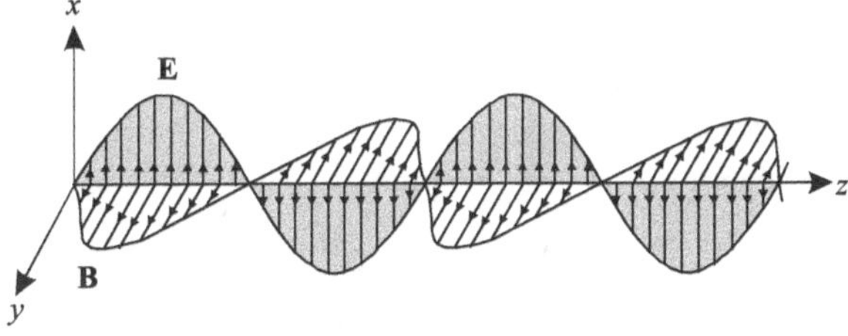

Fig.: A linearly polarised electromagnetic wave, propagating in the z-direction with the oscillating electric field $\mathbf{E}$ along the x-direction and the oscillating magnetic field $\mathbf{B}$ along the y-direction.

- We can write E_x and B_y as follows:

$E_x = E_0 \sin(kz - \omega t)$ ...(i)

$B_y = B_0 \sin(kz - \omega t)$ ...(ii)

- In free space, speed of EM waves

$$c = 1/\sqrt{\mu_0 \varepsilon_0}$$

- Magnitude of the electric and the magnetic fields in an electromagnetic wave are related as

$$B_0 = (E_0/c)$$

They are self-sustaining oscillations of electric and magnetic fields in free space, or vacuum.

- No material medium is involved in the vibrations of the electric and magnetic fields.

- In a material medium of permittivity ε and magnetic permeability μ, the velocity of light becomes,

$$v = \frac{1}{\sqrt{\mu\varepsilon}}$$

- It has been shown by experiments on electromagnetic waves of different wavelengths that this velocity is the same (independent of wavelength) of 3×10^8 m/s.

- Electromagnetic waves carry energy and momentum like other waves.

- In a region of free space with electric field E, there is an energy density $(\varepsilon_0 E^2/2)$. Similarly, associated with a magnetic field B is a magnetic energy density $(B^2/2\mu_0)$.

- If the total energy transferred to a surface in time t is U, it can be shown that the magnitude of the total momentum delivered to this surface (for complete absorption) is, $p = \dfrac{U}{c}$

Electromagnetic Spectrum

- Electromagnetic waves include visible light waves, X-rays, gamma rays, radio waves, microwaves, ultraviolet and infrared waves. The classification of em waves according to frequency is the electromagnetic spectrum (fig.).

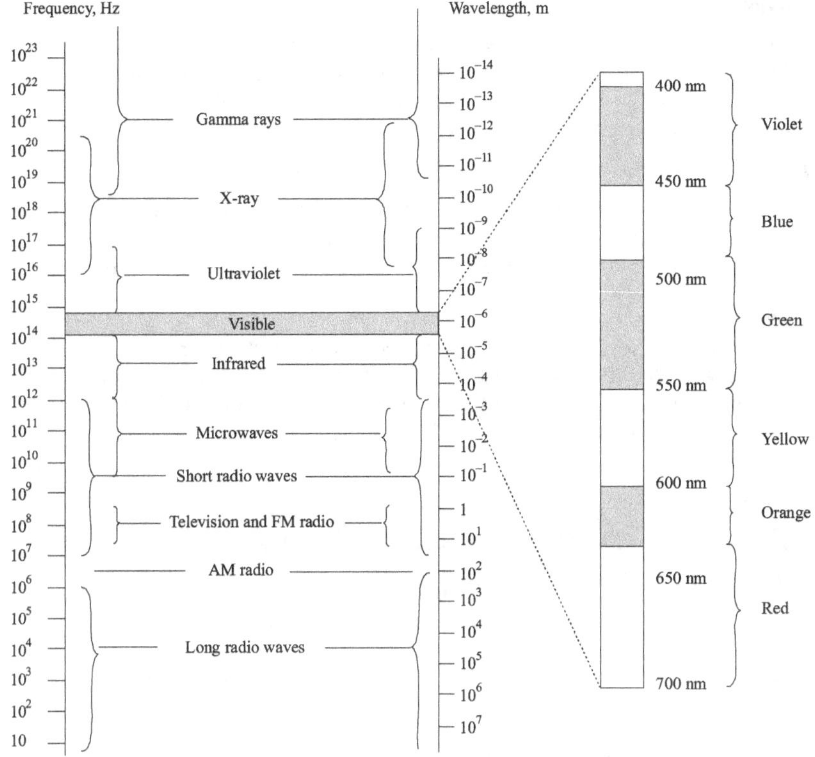

Fig.: The electromagnetic spectrum, with common names for various part of it. The various regions do not have sharply defined boundaries.

Radio Waves

♦ They are generally in the frequency range from 500 kHz to about 1000 MHz. Radiowaves are use in telecommunication.

Microwaves

♦ Microwaves (short-wavelength radio waves), with frequencies in the gigahertz (GHz) range, are produced by special vacuum tubes. They are suitable for the radar systems.

Infrared Waves

♦ Infrared waves are produced by hot bodies and molecules. This band lies adjacent to long-wavelength end of the visible spectrum. Infrared waves are sometimes referred to as *heat waves*.

♦ Infrared radiation plays an important role in greenhouse effect and to treat muscular strain.

Visible Rays

♦ It runs from about 4×10^{14} Hz to about 7×10^{14} Hz or a wavelength range of about 700 – 400 nm.
Uses-to see objects.

Ultraviolet Rays

- It covers wavelengths ranging from about 4×10^{-7} m (400 nm) down to 6×10^{-10} m (0.6 nm). The sun is source of ultraviolet light. But most of it is absorbed in the ozone layer in the atmosphere.
- UV-rays are used to preserve food, sterilizing the surgical instruments.

X-Rays

- It covers wavelengths from about 10^{-8} m (10 nm) down to 10^{-13} m (10^{-4} nm). X-rays damage or destroy living tissues and organisms, care must be taken to avoid unnecessary or over exposure. X-rays are used in medical diagonosis.

Gamma Rays

- They lie in the upper frequency range of the electromagnetic spectrum and have wavelengths of from about 10^{-10} m to less than 10^{-14} m. This high frequency radiation is produced in nuclear reactions and also emitted by radioactive nuclei. They are used in medicine to destroy cancer cells.

Past Years ONE-LINERS
NEET/JEE Main/Board

- Displacement current, $I_D = \dfrac{dq}{dt}$, q is charge on capacitor plate.

- Direction of $\overline{E} \times \overline{B}$ in EM wave gives direction of its propogation.

- Energy in EM wave is equally divided between electric & magnetic fields.

- Among colours VIBGYOR , red light has longest wavelength.

- In EM wave electric field & magnetic field are related by $\vec{E} \times \vec{B} = \vec{C}$.

- In EM wave ratio of electric field magnitude to magnetic field magnitude is equal to speed of light.

- An accelerating charge produces EM waves.

- Energy of x-ray is of the order of 100 ev to 100 kev.

- Velocity of EM wave in a medium of permittivity ε & permeability μ is $V = \dfrac{1}{\sqrt{\mu\varepsilon}}$.

- In EM wave electric field & magnetic field magnitude are related by $\vec{E} \times \vec{B} = \vec{C}$.

- For $\overline{B} = B_0 \cos\omega t\, \hat{i} + B_1 \cos\omega t\, \hat{j}$, magnetic field amplitude $= \sqrt{B_0^2 + B_1^2}$.

- Among non magnetic medium velocity of EM wave $= \dfrac{1}{\sqrt{\varepsilon\mu}}$.

- Radio wave < yellow light < blue light < X-rays (Increasing order of energy).

Tips/Tricks/Tecchniques ONE-LINERS
(Exam Sample)

- Displacement current can produce magnetic field.
- Displacement current is set up in a region where the electric field is changing with time.
- During charging of a capacitor, the conduction current in a wire connected to a capacitor is equal to the displacement current between the plates of capacitor.
- When a wave of energy U is totally reflected from the surface, the momentum delivered to the surface is given by $\dfrac{2U}{c}$.

  But in general, the momentum of the wave $= \dfrac{\text{energy (U)}}{\text{velocity (c)}} = \dfrac{U}{c}$

- The electric and magnetic fields satisfy the following wave equations, which can be obtained from Maxwell's third and fourth equations.

$$\frac{\partial^2 E}{\partial x^2} = \mu_0 \varepsilon_0 \frac{\partial^2 E}{\partial t^2} \text{ and } \frac{\partial^2 B}{\partial x^2} = \mu_0 \varepsilon_0 \frac{\partial^2 B}{\partial t^2}$$

  E and B are electric and magnetic field respectively.

- The electric and magnetic field of a sinusoidal plane electromagnetic wave propagating in the positive x-direction can also be written as
  $E = E_m \sin (kx - \omega t)$; $B = B_m \sin (kx - \omega t)$
  ω is the angular frequency of the wave and k is wave number which are given by

$$\omega = 2\pi f \text{ and } k = \frac{2\pi}{\lambda}$$

- The intensity of a sinusoidal plane electro-magnetic wave is defined as the average value of Poynting vector taken over one cycle.

$$S_{av} = \frac{E_m B_m}{2\mu_0} = \frac{E^2{}_m}{2\mu_0 c} = \frac{c}{2\mu_0} B^2{}_m$$

- For a perfectly refelcting surface, the average force exerted on the surface is

$$F = \frac{2IA}{C}$$

  where, I = energy flux incident on perfectly reflecting surface
  A = Area of surface

- The basic difference between various types of electromagnetic waves lies in their wavelengths or frequencies since all of them travel through vacuum with the same speed. Consequently, the waves differ considerably in their mode of interaction with matter.

24 Ray Optics and Optical Instruments

Reflection of Light by Spherical Mirrors

- Electromagnetic radiation (wavelength of about 400 nm to 750 nm) is called **light**.
- A light wave can be considered to travel from one point to another, along a straight line joining them. The path is called a **ray of light**, and a bundle of such rays constitutes a **beam of light**.
- The acceptable value of light in vacuum is
  $c = 2.99792458 \times 10^8 \, \text{m/s} = 3 \times 10^8 \, \text{m/s}$.
- **The laws of reflection**
  (i) The angle of reflection (i.e., the angle between reflected ray and the normal to the reflecting surface or the mirror) equals the angle of incidence (angle between incident ray and the normal).
  (ii) Also that *the incident ray, reflected ray and the normal to the reflecting surface at the point of incidence lie in the same plane*. These laws are valid at each point on any reflecting surface whether plane or curved.
- The geometric centre of a spherical mirror is called its **pole** while that of a spherical lens is called its **optical centre**. The line joining the pole and the centre of curvature of the spherical mirror is known as the **principal axis**.

Sign Convention

- According to this convention, all distances are measured from the pole of the mirror or the optical centre of the lens.
- The distances measured in the same direction as the incident light are taken as positive and those measured in the direction opposite to the direction of incident light are taken as negative.
- The heights measured upwards with respect to x-axis and normal to the principal axis (x-axis) of the mirror/ lens are taken as positive. The heights measured downwards are taken as negative.

Focal Length of Spherical Mirrors

- The distance between the focus F and the pole P of the mirror is called the **focal length** of the mirror, denoted by f. $f = R/2$, where R is the **radius of curvature** of the mirror.

The Mirror Equation

♦ The ray incident at any angle at the pole. The reflected ray follows laws of reflection.

$$\frac{1}{v} + \frac{1}{u} = \frac{1}{f}$$

This relation is known as the *mirror equation*.

♦ Linear magnification (m) as the ratio of the height of the image (h') to the height of the object (h):

$$m = \frac{h'}{h}$$

h and h' will be taken positive or negative in accordance with the accepted sign convention.

$$m = \frac{h'}{h} = -\frac{v}{u}$$

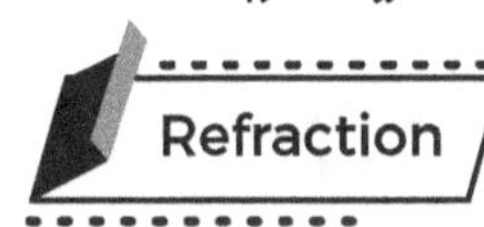

♦ The direction of propagation of an obliquely incident ($0° < i < 90°$) ray of light that enters the other medium, changes at the interface of the two media. This phenomenon is called **refraction of light**.

♦ Snell experimentally obtained the following laws of refraction:
  (i) The incident ray, the refracted ray and the normal to the interface at the point of incidence, all lie in the same plane.
  (ii) The ratio of the sine of the angle of incidence to the sine of angle of refraction is constant.

$$\frac{\sin i}{\sin r} = n_{21}$$

where n_{21} is a constant, called the **refractive index** of the second medium with respect to the first medium.

♦ If $n_{21} > 1$, $r < i$, i.e., the refracted ray bends towards the normal. In such a case medium 2 is said to be **optically *denser*** (or ***denser***, in short) than medium 1.

♦ If $n_{21} < 1$, $r > i$, the refracted ray bends away from the normal. This is the case when incident ray in a denser medium refracts into a rarer medium.

♦ If n_{21} is the refractive index of medium 2 with respect to medium 1 and n_{12} the refractive index of medium 1 with respect to medium 2, then

$$n_{12} = \frac{1}{n_{21}}$$

♦ If n_{32} is the refractive index of medium 3 w.r.t. medium 2 then $n_{32} = n_{31} \times n_{12}$.

♦ Some elementary results based on the laws of refraction. For a rectangular slab, refraction takes place at two interfaces (air-glass and glass-air).

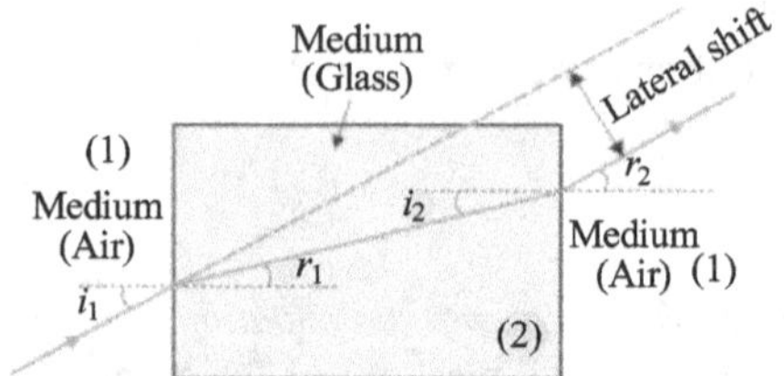

Fig. : Lateral shift of a ray refracted through
a parallel-sided slab.

- When $r_2 = i_1$, i.e., the emergent ray is parallel to the incident ray — there is no deviation, but it does suffer lateral displacement/ shift with respect to the incident ray.
- Another familiar observation is that the bottom of a tank filled with water appears to be raised.

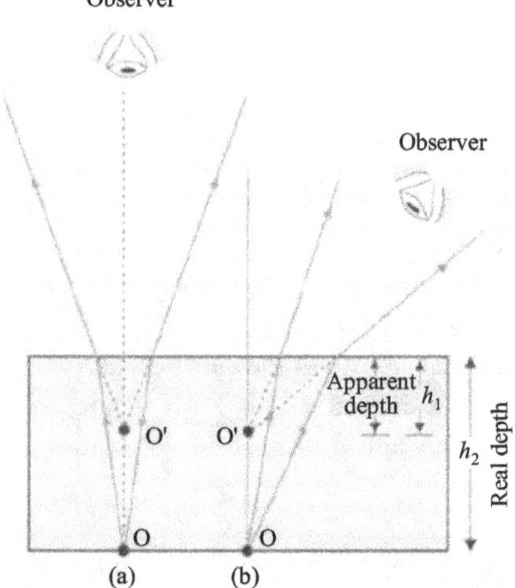

Fig. : Apparent depth for (a) normal, and (b) oblique viewing.

Total Internal Reflection

- When light travels from an optically denser medium to a rarer medium at the interface, it is partly reflected back into the same medium and partly refracted to the second medium. This reflection is called the **internal reflection**.

- When a ray of light enters from a denser medium to a rarer medium, it bends away from the normal.

- The incident ray AO_1 is partially reflected (O_1C) and partially transmitted (O_1B) or refracted, the angle of refraction (r) being larger than the angle of incidence (i). As the angle of incidence increases, so does the angle of refraction, till for the ray AO_3, the angle of refraction is $\pi/2$.

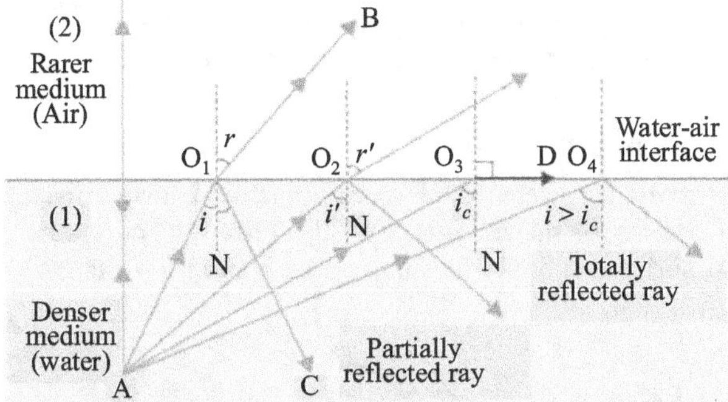

Fig. : Refraction and internal reflection of rays from a point A in the denser medium (water) incident at different angles at the interface with a rarer medium (air).

- If the angle of incidence is increased still further, refraction is not possible, and the incident ray is totally reflected. This is called **total internal reflection**.
- The angle of incidence corresponding to an angle of refraction 90°, say $\angle AO_3N$, is called the *critical angle* (i_c) for the given pair of media.
- The refractive index of denser medium 1 with respect to rarer medium 2 will be $n_{12} = 1/\sin i_c$.

Total Internal Reflection in Nature and its Technological Applications

- **Mirage** a distant patch of road, especially on a highway, appears to be wet.
- Diamonds are known for their spectacular brilliance. Their brilliance is mainly due to the total internal reflection of light inside them. The critical angle for diamond-air interface ($\cong 24.4°$) is very small.

  By cutting the diamond suitably, multiple total internal reflections can be made to occur.
- Prisms designed to bend light by 90° or by 180° make use of total internal reflection
- **Optical fibres** are extensively used for transmitting audio and video signals through long distances. Optical fibres are fabricated with high quality composite glass/quartz fibres. Each fibre consists of a core and cladding. The refractive index of the material of the core is higher than that of the cladding.

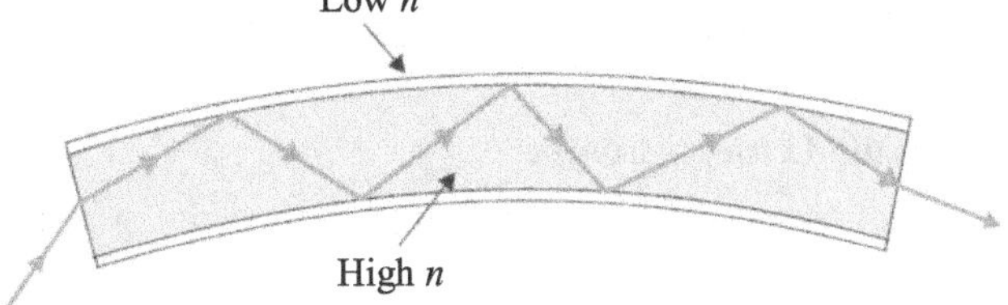

Fig. : Light undergoes successive total internal reflections as it moves through an optical fibre.

- Optical fibres are fabricated such that light reflected at one side of inner surface strikes the other at an angle larger than the critical angle. Even if the fibre is bent, light can easily travel along its length. An optical fibre can be used to act as an **optical pipe**.

Refraction at Spherical Surfaces and by Lenses

Refraction at a Spherical Surface

♦ Equation gives us a relation between object and image distance in terms of refractive index of the medium and the radius of curvature of the curved spherical surface. It holds for any curved spherical surface.

$$\frac{n_2}{v} - \frac{n_1}{u} = \frac{n_2 - n_1}{R}$$

Refraction by a Lens

♦ $$\frac{1}{f} = (n_{21} - 1)\left(\frac{1}{R_1} - \frac{1}{R_2}\right) \quad \left(\because n_{21} = \frac{n_2}{n_1}\right)$$

This equation is known as the *lens maker's formula*.

♦ Equation $\frac{1}{v} - \frac{1}{u} = \frac{1}{f}$ is the familiar *thin lens formula*.

♦ Magnification (m) produced by a lens is defined, as the ratio of the size of the image to that of the object.

$$m = \frac{h'}{h} = \frac{v}{u}$$

♦ For erect (and virtual) image formed by a convex or concave lens, m is positive, while for an inverted (and real) image, m is negative.

Power of a Lens

♦ The *power P* of a lens is defined as the tangent of the angle by which it converges or diverges a beam of light parallel to the principal axis falling at unit distance from the optical centre.

$$P = \frac{1}{f}$$

The SI unit for power of a lens is **dioptre (D): 1D = 1m^{-1}**.

Power of a lens is positive for a converging lens and negative for a diverging lens.

Combination of Thin Lenses in Contact

♦ If several thin lenses of focal length $f_1, f_2, f_3,...$ are in contact, the effective focal length of their combination is

$$\frac{1}{f} = \frac{1}{f_1} + \frac{1}{f_2} + \frac{1}{f_3} + ...$$

In terms of power,
$$P = P_1 + P_2 + P_3 + ...$$
where P is the net power of the lens combination.

Refraction through a Prism

♦ The angle between the emergent ray RS and the direction of the incident ray PQ is called the **angle of deviation, δ**.

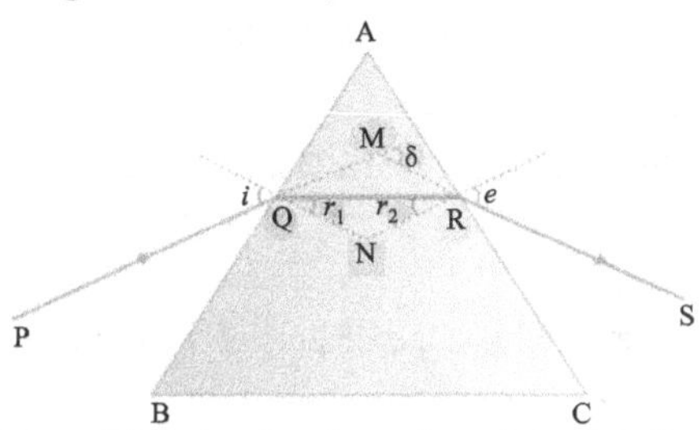

Fig. : A ray of light passing through a triangular glass prism.

♦ The total deviation δ is the sum of deviations at the two faces,

$$\delta = i + e - A$$
$$r_1 + r_2 = A$$

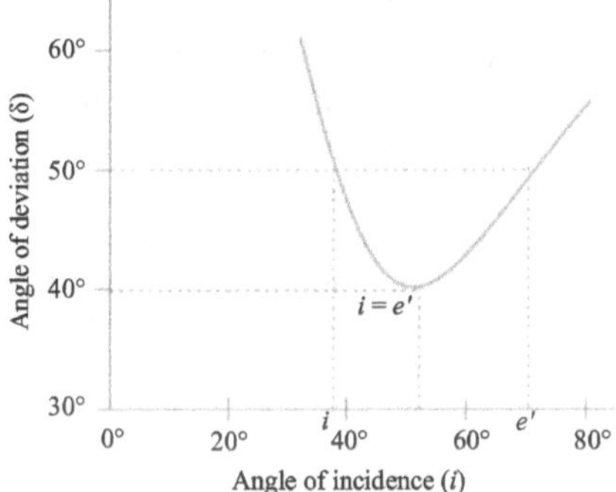

Fig. : Plot of angle of deviation (δ) versus angle of incidence (i) for a triangular prism.

♦ At the minimum deviation D_m, the refracted ray inside the prism becomes parallel to its base.

♦ For a small angle prism, i.e., a thin prism, D_m is also very small, and we get

$$n_{21} = \frac{\sin[(A + D_m)/2]}{\sin[A/2]} \simeq \frac{(A + D_m)/2}{A/2}$$

$$D_m = (n_{21} - 1)A$$

It implies that, thin prisms do not deviate light much.

Dispersion by a Prism

♦ When a narrow beam of sunlight or white light is incident of glass prism, it splits into consituents colour **Violet, Indigo, Blue, Green, Yellow, Orange, Red**. The phenomenon of splitting of light into its component colours is known as **dispersion**.

- The pattern of colour components of light is called the **spectrum of light**.
- The red light bends the least and the violet light bends the most.
- Dispersion takes place because the refractive index of medium for different wavelengths (colours) is different.
- $\lambda_{Red} > \lambda_{Violet}$ and $\mu_{Red} < \mu_{Violet}$.
- In vacuum (or air) the speed of light is independent of wavelength.

Some Natural Phenomena due to Sunlight

The Rainbow

- The rainbow is an example of the dispersion of sunlight by the water drops in the atmosphere.
- This is a phenomenon due to combined effect of dispersion, refraction and reflection of sunlight by spherical water droplets of rain.

Scattering of Light

- The amount of scattering is inversely proportional to the fourth power of the wavelength. This is known as **Rayleigh scattering**.
- Large particles like dust and water droplets present in the atmosphere behave differently. The relevant quantity here is the relative size of the wavelength of light λ, and the scatterer (of typical size, say, a). For $a \ll \lambda$, one has Rayleigh scattering which is proportional to $1/\lambda^4$. For $a \gg \lambda$, i.e., large scattering objects (for example, raindrops, large dust or ice particles) this is not true, all wavelengths are scattered nearly equally.

Optical Instruments

The Eye

- Light enters the eye through a curved front surface, the cornea. It passes through the pupil which is the central hole in the iris. The size of the pupil can change under control of muscles. The light is further focussed by the eye lens on the retina.
- The retina is a film of nerve fibres covering the curved back surface of the eye. The retina contains rods and cones which sense light intensity and colour, respectively, and transmit electrical signals via the optic nerve to the brain which finally processes this information.
- The shape (curvature) and therefore the focal length of the lens can be modified somewhat by the ciliary muscles.
- When the muscle is relaxed, the focal length is about 2.5 cm and objects at infinity are in sharp focus on the retina.
- If an elderly person tries to read a book at about 25 cm from the eye, the image appears blurred. This condition (defect of the eye) is called *presbyopia*. It is corrected by using a converging lens for reading.

- The light from a distant object arriving at the eye-lens may get converged at a point in front of the retina. This type of defect is called *nearsightedness* or *myopia*.
- To compensate this, we interpose a concave lens between the eye and the object, with the diverging effect desired to get the image focussed on the retina [Fig. (b)].

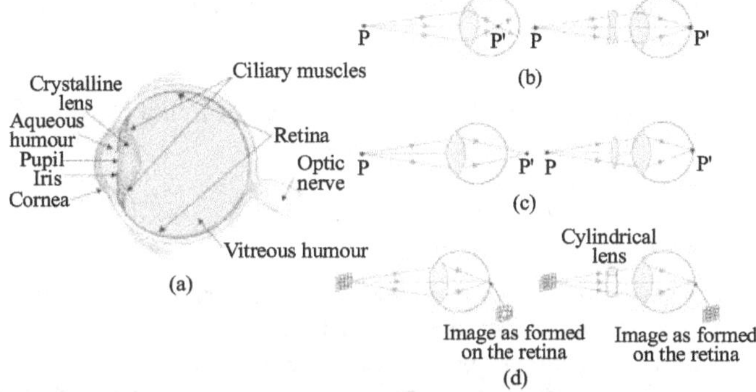

Fig. : (a) The structure of the eye; (b) shortsighted or myopic eye and its correction; (c) farsighted or hypermetropic eye and its correction; and (d) astigmatic eye and its correction.

- If the eye-lens focusses the incoming light at a point behind the retina, a convergent lens is needed to compensate for the defect in vision. This defect is called *farsightedness* or *hypermetropia* [Fig. (c)].
- Another common defect of vision is called *astigmatism*. This occurs when the cornea is not spherical in shape. For example, the cornea could have a larger curvature in the vertical plane than in the horizontal plane or vice-versa.

The Microscope

- A simple magnifier or microscope is a converging lens of small focal length
- The linear magnification m, for the image formed at the near point D, by a simple microscope

$$m = \left(1 + \frac{D}{f}\right)$$

- Magnification when the image is at infinity.

$$m = \left(\frac{\theta_i}{\theta_0}\right) = \frac{D}{f}$$

- A simple microscope has a limited maximum magnification (≤ 9) for realistic focal lengths.

Compound Microscope

- *Compound microscope* produces the final image, which is enlarged and virtual.
- Magnification due to a compound microscope.
  Magnification due to the objective,

$$m_0 = \frac{h'}{h} = \frac{L}{f_0}$$

when the final image is formed at the near point,

$$m_e = \left(1 + \frac{D}{f_e}\right)$$

- When the final image is formed at infinity, the angular magnification due to the eyepiece.

$$m_e = (D/f_e)$$

Total magnification, when the image is formed at infinity,

$$m = m_0 m_e = \left(\frac{L}{f_0}\right)\left(\frac{D}{f_e}\right)$$

Telescope

- The telescope is used to provide angular magnification of distant objects. It has an objective and an eyepiece. But here, the objective has a large focal length and a much larger aperture than the eyepiece.
- The magnifying power m is the ratio of the angle β subtended at the eye by the final image to the angle α which the object subtends at the lens or the eye.

$$m \approx \frac{\beta}{\alpha} \approx \frac{h}{f_e} \cdot \frac{f_o}{h} = \frac{f_o}{f_e}$$

In this case, the length of the telescope tube is $f_o + f_e$.

- The main considerations with an astronomical telescope are its light gathering power and its resolution or resolving power. The former clearly depends on the area of the objective. With larger diameters, fainter objects can be observed. The resolving power, or the ability to observe two objects distinctly, which are in very nearly the same direction, also depends on the diameter of the objective.
- Telescopes with mirror objectives are called reflecting telescopes. There is no chromatic aberration in a mirror.

Past Years ONE-LINERS
NEET/JEE Main/Board

- Lens formula, $\dfrac{1}{v} - \dfrac{1}{u} = \dfrac{1}{f}$.

- When angle of prism A > C (critical angle) then no ray emerges from second surface of the prism.

- When convex lens and concave lens are kept along the same axis, light refracted from convex lens
  virtually meet at focus of concave lens.

- From Snell's law, $\mu_0 \sin i = \mu_2 \sin r$.

- Equivalent focal length of two thin equi-convex lens of focal length f each in air $\dfrac{1}{F_1} = \dfrac{1}{f} + \dfrac{1}{f} = \dfrac{2}{f}$.

- Rainbow will be observed only when the sun is at the back side of observer.

- Mirror formula, $\dfrac{1}{f} = \dfrac{1}{v_1} + \dfrac{1}{u}$.

- For retracing the path, light ray should be normally incident.

- For telescope, angular magnification $= \dfrac{f_0}{f_E}$.

- For dispersion without deviation $(\mu-1)A_1 + (\mu'-1)A_2 = 0$.

- When mirror is rotated by angle θ reflected ray will be rotated by 2θ.

- Tube length of astronomical telescope $\ell = |v_0| + f_e$.

- Refractive index of material of prism, $\mu = \dfrac{\sin\left(\dfrac{A+\delta_m}{2}\right)}{\sin A/2}$.

- For total internal reflection, incident angle (i) > critical angle (i_c).

- Image will coincide with object if light fall perpendiculary to mirror.

- Magnification of compound microscope, $M \simeq \dfrac{L}{f_0}\left(1 + \dfrac{D}{f_e}\right)$.

- Using mirror formula $\dfrac{1}{v} + \dfrac{1}{u} = \dfrac{1}{f}$.

- A telescope magnifies by making the object appearing closer.

Tips/Tricks/Tecchniques ONE-LINERS
(Exam Sample)

- When light is reflected, velocity, wavelength and frequency of light remains same but intensity decreases.

- Images formed by mirrors is free from chromatic aberration.

- For concave mirror, minimum distance between a real object and its real image is zero when $u = v = 2f$.

- When mirror is rotated by angle θ, reflected ray will be rotated by 2θ.

- For two plane mirrors inclined at an angle θ, multiple reflections occur, if an object is placed between two mirrors.

  Number of images formed $n = \dfrac{360}{\theta} - 1$ $\left[\text{if } \dfrac{360}{\theta} = \text{even}\right]$

  and $n = \dfrac{360}{\theta}$ $\left[\text{if } \dfrac{360}{\theta} = \text{odd}\right]$

♦ If a source of light is situated at depth h in a liquid of refractive index μ, it will spread light in a circle of radius R such that $\mu = \sqrt{1 + h^2/R^2}$

♦ If the size of image produced by a spherical mirror is 'm' times the size of the object (m = magnification) then relation between u, v and f are given by the followings

$$u = \left(\frac{m-1}{m}\right)f, \quad v = -(m-1)f \quad \text{and} \quad f = \left(\frac{m}{m-1}\right)u$$

♦ Consider a lens is made of materials of refractive index μ_1, μ_2, μ_3, μ_4, μ_5 respectively. In such cases

Number of images formed = Number of materials used

Thus, total number of images = 5

♦ In a telescope, aperture of the field lens is made large to increase its resolving power as resolving power of a telescope varies directly with aperure of the field lens. Large aperture of objective also helps in improving the brightness of image by gathering more light from distant object.

♦ Magnification produced by telescope for normal setting is given by (f_o / f_e), so we can increase magnification, by taking f_o as large as practically possible and f_e small. This is why in a telescope, objective of large focal length is used while eye piece is small.

♦ If an object is moved with speed v_0 towards a spherical mirror along its axis then speed of image moving away from mirror is

$$\left| v_i \right| = -\left(\frac{f}{u-f}\right)^2 \cdot v_0$$

♦ If a sphere of radius R and refractive index μ_2 is placed in a medium of refractive index μ_1, then for an object placed at a distance $\left(\dfrac{\mu_1}{\mu_2 - \mu_1}\right)R$ from the pole, the real image will form at equidistant from the sphere.

♦ If two thin lenses of focal length f_1 and f_2 are separated co-axially by a distance x, then, formula of equivalent focal length F is given by

$$\frac{1}{F} = \frac{1}{f_1} + \frac{1}{f_2} - \frac{x}{f_1 f_2}$$

♦ For a system of lenses, net focal length is given by

$$\frac{1}{F} = \frac{1}{F_1} + \frac{1}{F_2} + \frac{1}{F_3} + \ldots\ldots$$

♦ Rainbow is a combined effect of dispersion, refraction and reflection of sunlight.

♦ To see the rainbow, the sun should be backside of observer.

♦ The laws of reflection and refraction are true for all surfaces and pairs of media at the point of the incidence.

25   Wave Optics

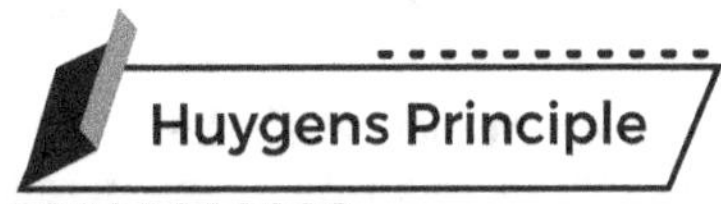

- The branch of optics in which one completely neglects the finiteness of the wavelength is called geometrical optics and a ray is defined as the path of energy propagation in the limit of wavelength tending to zero.

- A locus of points, which oscillate in phase is called a *wavefront*; thus *a wavefront is defined as a surface of constant phase*. The speed with which the wavefront moves outwards from the source is called the speed of the wave. The energy of the wave travels in a direction perpendicular to the wavefront.

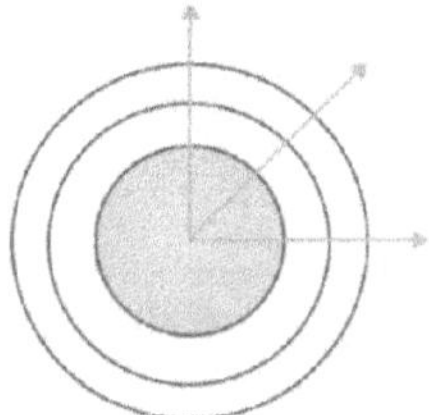

Fig.: A diverging spherical wave emanating from a point source. The wavefronts are spherical.

- If we have a point source emitting waves uniformly in all directions, then the locus of points which have the same amplitude and vibrate in the same phase are spheres and is known as a *spherical wave*.

- At a large distance from the source, a small portion of the sphere can be considered as a plane and we is known as a *plane wave*.

- According to **Huygens principle**, *each point of the wavefront is the source of a secondary disturbance and the wavelets emanating from these points spread out in all directions with the speed of the wave. These wavelets emanating from the wavefront are usually referred to as secondary wavelets and if we draw a common tangent to all these spheres, we obtain the new position of the wavefront at a later time.*

Refraction and Reflection of Plane Waves Using Huygens Principle

Refraction of a plane wave

♦ When a wave gets refracted into a denser medium ($v_1 > v_2$) the wavelength and the speed of propagation decrease but the *frequency* $\nu(= v/\lambda)$ *remains the same.*

The doppler effect

♦ When the source moves away from the observer the frequency as measured by the source will be smaller. This is known as the *Doppler effect.* Astronomers call the increase in wavelength due to doppler effect as *red shift* since a wavelength in the middle of the visible region of the spectrum moves towards the red end of the spectrum.

♦ When waves are received from a source moving towards the observer, there is an apparent decrease in wavelength, this is referred to as *blue shift.*

♦ The fractional change in frequency $\Delta\nu/\nu$ is given by $-v_{radial}/c$, where v_{radial} is the component of the source velocity along the line joining the observer to the source relative to the observer; v_{radial} is considered positive when the source moves away from the observer. Doppler shift

$$\frac{\Delta\nu}{\nu} = -\frac{v_{radial}}{c}$$

This formula is valid only when the speed of the source is small compared to that of light.

Coherent and Incoherent Addition of Waves

♦ *Superposition principle according to which at a particular point in the medium, the resultant displacement produced by a number of waves is the vector sum of the displacements produced by each of the waves.*

♦ If the displacement produced by the source S_1 is

$y_1 = a \cos \omega t$

Displacement produced by the source S_2

$y_2 = a \cos \omega t$

Thus, the resultant of displacement at a point

$y = y_1 + y_2 = 2\,a \cos \omega t$

♦ Since the intensity is proportional to the square of the amplitude, the resultant intensity

$I = 4\,I_0$

Where I_0 represents the intensity produced by each one of the individual sources; I_0 is proportional to a^2. At any point on the perpendicular bisector of S_1S_2, the intensity will be $4I_0$. The two sources are said to interfere constructively referred to as *constructive interference.*

- If the displacement produced by S_1 is

$y_1 = a \cos \omega t$

The displacement produced by S_2

$y_2 = a \cos (\omega t + 5\pi) = -a \cos \omega t$

Where we have used the fact that a path difference of 2.5λ corresponds to a phase difference of 5π. The two displacements are now out of phase and the two displacements will cancel out to give zero intensity. This is referred to as *destructive interference.*

- If we have two coherent sources S_1 and S_2 vibrating in phase, then for an arbitrary point P whenever the path difference,

$S_1P \sim S_2P = n\lambda \ (n = 0, 1, 2, 3,...)$

We will have constructive interference and the resultant intensity will be $4I_0$.

- If the point P is such that the path difference,

$$S_1P \sim S_2P = (n + \frac{1}{2})\lambda \ (n = 0, 1, 2, 3, ...)$$

We will have *destructive interference* and the resultant intensity will be zero.

- For any other arbitrary point G let the phase difference between the two displacements be ϕ. Thus, if the displacement produced by S_1 is

$y_1 = a \cos \omega t$

And, the displacement produced by S_2 would be

$y_2 = a \cos (\omega t + \phi)$

and the resultant displacement

$y = y_1 + y_2$

$\quad = a \left[\cos \omega t + \cos (\omega t + \phi)\right]$

$\quad = 2 a \cos (\phi/2) \cos (\omega t + \phi/2)$

The amplitude of the resultant displacement is $2a \cos (\phi/2)$ and therefore the intensity at that point will be

$I = 4 I_0 \cos^2 (\phi/2)$

- If $\phi = 0, \pm 2\pi, \pm 4\pi,...$ which corresponds to the condition given by constructive interference leading to maximum intensity. On the other hand, if $\phi = \pm \pi, \pm 3\pi, \pm 5\pi...$ destructive interference leading to zero intensity.

Interference of Light Waves and Young's Experiment

- Constructive interference resulting in a bright region when $\dfrac{xd}{D} \ n\lambda$

That is,

$$x = x_n = \frac{n\lambda D}{d}; \ n = 0, \pm 1, \pm 2, ...$$

Destructive interference resulting in a dark region when $\dfrac{xd}{D} = \left(n + \dfrac{1}{2} \right) \lambda$ that is

$$x = x_n = \left(n + \dfrac{1}{2} \right) \dfrac{\lambda D}{d}; \ n = 0, \pm 1, \pm 2$$

dark and bright bands appear on the screen are called *fringes*.

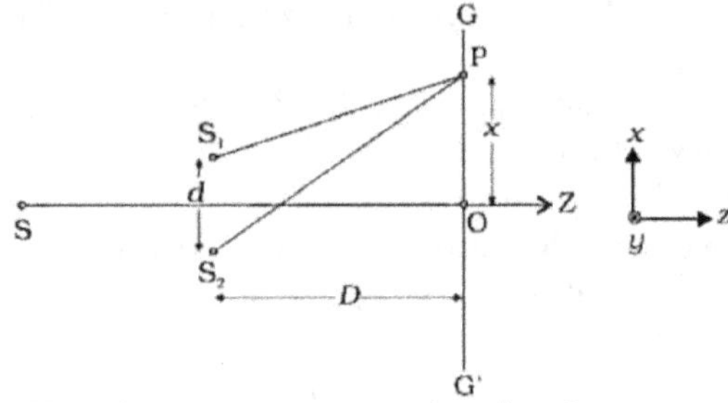

Fig.: Young's arrangement to produce interference pattern.

- The distance between two consecutive bright and dark fringes is given by

$$\beta = x_{n+1} - x_n \ \text{or} \ \beta = \dfrac{\lambda D}{d}$$

This is the expression for the *fringe width*.

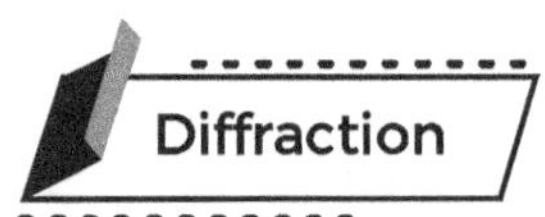

Diffraction

- Diffraction is a general characteristic exhibited by all types of waves, be it sound waves, light waves, water waves or matter waves.
- The colours that you see when a CD is viewed is due to diffraction effects.

The single slit

- Light spreads out from narrow holes and slits. It seems to turn around corners and enter regions where we would expect a shadow. These effects, known as *diffraction*.
- The path difference NP – LP between the two edges of the slit

$$NP - LP = NQ = a \sin \theta$$
$$\approx a \ \theta \ \text{(for smaller angles)}$$

- At the central point C on the screen, the angle θ is zero. All path differences are zero and hence all the parts of the slit contribute in phase. This gives maximum intensity at C.
- Fig. indicates that the intensity has a central maximum at $\theta = 0$ and other secondary maxima at $\theta \approx (n + 1/2) \lambda/a$, and has minima (zero intensity) at $\theta \approx n\lambda/a$, $n = \pm 1$, $\pm 2, \pm 3, ...$
- Consider first the angle θ where the path difference $a\theta$ is λ. Then,
$$\theta \approx \lambda/a.$$

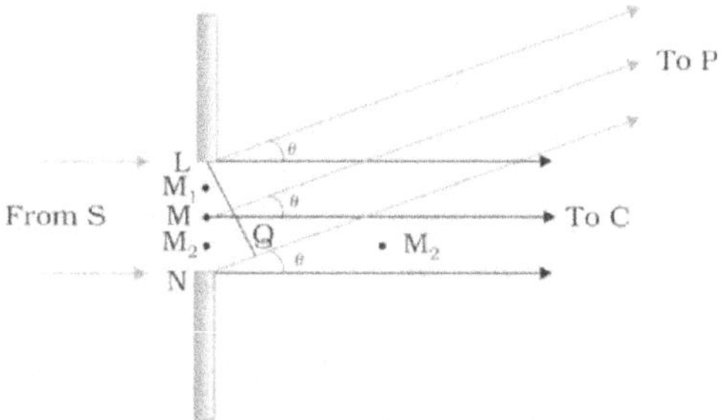

Fig.: The geometry of path differences for diffraction by a single slit.

- One can similarly show that the intensity is zero for $\theta = n\lambda/a$, with n being any integer (except zero!).

- There are maxima at $(n + 1/2)\,\lambda/a$ with $n = 2, 3$, etc.

- *In interference and diffraction, light energy is redistributed. If it reduces in one region, producing a dark fringe, it increases in another region, producing a bright fringe. There is no gain or loss of energy, which is consistent with the principle of conservation of energy.*

Resolving power of optical instruments

- Resolving power of microscope, $R.P. = \dfrac{2\mu\sin\theta}{\lambda}$

- Resolving limit of telescope, $d\theta = \dfrac{1.22\lambda}{a}$

- Resolving power, $RP = \dfrac{1}{d\theta} = \dfrac{a}{1.22\lambda}$

The validity of ray optics

- An aperture of size a illuminated by a parallel beam sends diffracted light into an angle of approximately $\approx \lambda/a$. This is the angular size of the bright central maximum. In travelling a distance z, the diffracted beam therefore acquires a width $z\lambda/a$ due to diffraction.

- The distance beyond which divergence of the beam of width a becomes significant.

$$z \approx \frac{a^2}{\lambda}$$

- A quantity z_F called the *Fresnel distance*

$$z_F = a^2/\lambda$$

- For distances much smaller than z_F, the spreading due to diffraction is smaller compared to the size of the beam. It becomes comparable when the distance is approximately z_F. For distances much greater than z_F, the spreading due to diffraction dominates over that due to ray optics (i.e., the size a of the aperture) z

$$\approx \frac{a^2}{\lambda}$$ also shows that ray optics is valid in the limit of wavelength tending to zero.

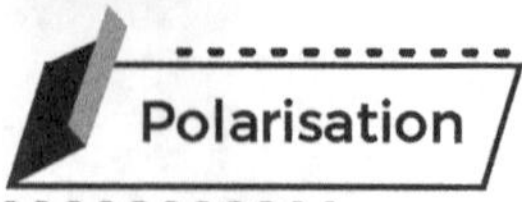

Polarisation

- The displacement (which is along the y direction) is at right angles to the direction of propagation of the wave, known as a *transverse wave*.

- If the plane of vibration of the string is changed randomly in very short intervals of time, then we have what is known as an *unpolarised wave*.

- For an unpolarised wave the displacement will be randomly changing with time though it will always be perpendicular to the direction of propagation.

- Light waves are transverse in nature; i.e., the electric field associated with a propagating light wave is always at right angles to the direction of propagation of the wave.

- A polaroid consists of long chain molecules aligned in a particular direction.

- The electric vectors (associated with the propagating light wave) along the direction of the aligned molecules get absorbed.

- If an unpolarised light wave is incident on such a polaroid then the light wave will get linearly polarised with the electric vector oscillating along a direction perpendicular to the aligned molecules; this direction is known as the pass-axis of the polaroid.

- If the light from an ordinary source (like a sodium lamp) passes through a polaroid sheet P_1, it is observed that its intensity is reduced by half.

- Rotating P_1 has no effect on the transmitted beam and transmitted intensity remains constant.

- Now, let an identical piece of polaroid P_2 be placed before P_1. As expected, the light from the lamp is reduced in intensity on passing through P_2 alone.

- But now rotating P_1 has a dramatic effect on the light coming from P_2. In one position, the intensity transmitted by P_2 followed by P_1 is nearly zero.

- When turned by 90° from this position, P_1 transmits nearly the full intensity emerging from P_2.

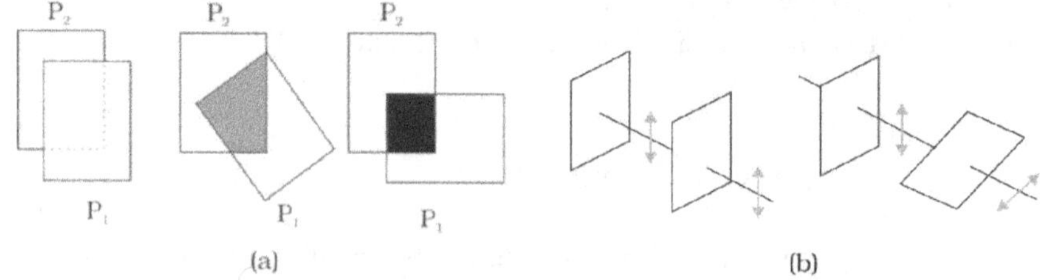

Fig.: (a) Passage of light through two polaroids P_2 and P_1. The transmitted fraction falls from 1 to 0 as the angle between them varies from 0° to 90°. Notice that the light seen through a single polaroid P_1 does not vary with angle. (b) Behaviour of the electric vector when light passes through two polaroids. The transmitted polarisation is the component parallel to the polaroid axis. The double arrows show the oscillations of the electric vector.

- As we rotate the polaroid the intensity will vary as:

$$I = I_0 \cos^2\theta$$

Where I_0 is the intensity of the polarized light after passing through P_1. This is known as *Malus' law*.

Polarisation by scattering

- The light from a clear blue portion of the sky shows a rise and fall of intensity when viewed through a polaroid which is rotated. This is nothing but sunlight, which has changed its direction (having been scattered) on encountering the molecules of the earth's atmosphere.

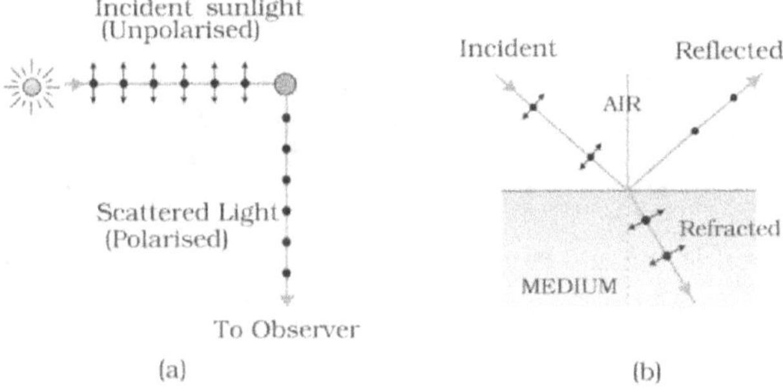

Fig.: (a) Polarisation of the blue scattered light from the sky. The incident sunlight is unpolarised (dots and arrows). A typical molecule is shown. It scatters light by 90° polarised normal to the plane of the paper (dots only).

(b) Polarisation of light reflected from a transparent medium at the Brewster angle (reflected ray perpendicular to refracted ray).

Polarisation by reflection

- Figure shows situation in which the reflected wave travels at right angles to the refracted wave. The oscillating electrons in the water produce the *reflected wave*. These move in the two directions transverse to the radiation from wave in the medium, i.e., the refracted wave. The arrows are parallel to the direction of the reflected wave. Motion in this direction does not contribute to the reflected wave.

- The reflected light is therefore linearly polarised perpendicular to the plane of the figure (represented by dots). This can be checked by looking at the reflected light through an analyser. The transmitted intensity will be zero when the axis of the analyser is in the plane of the figure, i.e., the plane of incidence.

- When unpolarised light is incident on the boundary between two transparent media, the reflected light is polarised with its electric vector perpendicular to the plane of incidence when the refracted and reflected rays make a right angle with each other.

- When reflected wave is perpendicular to the refracted wave, the reflected wave is a totally polarised wave. The angle of incidence in this case is called *Brewster's angle* and is denoted by i_B.

$$\mu = \frac{\sin i_B}{\sin r} = \frac{\sin i_B}{\sin (\pi/2 - i_B)} = \frac{\sin i_B}{\cos i_B} = \tan i_B$$

This is known as *Brewster's law*.

- When an unpolarised beam of light is incident at the Brewster's angle on an interface of two media, only part of light with electric field vector perpendicular to the plane of incidence will be reflected.

Past Years ONE-LINERS
NEET/JEE Main/Board

- A large focal length and large aperture of an objective of an astronomical telescope, ensures better light gathering power, and resolution.

- Fringe width $\beta = \dfrac{\lambda D}{d}$

- According to Brewster's law, when a beam of unpolarised light is reflected from a transparent medium of refractive index (μ_2), the reflected light is completely polarised at certain angle of incidence called the angle of polarisation (i_b).

$$\tan i_b = \frac{\mu_2}{\mu_1}$$

- Limit of resolution of telescope, $\theta = \dfrac{1.22\lambda}{d}$

- For double slit experiment angular fringe width $\theta_0 = \dfrac{\beta}{D}$

  Angular fringe width (in water) $\theta_w = \dfrac{\beta}{\mu D} = \dfrac{\theta_0}{\mu}$

- From Brewester law, $\tan i = \mu$ (i = Brewester angle)

- Angular width in Young's double slit experiment $= \dfrac{\lambda}{d}$

- Resolving power of a microscope $= \dfrac{2\mu \sin\theta}{\lambda}$

- According to malus law, $I = I_0\cos^2\theta$

- For common maxima, $n_1\lambda_1 = n_2\lambda_2$

Tips/Tricks/Tecchniques ONE-LINERS
(Exam Sample)

- When light goes from one medium to another, frequency of light wave remains constant. But wavelength and velocity both becomes $\dfrac{1}{\mu}$ time.

- Interference is the redistribution of light energy in the form of maxima and minima.

- The angular fringe width δ is given by $\delta = \dfrac{\beta}{D} = \dfrac{\lambda}{d}$.

- A substance (like calcite quartz) which exhibits different properties in different direction is called anisotopic substance.

- Ratio of maximum and minimum intensities :

$$\frac{I_{max}}{I_{min}} = \left(\frac{\sqrt{I_1} + \sqrt{I_2}}{\sqrt{I_1} - \sqrt{I_2}}\right)^2 = \left(\frac{\sqrt{I_1/I_2} + 1}{\sqrt{I_1/I_2} - 1}\right)^2$$

$$= \left(\frac{a_1 + a_2}{a_1 - a_2}\right)^2 = \left(\frac{a_1/a_2 + 1}{a_1/a_2 - 1}\right)^2 \text{ also } \sqrt{\frac{I_1}{I_2}} = \frac{a_1}{a_2} = \left(\frac{\sqrt{\dfrac{I_{max}}{I_{min}}} + 1}{\sqrt{\dfrac{I_{max}}{I_{min}}} - 1}\right)$$

- If two waves having equal intensity ($I_1 = I_2 = I_0$) meets at two locations A and B. Let Δ_1 and Δ_2 be the phase difference at A and B respectively, then the ratio of resultant intensity at point A and B will be

$$\frac{I_A}{I_B} = \frac{\cos^2 \dfrac{\phi_1}{2}}{\cos^2 \dfrac{\phi_2}{2}} = \frac{\cos^2\left(\dfrac{\pi\Delta_1}{\lambda}\right)}{\cos^2\left(\dfrac{\pi\Delta_2}{\lambda}\right)}$$

- If for two interfering wave initial phase difference between them is ϕ_0 and phase difference due to path difference between them is ϕ. Then total phase difference will be

$$\phi = \phi_0 + \phi' = \phi_0 + \frac{2\pi}{\lambda}\Delta$$

- If two coherent sources S_1 and S_2 are held at distance d apart horizontally in young's double slit experiment, then the path difference = d cos θ. Also, the condition for nth bright fringe will be $d \cos \theta = n\lambda$

♦ In YDSE, if D > d, then wavelengths absent in front of one of the slits will be given by

$$\lambda = \frac{d^2}{D}, \frac{d^2}{3D}, \frac{d^2}{5D} \text{ and so on.}$$

♦ Fringe visibility (V) is given by

$$V = \frac{I_{\max} - I_{\min}}{I_{\max} + I_{\min}} = \frac{2\sqrt{I_1 I_2}}{I_1 + I_2}$$

♦ Velocity of light using doppler's effect of light is given by

$$V = \pm \frac{\Delta v}{v} c = \frac{\Delta \lambda}{\lambda} c$$

♦ If two waves of intensity I_1 and I_2 and phase difference ϕ between them, resultant intensity is given by

$$I = I_1 + I_2 + 2\sqrt{I_1 I_2} \ \cos \phi$$

For two identical source, $I_1 = I_2 = I_0$

$$I = I_0 + I_0 + 2\sqrt{I_0 I_0} \ \cos \phi$$

$$= 4I_0 \cos^2 \frac{\phi}{2} \qquad \left(\because 1 + \cos \phi = 2\cos^2 \frac{\phi}{2} \right)$$

♦ If whole YDSE set up is taken in another medium then wavelength λ changes So β changes.

$$\beta_w = \frac{\beta_a}{\mu_w} \text{ [Here } b_a = \text{fringe width in air]}$$

μ_w = refractive index of water.

♦ Resolving power of microscope $= \dfrac{2\mu \sin \theta}{\lambda}$

Here, λ = wavelength of light

 μ = refractive index of the medium between the object and the objective.

$\sin \theta$ = half angle (θ) of the cone of light from the objects.

26 Dual Nature of Radiation and Matter

Electron Emission

- A certain minimum amount of energy is required to be given to an electron to pull it out from the surface of the metal. This minimum energy required by an electron to escape from the metal surface is called the **work function** of the metal. It is generally denoted by ϕ_0 and measured in eV (electron volt).
- One electron volt is the energy gained by an electron when it has been accelerated by a potential difference of 1 volt, so that $1 \text{ eV} = 1.602 \times 10^{-19}$ J.
- The minimum energy required for the electron emission from the metal surface can be supplied to the free electrons by any one of the following physical processes:
    - (i) **Thermionic emission**: By suitably heating, sufficient thermal energy can be imparted to the free electrons to enable them to come out of the metal.
    - (ii) **Field emission**: By applying a very strong electric field (of the order of 10^8 V m^{-1}) to a metal, electrons can be pulled out of the metal, as in a spark plug.
    - (iii) **Photoelectric emission**: When light of suitable frequency illuminates a metal surface, electrons are emitted from the metal surface. These photo (light)-generated electrons are called *photoelectrons*.

Experimental Study of Photoelectric Effect

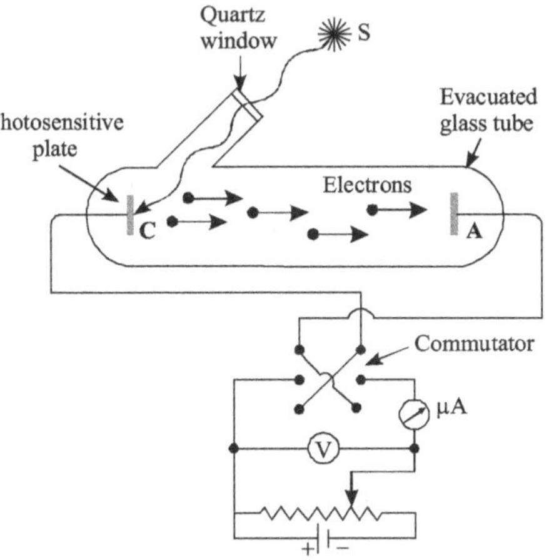

Fig.: Experimental arrangement for study of photoelectric effect.

Effect of Intensity of Light on Photocurrent

♦ Keeping the frequency of the incident radiation and the potential fixed, the intensity of light is varied and the resulting photoelectric current is measured each time. It is found that the photocurrent increases linearly with intensity of incident light as shown graphically.

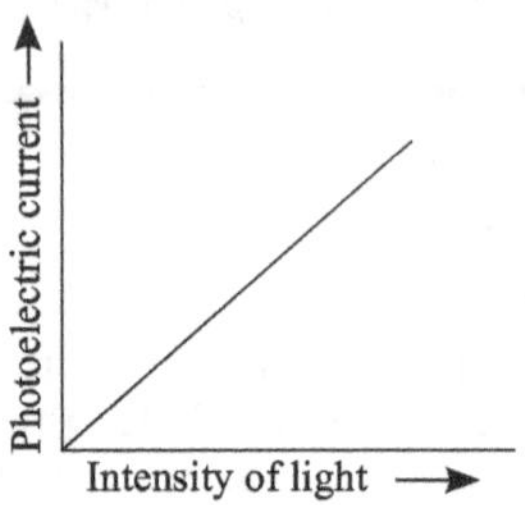

Fig.: Variation of Photoelectric current with intensity of light.

♦ The photocurrent is directly proportional to the number of photoelectrons emitted per second. This implies that *the number of photoelectrons emitted per second is directly proportional to the intensity of incident radiation.*

Effect of Potential on Photoelectric Current

♦ For a particular frequency of incident radiation, *the minimum negative (retarding) potential V_0 given to the plate A for which the photocurrent stops or becomes zero is called the **cut-off or stopping potential.***

♦ All the photoelectrons emitted from the metal do not have the same energy. Photoelectric current is zero when the stopping potential is sufficient to repel even the most energetic photoelectrons, with the maximum kinetic energy (K_{max}), so that

$$K_{max} = e\,V_0$$

♦ *For a given frequency of the incident radiation, the stopping potential is independent of its intensity.*

♦ The maximum kinetic energy of photoelectrons depends on the light source and the emitter plate material, but is independent of intensity of incident radiation.

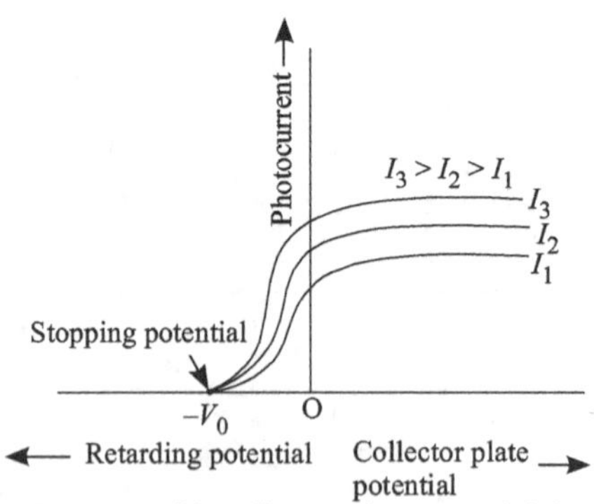

Fig.: Variation of photocurrent with collector plate potential for different intensity of incident radiation.

Effect of Frequency of Incident Radiation on Stopping Potential

♦ If we plot a graph between the frequency of incident radiation and the corresponding stopping potential for different metals we get a straight line.

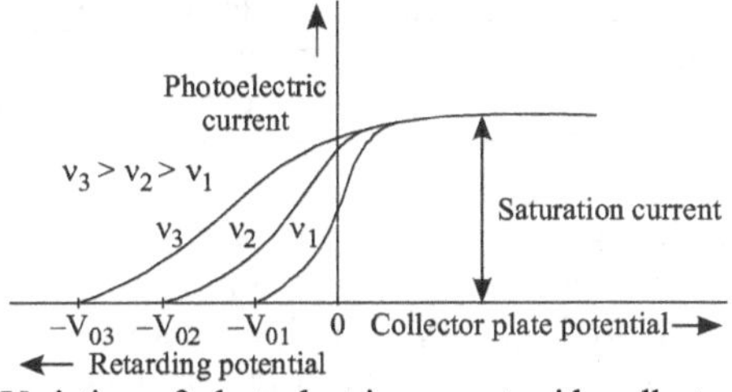

Fig.: Variation of photoelectric current with collector plate
potential for different frequencies of incident radiation.

♦ **Saturation Current** is the maximum value of photoelectric current which corresponds to the case when all photoelectrons emitted by emitter plate reach the collector plate.

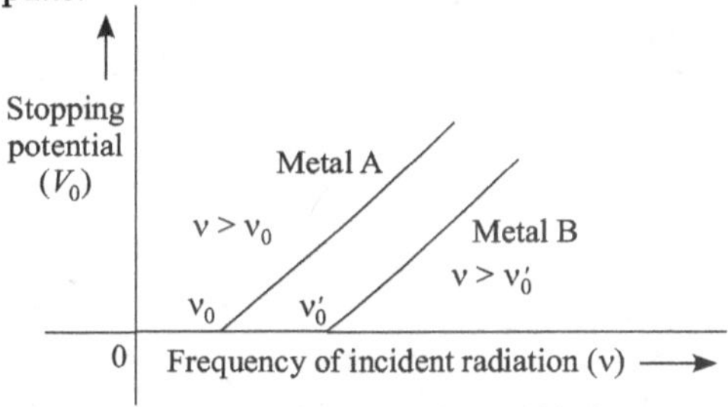

Fig.: Variation of stopping potential V_0 with frequency v of
incident radiation for a given photosensitive material.

♦ The graph shows that
  (i) the stopping potential V_0 varies linearly with the frequency of incident radiation for a given photosensitive material.
  (ii) There exists a certain minimum cut-off frequency n0 for which the stopping potential is zero.

♦ *These observations have two implications:*
  (i) *The maximum kinetic energy of the photoelectrons varies linearly with the frequency of incident radiation, but is independent of its intensity.*
  (ii) *For a frequency v of incident radiation, lower than the cut-off frequency v_0, no photoelectric emission is possible even if the intensity is large.*

♦ This minimum, cut-off frequency v_0, is called the **threshold frequency**.
♦ It is different for different metals.

Photoelectric Effect and Wave Theory of Light

♦ The phenomena of interference, diffraction and polarisation were explained in a natural and satisfactory way by the wave picture of light.
♦ According to wave picture of light, light is an electromagnetic wave consisting of electric and magnetic fields with continuous distribution of energy over the region of space over which the wave is extended.

258

♦ According to the wave picture of light, the free electrons at the surface of the metal (over which the beam of radiation falls) absorb the radiant energy continuously. The greater the intensity of radiation, the greater are the amplitude of electric and magnetic fields. Consequently, the greater the intensity, the greater should be the energy absorbed by each electron.

♦ In this picture, the maximum kinetic energy of the photoelectrons on the surface is then expected to increase with increase in intensity. Also, no matter what the frequency of radiation is, a sufficiently intense beam of radiation (over sufficient time) should be able to impart enough energy to the electrons, so that they exceed the minimum energy needed to escape from the metal surface. So, threshold frequency should not exist.

♦ The absorption of energy by electron takes place continuously over the entire wavefront of the radiation. Since a large number of electrons absorb energy, the energy absorbed per electron per unit time turns out to be small. Explicit calculations estimate that it can take hours or more for a single electron to pick up sufficient energy to overcome the work function and come out of the metal. This conclusion is again in striking contrast to observation that the photoelectric emission is instantaneous.

In short, the wave picture is unable to explain the most basic features of photoelectric emission.

Einstein's Photoelectric Equation: Energy Quantum of Radiation

♦ Radiation energy is built up of discrete units – the so called *quanta of energy of radiation*. Each quantum of radiant energy has energy $h\nu$, where h is Planck's constant and ν the frequency of light.

♦ According to Einstein, energy $h\nu$ of each quanta of radiation (photon) of incident light is partially utilised by an electron to overcome work function ϕ_0 and rest provides the maximum kinetic energy K_{max} to photoelectron during the emission. Equation given below is known as *Einstein's photoelectric equation*.

$$K_{max} = h\nu - \phi_0$$

♦ Photoelectric emission is possible only if $h\nu > \phi_0$
or $\nu > \nu_0$, where

$$\nu_0 = \frac{\phi_0}{h}$$

♦ The Einstein's photoelectric equation, can also be written as
$$eV_0 = h\nu - \phi_0; \text{ for } \nu \geq \nu_0$$

$$\Rightarrow \quad V_0 = \left(\frac{h}{e}\right)\nu - \frac{\phi_0}{e}$$

♦ On comparing the above equation with $y = mx + c$ we get slope $\left(= \frac{h}{e}\right)$.

♦ Thus, ν_0 vs ν graph is straight line with slope $\left(= \frac{h}{e}\right)$.

Particle Nature of Light: The Photon

- Einstein proposed that the light quantum can also be associated with momentum ($h\nu/c$). A definite value of energy as well as momentum associated with a particle. This particle was named *photon*.
- In interaction of radiation with matter, radiation behaves as if it is made up of particles called photons.
- Each photon has energy E ($= h\nu$) and momentum p ($= h\,\nu/c$), where speed c is the speed of light.
- All photons of light of a particular frequency ν, or wavelength λ, have the same energy E ($= h\nu = hc/\lambda$) and momentum p ($= h\nu/c = h/\lambda$), whatever the intensity of radiation may be.

  By increasing the intensity of light of given wavelength, there is only an increase in the number of photons per second crossing a given area, with each photon having the same energy. Thus, photon energy is independent of intensity of radiation.
- Photons are electrically neutral and are not deflected by electric and magnetic fields.
- In a photon-particle collision (such as photon-electron collision), the total energy and total momentum are conserved. However, the number of photons may not be conserved in a collision. The photon may be absorbed or a new photon may be created.

Wave Nature of Matter

- The wave nature of light shows up in the phenomena of interference, diffraction and polarisation. On the other hand, in photoelectric effect and Compton effect which involve energy and momentum transfer, radiation behaves as if it is made up of a bunch of particles – the photons.
- De Broglie proposed that the wavelength λ associated with a particle of momentum p is given as

$$\lambda = \frac{h}{p} = \frac{h}{m\nu}$$

  Where m is the mass of the particle and v its speed. This relation is called de-Broglie relation. The wavelength λ of the *matter wave is called de Broglie wavelength*.
- An electron (mass m, charge e) accelerated from rest through a potential V. The kinetic energy K of the electron equals the work done (eV) on it by the electric field:

$$K = e\,V$$
$$K = \frac{1}{2}m\,v^2 = \frac{p^2}{2m}$$
$$p = \sqrt{2mK} = \sqrt{2meV}$$

The de Broglie wavelength λ of the electron is then

$$\lambda = \frac{h}{p} = \frac{h}{\sqrt{2mK}} = \frac{h}{\sqrt{2meV}}$$

Substituting the numerical values of h, m, e, we get

$$\lambda = \frac{1.227}{\sqrt{V}}\ \text{nm}$$

♦ According to Heisenberg's uncertainity principle, it is not possible to measure both the position and momentum of an electron (or any other particle) at the same time exactly. There is always some uncertainty (Δx) in the specification of position and some uncertainty (Δp) in the specification of momentum. The product of Δx and Δp is of the order of $\hbar$ (with $\hbar = \hbar/2\pi$), i.e.,

$$\Delta x\,\Delta p \approx \hbar$$

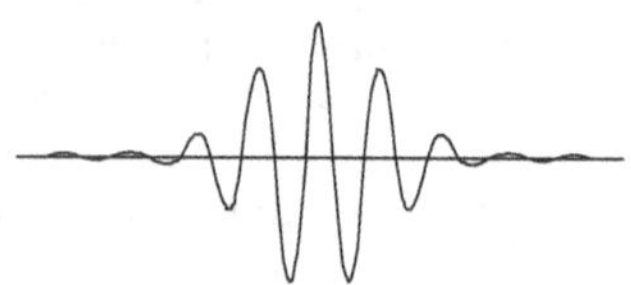

Fig.: The wave packet description of an electron. The wave packet corresponds to a spread of wavelength around some central wavelength (and hence by de Broglie relation, a spread in momentum). Consequently, it is associated with an uncertainty in position (Δx) and an uncertainty in momentum (Δp).

Davisson and Germer Experiment

♦ The experimental arrangement used by Davisson and Germer is schematically shown in fig. It consists of an electron gun which comprises of a tungsten filament F, coated with barium oxide and heated by a low voltage power supply (L.T. or battery). Electrons emitted by the filament are accelerated to a desired velocity by applying suitable potential/voltage from a high voltage power supply (H.T. or battery).

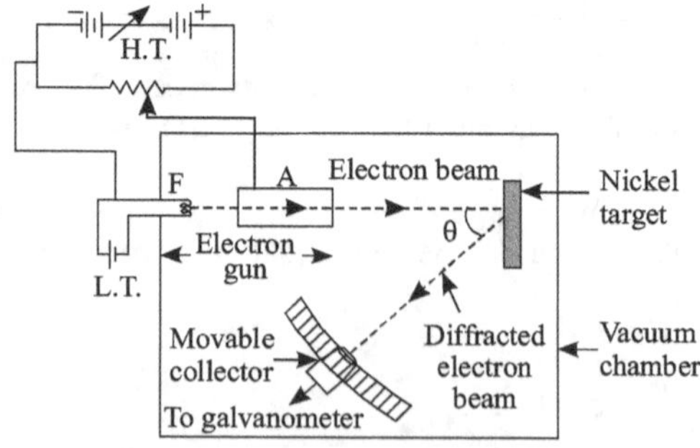

Fig.: Davisson-Germer electron diffraction arrangement.

- The experiment was performed by varying the accelerating voltage from 44 V to 68 V. It was noticed that a strong peak appeared in intensity (I) of the scattered electron for an accelerating voltage of 54V at a scattering angle θ = 50°.
- The appearance of the peak in a particular direction is due to the constructive interference of electrons scattered from different layers of the regularly spaced atoms of the crystals. From the electron diffraction measurements, the wavelength of matter waves was found to be 0.165 nm.
- The de Broglie wavelength λ associated with electrons, for V = 54 V is given by

$$\lambda = h / p = \frac{1227}{\sqrt{V}}\,\text{nm}$$

$$\lambda = \frac{1227}{\sqrt{54}}\,\text{nm} = 0.167\,\text{nm}$$

- Thus, there is an excellent agreement between the theoretical value and the experimentally obtained value of de Broglie wavelength.
- Davisson-Germer experiment thus strikingly confirms the wave nature of electrons and the de Broglie relation.

Past Years ONE-LINERS
NEET/JEE Main/Board

- From Einstein's photoelectric equation

$$\frac{hc}{\lambda} = \phi_0 + k$$

Where ϕ_0 = work function

k = maximum kinetic energy of photoelectrons

- No. of photons / second, $\dfrac{n}{t} = \dfrac{P}{\left(\dfrac{hc}{\lambda}\right)}$

- For photoelectric emission, frequency of incident light should be greater than threshold frequency.

- de-Broglie wavelength of electron, $\lambda = \dfrac{12.27}{\sqrt{V}}\,\text{Å}$

- de-Broglie wavelength of electron $\lambda = \dfrac{12.27}{\sqrt{V}}\,\text{Å}.$

- de-Broglie wavelength, $\lambda_{min} = \dfrac{h}{p} = \dfrac{h}{\sqrt{2m(KE)_{max}}}$

- From the Einstein's photoelectric equation

$$KE = h\nu - W_0 \Rightarrow eV = \dfrac{hc}{\lambda} - W_0$$

- Energy of proton, $E = \dfrac{hc}{\lambda}$

- Using Einstein's photoelectric equation, $E = W_0 + eV_s$

- In X-ray tube, $\lambda_{min} = \dfrac{hc}{eV}$ $\qquad$ In $\lambda_{min} = In\left(\dfrac{hc}{e}\right) - InV$

- de-Broglie wavelength, $\lambda = \dfrac{h}{mv}$

- From Einstein's photoelectric equation, $K.E. = E - W_0$.

Tips/Tricks/Tecchniques ONE-LINERS
(Exam Sample)

- The value of specific charge is same for all the particles of the cathode rays.
- The de-Broglie waves are not electromagnetic waves. It is also independent of the nature and charge of the material particle.
- De-broglie hypothesis established the wave nature of moving charged particle.
- Work function of metal increases with increase in temperature. Also, on increasing the atomic number of elements, work function decreases.
- De-Broglie wavelength of a particle having rest mass m_0 and moving with a speed v, which is comparable with the speed of light c is given by

$$\lambda = \dfrac{h\left(\dfrac{1-v^2}{c^2}\right)^{1/2}}{m_0 v}$$

- Number of photons having wavelength λ emitted from a lamp of power P in time t second is given by

$$n = \dfrac{Pt\lambda}{hc}$$

- The shortest wavelength emitted from the target when a high energy electrons falls on it, is given by

$$\lambda = \dfrac{hc}{eV} = \dfrac{1240}{V} nm$$

- According to Bragg's law,

  $2d \sin \theta = n\lambda$, where $n = 1, 2, 3\ldots\ldots$

  Here θ is the angle of diffraction of diffracted X-rays.

  d = space between the crystal planes.

- The wavelength of k_α line of characteristic X-rays (λ) is given by

$$\frac{1}{\lambda} = R(Z-1)^2\left(\frac{1}{1^2} - \frac{1}{2^2}\right)$$

  Similarly for L_α line of wavelength λ is given by

$$\frac{1}{\lambda} = R(Z-7.4)^2\left(\frac{1}{2^2} - \frac{1}{3^2}\right)$$

- The slope of graph between stopping potential and frequency of the incident light gives the ratio of Planck's constant to electronic charge.

Alpha-particle Scattering and Rutherford's Nuclear Model of Atom

♦ At the suggestion of Ernst Rutherford, in 1911, H. Geiger and E. Marsden performed some experiments.

In one of their experiments, as shown, they directed a beam of 5.5 MeV α-particles emitted from a $^{214}_{83}\text{Bi}$ radioactive source at a thin metal foil made of gold.

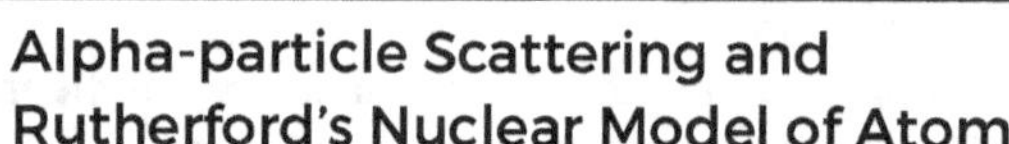

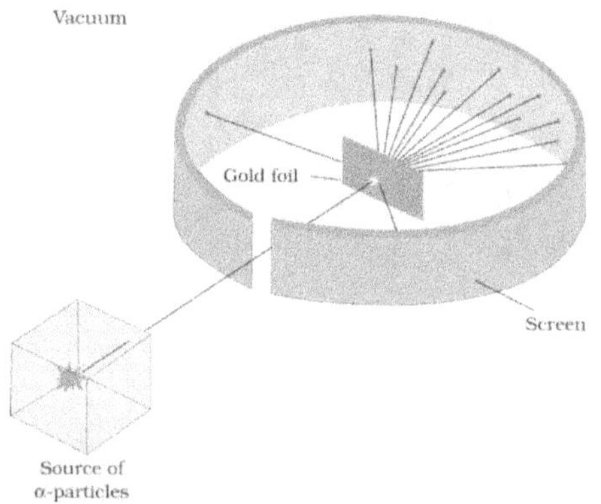

Fig.: Geiger-Marsden scattering experiment.
The entire apparatus is placed in a vacuum chamber
(not shown in this figure).

Alpha-particles emitted by a $^{214}_{83}\text{Bi}$ radioactive source were collimated into a narrow beam by their passage through lead bricks.

♦ The beam was allowed to fall on a thin foil of gold of thickness 2.1×10^{-7} m. The scattered alpha-particles were observed through a rotatable detector consisting of zinc sulphide screen and a microscope.

♦ The scattered alpha-particles on striking the screen produced brief light flashes or scintillations.

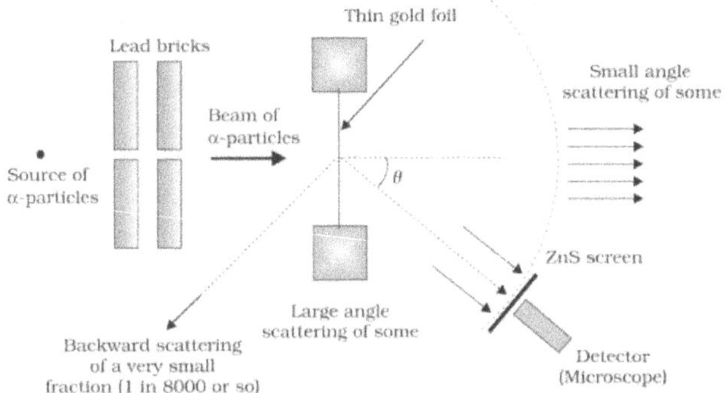

Fig.: Schematic arrangement of the Geiger-Marsden experiment.

- Many of the α-particles pass through the foil. It means that they do not suffer any collisions. Only about 0.14% of the incident α-particles scatter by more than 1° and about 1 in 8000 deflect by more than 90°.
- Rutherford argued that, to deflect the α-particle backwards, it must experience a large repulsive force. This force could be provided if the greater part of the mass of the atom and its positive charge were concentrated tightly at its centre.
- In Rutherford's nuclear model of the atom, the entire positive charge and most of the mass of the atom are concentrated in the nucleus with the electrons some distance away. The electrons would be moving in orbits about the nucleus just as the planets do around the sun.
- Rutherford's experiments suggested the **size of the nucleus** to be about 10^{-15} m to 10^{-14} m and most of an atom is empty space.
- The trajectory of an alpha-particle can be computed employing Newton's second law of motion and the Coulomb's law for electrostatic force of repulsion between the alpha-particle and the positively charged nucleus. The magnitude of this force is

$$F = \frac{1}{4\pi\varepsilon_0}\frac{(2e)(Ze)}{r^2}$$

Where r is the distance between the α-particle and the nucleus. The force is directed along the line joining the α-particle and the nucleus.

Alpha-particle trajectory

The ***impact parameter*** is the perpendicular distance of the initial velocity vector of the α-particle from the centre of the nucleus.

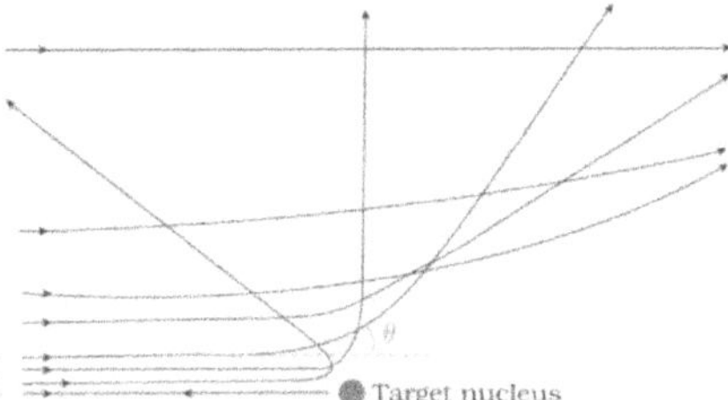

Fig.: Trajectory of α-particles in the coulomb field of a target nucleus. The impact parameter, b and scattering angle θ are also depicted.

- It is seen that an α-particle close to the nucleus (small impact parameter) suffers large scattering.
- In case of head-on collision, the impact parameter is minimum and the α-particle rebounds back ($\theta \cong \pi$).
- For a large impact parameter, the α-particle goes nearly undeviated and has a small deflection ($\theta \cong 0°C$).

Electron orbits

- For a dynamically stable orbit in a hydrogen atom

$$F_e = F_c$$

$$\frac{1}{4\pi\varepsilon_0} \frac{e^2}{r^2} = \frac{mv^2}{r}$$

Thus the relation between the orbit radius and the electron velocity is

$$r = \frac{e^2}{4\pi\varepsilon_0 mv^2}$$

- The **kinetic energy (K)** and **electrostatic potential energy (U)** of the electron in hydrogen atom are

$$K = \frac{1}{2}mv^2 = \frac{e^2}{8\pi\varepsilon_0 r} \text{ and } U = -\frac{e^2}{4\pi\varepsilon_0 r}$$

- The total energy E of the electron in a hydrogen atom is

$$E = K + U = \frac{e^2}{8\pi\varepsilon_0 r} - \frac{e^2}{4\pi\varepsilon_0 r} = -\frac{e^2}{8\pi\varepsilon_0 r}$$

The total energy of the electron is negative. This implies the fact that the electron is bound to the nucleus.

Spectral series

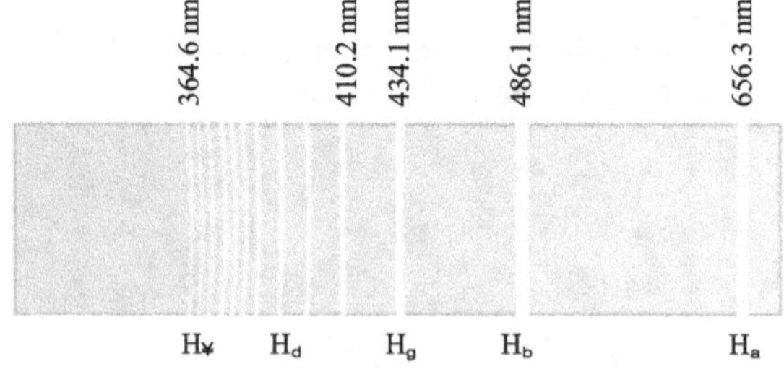

Fig.: Balmer series in the emission spectrum of hydrogen.

- Balmer found a simple *empirical formula* for the observed wavelengths

$$\frac{1}{\lambda} = R\left(\frac{1}{2^2} - \frac{1}{n^2}\right)$$

where λ is the wavelength, R is a constant called the **Rydberg constant**, and n may have integral values 3, 4, 5, etc. The value of R is 1.097×10^7 m^{-1}. This equation is also called **Balmer formula**.

♦ Other series of spectra for hydrogen were

Lyman series:

$$\frac{1}{\lambda} = R\left(\frac{1}{1^2} - \frac{1}{n^2}\right) \qquad n = 2,3,4...$$

Paschen series:

$$\frac{1}{\lambda} = R\left(\frac{1}{3^2} - \frac{1}{n^2}\right) \qquad n = 4,5,6...$$

Brackett series:

$$\frac{1}{\lambda} = R\left(\frac{1}{4^2} - \frac{1}{n^2}\right) \qquad n = 5,6,7...$$

Pfund series:

$$\frac{1}{\lambda} = R\left(\frac{1}{5^2} - \frac{1}{n^2}\right) \qquad n = 6,7,8...$$

♦ The Lyman series is in the ultraviolet, and the Paschen, Brackett, and Pfund series are in the infrared region.

♦ The **Balmer formula** may be written in terms of frequency of the light as

$$c = v\lambda$$

or $$\frac{1}{\lambda} = \frac{v}{c}$$

$$v = Rc\left(\frac{1}{2^2} - \frac{1}{n^2}\right)$$

Bohr Model of the Hydrogen Atom

♦ **Bohr** combined classical and early quantum concepts and gave his theory in the form of **three postulates**. These are:

(i) Bohr's first postulate was that *an electron in an atom could revolve in certain stable orbits without the emission of radiant energy.*

(ii) Bohr's second postulate states that the electron revolves around the nucleus *only in those orbits for which the angular momentum is some integral multiple of h/2π* where h is the Planck's constant ($= 6.6 \times 10^{-34}$ J s). Thus the angular momentum (L) of the orbiting electron is quantised. That is

$$L = nh/2\pi$$

(iii) Bohr's third postulate states that *an electron might make a transition from one of its specified non-radiating orbits to another of lower energy. When it does so, a photon is emitted having energy equal to the energy difference between the initial and final states. The frequency of the emitted photon is then given by*

$$hv = E_i - E_f$$

where E_i and E_f are the energies of the initial and final states and $E_i > E_f$

Energy levels

♦ The minimum energy required to free the electron from the ground state of the hydrogen atom is called the ***ionisation energy*** of the hydrogen atom.

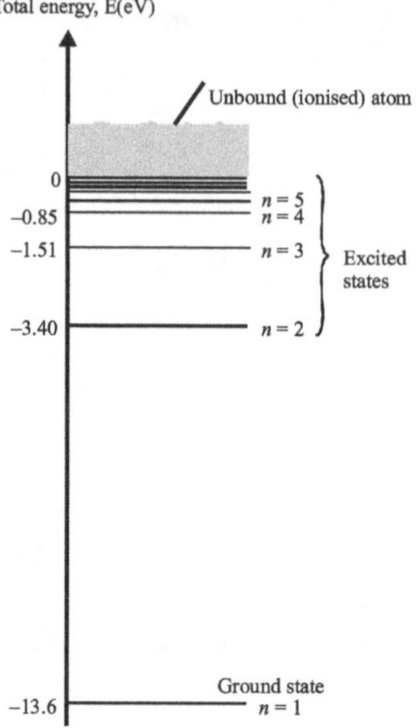

Fig.: The energy level diagram for the hydrogen atom. The electron in a hydrogen atom at room temperature spends most of its time in the ground state. To ionise a hydrogen atom an electron from the ground state, 13.6 eV of energy must be supplied. (The horizontallines specify the presence of allowed energy states.)

The Line Spectra of the Hydrogen Atom

♦ When an atom makes a transition from the higher energy state with quantum number n_i to the lower energy state with quantum number $n_f (n_f < n_i)$, the difference of energy is carried away by a **photon of frequency** v_{if} such that

$$hv_{if} = En_i - En_f$$

$$hv_{if} = \frac{me^4}{8\varepsilon_0^2 h^2}\left(\frac{1}{n_f^2} - \frac{1}{n_i^2}\right) \text{ or } v_{if} = \frac{me^4}{8\varepsilon_0^2 h^3}\left(\frac{1}{n_f^2} - \frac{1}{n_i^2}\right)$$

♦ The Rydberg constant R is readily identified to be

$$R = \frac{me^4}{8\varepsilon_0^2 h^3 c}$$

If we insert the values of various constants, we get $R = 1.03 \times 10^7 \text{ m}^{-1}$.

This is a value very close to the value $(1.097 \times 10^7 \text{ m}^{-1})$ obtained from the empirical Balmer formula.

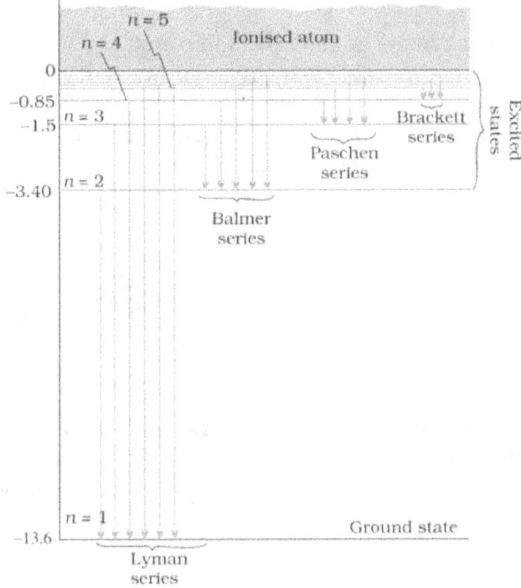

Fig.: Line spectra originate in transitions between energy levels.

- - - - - - - - - - -

De Broglie's Explanation of Bohr's Second Postulate of Quantisation

- - - - - - - - - - - -

♦ Louis de Broglie argued that the electron in its circular orbit, as proposed by Bohr, must be seen as a particle wave.

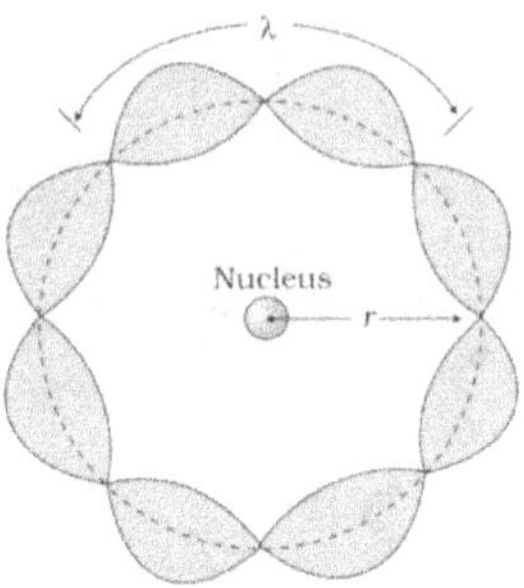

Fig.: A standing wave is shown on a circular orbit where four de Broglie wavelengths fit into the circumference of the orbit.

♦ For an electron moving in n^{th} circular orbit of radius r_n, the total distance is the circumference of the orbit, $2\pi r_n$. Thus
$$2\pi r_n = n\lambda, n = 1, 2, 3...$$

♦ If the speed of the electron is much less than the speed of light, the momentum is mv_n. Thus, $\lambda = h/mv_n$. We have
$$2\pi r_n = n\,h/mv_n \qquad \text{or} \qquad m\,v_n\,r_n = nh/2\pi$$

This is the quantum condition proposed by Bohr for the angular momentum of the electron.

♦ **Bohr's model** has many limitations. Some are:

(i) The Bohr model is applicable to hydrogenic atoms. It cannot be extended even to two electron atoms such as helium.

(ii) While the Bohr's model correctly predicts the frequencies of the light emitted by hydrogenic atoms, the model is unable to explain the relative intensities of the frequencies in the spectrum.

Past Years ONE-LINERS
NEET/JEE Main/Board

♦ Bohr model is only valid for single electron species i.e., Hydrogen or hydrogen like atom – He^+, deuteron, etc.

♦ The relation between kinetic energy, potential energy and total energy

$$K.E. = |TE| = \frac{|P.E.|}{2}$$

♦ In a Bohr orbit of the hydrogen atom, Kinetic energy, $k = \dfrac{kze^2}{2r_n}$. Total energy, E

$$= \frac{-kze^2}{2r_n}$$

♦ For last line of Balmer series : $n_1 = 2$ and $n_2 = \infty$

and wave number $\dfrac{1}{\lambda} = RZ^2 \left[\dfrac{1}{n_1{}^2} - \dfrac{1}{n_2{}^2} \right]$

♦ Wave number, $\dfrac{1}{\lambda} = RZ^2 \left(\dfrac{1}{n_2^2} - \dfrac{1}{n_1^2} \right)$ For hydrogen atom $z = 1$

♦ At closest distance of approach, the kinetic energy of the particle will convert completely into electrostatic potential energy.

♦ Wave number, $\dfrac{1}{\lambda} = R_e \left(\dfrac{1}{n_1^2} - \dfrac{1}{n_2^2} \right)$

For Lyman series, $n_1 = 1$ and $n_2 = 2, 3, 4...$
For Balmer series $n_1 = 2$ and $n_2 = 3, 4, 5...$

♦ The wave number is given by $\dfrac{1}{\lambda} = RZ^2 \left[\dfrac{1}{n_2^2} - \dfrac{1}{n_1^2} \right]$

♦ Time period of revolution of electron in ground state orbit in hydrogen atom,

$$T \propto \frac{n^3}{z^2}$$

- Wave number, $\dfrac{1}{\lambda} = R\left(\dfrac{1}{n_2} - \dfrac{1}{n_1}\right)$

- Energy of electron in ground state of hydrogen atom, $E \propto \dfrac{z^2}{n^2}$

- Wavelength of emitted photon from n^{th} state to the ground state,
$$\frac{1}{\Lambda_n} = RZ^2\left(\frac{1}{1^2} - \frac{1}{n^2}\right)$$

- Potential energy of electron in hydrogen atom, $U = -K\dfrac{ze^2}{r}$,

  total energy of electron in hydrogen atom, $T.E = -\dfrac{k}{2}\dfrac{ze^2}{r}$

Tips/Tricks/Tecchniques ONE-LINERS
(Exam Sample)

- We can obtain Lyman series in both emission as well as absorption spectrum. But other spectra are obtained in the emission spectrum.
- At minimum potential energy, an atom achieves most stable state.
- Spectrum of hydrogen has fine structure. For example, each spectral line of hydrogen atom consists of a large number of fine lines.
- For hydrogen atom, binding energy is the sum of kinetic energy and potential energy of the orbital electron.
- In hydrogen atom, when an electron Jumps from the excited state to the ground state, its kinetic energy increases but potential and total energy decreases.
- On increasing the principal quantum number, the energy difference between the two successive energy level decreases, but wavelength of spectral line increases.
- Bohr's theory is applicable for hydrogen and hydrogen like atoms or ions. For example the atoms or ions having number of electron = 1 but atomic number z may be different.
- The maximum number of electrons in a shell = $2n^2$.
- The wavelength of spectral line increases in the order
  λ P fund > λ brackett > λ paschen > λ balmer > λ lyman
- The excitation potential of an electron

$$= 13.6\, Z^2\left[\frac{1}{n^2} - \frac{1}{(n+1)^2}\right]$$

- Electric current due to electron motion

$$I_n = ef_n = \frac{1.06Z^2}{n^3}\, mA$$

- Ionisation potential of electron

$$= \frac{E_n}{e}(V) = -\frac{13.6\,Z^2}{en^2}(V)$$

- If an electron is revolving in n^{th} Bohr's orbit, then use following proportionality relation to solve problems
  Radius $(r_n) \propto n^2/Z$, Speed $(v_n) \propto Z/n$, Potential energy $(U_n) \propto Z^2/n^2$, Kinetic energy $(E_k) \propto Z^2/n^2$, Angular speed $(w_n) \propto Z^2/n^3$, Frequency $(v_n) \propto Z^2/n^3$, Time period $(T_n) \propto n^3/Z^2$, Angular momentum $(L_n) \propto n$, Magnetic field $(B_n) \propto Z^2/n^5$, Centripetal force $(F_n) \propto Z^3/n^4$

- Both the Thomson's as well as the Rutherford's models constitute an unstable system. Thomson's model is unstable electrostatically, while Rutherford's model is unstable because of electromagnetic radiation of orbiting electrons.

28 Nuclei

Atomic Masses and Composition of Nucleus

- **Atomic mass unit (u)**, defined as $1/12^{th}$ of the mass of the carbon (^{12}C) atom.

$$1u = \frac{\text{mass of one } ^{12}C \text{ atom}}{12}$$

$$= \frac{1.992647 \times 10^{-26} \text{ kg}}{12}$$

$$= 1.660539 \times 10^{-27} \text{ kg}$$

- Atomic species of the same element differing in mass bnt same atomic number are called **isotopes**.

Discovering of Neutron

- James chadwick discovered neutron in 1932. A free neutron, unlike a free proton, is unstable. It decays into a proton, an electron and a antineutrino (another elementary particle), and has a mean life of about 1000s. It is, however, stable inside the nucleus.
- Mass of neutron, $m_n = 1.00866u = 1.6749 \times 10^{-27}$ kg
  Mass of Proton, $m_p = 1.00727u = 1.67262 \times 10^{-27}$ kg
- The composition of a nucleus can now be described using the following terms and symbols:
  Z - *atomic number* = number of protons
  N = number of neutrons
  A - *mass number* $= Z + N$
  = total number of protons and neutrons = no. of **nucleons.**
- Nuclear species or nuclides are shown by the notation $^A_Z X$ where X is the chemical symbol of the species.
- The nuclei of isotopes of a given element contain the same number of protons, but differ from each other in their number of neutrons. Deuterium, $^2_1 H$, which is an isotope of hydrogen, contains one proton and one neutron. Its other isotope tritium, $^2_1 H$, contains one proton and two neutrons.
- All nuclides with same mass number A are called *isobars*. For example, the nuclides $^3_1 H$ and $^3_2 He$ are **isobars**.

♦ Nuclides with same neutron number N but different atomic number Z, for example $^{198}_{80}$Hg and $^{197}_{79}$Au are called **isotones**.

Size of the Nucleus

♦ Nucleus of mass number A has a radius $\mathbf{R = R_0 A^{1/3}}$
where $R_0 = 1.2 \times 10^{-15}$ m ($=1.2$ fm; 1 fm $= 10^{-15}$ m).
♦ This means the volume of the nucleus, which is proportional to R^3 is proportional to A. Thus the density of nucleus is a constant, independent of A, for all nuclei.
♦ The density of nuclear matter is approximately 2.3×10^{17} kg m^{-3}.

Mass-Energy and Nuclear Binding Energy

Mass-Energy

♦ Einstein showed that mass is another form of energy and one can convert mass-energy into other forms of energy, say kinetic energy and vice-versa. Einstein gave the famous mass-energy equivalence relation
$E = mc^2$
C is the velocity of light in vacuum and is approximately equal to 3×10^8 m s^{-1}.

Nuclear binding energy

♦ The difference in mass of a nucleus and its constituents, ΔM, is called the **mass defect**, and is given by
$\Delta M = [Zm_p + (A - Z)m_n] - M$
♦ If a certain number of neutrons and protons are brought together to form a nucleus of a certain charge and mass, an energy E_b will be released in the process. The energy E_b is called the **binding energy** $= \Delta Mc^2$ of the nucleus.
♦ A more useful measure of the binding between the constituents of the nucleus is the **binding energy per nucleon**, E_{bn}, which is the ratio of the binding energy E_b of a nucleus to the number of the nucleons, A, in that nucleus:
$E_{bn} = E_b / A$
♦ The main features of the binding energy per nucleon as a function of mass number plot:
(i) the binding energy per nucleon, E_{bn}, is practically constant, i.e. practically independent of the atomic number for nuclei of middle mass number ($30 < A < 170$). The curve has a maximum of about 8.75 MeV for A = 56 and has a value of 7.6 MeV for A = 238.

(ii) E_{bn} is lower for both light nuclei (A<30) and heavy nuclei (A>170).

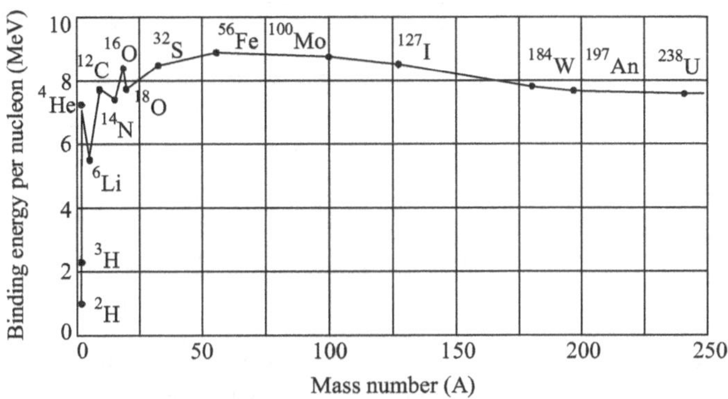

Fig.: The binding energy per nucleon as a function of mass number.

♦ The force is attractive and sufficiently strong to produce a binding energy of a few MeV per nucleon.

♦ The constancy of the binding energy in the range 30 < A < 170 is a consequence of the fact that the nuclear force is short-ranged.

♦ The property that a given nucleon influences only nucleons close to it is also referred to as saturation property of the nuclear force.

Nuclear Force

♦ To bind a nucleus together there must be a strong attractive force of a totally different kind. It must be strong enough to overcome the repulsion between the (positively charged) protons and to bind both protons and neutrons into the tiny nuclear volume.

♦ The nuclear force is much stronger than the Coulomb force acting between charges or the gravitational forces between masses.

♦ The nuclear force between two nucleons falls rapidly to zero as their distance is more than a few femtometres. This leads to *saturation of forces* in a medium or a large-sized nucleus, which is the reason for the constancy of the binding energy per nucleon.

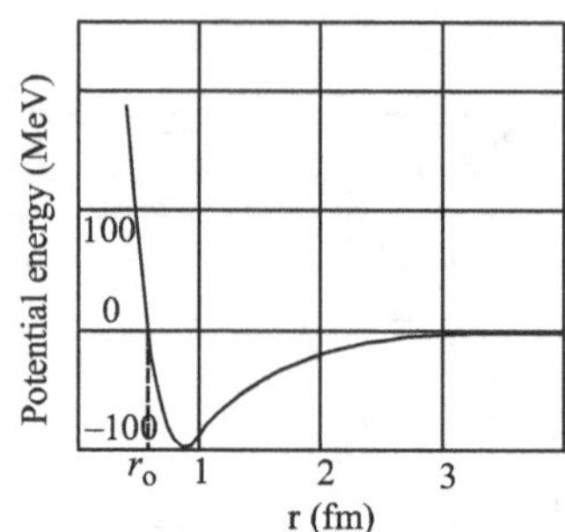

Fig.: Potential energy of a pair of nucleons as a function of their separation. For a separation greater than r_0, the force is attractive and for separations less than r_0, the force is strongly repulsive.

♦ The nuclear force between neutron-neutron, proton-neutron and proton-proton is approximately the same. The nuclear force does not depend on the electric charge.

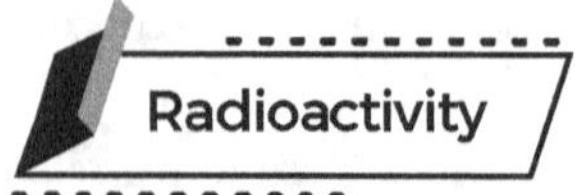

♦ Radioactivity is a nuclear phenomenon in which an unstable nucleus undergoes a decay. This is referred to as *radioactive decay*.

Law of radioactive decay

♦ The number of nuclei undergoing the decay per unit time is proportional to the total number of nuclei in the sample. If N is the number of nuclei in the sample and ΔN undergo decay in time Δt then

$$\frac{\Delta N}{\Delta t} \propto N \quad \text{or,} \quad \Delta N / \Delta t = \lambda N,$$

where λ is called the radioactive **decay constant or disintegration constant**.

$$N(t) = N_0 \, e^{-\lambda t} \text{ and } R = R_0 \, e^{-\lambda t}$$

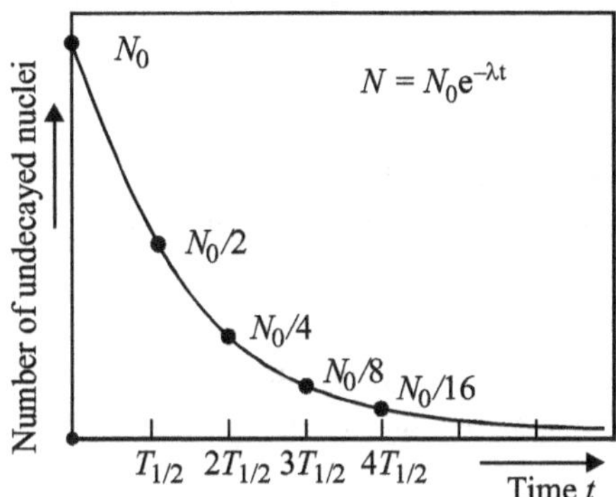

Fig.: Exponential decay of a radioactive species. After a lapse of $T_{1/2}$, population of the given species drops by a factor of 2.

♦ The decay rate R at a certain time t and the number of undecayed nuclei N at the same time are related by $R = \lambda N$

♦ The **SI unit for activity is becquerel,** named after the discoverer of radioactivity, Henry Becquerel.

1 becquerel is simply equal to 1 disintegration or decay per second.

1 curie = 1 Ci = 3.7×10^{10} decays per second = 3.7×10^{10} Bq

♦ **Half-life of a radionuclide** (denoted by $\mathbf{T_{1/2}}$) is the time it takes for a sample that has initially, say N_0 radionuclei to reduce to $N_0/2$.

$$T_{1/2} = \frac{\ln 2}{\lambda} = \frac{0.693}{\lambda}$$

Mean or **average life** $\tau = \dfrac{\lambda N_0 \displaystyle\int_0^\infty t e^{-\lambda t}\, dt}{N_0} = \lambda \int_0^\infty t e^{-\lambda t}\, dt$

Alpha decay

♦ Alpha decay is the decay of uranium $^{238}_{92}U$ to thorium $^{234}_{90}$Th with the emission of a helium nucleus $^4_2$He

$$^{238}_{92}U \rightarrow {}^{234}_{90}\text{Th} + {}^4_2\text{He} \qquad (\alpha\text{-decay})$$

♦ In α-decay, the mass number of the product nucleus (daughter nucleus) is four less than that of the decaying nucleus (parent nucleus), while the atomic number decreases by two. In general, α-decay of a parent nucleus ${}_{Z}^{A}X$ results in a daughter nucleus ${}_{Z-2}^{A-4}Y$

$${}_{Z}^{A}X \rightarrow {}_{Z-2}^{A-4}Y + {}_{2}^{4}He$$

♦ The disintegration energy or the Q-value of a nuclear reaction is the difference between the initial mass energy and the total mass energy of the decay products. For α-decay $Q = (m_X - m_Y - m_{He})\, c^2$

Beta decay

♦ In beta decay, a nucleus spontaneously emits an electron (β^- decay) or a positron (β^+ decay). A common example of β^- decay is

$${}_{15}^{32}P \rightarrow {}_{16}^{32}S + e^- + \bar{v}$$

and that of β^+ decay is

$${}_{11}^{22}Na \rightarrow {}_{10}^{22}Ne + e^+ + v$$

♦ The emission of electron in β^- decay is accompanied by the emission of an antineutrino ($\bar{v}$); in β^+ decay, instead, a neutrino (v) is generated. Neutrinos are neutral particles with very small (possiblly, even zero) mass compared to electrons.

♦ They have only weak interaction with other particles. They are, therefore, very difficult to detect, since they can penetrate large quantity of matter (even earth) without any interaction.

♦ The basic nuclear process underlying β^- decay is the conversion of neutron to proton

$$n \rightarrow p + e^- + \bar{v}$$

while for β^+ decay, it is the conversion of proton into neutron

$$p \rightarrow n + e^+ + v$$

Gamma decay

♦ When a nucleus in an excited state spontaneously decays to its ground state (or to a lower energy state), a photon is emitted with energy equal to the difference in the two energy levels of the nucleus. This is the so-called *gamma decay*.

♦ A gamma ray is emitted when a α or β decay results in a daughter nucleus in an excited state. This then returns to the ground state by a single photon transition or successive transitions involving more than one photon.

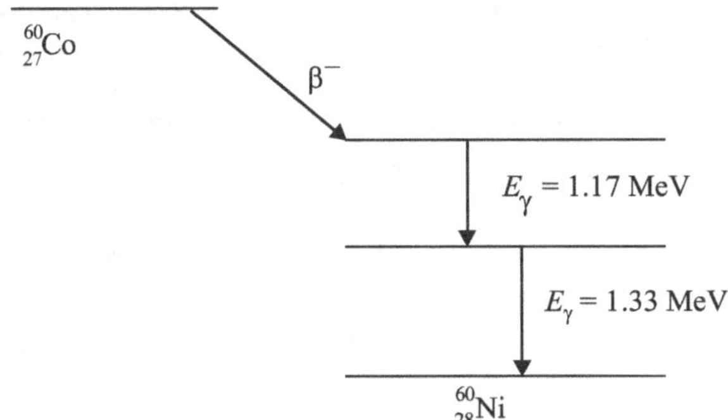

Fig.: β-decay of ${}^{60}_{28}Ni$ nucleus followed by emission of two γ rays from deexcitation of the daughter nucleus ${}^{60}_{28}Ni$.

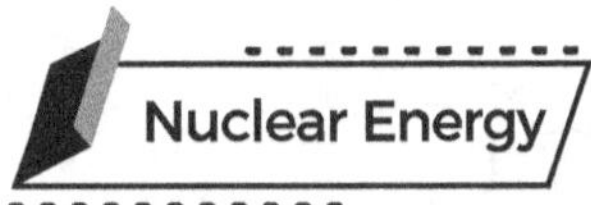

- Nuclear energy is released, when a heavy nucleus decays into two or more intermediate mass fragments (*fission*) or when light nuclei fuse into a havier nucleus (*fusion.*)

Fission

- When a heavy nucleus like uranium isotope ${}^{235}_{92}U$ bombarded with a neutron, it breaks into two intermediate mass nuclear fragments

$${}^{1}_{0}n + {}^{235}_{92}U \rightarrow {}^{236}_{92}U \rightarrow {}^{144}_{56}Ba + {}^{89}_{36}Kr + 3{}^{1}_{0}n$$

The same reaction can produce other pairs of intermediate mass fragments

$${}^{1}_{0}n + {}^{235}_{92}U \rightarrow {}^{236}_{92}U \rightarrow {}^{133}_{51}Sb + {}^{99}_{41}Nb + 4{}^{1}_{0}n$$

Or, as another example,

$${}^{1}_{0}n + {}^{235}_{92}U \rightarrow {}^{140}_{54}Xe + {}^{94}_{38}Sr + 2{}^{1}_{0}n$$

- The source of energy in nuclear reactors, which produce electricity, is nuclear fission. The enormous energy released in an atom bomb comes from uncontrolled nuclear fission.

Nuclear reactor

- If the chain reaction is controlled suitably, we can get a steady energy output. This is what happens in a nuclear reactor. If the chain reaction is uncontrolled, it leads to explosive energy output, as in a nuclear bomb.
- In reactors, light nuclei called **moderators** are provided along with the fissionable nuclei for slowing down fast neutrons. The moderators commonly used are water, heavy water (D_2O) and graphite.
- Ratio, K, of number of fission produced by a given generation of neutrons to the number of fission of the preceeding generation may be greater than one. This ratio is called the *multiplication factor*; it is the measure of the growth rate of the neutrons in the reactor.

- For $K = 1$ the operation of the reactor is said to be *critical*, which is what we wish it to be for steady power operation. If K > 1 the reaction rate and the reactor power increases exponentially. Unless the factor K is brought down very close to unity, the reactor will become supercritical and can even explode.

- The reaction rate is controlled through **control rods** made out of neutron-absorbing material such as cadmium.

- **Safety rods** when required can be inserted into the reactor and can be reduced rapidly to less than unity.

- The energy (heat) released in fission is continuously removed by a suitable **coolant**.

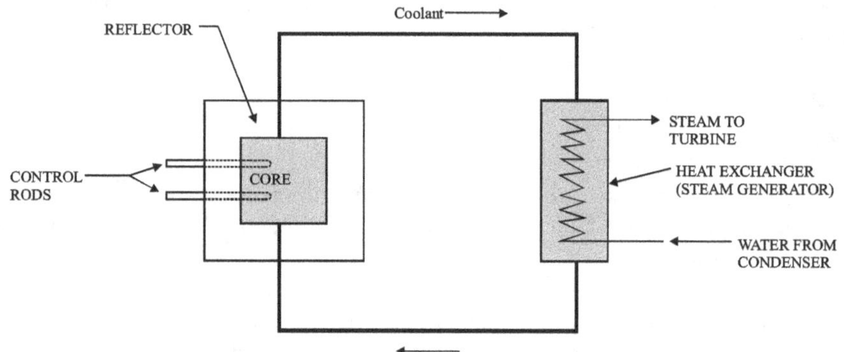

Fig.: Schematic diagram of a nuclear reactor based on thermal neutron fission.

- The *core* of the reactor is the site of nuclear fission. It contains the fuel elements in suitably fabricated form.

Nuclear fusion – energy generation in stars

- When fusion is achieved by raising the temperature of the system so that particles have enough kinetic energy to overcome the coulomb repulsive behaviour, it is called *thermonuclear fusion*.

Controlled thermonuclear fusion

- In controlled fusion reactors, the aim is to generate steady power by heating the nuclear fuel to a temperature in the range of 10^8 K. At these temperatures, the fuel is a mixture of positive ions and electrons (plasma).

- The challenge is to confine this plasma, since no container can stand such a high temperature.

- Several countries around the world including India are developing techniques in this connection. If successful, fusion reactors will hopefully supply almost unlimited power to humanity.

Past Years ONE-LINERS
NEET/JEE Main/Board

- Gain in BE = (BE) of products − (BE) of reactants.

- Activity of a radioactive substance $A = A_0 \left(\dfrac{1}{2}\right)^{\frac{t}{T_{1/2}}}$

- Atomic number (z) decreases by 1 after one β^+ decay
  Atomic number (z) increases by 1 after one β^- decay
  Atomic number (z) decreases by 2 after one α decay
- In Nuclear fission, heavy nuclei splits into smaller nuclei.
- α-particle is nucleus of helium He^{++} which has two protons and two neutrons.
- From the law of radioactive decay, $N = N_0 e^{-\lambda t}$
- Law of radioactive decay, $N_t = N_0 e^{-\lambda t}$
- In an explosion a body breaks up into two pieces of unequal masses both part will have
  numerically equal momentum and lighter part will have more velocity.
- From the law of radioactive decay $N_t = N_0 e^{-\lambda t}$

  Average life time, $t_{avg} = \dfrac{1}{\lambda}$

- Activity, $A = A_0 e^{-\lambda t}$
- From the law of radioactive decay $N_t = N_0 e^{-\lambda t}$

Tips/Tricks/Tecchniques ONE-LINERS
(Exam Sample)

- For a nucleus, density is maximum at its centre and decreases as we move outwards from the nucleus.
- If two small nuclei is combined to form a relatively heavy nucleus, then binding energy per nucleon increases.

♦ In every nuclear reaction, following conservation laws are obeyed
  (i) Conservation of charge number
  (ii) Conservation of nucleons
  (iii) Conservation of energy
  (iv) Conservation of linear momentum

♦ Nuclear force act inside the nucleus only. The nuclear force is 10^{38} times stronger than electrostatic forces.

♦ Radioactivity is a spontaneous process.

♦ Heavy water is an ideal moderator.

♦ An ideal moderator should have
  (i) low atomic weight
  (ii) should not absorb neutrons
  (iii) should undergo elastic collisions with neutrons

♦ Fusion reactors are better than fission reactors since they do not produce any unwanted radioactive substances.

♦ Number of atoms left undecayed after n half lives is given by

$$N = \frac{N_0}{2^n} \Rightarrow \frac{N}{N_0} = \left(\frac{1}{2}\right)^n$$

♦ The slope of N-t curve gives the value of decay constant.

♦ Number of atoms decayed after n half lives is given by

$$= N_0 - N = N_0\left[1 - \frac{1}{2^n}\right]$$

♦ Percentage of radioactive material left undecayed at time t is given by

$$\frac{N}{N_0} \times 100 = \frac{1}{2^n} \times 100 \left(\text{where} \quad n = \frac{t}{T}\right)$$

♦ If rate of decay of daughter nucleus is equal to the rate of decay of parent nucleus, then

$$\lambda_1 N_1 = \lambda_2 N_2$$

♦ Relation between average life and mean life is given by

$$\tau = 1.44\ T \qquad (\text{Here, } \tau = \text{average life, } T = \text{mean life})$$

♦ Effective half life (t) for two different process of radioactive decays for a sample is given by

$$\frac{1}{t} = \frac{1}{t_1} + \frac{1}{t_2} \Rightarrow t = \frac{t_1 t_2}{t_1 + t_2}$$

- The energy absorbed or released during nuclear reaction is known as θ value of nuclear reactin.

  θ-value = (Mass of reactants – mass of products)C^2 joules

  $\qquad$ = (Mass of reactants – mass of products) amu

- Activity of a substance after time t is given by

  $$A = A_0 e^{-\lambda t}$$

  Here, λ = distintegration constant

  $\qquad A_0$ = activity at $t = 0$

- The density of nuclear matter is independent of the size of the nucleus. The mass density of the atom does not follow this rule.

Classification of Metals, Conductors and Semiconductors

- On the basis of conductivity

  On the basis of the relative values of electrical conductivity (σ) or resistivity ($\rho = 1/\sigma$), the solids are broadly classified as:

  (i) **Metals:** They possess very low resistivity (or high conductivity).

  $\rho \sim 10^{-2} - 10^{-8}\ \Omega\ m$

  $\sigma \sim 10^{2} - 10^{8}\ S\ m^{-1}$

  (ii) **Semiconductors:** They have resistivity or conductivity intermediate to metals and insulators.

  $\rho \sim 10^{-5} - 10^{6}\ \Omega\ m$

  $\sigma \sim 10^{5} - 10^{-6}\ S\ m^{-1}$

  (iii) **Insulators:** They have high resistivity (or low conductivity).

  $\rho \sim 10^{11} - 10^{19}\ \Omega\ m$

  $\sigma \sim 10^{-11} - 10^{-19}\ S\ m^{-1}$

On the basis of energy bands

- Inside the crystal each electron has a unique position and no two electrons see exactly the same pattern of surrounding charges. Because of this, each electron will have a different energy level. These different energy levels with continuous energy variation form what are called *energy bands*.
- The energy band which includes the energy levels of the valence electrons is called the *valence band*.
- The energy band above the valence band is called the *conduction band*.
- With no external energy, all the valence electrons will reside in the valence band. If the lowest level in the conduction band happens to be lower than the highest level of the valence band, the electrons from the valence band can easily move into the conduction band. Normally the conduction band is empty. But when it overlaps on the valence band electrons can move freely into it. This is the case with **metallic conductors**.
- If there is some gap between the conduction band and the valence band, electrons in the valence band all remain bound and no free electrons are available in the conduction band. This makes the material an **insulator**.
- The gap between the top of the valence band and bottom of the conduction band is called the **energy band gap (Energy gap E_g)**. It may be large, small, or zero, depending upon the material.
- One can have a **metal** either when the conduction band is partially filled and the valance band is partially empty or when the conduction and valance bands overlap. When there is overlap electrons from valence band can easily move into the conduction band.

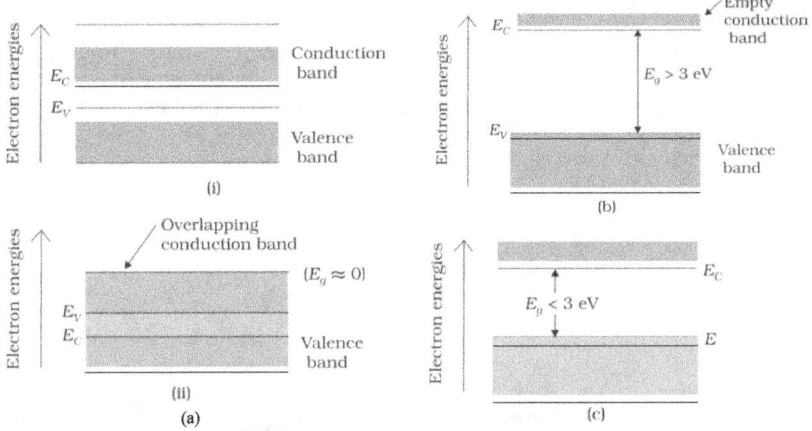

Fig.: Difference between energy bands of (a) metals,
(b) insulators and (c) semiconductors.

♦ **In case of insulators**-A large band gap E_g exists ($E_g > 3$ eV). There are no electrons in the conduction band, and therefore no electrical conduction is possible. Note that the energy gap is so large that electrons cannot be excited from the valence band to the conduction band by thermal excitation. This is the case of *insulators*.

♦ Incase of **Semi-conductors**-A finite but small band gap ($E_g < 3\ eV$) exists. Because of the small band gap, at room temperature some electrons from valence band can acquire enough energy to cross the energy gap and enter the conduction band. These electrons (though small in numbers) can move in the conduction band. Hence, the resistance of semiconductors is not as high as that of the insulators.

Intrinsic Semiconductor

♦ In its crystalline structure, every Si or Ge atom tends *to* share one of its four valence electrons with each of its four nearest neighbour atoms, and also *to take share* of one electron from each such neighbour. These shared electron pairs are referred to as forming a *covalent bond* or simply a *valence bond*.

♦ In intrinsic semiconductors, the number of free electrons, n_e is equal to the number of holes, n_h. That is
$$n_e = n_h = n_i$$
where n_i is called intrinsic carrier concentration.

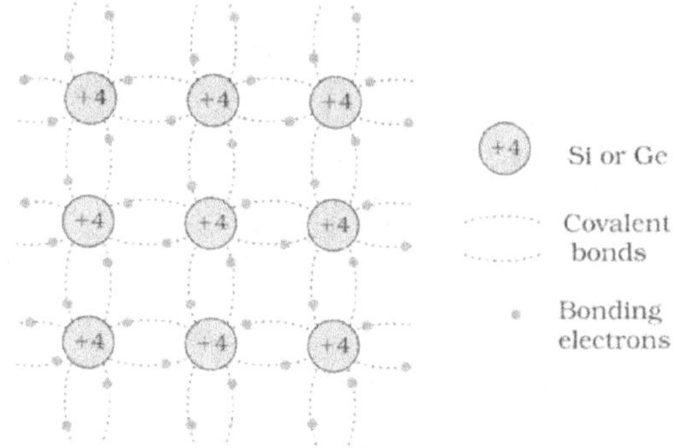

Fig.: Schematic two-dimensional representation of Si or Ge structure showing covalent bonds at low temperature (all bonds intact). +4 symbol indicates inner cores of Si or Ge.

- The total current, I is thus the sum of the electron current I_e and the hole current I_h:
  $I = I_e + I_h$.
- An intrinsic semiconductor will behave like an insulator at $T = 0\,K$ as shown in Fig. (a). It is the thermal energy at higher temperatures ($T > 0\,K$), which excites some electrons from the valence band to the conduction band. These thermally excited electrons at $T > 0\,K$, partially occupy the conduction band. Therefore, the energy-band diagram of an intrinsic semiconductor will be as shown in Fig. (b).

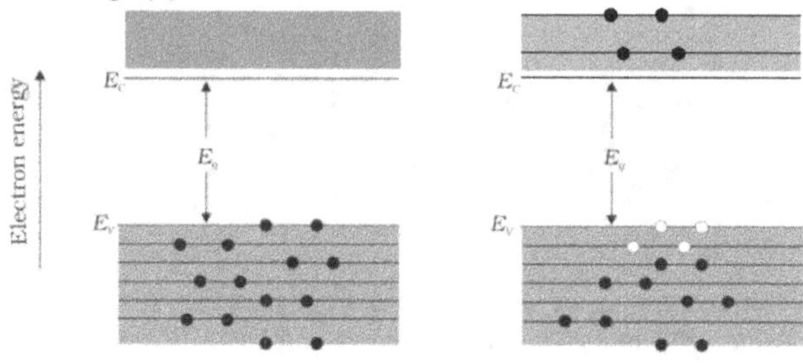

Fig.: (a) An intrinsic semiconductor at $T = 0\,K$ behaves like insulator. (b) At $T > 0\,K$, four thermally generated electron-hole pairs. The filled circles (•) represent electrons and empty/filled circles (○) represent holes.

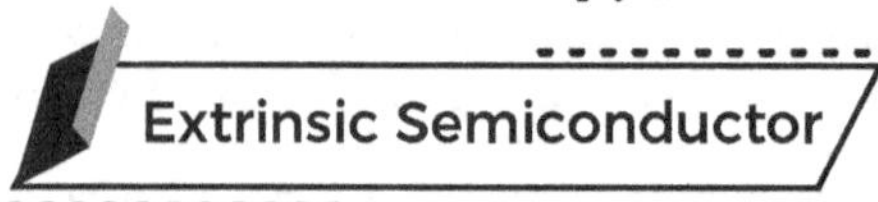

Extrinsic Semiconductor

- To improve the conductivity of semiconductors, impurities are used. When a small amount, say, a few parts per million (ppm), of a suitable impurity is added to the pure semiconductor, the conductivity of the semiconductor is increased manifold. Such materials are known as *extrinsic semiconductors* or *impurity semiconductors*.
- The deliberate addition of a desirable impurity is called *doping* and the impurity atoms are called *dopants*. Such a material is also called a *doped semiconductor*.
- There are two types of dopants used in doping the tetravalent intrinsio semiconductors Si or Ge
  (i) Pentavalent (valency 5); like Arsenic (As), Antimony (Sb), Phosphorous (P), etc.
  (ii) Trivalent (valency 3); like Indium (In), Boron (B), Aluminium (Al), etc.

n-type semiconductor

- The pentavalent dopant is donating one extra electron for conduction and hence is known as donor impurity. The number of electrons made available for conduction by dopant atoms depends strongly upon the doping level and is independent of any increase in ambient temperature.
- In an extrinsic semiconductor doped with pentavalent impurity, electrons become the majority carriers and holes the *minority carriers*. These semiconductors are, therefore, known as n-type semiconductors. For n-type semiconductors, we have,
  $n_e \gg n_h$

p-type semiconductor

- Extrinsic semiconductors doped with trivalent impurity are called p-type semiconductors. For p-type semiconductors, the recombination process will reduce the number (n_i) of intrinsically generated electrons to n_e. We have, for p-type semiconductors
  $n_h \gg n_e$

♦ The electron and hole concentration in a semiconductor in thermal equilibrium is given by

$$n_e n_h = n_i^2$$

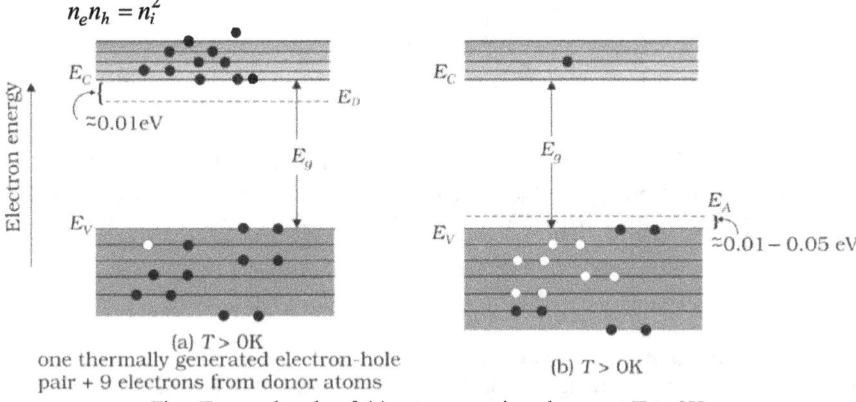

Fig.: Energy bands of (a) n-type semiconductor at T > 0K,
(b) p-type semiconductor at T > 0K.

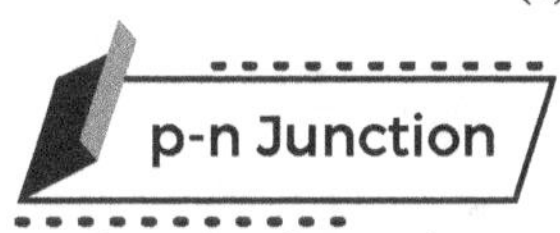

p-n Junction

p-n junction formation

♦ During the formation of p-n junction, and due to the concentration gradient across p-, and n- sides, *holes diffuse from p-side to n-side (p →n) and electrons diffuse from n-side to p-side (n →p)*. This motion of charge carries gives rise to diffusion current across the junction.

♦ When a hole diffuses from p → n due to the concentration gradient, it leaves behind an ionised acceptor (negative charge) which is immobile. As the holes continue to diffuse, a layer of negative charge (or negative space-charge region) on the p-side of the junction is developed. This space-charge region on either side of the junction together is known as ***depletion region***.

♦ Due to the positive space-charge region on n-side of the junction and negative space charge region on p-side of the junction, an electric field directed from positive charge towards negative charge develops.

♦ Due to this field, an electron on p-side of the junction moves to n-side and a hole on n-side of the junction moves to p-side. The motion of charge carriers due to the electric field is called **drift**.

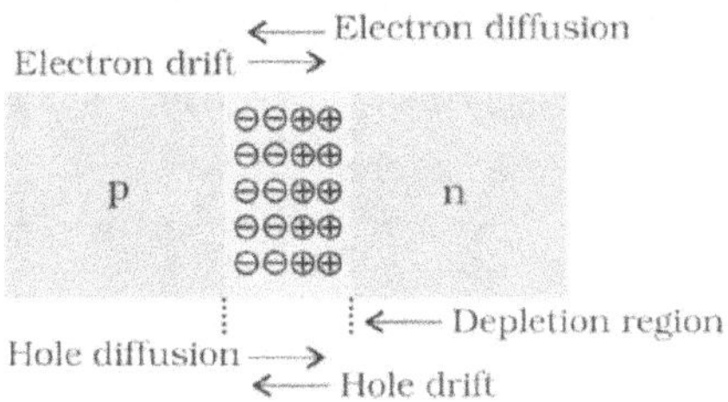

Fig.: p-n junction formation process.

♦ In a p-n junction under equilibrium there is no net current.

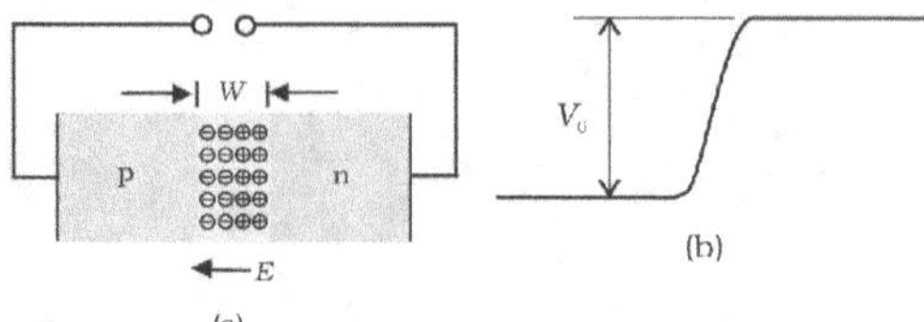

Fig.: (a) Diode under equilibrium (V = 0), (b) Barrier potential under no bias.

♦ Potential tends to prevent the movement of electron from the n-region into the p-region, it is often called a *barrier potential*.

Semiconductor Diode

p-n junction diode under forward bias

♦ When an external voltage V is applied across a semiconductor diode such that p-side is connected to the positive terminal of the battery and n-side to the negative terminal [Fig. (a)], it is said to be *forward biased*.

Fig.: (a) Semiconductor diode, (b) Symbol for p-n junction diode.

♦ The applied voltage mostly drops across the depletion region and the voltage drop across the p-side and n-side of the junction is negligible.

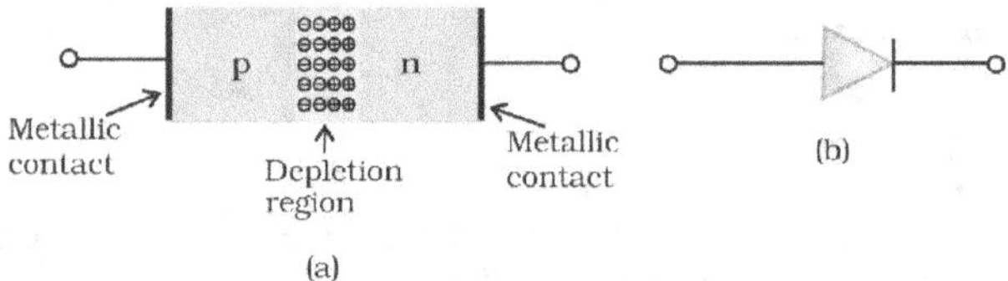

Fig.: (a) p-n junction diode under forward bias, (b) Barrier potential (1) without battery, (2) Low battery voltage, and (3) High voltage battery.

♦ The direction of the applied voltage (V) is opposite to the built-in potential V_0. As a result, the depletion layer width decreases and the barrier height is reduced fig. (b). The effective barrier height under forward bias is $(V_0 - V)$.

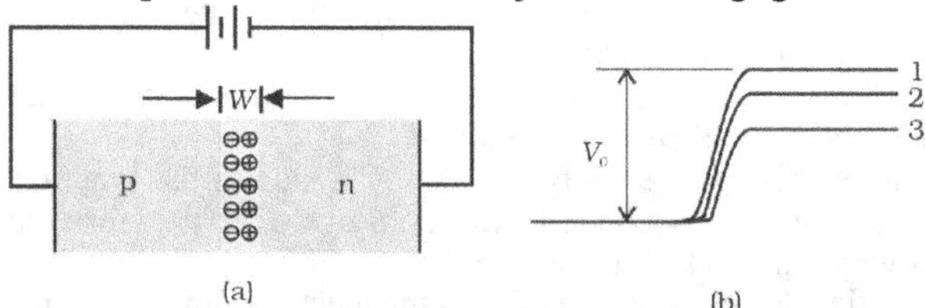

Fig.: Forward bias minority carrier injection.

p-n junction diode under reverse bias

♦ When an external voltage (V) is applied across the diode such that n-side is positive and p-side is negative, it is said to be reverse biased.

♦ The applied voltage mostly drops across the depletion region.

♦ The direction of applied voltage is same as the direction of barrier potential. As a result, the barrier height increases and the depletion region widens due to the change in the electric field. The effective barrier height under reverse bias is ($V_0 + V$).

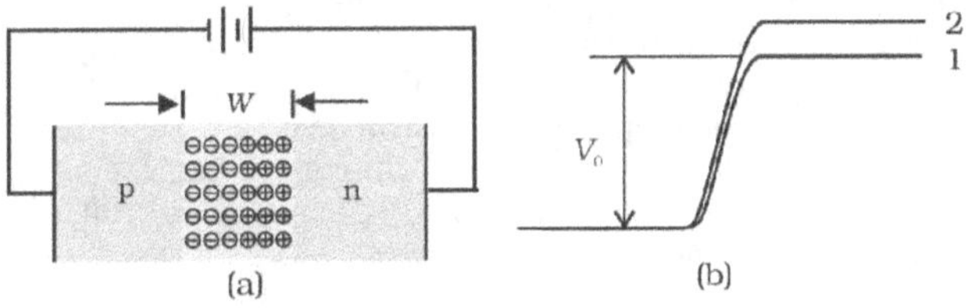

Fig.: (a) Diode under reverse bias,

(b) Barrier potential under reverse bias.

♦ The current under reverse bias is essentially voltage independent upto critical reverse bias votage known as **breakdown voltage (V_{br})**. When $V = V_{br}$ the diode reverse current increases sharply.

♦ In forward bias, the current first increases very slowly, almost negligibly, till the voltage across the diode crosses a certain value. After the characteristic voltage, the diode current increases significantly (exponentially), even for a very small increase in the diode bias voltage. This voltage is called the *threshold voltage* or cut-in voltage (~0.2V for germanium diode and ~0.7 V for silicon diode).

♦ Typical **V-I characteristics** of a silicon diode

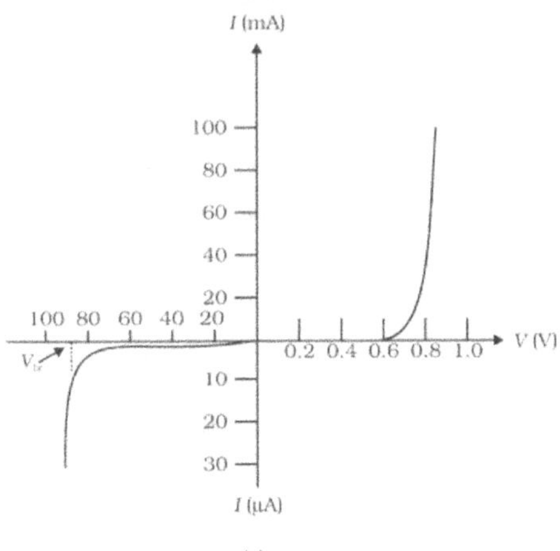

Fig.: Typical V-I characteristics of a silicon diode.

♦ For the diode in reverse bias, the current is very small (~μA) and almost remains constant with change in bias. It is called **reverse saturation current**.

- For diodes, we define a quantity called **dynamic resistance** as the ratio of small change in voltage ΔV to a small change in current ΔI:

$$r_d = \frac{\Delta V}{\Delta I}$$

Application of Junction Diode as a Rectifier

- If an alternating voltage is applied across a diode the current flows only in that part of the cycle when the diode is forward biased. This property is used to rectify alternating voltages and the circuit used for this purpose is called a *rectifier*.
- If an alternating voltage is applied across a diode in series with a load, a pulsating voltage will appear across the load only during the half cycles of the ac input during which the diode is forward biased. Such rectifier circuit, as shown in fig. is called a **half-wave rectifier**.

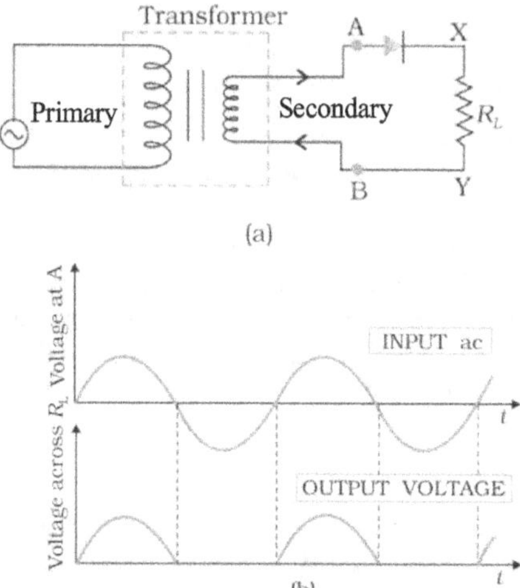

Fig.: (a) Half-wave rectifier circuit, (b) Input ac voltage and output voltage waveforms from the rectifier circuit.

- The circuit using two diodes, gives output rectified voltage corresponding to both the positive as well as negative half of the ac cycle. Hence, it is known as *full-wave rectifier*.
- Each diode rectifies only for half the cycle, but the two do so for alternate cycles. Thus, the output between their common terminals and the centre-tap of the transformer becomes a full-wave rectifier output.

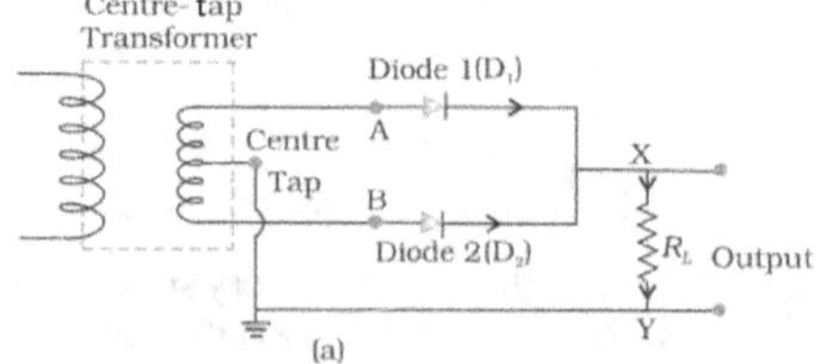

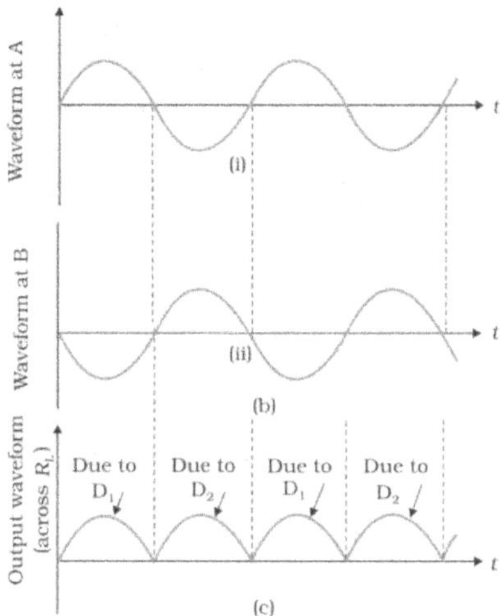

Fig.: (a) A full-wave rectifier circuit; (b) Input wave forms given to the diode D_1 at A and to the diode D_2 at B; (c) Output waveform across the load R_L connected in the full-wave rectifier circuit.

♦ The rectified voltage is in the form of pulses of the shape of half sinusoids. Though it is unidirectional it does not have a steady value.

♦ To get steady dc output from the pulsating voltage normally a capacitor is connected across the output terminals (parallel to the load R_L).

♦ One can also use an inductor in series with R_L for the same purpose. Since these additional circuits appear to filter out the ac ripple and give a pure dc voltage, so they are called **filters**.

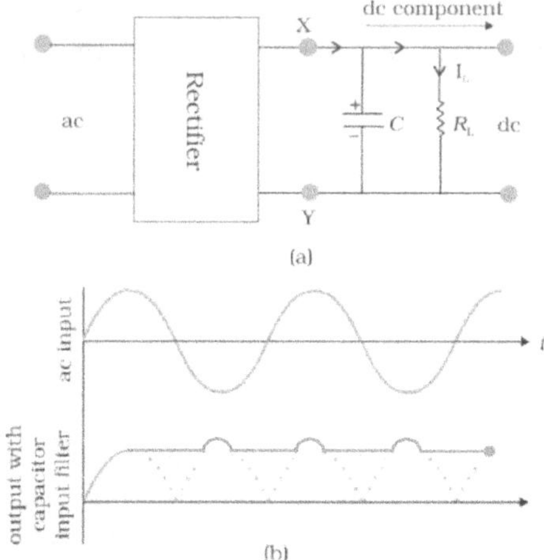

Fig.: (a) A full-wave rectifier with capacitor filter,
(b) Input and output voltage of rectifier in (a).

Special Purpose P-n Junction Diodes

Zener diode

♦ It is designed to operate under reverse bias in the breakdown region and used as a voltage regulator.

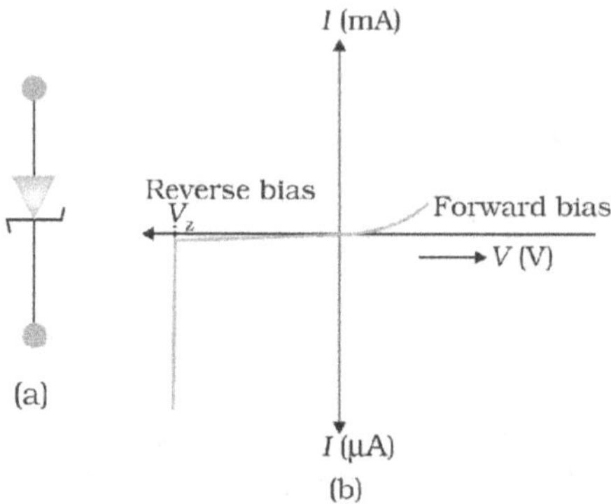

Fig.: Zener diode, (a) symbol, (b) *I-V* characteristics.

♦ Zener diode is fabricated by heavily doping both p-, and n-sides of the junction. Due to this, depletion region formed is very thin ($<10^{-6}$ m) and the electric field of the junction is extremely high ($\sim 5\times10^6$ V/m) even for a small reverse bias voltage of about 5V.

Zener diode as a voltage regulator

♦ When the ac input voltage of a rectifier fluctuates, its rectified output also fluctuates. To get a constant dc voltage from the dc unregulated output of a rectifier, we use a Zener diode.

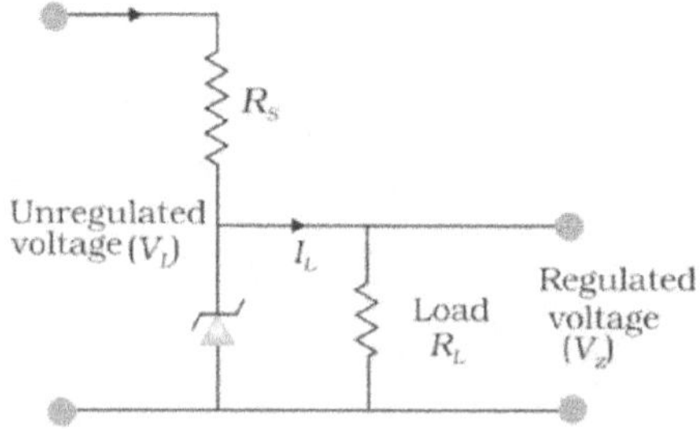

Fig.: Zener diode as DC voltage regulator to be corrected

Optoelectronic junction devices
(i) Photodiode

♦ A photodiode is again a special purpose p-n junction diode fabricated with a transparent window to allow light to fall on the diode. It is operated under reverse bias.

♦ The magnitude of the photocurrent depends on the intensity of incident light (photocurrent is proportional to incident light intensity).

♦   It is easier to observe the change in the current with change in the light intensity, if a reverse bias is applied. Thus photodiode can be used as a photodetector to detect optical signals.

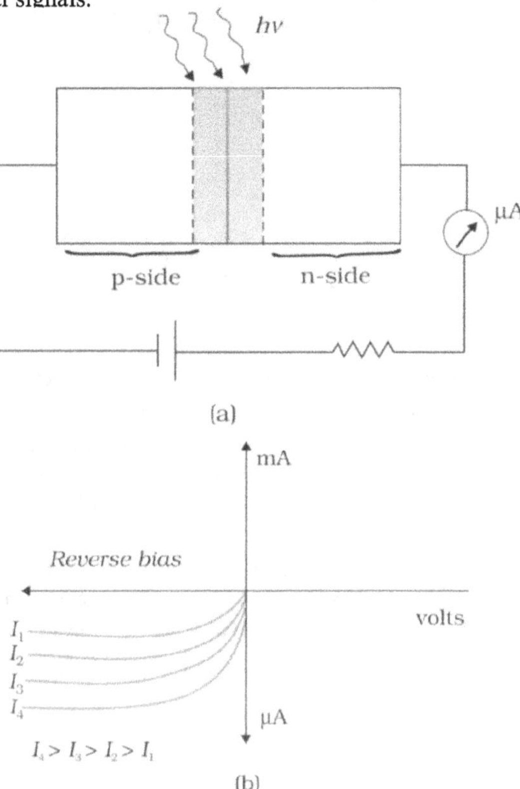

Fig.: (a) An illuminated photodiode under reverse bias,
(b) I-V characteristics of a photodiode for different illumination intensity $I_4 > I_3 > I_2 > I_1$.

♦   Photodiode used for detecting optical signal (photodetectors)

(ii) Light emitting diode

♦   It is a heavily doped p-n junction which under forward bias emits spontaneous radiation.

♦   The semiconductor used for fabrication of visible LEDs must at least have a band gap of 1.8 eV.

♦   The compound semiconductor Gallium Arsenide – Phosphide ($GaAs_{1-x}P_x$) is used for making LEDs of different colours.

♦   LEDs have the following advantages over conventional incandescent low power lamps:

- Low operational voltage and less power.
- Fast action and no warm-up time required.
- The bandwidth of emitted light is 100 Å to 500 Å or in other words it is nearly (but not exactly) monochromatic.
- Long life and ruggedness.

- Fast on-off switching capability.
♦ LED convert electrical energy into light.

(iii) Solar cell Photovoltaic devices

Which convert optical radiation into electricity.

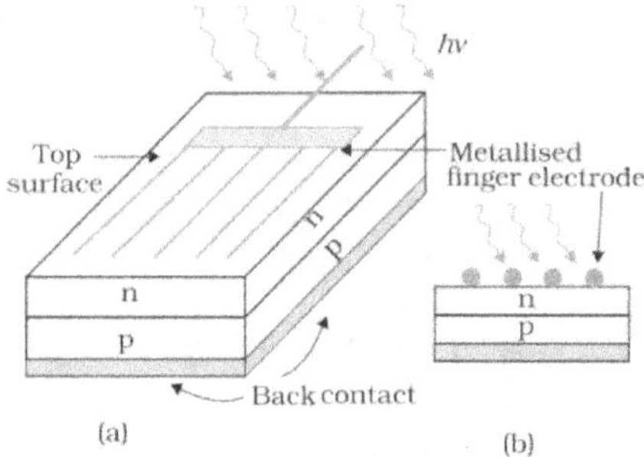

Fig.: (a) Typical p-n junction solar cell; (b) Cross-sectional view.

♦ The generation of emf by a solar cell, when light falls on, it is due to the following three basic processes: generation, separation and collection—

  (i) generation of e-h pairs due to light (with $h\nu > E_g$) close to the junction;

  (ii) separation of electrons and holes due to electric field of the depletion region. Electrons are swept to n-side and holes to p-side;

  (iii) the electrons reaching the n-side are collected by the front contact and holes reaching p-side are collected by the back contact. Thus p-side becomes positive and n-side becomes negative giving rise to photovoltage.

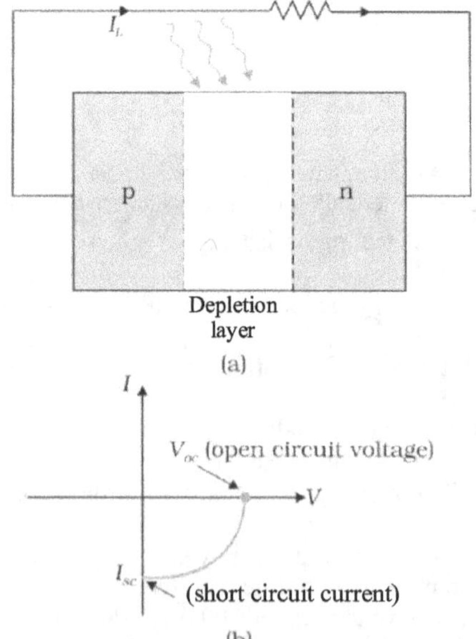

Fig.: (a) A typical illuminated p-n junction solar cell;
(b) *I-V* characteristics of a solar cell.

Transistor: Structure and Action

♦ A transistor has three doped regions forming two p-n junctions between them.

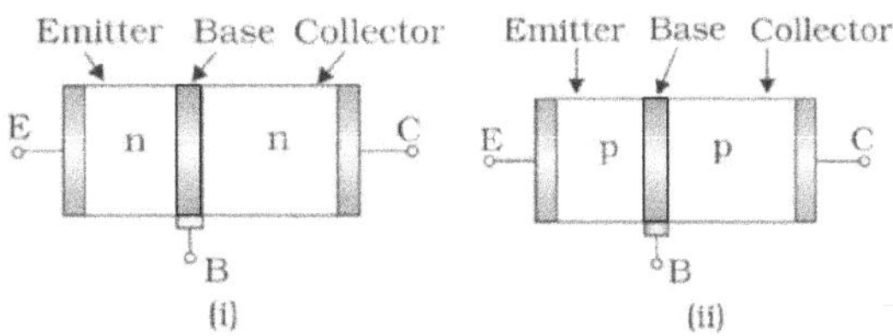

Fig.: (a) Schematic representations of a n-p-n transistor and p-n-p transistor

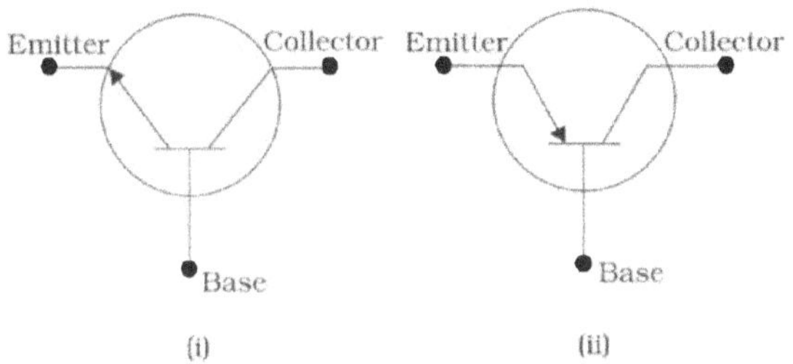

(b) Symbols for n-p-n and p-n-p transistors.

♦ There are two types of transistors,
  - **n-p-n transistor:** Here two segments of n-type semiconductor (emitter and collector) are separated by a segment of p-type semiconductor (base).
  - **p-n-p transistor:** Here two segments of p-type semiconductor (termed as emitter and collector) are separated by a segment of n-type semiconductor (termed as base).
♦ Three segments of a transistor is
  - **Emitter:** This is the segment on one side of the transistor shown in fig. It is of moderate size and heavily doped.
  - **Base:** This is the central segment. *It is very* thin and lightly doped.
  - **Collector:** This segment collects a major portion of the majority carriers supplied by the emitter. The collector side is moderately doped and larger in size as compared to the emitter.
♦ Emitter current is the sum of collector current and base current:
$$I_E = I_C + I_B$$
We also see that $I_C \approx I_E$.

Basic transistor circuit configurations and transistor characteristics
♦ The transistor can be connected in either of the following three configurations: *Common Emitter (CE), Common Base (CB), Common Collector (CC).*
♦ The transistor is most widely used in the CE configuration.
♦ More commonly used transistors are n-p-n Si transistors.

Common emitter transistor characteristics
♦ When a transistor is used in CE configuration, the input is between the base and the emitter and the output is between the collector and the emitter.

- The variation of the base current I_B with the base-emitter voltage V_{BE} is called the input characteristic.
- Similarly, the variation of the collector current I_C with the collector-emitter voltage V_{CE} is called the output characteristic.

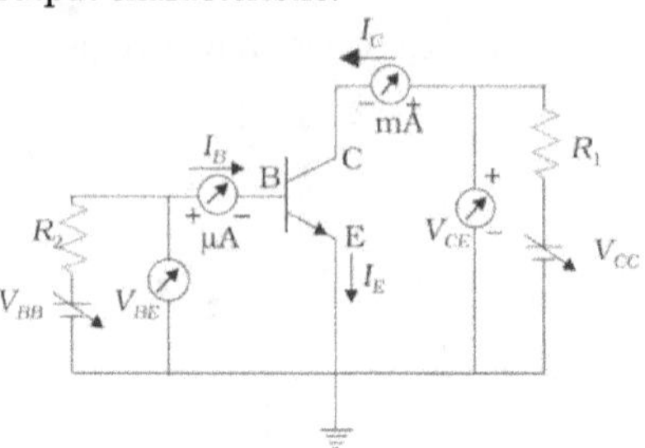

Fig.: Circuit arrangement for studying the input and output characteristics of n-p-n transistor in CE configuration.

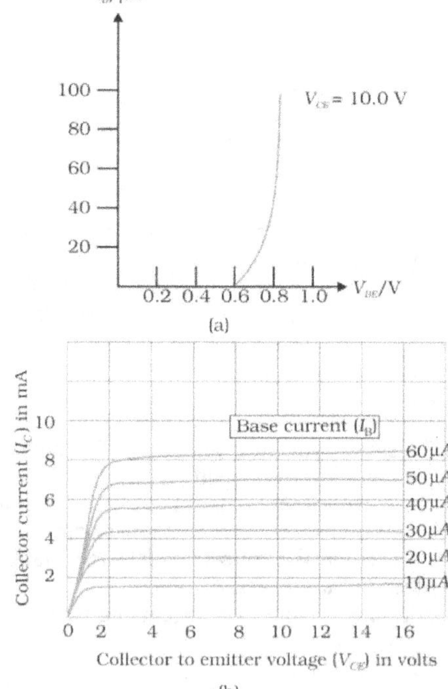

Fig.: (a) Typical input characteristics, and (b) Typical output characteristics.

- Ac parameters of transistors as shown below:
  - ***Input resistance (r_i):*** This is defined as the ratio of change in base-emitter voltage (ΔV_{BE}) to the resulting change in base current (ΔI_B) at constant collector-emitter voltage (V_{CE}).

$$r_i = \left(\frac{\Delta V_{BE}}{\Delta I_B}\right)_{V_{CE}}$$

- **Output resistance (r_o):** This is defined as the ratio of change in collector-emitter voltage (ΔV_{CE}) to the change in collector current (ΔI_C) at a constant base current I_B.

$$r_0 = \left(\frac{\Delta V_{CE}}{\Delta I_C}\right)_{I_B}$$

- **Current amplification factor (β):** This is defined as the ratio of the change in collector current to the change in base current at a constant collector-emitter voltage (V_{CE}) when the transistor is in active state.

$$\beta_{ac} = \left(\frac{\Delta I_C}{\Delta I_B}\right)_{V_{CE}} \quad \text{and} \quad B_{dc} = \frac{I_C}{I_B}$$

Transistor as a device
- When the transistor is used in the cutoff or saturation state it acts as a **switch**.
- And for using the transistor as an amplifier, it has to-operate in the **active** region.

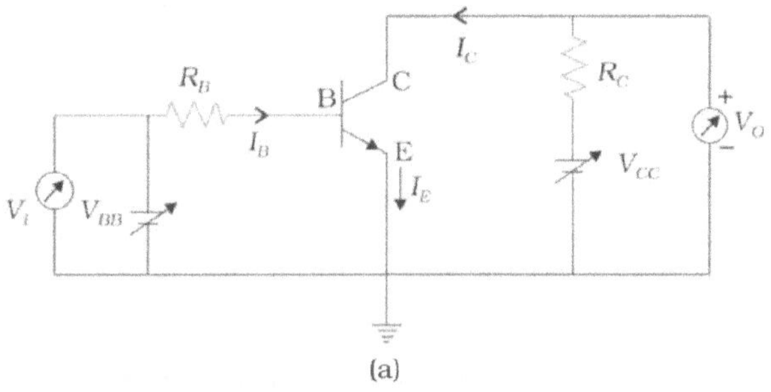

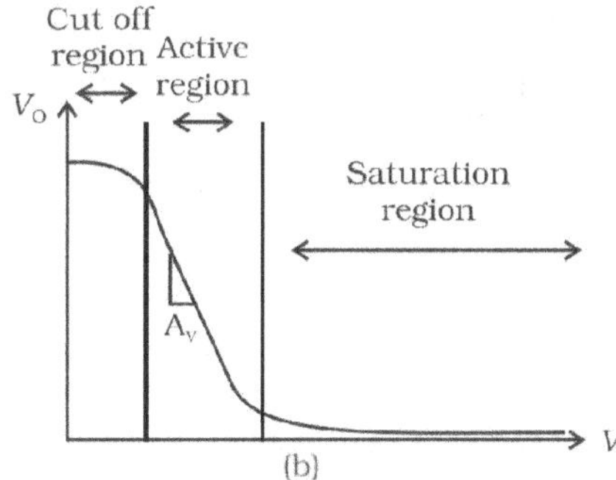

Fig.: (a) Base-biased transistor in CE configuration,
(b) Transfer characteristic.

- As long as V_i is low and unable to forward-bias the transistor, V_o is high (at V_{CC}). If V_i is *high* enough to drive the transistor into saturation, then V_o is low, very near to zero.

♦ When the transistor is not conducting it is said to be switched off and when it is driven into saturation it is said to be switched on.

♦ This shows that if we define low and high states as below and above certain voltage levels corresponding to cut off and saturation of the transistor, then we can say that a low input switches the transistor off and a high input switches it on.

♦ A low input to the transistor gives a high output and a high input gives a low output.

Transistor as an Amplifier (CE-Configuration)

♦ To operate the transistor as an amplifier it is necessary to fix its operating point somewhere in the middle of its active region.

♦ If we fix the value of V_{BB} corresponding to a point in the middle of the linear part of the transfer curve then the dc base current I_B would be constant and corresponding collector current I_C will also be constant.

♦ The dc voltage $V_{CE} = V_{CC} - I_C R_C$ would also remain constant. The operating values of V_{CE} and I_B determine the operating point, of the amplifier.

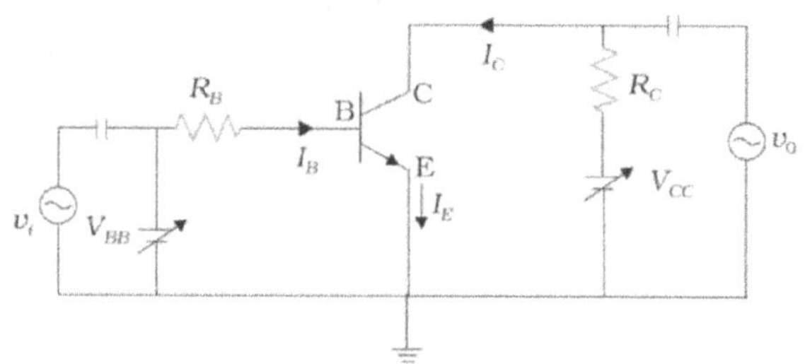

Fig.: A simple circuit of a CE-transistor amplifier.

♦ The **voltage gain** of the amplifier is

$$A_v = \frac{V_o}{V_i} = \frac{\Delta V_{CE}}{r \Delta I_B} = -\frac{\beta_{ac} R_L}{r}$$

♦ The **power gain** A_p can be expressed as the product of the current gain and voltage gain.

♦ Mathematically

$$A_p = \beta_{ac} \times A_v$$

Since β_{ac} and A_v are greater than 1, we get ac power gain.

Feedback amplifier and transistor oscillator

♦ In an oscillator, we get ac output without any external input signal. In other words, the output in an oscillator is self-sustained.

To attain this, an amplifier is taken. A portion of the output power is returned back (feedback) to the input in phase with the starting power (this process is termed positive feedback).

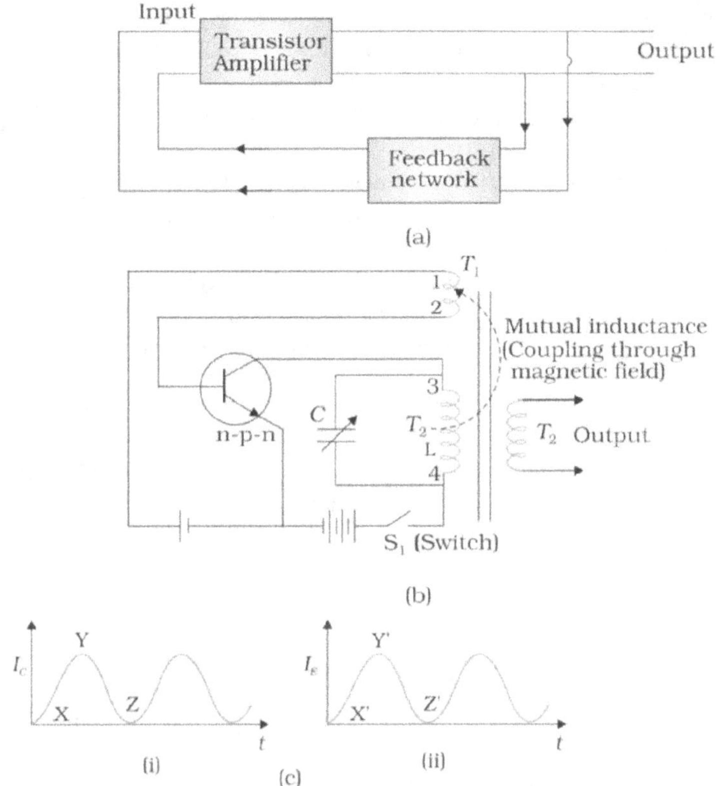

Fig.: (a) Principle of a transistor amplifier with positive feedback working as an oscillator and (b) Tuned collector oscillator, (c) Rise and fall (or built up) of current I_c and I_e due to the inductive coupling.

- The feedback can be achieved by inductive coupling (through mutual inductance) or LC or RC networks.
- Different types of oscillators essentially use different methods of coupling the output to the input (feedback network), apart from the resonant circuit for obtaining oscillation at a particular frequency.
- The resonance frequency (v) of this tuned circuit determines the frequency at which the oscillator will oscillate.

$$v = \left(\frac{1}{2\pi\sqrt{LC}} \right)$$

Digital Electronics and Logic Gates

- The signal (current or voltage) has been in the form of continuous, time-varying voltage or current. Such signals are called continuous or **analogue signals**.

- A binary number has only two digits '0' (say, 0V) and '1' (say, 5V). In digital electronics we use only these two levels of voltage. Such signals are called **Digital Signals**.
- In digital circuits only two values (represented by 0 or 1) of the input and output voltage are permissible.
- Logic gates are used in calculators, digital watches, computers, robots, industrial control systems, and in telecommunications.

Logic gates

- A **logic** gate is a digital circuit that follows certain logical relationship between the input and output voltages. Therefore, they are generally known as logic gates — gates because they control the flow of information.

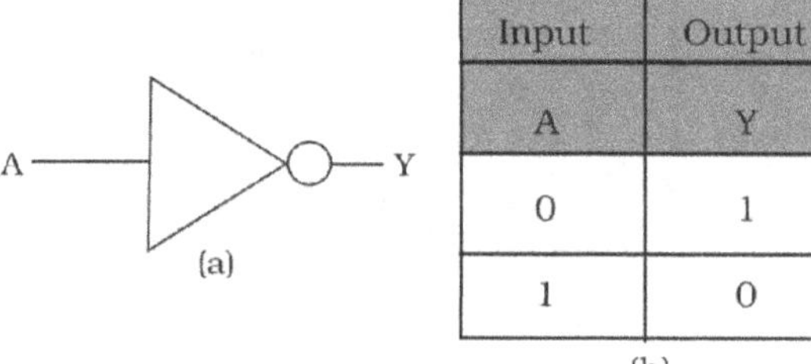

Input	Output
A	Y
0	1
1	0

(b)

Fig.: (a) Logic symbol, (b) Truth table of NOT gate.

- This is the most basic gate, with one input and one output. It produces a '1' output if the input is '0' and vice-versa.
- It is also known as an **inverter**.
- An **OR gate** has two or more inputs with one output.
- The output Y is 1 when either input A or input B or both are 1s, that is, if any of the input is high, the output is high.

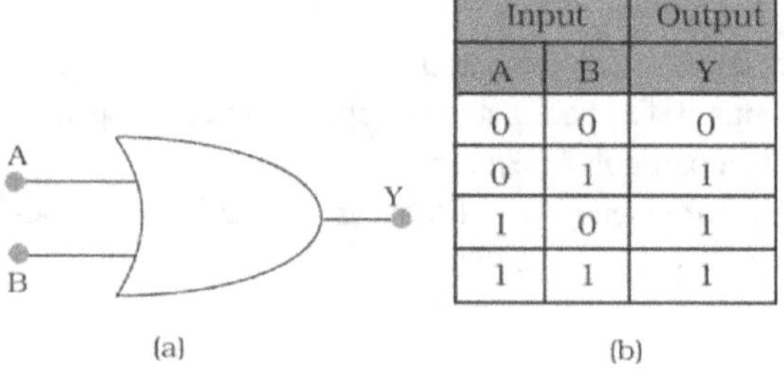

Input		Output
A	B	Y
0	0	0
0	1	1
1	0	1
1	1	1

(a)   (b)

Fig.: (a) Logic symbol (b) Truth table of OR gate.

- An **AND gate** has two or more inputs and one output. The output Y of **AND** gate is 1 only when input A and input B are both 1.

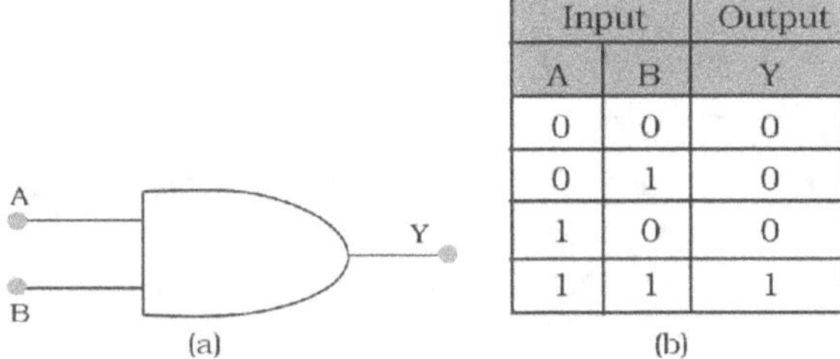

Fig.: (a) Logic symbol, (b) Truth table of AND gate.

♦ **NAND gate:** This is an AND gate followed by a NOT gate. If inputs A and B are both '1', the output Y is not '1'.

♦ NAND gates are also called Universal Gates since by using these gates you can realise other basic gates like OR, AND and NOT.

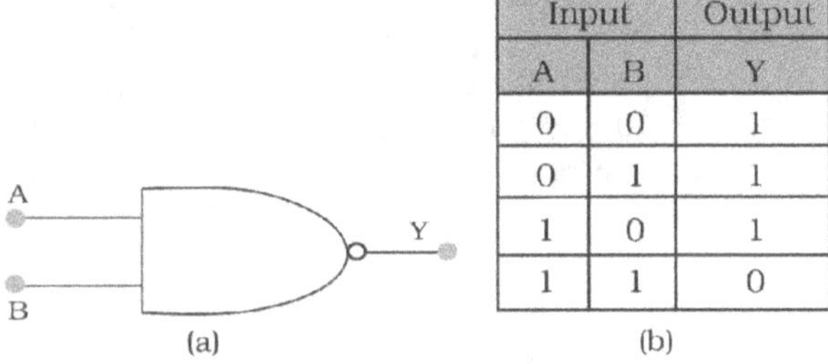

Fig.: (a) Logic symbol, (b) Truth table of NAND gate.

♦ **NOR gate:** It has two or more inputs and one output. A NOT- operation applied after OR gate gives a NOT-OR gate (or simply NOR gate).

♦ Its output Y is '1' only when both inputs A and B are '0', i.e., neither one input nor the other is '1'.

Input		Output
A	B	Y
0	0	1
0	1	0
1	0	0
1	1	0

Fig.: (a) Logic symbol, (b) Truth table of NOR gate.

♦ NOR gates are considered as universal gates because you can obtain all the gates like AND, OR, NOT by using only NOR gates.

Integrated Circuits

- The concept of fabricating an entire circuit (consisting of many passive components like R and C and active devices like diode and transistor) on a small single block (or chip) of a semiconductor has revolutionised the electronics technology. Such a circuit is known as *Integrated Circuit* (IC).
- The entire circuit is formed on a single silicon crystal (or *chip*). The chip dimensions are as small as 1mm × 1mm or it could even be smaller.
- Depending on nature of input signals, IC's can be grouped in two categories: (a) *linear* or *analogue IC's* and (b) **digital IC's**.
- The linear IC's process analogue signals which change smoothly and continuously over a range of values between a maximum and a minimum.
- The output is more or less directly proportional to the input, i.e., it varies linearly with the input.
- Depending upon the level of integration. The ICs are termed as Small Scale Integration, SSI (logic gates ≤ 10); Medium Scale Integration, MSI (logic gates ≤ 100); Large Scale Integration, LSI (logic gates ≤ 1000); and Very Large Scale Integration, VLSI (logic gates > 1000).

Past Years ONE-LINERS
NEET/JEE Main/Board

- Boolean expression for combination of logic gates Output, $y = A.B + \overline{B}.C$
- Current $\dfrac{I_n}{I_p} = \dfrac{\mu_e}{\mu_h}$
- A zener diode is connected in reverse biased when used as voltage regulator as in reverse biased after breakdown, voltage becomes constant.
- $Y = \overline{\overline{A} + \overline{B}} = \overline{\overline{A \cdot B}} = A \cdot B \Rightarrow$ AND Gate
- In a transistor, emitter is heavily doped, the base region is lightly doped and thin. The size of collector region is larger than other two regions.
- Due to reverse biasing, the width of the depletion region increases in a *p-n* junction diode.
- In p-type semiconductor, trivalent impurities are added to intrinsic semiconductor, which creates holes which are majority charge carriers.
- Boolean expression $Y = \overline{A.B}$ *i.e.*, circuit represents NAND gate.
- On heating, number of electron-hole pairs increases, so overall resistance of diode will change.

- $\beta = \dfrac{I_C}{I_b}$

- $Y = (A \cdot \overline{B} + \overline{A} \cdot B)$

- Voltage gain $(A_v) = \beta \dfrac{R_c}{R_b}$

- $y = \overline{y}_2 = \overline{A+B}$ i.e. NOR gate

- Voltage gain for common emitter configuration $A_v = \beta . \dfrac{R_L}{R_i}$, Power gain for common emitter configuration $P_v = \beta A_v$ Voltage gain for common base configuration $A_v = \alpha, \dfrac{R_L}{R_P}$ Power gain for common base configuration $P_v = A_v \alpha$

- Since diode is in forward bias, so the value of current flowing through AB $i = \dfrac{\Delta V}{R}$

- Current $I = \dfrac{V}{R}$

- For a common emitter transistor $I_E = I_C + I_B$ $\because \alpha = \dfrac{I_C}{I_E}, \beta = \dfrac{I_C}{I_B}$

- A logic gate is reversible if we can recover input data from the output. Hence NOT gate.

- Voltage gain $= \dfrac{\Delta I_c}{\Delta I_b} \times \dfrac{R_0}{R_i}$

- Current, $I = \dfrac{V - \Delta V}{R}$

- Graph (a) is for a simple diode. Graph (b) is showing the V Break down used for zener diode. Graph (c) is for solar cell which shows cut-off voltage and open circuit current. Graph (d) shows the variation of resistance h and hence current with intensity of light.

Tips/Tricks/Tecchniques ONE-LINERS
(Exam Sample)

- At absolute zero, a pure semiconductor behaves as an insulator as it has filled valence band and empty conduction band.
- Semiconductor devices are temperature sensitive current control devices.
- A P-N junction diode can be considered as a capacitor with P and N regions acting as the plates of the capacitor and depletion layer as the dielectric medium.
- A P-N junction acts as voltage controlled switch. During forward biasing of p-n

junction diode it acts like ON switch. When reverse biased, it acts like an OFF switch.

♦ We prefer common emitter transistor over common base transistor due to large current gain.

♦ In common base transistor amplifier, the input and output signal are in the same phase.

♦ In common emitter transistor amplifier, the input and output signals are out of phase by π or $180°$.

♦ NOR and NAND gates are called building blocks of digital system because they can be used to perform the basic logic function, AND, OR and NOT.

♦ A logic gate is seversible, if we can recover input data from the output.

♦ For a doped semiconductor, $n_e n_h = n_i^2$
n_e and n_h are the number density of electrons and holes respectively and n_i is number density of intrinsic carriers.

♦ The current in the junction diode
$I = I_0 \, (e^{ev/kT} - 1)$
k = Boltzmann constant
I_0 = reverse saturation current
In case of forward biasing, V is positive and low
So, forward current will be
$I_f = I_0 \, (e^{ev/kT} - 1)$ $\qquad$ $(\because e^{ev/kT} > 1)$
In case of reverse biasing, V is negative and high
$e^{-ev/kT} << 1$, So, reverse current
$I_r = -I_0$

♦ For Half wave rectifier : $i_{dc} = i_0 / \pi$, $i_{rms} = i_0 / \sqrt{2}$ $\quad P_{DC} = i_{dc}^2 R_L$.

$$P_{AC} = i^2_{rms}(R_L + R_f).$$

$$\eta_{rec} = \frac{P_{dc}}{P_{ac}} \times 100\% = \frac{40.6}{1 + \dfrac{R_f}{R_L}}$$

♦ For Full wave rectifier : $i_{dc} = 2i_0/\pi$, $i_{rms} = i_0/2$

$$P_{DC} = i_{dc}^2 R_L$$

$$P_{AC} = i^2_{rms}(R_L + R_f)$$

$$\eta_{rec} = \frac{P_{dc}}{P_{ac}} \times 100\% = \frac{81.2}{1 + \dfrac{R_f}{R_L}}.$$

♦ The energy bands (E_C or E_V) in the semiconductors are space delocalised which means that these are not located in any specific place inside the solid. The energies are the overall averages. When you see a picture in which E_C or E_V are drawn as straight lines, then they should be respectively taken simply as the bottom of conduction band energy levels and top of valence band energy levels.

30 Communication Systems

Elements of a Communication System

- *Communication is the act of transmission of information.*
- For communication to be successful, it is essential that the sender and receiver understand a common language.
- Languages and methods used in communication have kept evolving from prehistoric to modern times, to meet the growing demands in terms of speed and complexity of information.
- Every communication system has three essential elements-transmitter, medium/channel and receiver.
- The purpose of the **transmitter** is to convert the message signal produced by the source of information into a form suitable for transmission through the channel. If the output of the information source is a non-electrical signal like a voice signal, a transducer converts it to electrical form before giving it as an input to the transmitter.
- The **receiver** has the task of operating on the received signal. It reconstructs a recognisable form of the original message signal for delivering it to the user of information.
- There are two basic modes of communication: *point-to-point* and **broadcast**.
- In point-to-point communication mode, communication takes place over a link between a single transmitter and a receiver. Telephony is an example of such a mode of communication.
- In the broadcast mode, there are a large number of receivers corresponding to a single transmitter. Radio and television are examples of broadcast mode of communication.
- The block diagram depicting the general form of a communication system.

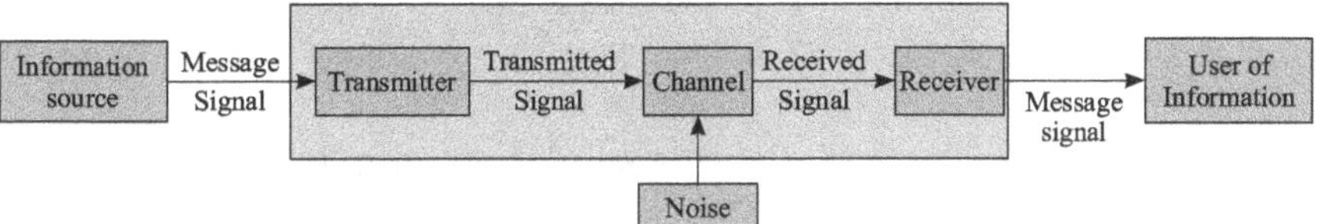

Fig. Block diagram of a generalised communication system

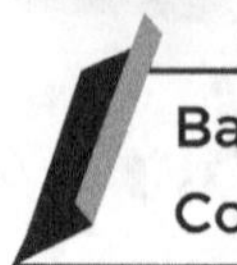

Basic Terminology used in Electronic Communication Systems

- *Transducer:* Any device that converts one form of energy into another can be termed as a transducer.

- *Signal:* Information converted in electrical form and suitable for transmission is called a signal. Signals can be either analog or digital. Analog signals are continuous variations of voltage or current. *They are essentially single-valued functions of time. Sine wave is a fundamental analog signal.*

- Digital signals are those which can take only discrete stepwise values. Binary system that is extensively used in digital electronics employs just two levels of a signal. '0' corresponds to a low level and '1' corresponds to a high level of voltage/current.

- American Standard Code for Information Interchange (ASCII) is a universally popular digital code to represent numbers, letters and certain characters.

- *Noise:* Noise refers to the unwanted signals that tend to disturb the transmission and processing of message signals in a communication system.

- *Transmitter:* A transmitter processes the incoming message signal so as to make it suitable for transmission through a channel and subsequent reception.

- *Receiver:* A receiver extracts the desired message signals from the received signals at the channel output.

- *Attenuation:* The loss of strength of a signal while propagating through a medium is known as attenuation.

- Amplification: It is the process of increasing the amplitude (and consequently the strength) of a signal using an electronic circuit called the amplifier.

- Amplification is necessary to compensate for the attenuation of the signal in communication systems.

- *Range:* It is the largest distance between a source and a destination up to which the signal is received with sufficient strength.

- *Bandwidth:* Bandwidth refers to the frequency range over which an equipment operates or the portion of the spectrum occupied by the signal.

- At the transmitter, information contained in the low frequency message signal is superimposed on a high frequency wave, which acts as a carrier of the information. This process is known as modulation.

- *Demodulation:* The process of retrieval of information from the carrier wave at the receiver is termed demodulation. This is the reverse process of modulation.

◆ *Repeater:* A repeater is a combination of a receiver and a transmitter. A repeater, picks up the signal from the transmitter, amplifies and retransmits it to the receiver sometimes with a change in carrier frequency. A communication satellite is essentially a repeater station in space.

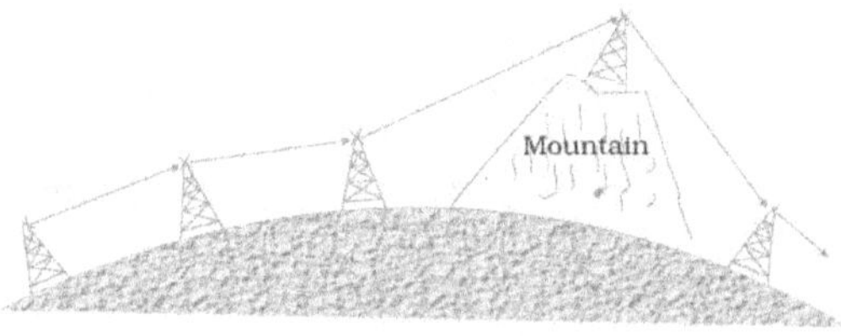

Fig. : Use of repeater station to increase the range of communication

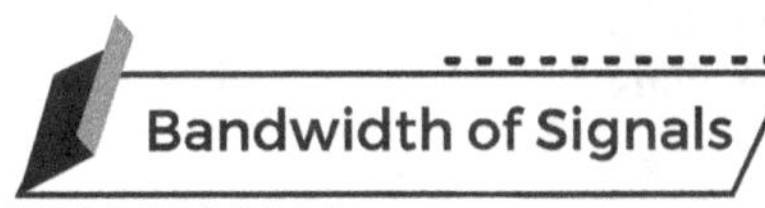

Bandwidth of Signals

◆ **Bandwidth:** The two side bands lie on either side of the carrier frequency at equal frequency interval fm.

◆ The type of communication system needed for a given signal depends on the band of frequencies which is considered essential for the communication process.

◆ Speech signal requires a bandwidth of 2800 Hz (3100 Hz – 300 Hz) for commercial telephonic communication. To transmit music, an approximate bandwidth of 20 kHz is required because of the high frequencies produced by the musical instruments.

◆ Video signals for transmission of pictures require about 4.2 MHz of bandwidth. A TV signal contains both voice and picture and is usually allocated 6 MHz of bandwidth for transmission.

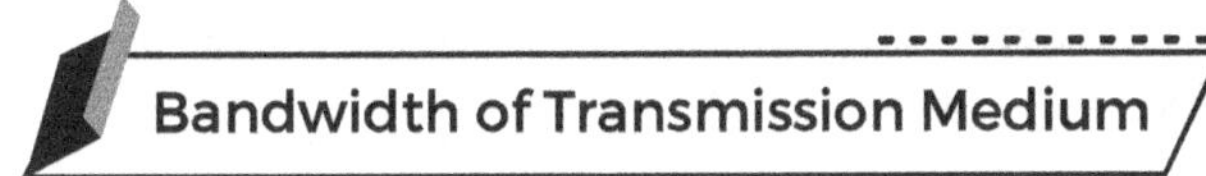

Bandwidth of Transmission Medium

◆ Different types of transmission media offer different bandwidths. Coaxial cable is a widely used wire medium, which offers a bandwidth of approximately 750 MHz. Such cables are normally operated below 18 GHz. Communication through free space using radio waves takes place over a very wide range of frequencies: from a few hundreds of kHz to a few GHz.

◆ Optical communication using fibers is performed in the frequency range of 1 THz to 1000 THz (microwaves to ultraviolet). An optical fiber can offer a transmission bandwidth in excess of 100 GHz.

Table: Some Important Wireless Communication Frequency Bands

Service	Frequency Bands	Comments
Standard AM broadcast	540 - 1600 kHz	
FM broadcast Television	88 - 108 MHz 54 - 72 MHz 76 - 88 MHz 174 - 216 MHz 420 - 890 MHz	 VHF (very high frequencies) TV UHF (ultra high frequencies) TV
Cellular Mobile Radio	896 - 901 MHz 840 - 935 MHz	Mobile to base station Base station to mobile
Satellite Communication	5.925 - 6.425 GHz 3.7 - 4.2 GHz	Uplink Downlink

Propagation of Electromagnetic Waves

Ground Wave

♦ To radiate signals with high efficiency, the antennas should have a size comparable to the wavelength l of the signal (at least ~ l/4). At longer wavelengths (i.e., at lower frequencies), the antennas have large physical size and they are located on or very near to the ground. In standard AM broadcast, ground based vertical towers are generally used as transmitting antennas. For such antennas, ground has a strong influence on the propagation of the signal. The mode of propagation is called **surface wave propagation** and the wave glides over the surface of the earth.

♦ The attenuation of surface waves increases very rapidly with increase in frequency. The maximum range of coverage depends on the transmitted power and frequency (less than a few MHz).

Sky Wave

♦ In the frequency range from a few MHz up to 30 to 40 MHz, long distance communication can be achieved by ionospheric reflection of radio waves back towards the earth. This mode of propagation is called **sky wave propagation**

♦ At some intermediate heights, there occurs a peak of ionisation density. The ionospheric layer acts as a reflector for a certain range of frequencies (3 to 30 MHz). Electromagnetic waves of frequencies higher than 30 MHz penetrate the ionosphere and escape.

- The phenomenon of bending of em waves so that they are diverted towards the earth is similar to total internal reflection in optics.

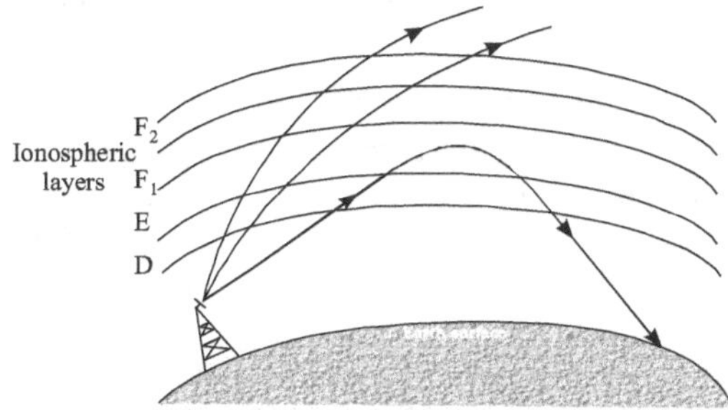

Fig. : Sky wave propagation. The layer nomenclature is given in Table 30.3

Space Wave

- A space wave travels in a straight line from transmitting antenna to the receiving antenna. Space waves are used for **line-of-sight (LOS) communication** as well as satellite communication.

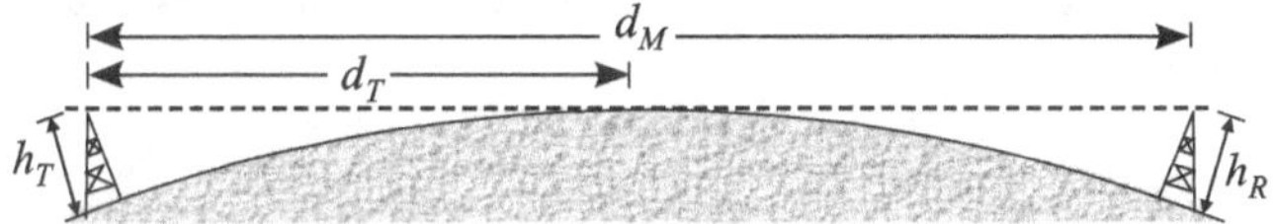

Fig. : Line of sight communication by space waves.

- If the transmitting antenna is at a height h_T, then you can show that the distance to the horizon h_T is given as $d_T = \sqrt{2Rh_T}$, where R is the radius of the earth (approximately 6400 km). dT is also called the radio horizon of the transmitting antenna. The **maximum line-of-sight distance** d_M between the two antennas having heights h_T and h_R above the earth is given by

$$d_M = \sqrt{2Rh_T} + \sqrt{2Rh_R}$$

where h_R is the height of receiving antenna.

- Television broadcast, microwave links and satellite communication are some examples of communication systems that use space wave mode of propagation.

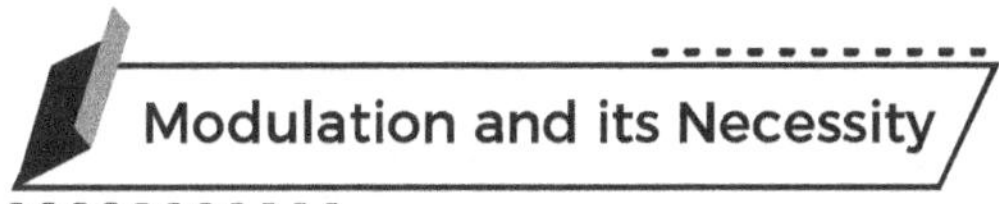

Modulation and its Necessity

- Message signals are also called baseband signals, which essentially designate the band of frequencies representing the original signal, no signal, in general, is a single frequency sinusoid, but it spreads over a range of frequencies called the signal *bandwidth*. we wish to transmit an electronic signal in the audio frequency (AF) range (baseband signal frequency less than 20 kHz) over a long distance directly.

Size of the Antenna or Aerial

♦ Antenna should have a size comparable to the wavelength of the signal (at least $\lambda/4$ in dimension) so that the antenna properly senses the time variation of the signal.

Effective Power Radiated by an Antenna

♦ Radiation from a linear antenna (length l) shows that the power radiated is proportional to $(l/\lambda)^2$. This implies that for the same antenna length, the power radiated increases with decreasing l, i.e., increasing frequency. Hence, the effective power radiated by a long wavelength baseband signal would be small.

♦ For a good transmission, we need high powers and hence this also points out to the need of using high frequency transmission.

Mixing up of Signals from Different Transmitters

♦ Suppose many people are talking at the same time or many transmitters are transmitting baseband information signals simultaneously. All these signals will get mixed up and there is no simple way to distinguish between them. This points out towards a possible solution by using communication at high frequencies and allotting a band of frequencies to each message signal for its transmission.

♦ There is a *need for translating the original low frequency baseband message or information signal into high frequency wave before transmission such that the translated signal continues to possess the information contained in the original signal.*

♦ Three types of modulation: (i) Amplitude modulation (AM), (ii) Frequency modulation (FM) and (iii) Phase modulation (PM).

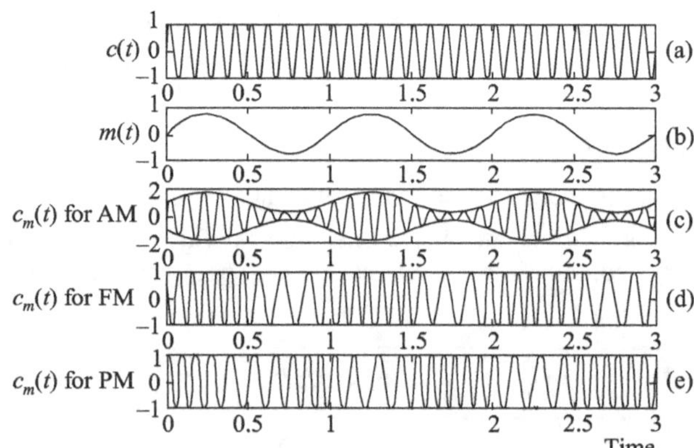

Fig. : Modulation of a carrier wave (a) a sinusoidal carrier wave; (b) a modulating signal; (c) amphtude modulation; (d) frequency modulation; and (e) phase modulation.

♦ Different types of pulse modulation are: (a) pulse amplitude modulation (PAM), (b) pulse duration modulation (PDM) or pulse width modulation (PWM), and (c) pulse position modulation (PPM).

Amplitude Modulation

♦ In amplitude modulation the amplitude of the carrier is varied in accordance with the information signal.

♦ Let $c(t) = A_c \sin \omega_c t$ represent carrier wave and $m(t) = A_m \sin \omega_m t$ represent the message or the modulating signal. The modulated signal $c_m(t)$ can be written as

$$c_m(t) = (A_c + A_m \sin \omega_m t)\sin \omega_c t$$

$$= A_c \left(1 + \frac{A_m}{A_c} \sin \omega_m t\right) \sin \omega_c t$$

$$c_m(t) = A_c \sin \omega_c t + \mu A_c \sin \omega_m t \sin \omega_c t$$

Here $\mu = A_m/A_c$ is the modulation index; in practice, μ is kept ≤ 1 to avoid distortion.

♦ Using the trignomatric relation $\sin A \sin B = \frac{1}{2}(\cos(A - B) - \cos(A + B))$, we can write c_m as

$$c_m(t) = A_c \sin \omega_c t + \frac{\mu A_c}{2} \cos(\omega_c - \omega_m)t - \frac{\mu A_c}{2} \cos(\omega_c + \omega_m)t$$

♦ $\omega_c - \omega_m$ and $\omega_c + \omega_m$ are respectively called the **lower side** and **upper side frequencies**.

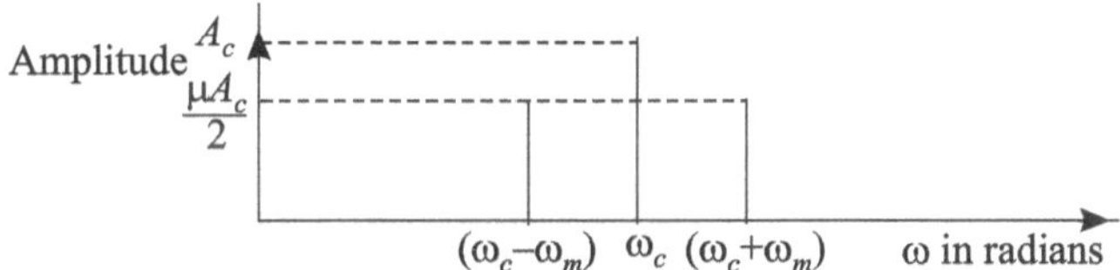

Fig. : A plot of amplitude versus ω for an amplitude modulated singnal.

Production of Amplitude Modulated Wave

♦ Block diagram of a simple modulator for obtaining an AM signal.

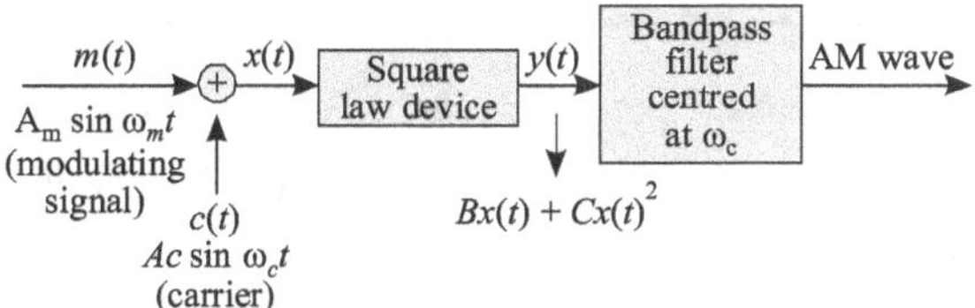

Fig. : A Block diagram of a simple modulator for obtaining an AM signal.

- The modulating signal $A_m \sin \omega_m t$ is added to the carrier signal $A_c \sin \omega_c t$ to produce the signal x(t). This signal $x(t) = A_m \sin\omega_m t + A_c \sin\omega_c t$ is passed through a square law device which is a non-linear device which produces an output

$$y(t) = Bx(t) + Cx^2(t)$$

where B and C are constants.

$$y(t) = BA_m \sin \omega_m t + BA_c \sin \omega_c t$$

$$+ CA_m^2 \sin^2 \omega_m t + A_c^2 \sin^2 \omega_c t + 2A_m A_c \sin \omega_m t \sin \omega_c t$$

$$= BA_m \sin \omega_m t + BA_c \sin \omega_c t$$

$$+ \frac{CA_m^2}{2} + A_c^2 - \frac{CA_m^2}{2} \cos 2\omega_m t \frac{CA_c^2}{2} \cos 2\omega_c t$$

$$+ CA_m A_c \cos(\omega_c - \omega_m)t - CA_m A_c \cos(\omega_c + \omega_m)t$$

- This signal is passed through a band pass filter* which rejects dc and the sinusoids of frequencies ω_m, $2\omega_m$ and $2\omega_c$ and retains the frequencies ω_c, $\omega_c - \omega_m$ and $\omega_c + \omega_m$.

- The modulator is to be followed by a power amplifier which provides the necessary power and then the modulated signal is fed to an antenna of appropriate size for radiation.

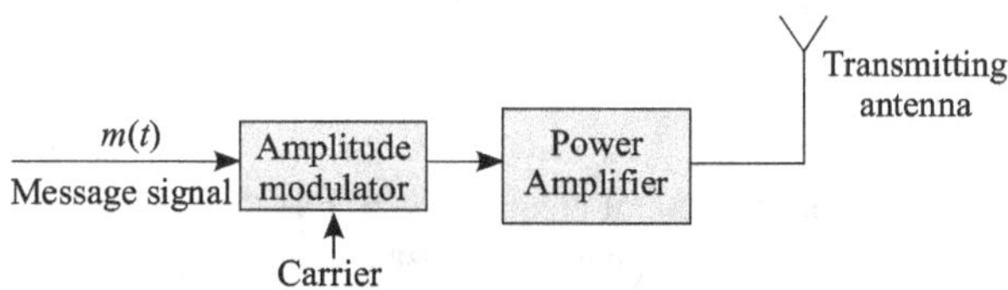

Fig. : Block diagram of a transmitter

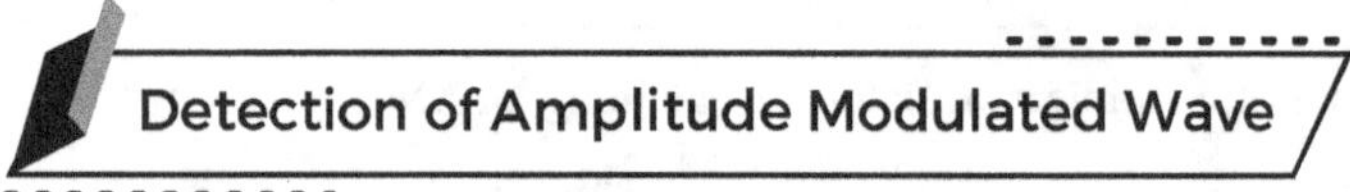

Detection of Amplitude Modulated Wave

- The transmitted message gets attenuated in propagating through the channel. The receiving antenna is therefore to be followed by an amplifier and a detector.

- The carrier frequency is usually changed to a lower frequency by what is called an intermediate frequency (IF) stage preceding the detection. The detected signal may not be strong enough to be made use of and hence is required to be amplified.

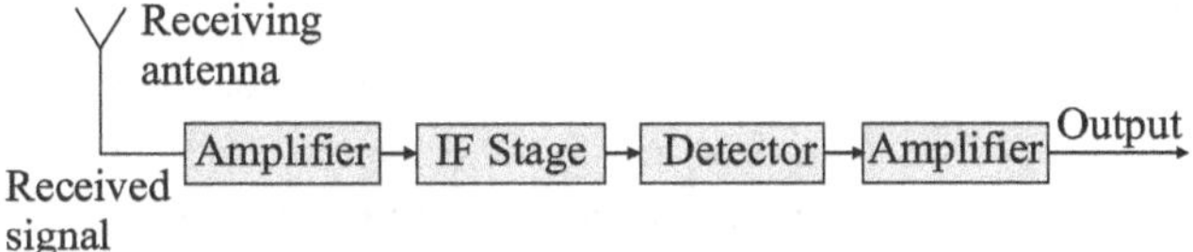

Fig. : Block diagram of a receiver.

♦ Detection is the process of recovering the modulating signal from the modulated carrier wave. Modulated carrier wave contains the frequencies ω_c and $\omega_c \pm \omega_m$. In order to obtain the original message signal m(t) of angular frequency ω_m.

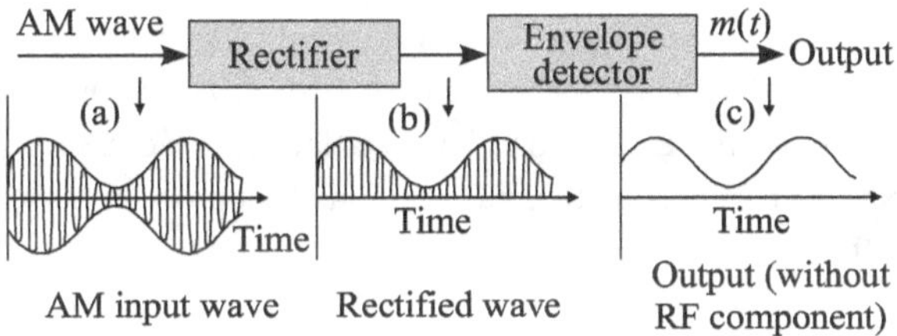

Fig. : Block diagram of a detector for AM signal.

The quantity on *y*-axis can be current or voltage.

♦ The modulated signal is passed through a rectifier to produce the output shown in (b). This envelope of signal (b) is the message signal. In order to retrieve m(t), the signal is passed through an envelope detector (which may consist of a simple RC circuit).

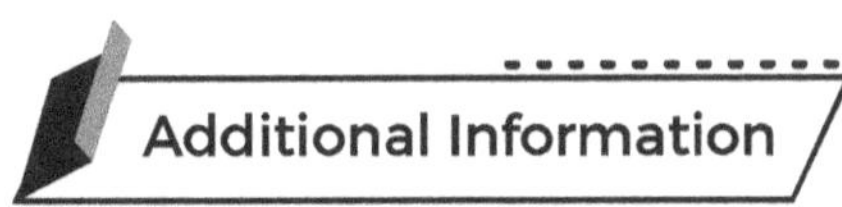

Additional Information

The Internet

♦ It permits communication and sharing of all types of information between any two or more computers connected through a large and complex network.

♦ *E mail* – It permits exchange of text/graphic material using email software.

♦ File transfer – A FTP (File Transfer Programmes) allows transfer of files/software from one computer to another connected to the Internet.

♦ *World Wide Web (WWW)* – Computers that store specific information for sharing with others provide websites either directly or through web service providers.

♦ *E-commerce* – Use of the Internet to promote business using electronic means such as using credit cards is called E-commerce.

♦ *Chat* – Real time conversation among people with common interests through typed messages is called chat.

Facsimile (FAX)

♦ It scans the contents of a document (as an image, not text) to create electronic signals. These signals are then sent to the destination (another FAX machine) in an orderly manner using telephone lines. At the destination, the signals are reconverted into a replica of the original document.

Mobile Telephony

♦ The central concept of this system is to divide the service area into a suitable number of cells centred on an office called *MTSO (Mobile Telephone Switching Office)*. Each cell contains a low-power transmitter called a base station and caters to a large number of mobile receivers (popularly called cell phones). Each cell could have a service area of a few square kilometers or even less depending upon the number of customers. When a mobile receiver crosses the coverage area of one base station, it is necessary for the mobile user to be transferred to another base station. This procedure is called handover or handoff.

Past Years ONE-LINERS
NEET/JEE Main/Board

♦ Bandwidth, $\beta = \dfrac{\omega_m}{\pi}$

♦ Modulation index, $\mu = \dfrac{A_m}{A_c}$

♦ The equation of amplitude modulated wave

$C_m = (v_0 + A\cos\omega t)\sin\omega t$

$= v_0\sin\omega_0 t + A\cos\omega t\,\sin\omega_0 t$

♦ Number of channel $= \dfrac{\text{Transmission frequency}}{\text{bandwidth of channel}}$

♦ Modulated carrier wave contains frequency $w_{c\text{ and }}\omega_c \pm \omega_m$

♦ In amplitude modulation, the amplitude of the high frequency carrier wave made to vary in proportional

to the amplitude of audio signal.

♦ Amplitude modulated wave consists of three frequencies are $\omega_c + \omega_m$, ω, $\omega_c - \omega_m$

Tips/Tricks/Tecchniques ONE-LINERS
(Exam Sample)

- In a digital signal, information is carried by the pattern of pulses and not by the shape of pulses.

- We use parallel wire lines for transmission of microwaves. This is because at this frequency, separation between the two wires approaches half a wavelength $\left(\dfrac{\lambda}{2}\right)$. Therefore radiation loss of energy becomes maximum.

- Optical fibres are hair-thin glass strands and use the principle of total internal reflection for transmission of light through them.

- Modems are the devices which convert digital signals into analog singals and vice-versa. It is used in two way communications.

- A satellite communication is a line of sight communication or space communication.

- Number of channel accommodated for transmission

$$= \frac{\text{Total bandwidth of channel}}{\text{Bandwidth needed per channel}}$$

- Critical angle is related with refractive index (μ) of central core of optical fiber by the relation

$$\cos\,\theta_c = \frac{\sqrt{\mu_1^2 - \mu_2^2}}{\mu_1}$$

- Acceptance angle for the optical fiber

$$\sin\,\theta_a = \frac{\sqrt{\mu_1^2 - \mu_2^2}}{\mu_0} \quad \Rightarrow \quad \theta_a = \sin^{-1}\left(\frac{\sqrt{\mu_1^2 - \mu_2^2}}{\mu_0}\right)$$

- The power radiated by an antenna $\propto \dfrac{1}{\lambda^2}$

♦ In amplitude modulation (AM), the amplitude of high frequency wave is changed in accordance with the intensity of the signal.

Modulation factor or modulation index,

$$m_a = \frac{\text{Amplitude change of carrier wave}}{\text{Normal carrier wave (unmodulated)}}$$

♦ Numerical aperture for step-index fiber

$$NA = \mu_0 \sin \theta_a = \left(\sqrt{\mu_1^2 - \mu_2^2} \right)$$

for air, $\mu_0 = 1$, therefore

$$NA = \sin \theta_a = \sqrt{\mu_1^2 - \mu_2^2}$$

$$m_a = \frac{A_{max} - A_{min}}{A_{max} + A_{min}}$$